KIDS AND MED

One important element necessary ... the use of mass media in the lives of young people is ... terns of media use. How much do they use which media and which media content, and under what circumstances? This book reports the only national random sample survey of U.S. children's and adolescents' use of all of the various media available to them conducted in at least the past thirty years. In addition to providing the first comprehensive look at how media-saturated our young people's lives have become, it is the first study to examine young people's overall media budgets and the first to attempt to describe distinctly different types of young media users. Extensive background information and chapters devoted to each of the various media, to the overall media budget, and to particular types of media users enable the authors to describe perhaps the most detailed map of U.S. young people's media behavior ever assembled.

Professor Donald F. Roberts has taught and conducted research on youth and media at Stanford University for more than thirty years. His books include *The Process and Effects of Mass Communication*, *Television and Human Behavior*, and *It's Not Only Rock and Roll: Popular Music in the Lives of Adolescents*.

Ulla G. Foehr is a Ph.D. candidate at Stanford University and spent the last year as a Fellow at Stanford's Center on Adolescence.

KIDS AND MEDIA
IN AMERICA

DONALD F. ROBERTS
ULLA G. FOEHR

Stanford University

With

VICTORIA J. RIDEOUT
MOLLYANNE BRODIE

Based on a Kaiser Family Foundation Study

CAMBRIDGE
UNIVERSITY PRESS

PUBLISHED BY THE PRESS SYNDICATE OF THE UNIVERSITY OF CAMBRIDGE
The Pitt Building, Trumpington Street, Cambridge, United Kingdom

CAMBRIDGE UNIVERSITY PRESS
The Edinburgh Building, Cambridge CB2 2RU, UK
40 West 20th Street, New York, NY 10011-4211, USA
477 Williamstown Road, Port Melbourne, VIC 3207, Australia
Ruiz de Alarcón 13, 28014 Madrid, Spain
Dock House, The Waterfront, Cape Town 8001, South Africa

http://www.cambridge.org

First published 2004

Printed in the United States of America

Typeface Goudy 10.5/13 pt.   *System* LATEX 2$_\varepsilon$ [TB]

A catalog record for this book is available from the British Library.

Library of Congress Cataloging in Publication Data
Roberts, Donald F.
Kids and media in America / Donald F. Roberts and Ulla G. Foehr ; with
Victoria J. Rideout and Mollyanne Brodie.
p.   cm.
"Based on a Kaiser Family Foundation Study."
Includes bibliographical references and index.
ISBN 0-521-82102-9 – ISBN 0-521-52790-2 (pb.)
1. Mass media and children – United States.   2. Mass media and teenagers –
United States.   3. Internet and children – United States.   4. Internet and
teenagers – United States.   5. Child consumers – United States.
6. Teenage consumers – United States.   I. Foehr, Ulla G.   II. Henry J. Kaiser
Family Foundation.   III. Title.

HQ784.M3R515   2003
305.23′083–dc21   2003046183

ISBN 0 521 82102 9 hardback
ISBN 0 521 52790 2 paperback

This book is dedicated to
our spouses,
Wendy and Matt,
and to "the second work in progress,"
Greta

CONTENTS

TABLES AND FIGURES

TABLES

Figures

Acknowledgments

A research project of the magnitude reported in this book is the result of the efforts of many individuals over a long period of time. First and foremost, credit must go to the Kaiser Family Foundation, which conducted the study, and particularly to Victoria Rideout, Vice President and Director of the Foundation's Program for the Study of Entertainment Media and Health. She conceived and shepherded the project from its inception.

One of the missions of the Kaiser Family Foundation is to inform and educate young people about various health issues relevant to them. In December 1997, Ms. Rideout convened a group of communication scholars at the Kaiser Family Foundation campus in Menlo Park to discuss the state of knowledge about the effects of sexual content in the media and to establish a research agenda in this area. One important gap in knowledge identified at that meeting was the lack of a comprehensive, up-to-date mapping of children's and adolescents' media use, a gap that Ms. Rideout believed the Kaiser Family Foundation could help to fill.

With the support of Drew Altman, the President and CEO of the Kaiser Family Foundation, and Matt James, Sr. Vice President and Director of Media and Public Education, Rideout assembled a research team to design and execute the study – the first-ever national random sample survey to focus on U.S. children and adolescents' use of all of the various mass media. That team consisted of Rideout herself, Dr. Mollyann Brodie, Vice President and Director of Public Opinion and Media Research, and the two senior authors of this book (at that time, Ms. Foehr was also employed by the Kaiser Family Foundation).

This team, with the able staff support of Ms. Theresa Boston, devoted several years to bringing the study to completion.

Once the broad outlines of the study and questionnaire were settled, Harris Interactive, Inc. (formerly Louis Harris and Associates), joined the project. Under the management of Dr. Dana Markow, Research Director, Harris Interactive assisted in the later stages of questionnaire construction, as well as designing (in conjunction with Kaiser staff and sampling consultant Dr. Marty Frankel) and carrying out the sampling, conducting all interviews and questionnaire administration, and providing the initial data set and top-line results. Thanks are due to the many people at Harris who were involved in this study.

The original data analysis for the Kaiser report was conducted at the Foundation by Ulla Foehr and Dr. Mollyann Brodie. Most of the data analysis for the book was conducted in the Department of Communication at Stanford University. At this stage, the assistance of Dr. Melissa Saphir must be acknowledged. Still a graduate student at the time, Dr. Saphir showed remarkable patience and skill during the early stages of organizing a massive data set into easily manageable form.

The task of turning the initial research findings, which were released by the Kaiser Family Foundation in November 1999, into a more comprehensive and accessible book was also facilitated by the administrative staff of Stanford's Department of Communication, who did much to assist our efforts on a day-to-day basis, and by Ms. Christina Yang, who served as a Research Intern for the authors. In addition, various other individuals contributed less directly, but no less importantly. Among these we count the faculty and graduate students in the Department of Communication, many of whose comments and suggestions are incorporated in the following pages. In particular, we are grateful for the conceptual and statistical advice of Professor Clifford Nass.

Finally, we must offer thanks to our two biggest supporters and cheerleaders – Wendy Roberts and Matt Foehr. Throughout the course of this study, they never failed to provide encouragement, assistance, and help. Each time the task seemed to become overwhelming (in a project of this size, those times do occur), they urged us on, held our hands, took us to dinner – whatever was needed to keep us on track. And last but not least, we must acknowledge one who did more than any other to keep us working on schedule – Miss Greta Foehr. As we struggled to bring this work in progress to a close, she was a second work in progress. Her impending arrival in the summer of 2002 served as a superb motivator.

Now that we are finished, she serves as a superb reward – not to mention a continuing work in progress.

Donald F. Roberts and Ulla G. Foehr

Stanford University
January 2003

CHAPTER ONE

The Changing Media Landscape

Of the many technological innovations the United States has witnessed during the latter half of the twenty-first century, arguably none have been more important in the lives of children and adolescents than the emergence and evolution of the new communication technologies. In a little over 50 years, we have moved from a media environment dominated by local newspapers and radio stations to one characterized by an almost continual diet of highly vivid, on-demand, audiovisual images, many with interactive capabilities.

Readers nearing retirement age probably recall a childhood media environment consisting of magazines and newspapers, radio (drama, game shows, music, 5-minute news broadcasts), possibly a phonograph, and an occasional Saturday matinee at a neighborhood movie theater – with two or three television channels perhaps joining the mix during adolescence. In contrast, most of today's high school students cannot recall a time when the universe of television channels was fewer than three dozen (even without cable or satellite, many homes can receive more than 20 broadcast channels), and their younger siblings have never known a world without interactive video games, personal computers, the World Wide Web, and instant messaging. Older readers probably remember when chocolate syrup dabbed on a shirt sleeve served convincingly as blood in Gene Autry westerns; youths today take for granted films and video games in which blood, gore, and severed limbs complete with spasmodic nerve endings are the norm. Some of us can still recall a time when adults were assumed to be advertisers' only targets and companies such as 3M and General Electric sponsored *The Mickey Mouse Club*. Today's teenagers, who spent in excess of

1

$155 billion in 2000 (Teens spend . . . , 2001), have never known a time when they were not viewed as consumers, thus when substantial portions of media and media content were not tailored expressly for them (Pecora, 1998).

In this modern media environment, how much time do American children devote to each of the different media? What content do they encounter, select, or ignore? What are the social conditions under which they consume different kinds of media content? Do different subgroups of youth select different media mixes? Do media-use patterns differ within different subgroups?

The importance of such seemingly straightforward questions cannot be underestimated. Without an accurate mapping of children's and adolescents' patterns of media use, we can never fully understand the role of mass mediated messages in the lives of youth. At bottom, any statement about how media content affects what youngsters believe and how they act rests on an assumption that those youngsters are exposed to the message. But what is the basis for such an assumption? Do we really have an accurate picture of children's and adolescents' patterns of media use?

Literally hundreds of empirical studies conducted over the past half-century leave little doubt that, given exposure, media content can and does influence youngsters' beliefs, attitudes, and behaviors. Indeed, the evidence is so ample that few mass communication scholars hesitate to list mass media as equal in importance to most other socialization agents (e.g., parents, schools, churches) in the lives of contemporary U.S. children (see, e.g., Calvert, 1999; Christenson & Roberts, 1998; Comstock, 1991; Strasburger & Wilson, 2002). This same body of research also tells us that the nature and degree of media influence depends on a wide array of factors, not the least of which are the various facets of media use characterized in the questions posed above: media choices, media mix, media time, content selection, consumption conditions, subgroup characteristics.

What is surprising, given the growing concern with the role of media in children's lives and the large number of empirical studies examining children and media, is the absence of comprehensive, current information about overall media use patterns among contemporary U.S. youth. In spite of numerous studies of young people's consumption of various individual media available today, we are aware of no research that has examined use of the full array of media among a representative sample of U.S. youth, let alone how young people have accepted, adopted, and begun to use the new media that have emerged over the past few years.

THE CHANGING MEDIA LANDSCAPE

Over the past several decades, young people's media environment has changed in several ways, each of which has affected the kinds of information available and/or how youth interpret that information and integrate it into their belief systems. Changes include increases in both the number and kinds of media available, in the number of choices each medium offers, in the fidelity with which symbols and images can be transmitted, and in the degree of privacy with which each medium can be experienced.

Clearly, the number of different kinds of media through which youngsters acquire information has exploded. The first large-scale examinations of children's media use in North America, conducted in the late 1950s and 1960s (e.g., Lyle & Hoffman, 1972a, 1972b; Schramm, Lyle & Parker, 1961; Steiner, 1963), needed to survey only a few media: television, radio and records, print (newspapers, magazines, books), and movies. By the 1980s, however, the media landscape looked quite different. By then it included broadcast, cable, and satellite television, the VCR, newspapers, a growing number of books and magazines aimed specifically at children and adolescents, numerous audio media (e.g., stereo systems, portable radios, tape and CD players), video games, and the personal computer (see Dorr & Kunkel, 1990). At the dawn of a new millennium, the media environment continues to change. Entire television channels now target children or adolescents. Both audio systems and video games have become miniaturized and highly portable. The personal computer now includes CD-Rom and DVD capabilities and serves as a gateway to the World Wide Web, and seemingly unlimited access to any and all human information. Technological advances have put young people in constant contact with their peers via cell phones, instant messaging, e-mail, and pagers. Cellular phones have merged with the World Wide Web, and mainstream virtual reality media loom just ahead.

Not only have new media appeared, but older media have evolved, offering more channels more vividly than ever before. In the mid-1950s, major television markets typically boasted five or six broadcast channels; today, cable and satellites make literally hundreds of channels a possibility in even the most isolated locations. At the half-century mark, a few of our larger cities hosted as many as eight or ten AM radio stations. In August 2001, the radio guide in San Francisco listed 28 AM and 45 FM stations. In the early 1950s *Billboard* magazine reported separate charts for three categories of music recordings; *Billboard* today charts more than 20 music genres. As recently as 1985, most personal computers were limited to whatever software one loaded on them; today they serve as portals to a worldwide network of content so vast and fluid that it is almost impossible to describe.

Along with rapid growth in media channels, digital technology is dramatically altering media experiences, providing sights and sounds that equal or – some would argue – surpass reality. Today's audiences hear orchestras in their own homes with the fidelity of the concert hall; they experience space travel in movie theaters so real that it can engender motion sickness; almost any screen they turn to can portray violence and mayhem so vividly that it leaves viewers ducking to avoid being spattered. And finally, the new interactive media have transformed listening and viewing audiences into active participants. Children no longer simply watch actors shoot at each other; they now take part in the action, blasting anything on screen that moves.

There is also good reason to believe that the proliferation and miniaturization of communication devices themselves is changing the social context of media use, turning what was once a family experience into an activity that, for many youngsters, is more and more private. The findings we report in this study show that almost nine out of 10 U.S. households (88%) have two or more television sets (61% have three or more), and about half of all children (54%) have a television in their bedrooms. Similarly, it is a rare adolescent who does not own a radio *and* a CD or tape player, also typically used in private, whether in the bedroom, the automobile, or through personal headphones. Nearly seven out of 10 (69%) households with children under 18 own a computer, and just under half (45%) have Internet access. Often youngsters sit at the computer terminal alone, many in the privacy of their bedrooms. In other words, although it has always been possible for youth, especially adolescents, to engage in various kinds of media use with some degree of privacy, the new media appear to have given today's kids a great deal more autonomy in their media selection, and a great deal more freedom from adult supervision of or comment about the messages they receive than was the case in even the very recent past. Moreover, continuing advances in miniaturization and portability (e.g., cell phones with Internet access) suggest that media experiences are likely to become even more private.

For much of the latter half of the twentieth century, then, and particularly during the last two decades, North American children's media environment has undergone revolutionary change. Today's youth have access to more media with more channels or outlets within each medium, offering more (and more varied) content, more vividly than even the most "outlandish" midcentury science-fiction novels once predicted. And perhaps most important, technological changes and contemporary social trends may be combining to create a media environment in which youth use these media largely independent of adult supervision or comment – indeed, often in the absence of adult awareness.

CHILDREN AND MEDIA: A HISTORY OF CONCERN

Expressions of concern about children and media – or, more accurately, about content from "outside" that media make available to children – can be traced back at least to Plato's defense of censorship in *The Republic*. They have continued with the introduction of each new medium. Regardless of historical period, whenever children have acquired access to "stories from outside" – whether from a storyteller, a book of fairy tales, or a screen of any kind – parents, educators, and social critics have worried (Roberts, 2003; Starker, 1989). Concern mounted significantly, however, with the introduction of electronic media (e.g., motion pictures and radio), and especially with the introduction of television in the 1950s. Electronic media, but particularly television, gave children both physical and psychological access to a much wider array of content than ever before available. Between 1948, when there were barely 100,000 television receivers in the United States, and the end of 1959, when seven out of eight homes (about 50 million) had acquired a TV set, young people entered a new world. Television was new in terms of the amounts and kinds of information, ideas, and images made easily available, and in terms of allowing children's growing "information independence" – that is, their ability to access and process such information freer from adult supervision than in any previous period. In the course of that single decade, the media environment changed from one in which parents could serve as relatively effective gatekeepers to one in which the gates began to leak at ever more alarming rates.

Prior to television, parents could exert at least some control over children's access to messages. The seven or eight years it took most children to learn to read provided time for parents to establish the "cognitive templates" that their offspring used to interpret the meaning of print and audio symbols. Television was different. With its easily accessed, easily interpreted audiovisual symbols, it created a new kind of symbolic environment. Once in the home, television was on much of the time (in some homes, most of the time). It provided even very young children both physical and psychological access (three-year-olds can operate the TV set and have little difficulty making some kind of sense of audiovisual symbols) to numerous stories from "outside" the home well before parents had time firmly to establish baseline definitions of the world. (Although motion pictures were available to youngsters before 1950, it was an unusual child who spent more than a couple of hours a week in a movie theater, and it was a time when most youngsters still asked parents for permission and money to attend the movies.) Small wonder that parental worry about the potential impact of content over which they had little or no control increased substantially during television's first ten years (Roberts, 2003), and continues to this day (Kaiser Family Foundation, 2001; Kaiser Family Foundation & YM Magazine, 1998).

Small wonder, too, that this same decade saw the real beginning of what has become a long tradition of scientific study on children and media, a tradition that has demonstrated clearly that media messages can influence children's and adolescents' beliefs, attitudes, and behavior across a wide range of topic areas. Although the 1930s had witnessed a brief spate of research activity concerned with motion pictures and youth (Charters, 1933), it was not until television had moved into a majority of U.S. households that sustained scientific examination of whether and how constant audiovisual images might influence youth took hold. Over the ensuing half-century, literally hundreds of studies examined media influence on children and adolescents.

Research concerning media effects on youth has proceeded from several different theoretical perspectives, but they assume in common that a necessary condition for any influence is some level of exposure. At issue, however, is how exposure is conceptualized and the degree to which amount of exposure and/or different exposure conditions play a role in the media effects process. On the one hand, as little as a single viewing of a brief screen display has been shown to influence young people's beliefs, attitudes, and behavior. On the other hand, both longitudinal field experiments and survey studies that attempt to measure typical media exposure over time have demonstrated that while for some youngsters effects occur following multiple exposures, for others even long-term exposure seems to have little impact (for reviews, see Comstock, 1991; Strasburger & Wilson, 2002).

Numerous experimental studies have documented that a brief exposure to screen portrayals affects children's beliefs and behaviors. For the most part, the experimental work has proceeded from either of two theoretical orientations: (1) Albert Bandura's social cognitive theory, particularly parts of the theory that concern observational learning processes (Bandura, 1986, 2002), and (2) "cognitive neo-associationist" examinations of how media portrayals may operate to "prime" other semantically related concepts and emotions, thereby influencing viewers' behavior (e.g., Berkowitz, 1984; Jo & Berkowitz, 1994; Josephson, 1987). Once early experiments had demonstrated that exposure to behavior portrayed on a screen can influence young viewers, subsequent research focused largely on how different attributes of a particular portrayal (e.g., Is an act portrayed as rewarded or punished? Justified or unjustified? Is there repetition?), of particular audience members (e.g., Are they boys or girls? Children or adolescents? Similar or dissimilar to the actors? From family environments that encourage or discourage exploration of new ideas?), and of particular reception conditions (e.g., Does the child watch alone, with peers, or with parents? In a public or private venue?) operate to mediate different effects of media exposure. By and large, this work has produced ample empirical evidence that, *assuming exposure*, media messages play a significant role in the socialization of youth (for reviews, see Bushman & Anderson, 2001; Calvert, 1999; Christenson & Roberts, 1983, 1998; Comstock, 1991; Comstock and Scharrer, 1999; Federman, Carbone, Chen & Munn, 1996; Huston, Donnerstein, Fairchild, Feshbach, et al., 1992; Paik & Comstock, 1994; Roberts, 1993, 2003; Roberts & Maccoby, 1985; Strasburger & Wilson, 2002; Wartella & Reeves, 1987). Unfortunately, outside the laboratory, assumptions about the amount or nature of exposure may be invalid, and factors that do not operate under experimental conditions may play an important role in mediating or moderating the effects of media exposure.

A third theoretical approach, George Gerbner's cultivation theory, posits that beliefs and attitudes about the real world are influenced by how television (or, theoretically, any other dominant medium) portrays the world as a rather straightforward function of amount of exposure (e.g., Gerbner & Gross, 1976; Gerbner, Gross, Morgan, Signorielli, & Shanahan, 2002). That is, cultivation theory posits that the more people (whether children, adolescents, or adults) attend to television's portrayal of the world, the more likely they are to accept that view as valid. Not surprisingly, one of the more hotly debated dimensions of Gerbner's work concerns the nature of exposure. Numerous questions about whether all exposure is equal, whether all content is equal, what constitutes heavy or light viewing, and so forth, have been raised (e.g., Gerbner, Gross, Morgan, & Signorielli, 1981; Hirsch, 1980; Potter, 1993). These are all issues that point to the importance of understanding audience exposure to media messages.[1]

In short, an important key to understanding media effects is understanding media exposure. If we are to integrate results from experimental studies of media effects on young people with data from surveys and field studies, then we need to map media exposure very carefully.

Previous Research on Children's Media Use

Surprisingly, in the midst of the growing body of research on youth and media there remain significant questions about real-world patterns of media use – questions regarding which kids encounter which messages, how often, from which sources, and under which conditions. Even more important given the explosion in new communication technologies and the evidence that youth are often among the early adopters of these new technologies (Center for Media Education, 2001), we know relatively little about how kids mix and balance the wide array of media available to them today. For example, might a youngster's fascination with the World Wide Web lead to a reduction in television viewing time? Do kids who read a lot ignore television?

Even though children and media have been a research focus for almost half a century, and even though a full understanding of the role of media in the lives of youth requires careful documentation of how they use each different medium, most of our information about children's media use patterns comes either from relatively small, nonrepresentative samples of U.S. children or from studies that have focused on relatively few media. A few recent national sample surveys have asked questions about children's use of several different media (e.g., Bower, 1985; Horatio

---

[1] Recently, Zillmann's exemplification theory has begun to explain the processes that might underlie cultivation effects, fundamentally by pointing to the power of examples, particularly concrete examples, of any issue to influence one's conceptualization of that issue. Concepts such as frequency and recency of exposure and concreteness of exemplars lie at the core of his theory – all concepts that point to the importance of mapping complex patterns of media exposure (Zillmann, 1999, 2002).

Alger Foundation, 1996; Kaiser Family Foundation & YM Magazine, 1998; Stanger, 1997; Stanger & Gridina, 1999), but these are more the exception than the rule. The majority of academic studies of children's use of media also tend to focus on just two or three (e.g., television, radio, computers) and to use small, and/or nonrepresentative samples of young respondents. Thus, for example, academic researchers often base conclusions on such samples as junior high school students in the southeast (Brown, Childers, Bauman & Koch, 1990), sixth and tenth graders from Michigan (Greenberg, Ku, & Li, 1989), high school students from the San Francisco Bay area (Roberts & Henriksen, 1990), or 6- through 12-year-olds from Portland, Oregon (Christenson, 1994).

We have found no study in the public domain that has surveyed a large, representative sample of U.S. youth *and* that has included items concerning a full array of media and media behaviors – that is, questions about amount of use, content selection, the social context in which use occurs, and the interrelationships among television (broadcast and cable), videos, motion pictures, radio, CDs and tapes, print (newspapers, magazines, books, comic books), video games, and the computer (including games, the Internet, and the World Wide Web).

Two of the most comprehensive U.S. studies of young people's media use were conducted in the late 1950s and the late 1960s. They offer insights into media use patterns of young people in the middle of the twentieth century, before many of today's communication technologies had been introduced. We know, for example, that by the end of the 1950s, sixth-grade children (12-year-olds) from the Rocky Mountain West were devoting about 3 hours per day to television and almost an hour and a quarter to radio and recordings (Schramm, Lyle, and Parker, 1961). A decade later, Los Angeles 12-year-olds reported 4 hours of daily TV viewing, and Los Angeles 16-year-olds claimed about 2 hours of daily music listening (Lyle & Hoffman, 1972a). Although dated, these numbers are remarkably similar to television and music use estimates obtained from today's young people.

More recently, a large sample of junior high school students (approximately 12 to 14 years old) from 10 Southeastern cities claimed to devote about 6 hours per day to television and another 5 hours to radio (Brown et al., 1990), and a national sample of high school students (13 to 17 years) reported about 4 and a half hours of daily viewing and 4 hours of radio listening (Horatio Alger Foundation, 1996). If we add to this the time spent reading (magazines, newspapers, nonschool books), attending motion pictures, watching videos, playing video games, working with personal computers both off-line and on-line, then any estimates that today's young adolescents are exposed to media as much as 8 to 10 hours per day (cf. Roberts, 2001; Roberts & Henriksen, 1990) do not seem extravagant. Nevertheless, to our knowledge, no study using a representative sample of U.S. youth and measuring exposure to most currently extant media has tested this claim.

Although past studies of children and adolescents have produced relatively consistent findings with regard to the relationship between some kinds of media use and various social and demographic variables, they have left several important gaps in our knowledge. Many earlier studies report the average amount of time children spend with one or another medium, but these averages conceal a great deal of variation. Some children watch no television on an average day, others view more than 8 hours. Some children have no access to a computer, others spend much of their free time online. Some children may hear one or two top-40 songs while being driven to soccer practice, while for others Walkman headphones serve as a standard part of the wardrobe and the latest hip hop hits wash over them continually. More interesting than either averages or the fact that children differ greatly in how they use media, however, is that much of the variation in children's media use is predictable. That is, the amount of time kids spend viewing, listening, or going on-line – as well as what they watch, hear, or access – is related to a wide variety of social and demographic factors.

For example, past research has demonstrated that the amount of time children and adolescents devote to each medium (as well as the ways in which they use each) depends on such factors as age (e.g., television viewing time increases until about 12 or 13 years, then tapers off throughout adolescence; music listening begins at around 9 to 10 years and steadily increases throughout adolescence), gender (e.g., boys spend more time than girls using computers and playing video games), race and ethnicity (e.g., African American adolescents use both television and radio more than their white counterparts), intelligence (e.g., as IQ increases, television viewing decreases and reading increases), social integration (e.g., youth with few friends spend more time with media than do those with many friends), geographical location, household socioeconomic status, and family size (see, e.g., Bower, 1985; Brown et al., 1990; Christenson & Roberts, 1998; Comstock, 1991; Comstock and Scharrer, 1999; Lyle & Hoffman, 1972a; Schramm et al., 1961).

In addition, large disparities among different estimates of the total amount of time children devote to the various media are quite common.

For example, within any 10-year period estimates of children's daily television viewing may range from about 2 hours (e.g., Stanger, 1997) to over 5 hours (e.g., Brown et al., 1990). Similarly, different studies have found that different media dominate. That is, although some researchers report that adolescents devote more time to television than to music media (e.g., Brown et al., 1990; Horatio Alger Foundation, 1996), others argue the reverse (e.g., Christenson & Roberts, 1998; Roberts & Henriksen, 1990). Large gaps in our knowledge of total media budgets and of the interrelationships among all of the various media also persist. Some of the reasons for these kinds of discrepancies are explored in Chapter 2.

In summary, then, although previous empirical studies have touched on a few of the important facets of children's and adolescent's media use, and have provided us with very good evidence that children devote a lot of time to all of the mass media, several factors limit the generalizations that can be drawn. Among these limiting factors we include:

- relatively few studies have used nationwide probability samples that are truly representative of U.S. children;
- those studies with representative samples have often tended to focus primarily on one particular medium, including only a few (if any) questions about other media for comparative purposes;
- sampling procedures that would promote studying media use within various minority racial/ethnic groups have been largely neglected;
- the variety of measurement techniques that has been used makes meaningful comparisons among different studies difficult at best.

As a result, there exists little public information about the overall mix of media that today's young people use, about how the emergence of new media has influenced the overall media mix for different children, about whether recent changes in the media environment have changed how much time youth devote to different media, and about how they use those media at the dawn of the twenty-first century.

The goal of this book is to address many of these gaps in our knowledge and to provide a more solid base on which to build future research concerning the effects of media on young people. In the following pages, we report a national, random-sample survey of U.S. young people's media behavior. We believe it is the first representative study to examine children's and adolescents' exposure to the full array of mass media available at the close of the twentieth century. The study was conceived and directed by the staff of the Kaiser Family Foundation, in conjunction with Harris Interactive, Inc. (formerly Louis Harris and Associates), and faculty and students in Stanford University's Department of Communication.

CHAPTER TWO

THE MEASUREMENT OF MEDIA

BEHAVIOR

In this chapter, we present the methods and procedures used to gather information about U.S. youth's media behavior leading into the twenty-first century. The study examines young people's leisure time exposure to television, videotapes, movies, video games, newspapers, magazines, books, radio, audio recordings (CDs and tapes), and the computer. The chapter briefly introduces a few of the obstacles that militate against collection of accurate information when surveying youth. It goes on to describe how we addressed those obstacles by collecting data from two distinct samples of youngsters and by constructing questionnaire items that made as few demands on memory as possible.

At its core, this book is about time – the time children and adolescents spend with various media. Although at first glance measuring media time might seem a relatively straightforward task, over the past several decades social scientists have come to view it as difficult at best. For example, because television typically comes packaged in convenient half-hour segments, TV exposure might seem, theoretically at least, relatively easy to measure. It is tempting to assume that when asked how much television they view, individuals will simply think of what programs they watched (or usually watch) on a typical day, add the half-hour and hour segments together, and thus arrive at an accurate answer. Moreover, we are used to seeing highly precise statements from organizations such as Nielsen Media Research regarding the average amount of television viewing time in U.S. households. Such accuracy would seem to attest to the apparent ease with which TV viewing can be measured. Unfortunately, we all too often overlook the fact that although the Nielsen ratings provide accurate statements about how much time household TV sets are in operation, their estimates of time spent viewing by different individuals within the household are open to question.

In their book entitled *Television*, George Comstock and Erica Scharrer (1999) note that, particularly in recent years, the measurement of TV viewing time has become quite controversial. They argue that because the proliferation of television channels and resulting fragmentation of the audience has increased the importance of leaving no viewer un-counted, sample sizes and procedures once deemed adequate to measure network audiences have been called into question. In addition, changes in the technology of measurement made partly in response to the new multichannel TV environment (e.g., the people meter) have resulted in substantial changes in audience statistics, most notably a drop in the proportion of viewers estimated to be tuning into one of the three major networks. The discrepancies with earlier estimates have raised fundamental questions about the validity of audience measurement.

When we move beyond television exposure to attempt to measure time spent with other media, time that is not so easily broken into con-venient half-hour units, the problems multiply. Even under the best of circumstances, the act of estimating time devoted to almost *any* activity is difficult. For example, consider the following question:

"On an average day, how much time do you, the reader, spend eat-ing?" After thinking of an answer, consider the following: Did you in-clude snacking while watching television or working or driving a car? Did you include or ignore the 10 minutes sitting at the breakfast table when, totally engrossed in the newspaper, no food passed your lips? Did you include or ignore time spent drinking (as opposed to eating)? What did you determine to be an average day? Did any of these subsequent questions motivate you to revise your initial estimate? Would your an-swer have been different if you had been asked this question in the context of a survey questionnaire that allowed you only a few seconds to respond?

Robinson and Godbey (1997) list a number of obstacles to obtaining accurate responses about time use. They note that any question about time devoted to an activity such as watching television assumes that a given respondent:

- interprets "watching television" in the same way as do others;
- separates the primary activity from other activities taking place simultaneously (e.g., when paying bills in front of the television, which activity is counted as the primary one?);

- adequately searches memory for all episodes of TV viewing during the period asked about (e.g., usually, yesterday, a typical day, last week);
- can and does add up all the episode lengths across the period asked about;
- feels comfortable disclosing or describing this duration when it may not be a typical day or week; and
- avoids reverting to presumed social norms, stereotypes, or images of themselves about how much a "normal" or average person ought to watch television.

As noted above, TV exposure is probably the easiest kind of media use to measure. With the possible exception of movies (and some radio), other kinds of media are seldom indexed in time-based units. Indeed, newer TV formats such as music videos and all-news formats, and even some traditional programs, are beginning to ignore the conventional 30-minute structure. Moreover, for many individuals a central characteristic of some kinds of media is that they cause one to lose track of time. It is not uncommon, for example, for people to report that they look up from a book or turn away from a video game or a web-surfing session to discover that literally hours have disappeared. Finally, it is also clear that other kinds of media use often constitute "background" activity, and it is legitimate to expect that people will have difficulty accurately estimating how much time they spend with media when used as a backdrop to other, more primary activities.

Another difficulty inherent in attempting to measure and compare different kinds of media exposure is that the nature of the symbols and/or content generally associated with each different medium typically elicits very different levels of cognitive engagement. Salomon (1979) referred to this as "depth of processing" and argued that in general audiovisual media (e.g., television) require less depth of processing than do print media. At the extremes, it seems intuitively reasonable that reading or playing a complex video game requires relatively more focused attention and active cognitive processing than does listening to popular music or watching television. George Comstock (1991), for example, has observed that children's and teenagers' experience of television is more accurately characterized as "monitoring" (scanning audio, visual, and social cues as to the desirability of paying attention to the screen) than as "viewing" (which implies greater attention to the screen).

Of course, depending on the nature of the content and on individual differences in interests and abilities, there can be a good deal of variation in depth of processing materials within any one medium. Sometimes we skim a newspaper; sometimes we read it carefully. Sometimes music provides background; sometimes we pay close attention to a particular composition or performance. Sometimes we are critically attentive to a TV show; sometimes (often?) TV viewing is casual and sporadic (see, e.g., Potter, 1998). In general, however, reading or engaging in any of several computer activities typically elicits more attention and cognitive activity than does listening to music or watching television. Such differences in depth of processing are important. For example, how deeply a user processes content surely plays a role in whether and how that individual may be affected (Comstock, 1991; Salomon, 1979), a factor that must be taken into account in any between-media comparison of effects. That is, when attempting to compare the effects of exposure to different media, equal units of time seldom ensure equal units of exposure, because identical content delivered by different media cannot be equated on the basis of exposure time alone. The amount of information processed and the depth at which it is processed is quite likely to be quantitatively and qualitatively different for 10 minutes of TV viewing versus 10 minutes of newspaper reading.

Similar obstacles to accuracy may apply to a wider variety of survey questions than just those pertaining to time. Almost any introductory text in survey methods warns novice researchers that respondents often do not respond accurately to queries about education or income levels, let alone about opinions or attitudes. Even such a seemingly straightforward question as one about race or ethnicity may not be as simple as it first appears, depending on how a particular mixed-race or multiethnic individual classifies him- or herself.

Measuring Young People's Media Behavior

The problem of accuracy becomes even more complex when children and adolescents are the target of study. Typically, the youngest cannot even tell time. For both younger and older children, the task of recalling "yesterday's" activities may be difficult; for some, the task of conceptualizing an "average" or "typical" day may be almost impossible. In addition, as most parents who have fielded a string of "How much longer . . . ?" queries from their offspring can attest, children and even adolescents (who presumably can "tell time") have different conceptions of time units than we might expect from adults. Young people also often lack accurate information about a variety of other relatively standard (and important) survey questions. For example, many youngsters have no idea of their parents' education or income level; others may have been given false information. Moreover, differences in interpretation of what a question asks may be even greater among children and adolescents than among a sample of adults. We suspect, for example, that variations in what "reading" means to 7-year-olds and 16-year-olds may be both qualitatively and quantitatively greater than the variations likely to be found among adults.

Without further belaboring the issue, suffice it to say that the task of surveying a large sample of children and adolescents about how they spend their media time poses a variety of measurement problems. Some we can deal with; some we must simply acknowledge.

This study employs two overarching strategies to address many of the measurement difficulties inherent in surveys of youth. First, the results reported here describe two different samples of young people – one consisting of younger children (2 to 7 years) and one consisting of older children and adolescents (8 to 18 years). Our use of two samples is based on the assumption that parents are better equipped than their young children to provide valid information about the media behavior of 2- to 7-year-olds, but that older youth can and will provide more accurate information about themselves and their behavior. Each sample was developed by Harris Interactive, Inc. (formerly Louis Harris and Associates) in consultation with staff at the Kaiser Family Foundation; each comprises a nationally representative sample.

Second, as much as possible questions were designed to minimize demands on memory and to avoid asking respondents to conceptualize "typical" media exposure. In particular, all questions about media exposure are phrased in terms of the previous day (i.e., "yesterday") or previous weekend day, with interviews and questionnaire administration spread in roughly equal proportions across the school days of the week. The following sections provide more details about the samples and sampling procedures and about questionnaire design and administration.

THE SAMPLES

The information in this study was obtained from two distinct and independent nationally representative samples that are briefly described here. Appendix 2.1 presents a more detailed description of sampling procedures.

The "in-home" sample consists of 1,090 young children, ages 2 through 7 years, and relies on parent responses to questionnaires administered in the home. The "in-school" sample consists of 2,014 older children and adolescents, ages 8 through 18 years, and relies on questionnaires completed in school by the young people themselves. To ensure large enough numbers of African American and Hispanic youth to permit reasonably stable subgroup analyses (e.g., examination of differences in media behavior as a function of race/ethnicity while controlling for age, or gender, or parent education), these two groups were oversampled. That is, extra numbers of children and adolescents from these racial and ethnic groups were included. Finally, in addition to the two representative samples providing the survey data, participants were also invited to complete a "media-use diary" detailing all of their media activities over the course of a 7-day week. This resulted in two self-selected supplemental samples: 134 diaries for 2- to 7-year-olds (parents completed or assisted with the young children's diaries) and 487 diaries completed by 8- to 18-year-olds.

YOUNG CHILDREN: THE IN-HOME SAMPLE

The sample of younger children (the in-home sample) was obtained using an area probability sampling procedure based on a U.S. Census list of 255,000 block groups in the continental United States. The sample was stratified by region, state, county, census tract, and block group. Depending on population density, a "block group" may range from a single city block (or group of blocks) in an urban area to a geographical area of land with identifiable boundaries such as streams, roads, or civil boundaries in a rural area. A random selection of block groups was drawn based on the number of households within each block group, after which an area probability sampling procedure was used to select individual households.

OLDER CHILDREN AND ADOLESCENTS: THE IN-SCHOOL SAMPLE

The sample of older children and adolescents (the in-school sample) was drawn from the Harris national probability samples of schools and students. The sample is based on a highly stratified two-stage sampling design. In the first stage, a sample of schools is selected from a list of approximately 80,000 public, private, and parochial schools in the United States. In the second stage, a class from within each of the chosen schools is randomly selected to participate. In junior and senior high schools, where students attend different classes for each subject, only English classes were used to make the class selection. (This procedure resulted in 2,065 completed questionnaires. However, subsequent examination of questionnaires revealed that 51 were suspect because of what we judged to be impossibly high reports of time spent with several of the media. These were eliminated, leaving a sample of 2,014 questionnaires as the basis for the analyses reported in this book).[1]

Each of the two final samples has been weighted to ensure that they are nationally representative. For the sample of 8- to 18-year-olds, the margin of error is +/− 3 percent. That is, readers can be confident that sample percentages reported for the in-school sample are within + or − 3 percent of the "true" population percentages. For the sample of 2- to 7-year-olds, the margin of error is +/− 5 percent.

QUESTIONNAIRES

Questionnaires were designed to elicit as much information about young people's media behavior as possible in a relatively brief time. Questions assessed which media children and adolescents have access to and use, how much time they spend with each medium, the kinds of content consumed, and the social context of media exposure. Several questions asked about attitudes toward the different media and about youngsters' general contentment or satisfaction with their lives. Finally, in order to look at possible differences in how various subgroups of children and adolescents use media, we included a number of relatively standard demographic questions.

QUESTIONNAIRE ADMINISTRATION

Our interest in obtaining information about the media habits of even very young children, in combination with the complex and

---

[1] Because of the elimination of these 51 questionnaires, some slight differences occur in the results presented in the original technical report describing this study and the results reported here.

comprehensive nature of the questionnaire, made it impractical (if not impossible) to administer questionnaires directly to the 2- to 7-year-olds. Thus, the information about the younger sample is based on individual, face-to-face interviews conducted in the home with parents or caregivers in the presence of the young child. Parents and children could and did consult on many of the questions, and at least one item – pertaining to the child's preferred medium – was usually completed by the child. Older children and adolescents, on the other hand, reported on their own behavior by completing self-administered questionnaires in their classrooms.

Two, highly similar questionnaires were developed. The two versions differed primarily in terms of question wording depending on whether parents or the students themselves were responding. A few items were asked only of parents about young children (e.g., parents were asked whether they spent time reading to their young child; older children did not encounter a similar question). Because of time constraints and differences in reading abilities, a few questions asked of parents in the in-home sample and of seventh through twelfth graders in the in-school sample were not included for third through sixth graders. For the most part, these concerned the kinds of media content consumed. All versions of the questionnaire were designed to require about 40 minutes to complete. Finally, through asking media questions about the preceding day or preceding weekend day (i.e., "Thinking only about yesterday . . . how much total time . . ."), care was taken to assure that roughly equal proportions of each sample responded each day of the school week.[2]

MEDIA EXPOSURE MEASURES

Media examined in this study include television, commercial videotapes, self-recorded videotapes, movies, video games, newspapers, magazines, books, radio, CDs and tapes, and computers (games, chat rooms, websites, e-mail). Questions assessed availability of each medium within the household, amount of exposure to each medium, type of content used, and the social context of use. With the exception of a few items asking about computer use in school, all media questions were phrased in terms of *leisure time* activity.

[2] Copies of the original questionnaire may be obtained from the Kaiser Family Foundation, 2400 Sand Hill Road, Menlo Park, CA 94025 (*www.kff.org*).

Key questions asked young people to report how much time, in minutes and hours, they were exposed to each medium. Following suggestions implicit in Comstock's (1991; Comstock & Scharrer, 1999) discussions of measuring young people's TV viewing, questions about media exposure were made as specific as possible. To minimize reliance on memory, respondents were asked about only the preceding day's (or weekend day's) media activities. In addition, questions asking about TV exposure divided the day into three subparts: morning, afternoon, and evening. Respondents were provided with a TV "grid," similar to the TV guides found in most newspapers, listing all of the previous day's programming and program times. This functioned as both a memory aid and as a means to obtain genre information. To capture brief instances of media use, respondents were given time scales in which the first hour was broken into several small units of time (i.e., none, 5 minutes, 15 minutes, 30 minutes, 45 minutes, 1 hour), then increased in half-hour increments to $7\frac{1}{2}$ hours. This type of time scale was designed to avoid forcing someone who might use a medium for 10 or 15 minutes to choose between 0 and 30 minutes, a problem in some earlier studies.

Young people who indicated they were exposed to a medium the preceding day were further asked to indicate the kinds of content consumed. For all but the TV questions this was accomplished by marking a list of content genres typically associated with each medium. For example, the list of music genres for CDs and tapes included alternative rock, top 40 rock, rap/hip hop, salsa, and so forth. Appendix 2.2 contains the genres used for each medium. Assessment of TV content was determined directly from the specific programs that children and adolescents indicated they had watched on the TV grids. Each TV program was classified as belonging to one of the television genres, also included in Appendix 2.2. In addition, youngsters who reported exposure to television, videos, movies, video games, and/or computers were asked to describe the social context of that exposure. That is, they were asked to indicate whether they used the medium alone or in the company of others, and to identify any "others." To reduce the amount of time required to complete the entire questionnaire, similar items about the social context of exposure to audio media and print media were eliminated. Our rationale for this omission was that print use, by its very nature, is highly solitary, and that prior research has demonstrated that the bulk of both print and music exposure occurs when individuals are alone (Kubey & Larson, 1990).

THE HOME MEDIA ENVIRONMENT

Several questions were designed to determine both the kinds of media young people have access to in their households and the "norms" that surround those media. Items concerning in-home access were straightforward. Respondents were asked how many of each of the following media were to be found (1) in their home, and (2) in their or their child's bedroom: television, VCR, radio, tape players, CD players, video game systems, computers, cable/satellite TV connections, premium cable channel subscriptions, computers with CD-Rom drives, and computers with Internet connections.

Other questions were designed to assess the norms surrounding media in the home. Several of these items were based on Medrich and his colleagues' concept of "constant television households" (Medrich, 1979; Medrich, Roizen, Rubin, & Buckley, 1982). They found that in some households an operating TV set is a relatively constant part of the environment, and that such "constant television households" manifest substantially different patterns of media exposure from those households where the television is not constantly on. Questions aimed at identifying constant TV households asked how often the TV set was "usually on in the home, even when no one was watching," and whether or not the television was "usually on during meals." An additional item assessing the household media environment asked whether or not there were any family rules regarding TV viewing.

MEDIA ATTITUDES

The in-school questionnaire included items designed to assess attitudes toward television and toward the computer. Older children and adolescents were asked to indicate how often they were "entertained," "just killing time," and "learn[ing] interesting things" when watching television and using the computer. Unfortunately, time constraints precluded inclusion of similar items for other media.

Another question determined young people's preferred medium. For the in-home sample (2- to 7-year-olds), parent and child were presented an array of five different pictures, including a book, a TV set, a radio/tape player, a computer, and a video-game console. The interviewer named the medium portrayed in each picture, then asked the child to select "the one thing that you like to use most." Youth in the in-school sample (8- to 18-year-olds) were invited to express their media preferences

by means of the following question: "If you were going to a desert island (OK, a desert island with electricity) and you could take only one
of the following things, what would you choose?" A list of eight options followed: books or magazines, CDs or tapes and a player, computer
with Internet access, radio, television, video games, videos and a VCR,
nothing.

SOCIAL/PSYCHOLOGICAL WELL-BEING

A small battery of items assessed respondents' sense of social/psycho-
logical well-being – an index tapping something like social adjustment
or personal sense of contentment with their current life. The index consisted of six first-person, self-descriptive statements. Both school children and the parents of the younger children were asked to indicate how
well each statement described them (their child) by circling one of four
responses: a lot like me, somewhat like me, not much like me, not at
all like me. Although somewhat skeptical about parents' ability to give
accurate responses about their young children's inner feelings, in the
interest of symmetry we included similar questions in both the in-home
questionnaire and the in-school questionnaires. These "contentedness"
items are presented in more detail in Chapter 9.

DEMOGRAPHIC AND BACKGROUND ITEMS

Demographic information obtained directly from respondents included
children's age, school grade level, gender, race/ethnicity, number of siblings, level of parent education, whether or not they lived with one or
two parents, and for 8- to 18-year-olds, self-reports of grades earned in
school.

Additional information was obtained from external sources. Classification of "residence locale," that is, whether respondents lived in
an urban, suburban, or rural area, was obtained from Harris Interactive
sample files, which contain information regarding the location of the
households and schools in the two samples. The index of family income,
perhaps the most problematic demographic variable in the study, is also
derived from external information. Because it is extremely difficult to
obtain accurate estimates of household income from school-aged youth,
we use federal estimates of median household income in the zip code area
of each participating household (for the in-home sample) or each participating school (for the in-school sample). In other words, the youth

in this study are classified as coming from low-, middle-, or high-income families depending on the federal classification of the postal zip code area in which their home (younger sample) or school (older sample) is located. It is important to acknowledge a problem inherent in combining aggregate-level data such as these with the individual-level information that supplies most of the data for this study. There is no question that some students from higher income households attend schools located in lower income zip code areas, and that some students from lower income households attend schools in relatively higher income zip code areas. Similarly, some higher income households may be located in lower income zip codes, and vice versa. This means, of course, that there is no way to avoid misclassification of some individuals on the income variable. It is important to keep in mind, then, that comparisons based on income level provide only rough estimates. That said, it is also worth noting that our data reveal that similar patterns of results are produced by several different variables that have been demonstrated in other studies to be highly correlated with more direct measures of household income. These include level of parent education and single-parent versus two-parent family status. Such results increase our confidence in the findings for various subgroup comparisons based on our proxy measure of income.

MEDIA-USE DIARIES

In addition to information obtained from the survey questionnaires, supplemental information was obtained from a self-selected subsample of children and adolescents who completed relatively demanding, 7-day media-use diaries. The diaries asked youngsters to respond to four primary questions for each half-hour of each day, beginning at 6 A.M. and finishing at midnight. The four primary questions were:

- What kind of media (if any) were you using?
- Where were you (when using any medium)?
- Who was with you?
- What else were you doing?

Finally, at the end of each diary day, respondents were asked to estimate about how much time they spent on each of the following activities: attending school; working at a job; doing chores; doing homework; participating in sports, a hobby, or a club; attending child care or a before- or after-school program. Because the diary sample is self-selected, the data obtained from these diaries primarily serve to supplement and/or elaborate results obtained from the survey questionnaires.

The findings reported in the narrative text of this book are based on standard statistical procedures, including tests for difference in population proportions, analyses of variance and associated t-tests, and various correlation analyses. For the most part, when the text refers to particular relationships and/or differences, statistical tests have shown those relationships and/or differences to be "statistically" significant. For narrative purposes, this means that differences or relationships reach *at least* the standard $p < .05$ level of significance. In other words, unless we comment to the contrary, any difference or relationship to which we refer, whether or not we use the term "significant," is strong enough that it would occur by chance fewer than one time in 20. For many analyses, the probability levels are even smaller (i.e., numerous differences and/or relationships we report would occur by chance fewer than one time in 100 or one in 1,000). Complete tables displaying proportions and means and the results of all statistical tests of significance are presented in the Appendixes.

To present the results of statistical tests of significance, we use a system of subscripts that indicate when differences between proportions or means are statistically significant. When proportions or means *share* a subscripted letter, they *do not* differ significantly. In other words, *numbers with no subscripted letter in common differ reliably*. To illustrate, in example 1 below, none of the numbers has subscripted letters in common. Thus, the first proportion (20%) differs significantly from both the second (35%) and the third (48%), and the second (35%) also differs significantly from the third (48%). In example 2, the first proportion (12%) differs significantly from the second (30%), but the third proportion (17%) does not differ from either the first or second. In example 3, the first (10%) and third (14%) proportions do not differ from each other, but both differ from the second (33%). When no subscripts appear, the numbers do not differ significantly, as illustrated in example 4.

Example 1: $20\%_a$ $35\%_b$ $48\%_c$
Example 2: $12\%_a$ $30\%_b$ $17\%_{ab}$
Example 3: $10\%_a$ $33\%_b$ $14\%_a$
Example 4: 62% 71% 67%

One further point about statistical tests is in order. Because of our necessary reliance on parent-proxy interviews, comparisons between responses pertaining to the sample of young children and those of their school-based counterparts must be tentative at best. There is good reason to expect parent estimates of their children's media exposure to be somewhat different than the children themselves might give (if they were able to provide accurate information themselves). Because parents frequently are not present when their children are engaged in media activities, they may be unaware of how much of which media and what content their children consume under what conditions. Moreover, in light of recent public discussion of the possibly negative role of media in children's lives, some parents may be inclined to give "socially desirable" responses to some of the questions. That is, parents may provide relatively conservative descriptions of their children's media behavior. For these reasons, the statistical analyses in this book keep the two samples separate. That is, we report no statistical comparisons between the in-home sample and the in-school sample.

AGE AS A BASELINE VARIABLE

Among young people, age is arguably the single most important variable associated with media behavior. Between the time they are old enough to turn on a TV set until they graduate from high school, young people change dramatically – in abilities, in needs, in interests, in tastes, and more. Numerous studies have shown that children and adolescents of different ages select different kinds of content from different media, for different lengths of time (see, e.g., Christenson & Roberts, 1998; Comstock, 1991; Subrahmanyam, Kraut, Greenfield, & Gross, 2001). For this reason, we begin our analyses of young people's exposure to each of the various media by looking at exposure as a function of age, dividing the samples into five smaller age subgroupings. The groupings, described below, are large enough to capture sufficient numbers of young people to render our estimates relatively stable, but small enough that we can look at some of the changes in media behavior that occur as a function of age. As we shall see, for example, a single number representing something like average TV exposure among 8- to 18-year-olds (in this study, 3:05), can mask substantial differences between narrower age groupings (e.g., in this study, 11- to 14-year-olds' television exposure exceeds that of 15- to 18-year-olds by more than an hour). When numbers are sufficient to allow it, we attempt to examine other variables, holding age constant.

That is, we try to look at the relationship between media exposure and gender or race within age groups). Unfortunately, for many analyses, the small number of youths in some subgroups limits us to looking at 8- to 18-year-olds as a single group.

Whenever possible, then, analyses in this book are based on five age groupings: 2- to 4-year-olds, 5- to 7-year-olds, 8- to 10-year-olds; 11- to 14-year-olds, and 15- to 18-year-olds. These groupings were determined by a combination of the year-by-year total media exposure patterns in Figure 8.1 (this figure, in Chapter 8, introduces our discussion of over-all media use and young people's media budgets) in combination with the following reasoning derived from principles of child and adolescent development.

2 TO 4 YEARS

Prior to age 5, children's daily activities and experiences depend on whether the child stays at home with a parent or other caregiver or is in some more structured setting, such as preschool or daycare. Thus, our youngest group spans the years from 2 through 4, and marks a period when children's experiences vary based on setting. During a typical week, about half of these youngest children are in child-care of some sort (35% in preschool) and the other half are at home.

5 TO 7 YEARS

At about 5 years, most U.S. children begin school, thus experience similar environments and activities for at least part of each weekday. This age landmark for beginning school points to a natural age break between 4 and 5 years. This group includes 5-, 6-, and 7-year-olds.

8 TO 10 YEARS

Another break is made between 7 and 8 years, both because the method of data collection differs for the older children, and because by 8 years children are typically in third grade, can read at a basic level, and have probably settled into the elementary school routine. The 8- to 10-year-old group consists of "tweens," youths still in elementary school and still largely dependent on parents, siblings, and some school-based activities for social experiences (Jackson & Rodriguez-Tomé, 1993).

11 TO 14 YEARS

The transition into early adolescence and all that comes along with it typically begins at about 11 years, when youngsters enter middle or junior high school. This period, which lasts until about 14 years, is characterized by the beginning and growth of interest in cross-gender relationships, increased contact with and reliance on peer groups, reduced interaction with family, some experience with part-time jobs, and more independence in general (see Feldman & Elliott, 1990; Jackson & Rodriguez-Tomé, 1993).

15 TO 18 YEARS

The 15- to 18-year-old group consists of high school youths who are firmly establishing independence from their families. These older teenagers are dating, holding jobs, and earning driver's licenses, thus extending their freedom and opportunity to explore the world around them. They exercise more choice than ever before in their lives, in the social and school-related activities in which they engage, and in the peer groups with which they associate.

With few exceptions, these five age groups serve as the foundation for the analyses of media consumption presented in the remainder of this book.

CHAPTER THREE

THE MEDIA ENVIRONMENT

The environment that young people inhabit strongly influences their media behavior. Clearly, which media are available in their homes, and the social and psychological context surrounding those media, affect how much time they spend reading, listening, or viewing, and the kinds of media content to which they are exposed. For example, children and adolescents from households equipped with a personal computer are more likely to use computers, hence become more computer literate and gain various educational and economic advantages, than are youngsters from households lacking a personal computer (National Telecommunications and Information Administration, 1998, 1999). It is clear throughout this book that access plays a powerful role in media behavior. Similarly, children from families that impose rules on television viewing tend to watch fewer than and/or different television programs from children from families in which there are no controls on viewing (Comstock & Scharrer, 1999; Stanger, 1997). Thus, household norms also influence media behavior in important ways. The point is that the household media environment matters.

In this chapter we examine the kinds of media to which U.S. children and adolescents have in-home access, as well as some dimensions of the social context within which that access takes place. We begin by describing the electronic media directly available to the young people in our sample. We look first at media in the household, then narrow the focus to media available in young people's own bedrooms (as well as the proportion of seventh through twelfth graders who subscribe to their own magazines). We assume that an environment in which young people possess their own TV sets, radios, computers, video-game players, or magazine subscriptions differs from one where media are shared with others in a more public room. Moreover, we assume that the differences are likely to influence a variety of media (and nonmedia) behaviors. Finally, we examine several indicators of "household television orientation," each of which is employed in subsequent chapters to examine aspects of media consumption. The focus is on "television orientation" because it is the medium with which families spend the most time and that they are most likely to attempt to control.

Media in the Home

OVERALL IN-HOME ACCESS

Given that we now live in a society where even automobiles have begun to feature video playback systems and cell phones are converging with computers, it is hardly surprising that the parents and children in our sample make it abundantly clear that they live in a media-rich environment. Table 3.1 presents the proportions of homes containing one, two, or three or more of each of the various electronic media, as well as several associated subscription services such as cable TV and Internet connections. Clearly, television has reached saturation levels. Not only do virtually all households with children or adolescents have at least one television and a VCR, but almost three-quarters subscribe to cable or satellite channels. In addition, most homes contain one or more "music media" – radios and CD or tape players (as we shall see in Chapter 5, for most young people radio functions primarily as a music source). When the three music media are combined, fewer than one-half of 1 percent of the households in our sample lack a music medium. The large majority of youths also live in homes with computers (62% of the younger group and 73% of the older group) and video game consoles (52% of the younger group and 82% of the older group). Indeed, in-home access falls below 50% only for "extra," more discretionary subscription services associated with television and the computer; 44 percent of households subscribe to premium cable channels and 45 percent report Internet connections. It is worth noting, however, that both computer access and Internet connections have continued to increase in the few years since these data were collected. For example, the U.S. census for 2000 estimates that 67 percent of households with school-age children now have a personal computer and 53 percent have an Internet connection (Newburger, 2001), and the numbers continue to grow. Similarly, data gathered in late 2001 indicate that 83 percent of U.S. 15- to 17-year-olds

Table 3.1. *Media Availability in Young People's Homes*

	Average	1+	2+	3+
Percent of 2- to 7-year-olds who live with . . .				
TV	2.5	100%	81%	45%
VCR	1.6	96	47	12
Radio	2.6	99	78	48
CD player	1.4	83	36	14
Tape player	1.8	91	53	26
Computer	.8	63	16	3
Video-game console	.8	53	18	5
Cable TV		73		
Premium channels		40		
Internet connection		40		
Percent of 8- to 18-year-olds who live with . . .				
TV	3.1	100%	93%	70%
VCR	2.0	99	64	26
Radio	3.4	98	91	73
CD player	2.6	95	74	48
Tape player	2.9	98	85	62
Computer	1.1	74	25	8
Video-game console	1.7	82	49	24
Cable TV		74		
Premium channels		45		
Internet connection		47		

live in homes with Internet connections (Kaiser Family Foundation, 2001).

Perhaps even more indicative of how media-saturated our society has become than simply the proportion of households equipped with each medium is the high proportion of households with *multiple instances* of each. For example, 88 percent of our combined samples (i.e., 2- to 18-year-olds) live in homes with at least two televisions (almost 12% report five or more TV sets!). Table 3.1 shows that most U.S. youth live with multiple media. Forty-four percent of the 2- to 7-year-olds and over two-thirds of the 8- to 18-year-olds report three or more TV sets. Almost half of younger children and three-quarters of older youth report at least three radios in their homes; when radios, CD players, and tape players are combined under the heading of "music media," 90 percent of 2- to

The typical child's home contains...

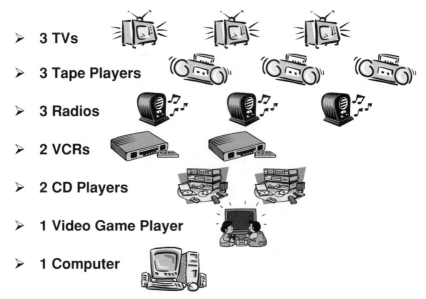

- ➢ **3 TVs**
- ➢ **3 Tape Players**
- ➢ **3 Radios**
- ➢ **2 VCRs**
- ➢ **2 CD Players**
- ➢ **1 Video Game Player**
- ➢ **1 Computer**

Figure 3.1. Media in the home.

7-year-olds and 97 percent of 8- to 18-year-olds live in homes with at least three music sources. When the data from both the younger and older samples are combined as in Figure 3.1, it is fair to say that a "typical" U.S. 2- to 18-year-old is likely to live in a household equipped with three TV sets, three radios, two VCRs, two tape players, two CD players, a video-game player, and a computer. "Media rich" is not an unreasonable characterization.

Because almost every child has access to a television, a VCR, and a music source of one kind or another, factors such as age, race/ethnicity, household income, and parent education locate few meaningful differences in access to at least one of each of the various "basic" electronic media.[1] However, for newer, more "optional" media and media-related services such as video-game consoles, cable and premium TV

---

[1] Because a much smaller difference is required to reach statistical significance near the tails of a distribution of proportions, some statistically significant differences are not what we would call "meaningful." For example, 97% of the 8- to 10-year-olds and 99% of the 11- to 14-year-olds live in homes with a CD or tape player. Although the difference is statistically significant, we do not view it as particularly meaningful.

subscriptions, personal computers, and Internet connections,[2] demographic variables do locate substantial differences in access. We summarize the most important of these relationships below; Appendix 3.1 presents data tables underlying this summary.

AGE AND IN-HOME ACCESS

In both the younger and older samples, the proportion of young people living in homes with a computer increases significantly with each successive increase in age. Among young children, there is no age-related difference in access to an Internet connection. Among older youth, however, both 11- to 14-year-olds and 15- to 18-year-olds are significantly more likely than 8- to 10-year-olds to report an Internet connection (see Appendix 3.1).

SOCIOECONOMIC STATUS AND IN-HOME ACCESS

Not surprisingly, both indicators of socioeconomic status – median household (or school district) income and level of parent education – locate significant differences in the proportion of youths with in-home access to these "extra" media. However, the nature of the relationship between these socioeconomic status indicators and in-home access is not always what one might expect. As can be seen in Figures 3.2 and 3.3, each successive level of household income locates substantial increases in the likelihood that U.S. youth live in a home equipped with a computer and that the computer has an Internet connection.[3] A positive relationship between cable access and household income also holds for the younger sample (see Fig. 3.2). Each of these results is consistent with an expectation that as household income increases, so too should the likelihood of bearing the extra expense of such "add-on" media. However, that expectation is not supported by the remaining results, particularly

---

[2] In many households, video-game consoles and subscriptions to cable or premium channels are considered "extras." For example, television can be enjoyed without their added expense. Similarly, even with recent price reductions, the cost of a computer (possibly in combination with a perception that it is quite possible to get along without one, at least insofar as home entertainment is concerned) arguably makes all these media and services extra "add-ons." We note, however, that computers and Internet connections may be rapidly evolving into "necessities."

[3] The same pattern of results emerges when Internet access is examined looking only at households with computers.

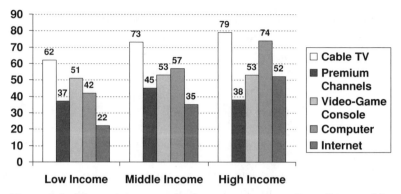

Figure 3.2. Discretionary media by income among 2- to 7-year-olds.

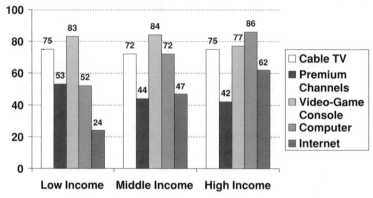

Figure 3.3. Discretionary media by income among 8- to 18-year-olds.

among older youth. Although there is no relationship between household income and cable access among 8- to 18-year-olds, low-income households are significantly more likely than either middle or higher income households to subscribe to premium channels. Similarly, video-game console ownership increases as household income decreases (low- and middle-income households are significantly more likely than high-income households to possess a video-game console). Among younger children, income locates no difference in access to video games, but there is a small (albeit statistically significant) difference for premium channels, with middle-income households more likely than either low- or high-income households to subscribe. In short, income is relatively strongly related to the most expensive of what we have labeled extra media (the computer and its associated Internet connection), but has no relationship (or even a reverse relationship) with TV-related "extras" (cable and premium subscriptions and video-game consoles).

Much the same pattern emerges when in-home access to media is examined as a function of parent education (see Appendix 3.1). That is, in both the younger and older samples, personal computer ownership and Internet access increase steadily as parent education increases. Cable access also increases with parent education in the younger sample,[4] but there is no relationship among older youth. Conversely, and also in line with findings for income, access to video-game consoles decreases as parent education increases in the younger sample (there is no relationship in the older sample), and premium channel subscriptions decrease as parent education increases in the older sample (there is no relationship in the younger sample). For the most part, these findings for parent education withstand controls for household income. For example, computer ownership and Internet access increase as parent education increases, regardless of household income.

Briefly, then, the optional, add-on media more typically associated with entertainment, escape, or play either are not related or are only slightly negatively related to our two socioeconomic indicators. On the other hand, computers and Internet connections, more expensive media that are often associated with reality content, information seeking, and education, are strongly and positively related to both household income and parent education. This may be a medium-related instance of Schramm et al.'s (1961) early observation that attraction to "reality content" increased as socioeconomic status increased, while the reverse was true for "fantasy content." We return to this point below.

RACE/ETHNICITY AND IN-HOME ACCESS

When access to "add-on" media is examined in relation to race and ethnicity, a complex pattern of results emerges. Race/ethnicity mediates differential access, depending on children's age and their parents' socioeconomic classification. The findings reported next begin a pattern that becomes more distinct in later analyses of multiple-media access and children's personal possession of media.

---

[4] When parent education is controlled for household income, cable access still tends to increase with parent education, but the differences are no longer statistically significant.

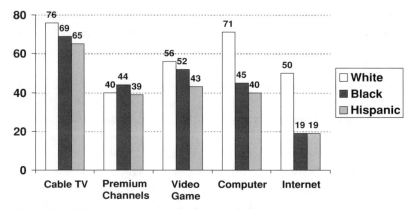

Figure 3.4. Discretionary media by race/ethnicity among 2- to 7-year-olds.

Looking first at TV-related add-ons, Figure 3.4 shows that although race or ethnicity locate no differences in premium TV subscriptions among 2- to 7-year-olds, there are significant differences in access to cable television and video-game consoles. More white than either African American or Hispanic children have cable access, and more white than Hispanic children live with video-game consoles. These relationships change, however, when socioeconomic controls are applied. The higher proportion of whites with cable access holds only for children from households earning less than $25,000 per year, or from households where parents report no more than a high school education. Similarly, when differences in video-game console ownership located by race and ethnicity are controlled for household income, the difference favoring white children remains statistically significant only for children from the lowest income category. In other words, white 2- to 7-year-olds from the lowest socioenonomic classifications are more likely than their African American or Hispanic counterparts to have access to cable television and to video-game consoles. As either income or parent education increases, however, differences related to race or ethnicity disappear.

A very different picture emerges for TV-related add-ons among 8- to 18-year-olds. Figure 3.5 shows that for older youths, race or ethnicity makes no difference to cable TV subscriptions, but is significantly related both to subscriptions to premium TV channels and to video-game console ownership. African American kids have more access. A substantially higher proportion of African American (62%) than either

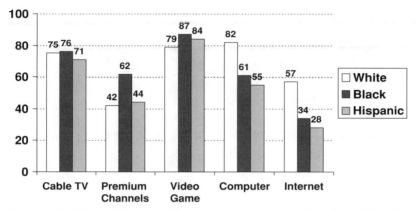

Figure 3.5. Discretionary media by race/ethnicity among 8- to 18-year-olds.

white (42%) or Hispanic youths (44%) live in homes with premium TV subscriptions. Moreover, the relationship is not affected by controls for either household income or parent education. Similarly, a significantly higher proportion of African American (87%) than white youths (79%) live in homes with video-game consoles, with Hispanic youths falling between (84%). This pattern remains largely the same when controlled for socioeconomic status, although the differences are statistically significant only at the highest income and education levels. That is, among 8- to 18-year-olds, whites are significantly less likely than blacks or Hispanics to have in-home access to a video-game console *only* in households earning more than $40,000 per year, or in homes where parents completed college.

The relationships between race or ethnicity and both personal computer ownership and Internet access are a bit more straightforward. Regardless of age, white youths are substantially more likely than either African Americans or Hispanics to live in a home with a computer. Among 2- to 7-year-olds, 71 percent of white children, 45 percent of black children, and 40 percent of Hispanic children live with a computer. Among 8- to 18-year-olds, 82 percent of white, 61 percent of black, and 55 percent of Hispanic children live with a computer. Much the same pattern holds for Internet connections. Among younger children, 51 percent of white children but only 19 percent of both African American and Hispanic children live with computers with Internet connections. Among older youth, 57 percent of whites, 34 percent of African Americans, and 25 percent of Hispanics have computers with

Internet connections. All of these differences withstand controls for both household income and parent education.

To summarize, white households are substantially more likely than African American or Hispanic households to provide access to the new digital media, regardless of household income or parent education. At the same time, there is a modest tendency for African American households to provide more access to TV-related "extras"; black youths are somewhat more likely than whites to report living with premium TV channels and video-game consoles.

GENDER AND IN-HOME ACCESS

Gender locates a meaningful difference in access only to video-game consoles. In both younger and older samples, boys are more likely than girls to live in homes with a video-game console (57% vs. 47% among younger children; 88% vs. 74% among older youths). This gender difference is very much in line with other work showing that boys spend more time than girls with video games (Funk & Buchman, 1996; Funk, Buchman & Germann, 2000), as well as with claims that the video-game industry targets most of its games at boys (Calvert, 1999; Oldenburg, 1995). This explanation receives support from our analysis of gender differences in time spent with video games (see Chapter 7). What strikes us as more interesting than the fact of a gender difference, however, is the sheer magnitude of the figure for girls. Gender-typed or not, almost half of 2- to 7-year-old girls and three-quarters of 8- to 18-year-old girls have access to a video-game console at home.

MULTIPLE-MEDIA HOMES

Obviously, households with several TV sets, VCRs, music sources, video-game consoles, and/or computers constitute different media environments than those with only one. It makes sense, therefore, to examine characteristics of multiple-media homes. We have already noted that substantial numbers of U.S. youth inhabit households with multiple instances of each medium (see Table 3.1). Indeed, it is only when the sample is divided on the basis of those who report three or more instances of most media that substantial numbers of respondents fall into the "low ownership" group. For this reason, we have made 3+ media the cut-off point for all but one of our multiple-media analyses. The exception is computer ownership. Since fewer than 25 percent of the participants in this study reported two or more computers in the home, 2+ serves as the cut-off for computers. Appendix 3.2 presents data underlying the following description.

Of the various demographic variables we have been considering, age emerges as the most consistent predictor of multiple media ownership. The proportion of youth reporting three or more household TV sets, radios, CD/tape players, or video-game consoles increases substantially and significantly at each successive age level. Multiple VCR ownership also increases with age among 8- to 18-year-olds, but not in the younger sample. Age fails to predict multiple ownership of only personal computers. Moreover, controls for socioeconomic status do little to change this overall finding. As children and adolescents get older, their likelihood of living with multiple instances of most media increases significantly regardless of level of household income or parent education. We suspect this is largely a function of two factors: (1) a greater likelihood that older children agitate for their own, personal media, and (2) greater household resources inherent in families with older children. Parents of older children are older themselves. They have had more years as wage earners and as heads of household, thus more opportunity to have "upgraded" in-home media. It is likely that multiple media ownership often occurs when a household purchases a new television (or replaces an analog clock radio with a digital model, and so on), moving the older but still operating set to a different room.

Both household income and parent education are strongly and positively related to ownership of multiple radios, CD/tape players, and computers. With few exceptions (e.g., similar percentages of middle- and high-income households have 3+ radios), the proportion of households reporting multiple ownership of each medium increases significantly at each successive level of household income and parent education. Moreover, even though household income and parent education are positively related,[5] examining the influence of parent education at each different level of household income does not change the overall relationship in any substantial way. In other words, both indicators of socioeconomic status independently influence the likelihood of multiple music media ownership and multiple computer ownership. Interestingly, this is not the case for visual media. The proportion of youth living with multiple televisions, VCRs, and video-game consoles is roughly equal regardless of household income or parent education.

[5] Pearson $r = .35$ and $r = .21$, $p < .001$, in the younger and older samples, respectively.

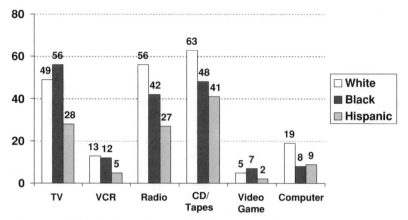

Figure 3.6. Multiple media availability by race/ethnicity: proportion of 2- to 7-year-olds' homes with *multiple* instances of each of six media.

Although preliminary analyses indicated that multiple media ownership is related to whether youngsters live with one or two parents (see Appendix 3.2), many of those differences are reduced or eliminated when controls for household income or parent education are applied. For example, initial findings that a smaller percentage of one-parent than of two-parent households contain three or more VCRs or two or more computers largely disappear when household income is held constant.[6] On the other hand, neither household income nor parent education greatly change the finding that higher proportions of two-parent households than one-parent households contain multiple televisions, radios, and CD/tape players. It appears that for these analyses the number of parents in the home operates as yet another indicator of socioeconomic status, sometimes independently, sometimes simply mirroring measures of income and parent education.

Probably the most interesting pattern of findings emerges when multiple media ownership is examined as a function of race or ethnicity. With but two exceptions, race or ethnicity is related to substantial differences in the likelihood that youths live with multiple instances of each of the media we have been considering.[7] However, as Figures 3.6

[6] Among 2- to 7-year-olds, multiple computer ownership remains higher in two-parent households provided that median household income exceeds $25,000.

[7] The two exceptions are: (1) among 2- to 7-year-olds, there is no difference in the proportion of white, African American, and Hispanic children with three or

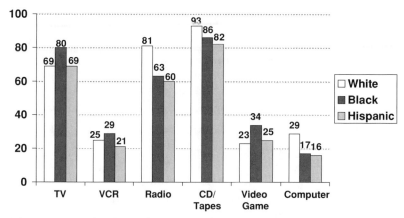

Figure 3.7. Multiple media availability by race/ethnicity: proportion of 8- to 18-year-olds' homes with *multiple* instances of each of six media.

and 3.7 reveal, race or ethnicity operates in different ways depending on the medium examined. Overall, African American youth are significantly more likely than either white or Hispanic youth to report three or more TV sets. In the younger sample, African American children are more likely than Hispanic children to report three or more VCRs. In the older sample, they are more likely than both whites and Hispanics to report three or more video-game consoles. For music media and computers, however, the pattern changes. In both the younger and the older samples, significantly higher proportions of white than either African American or Hispanic youths report multiple radios, CD/tape players, and computers. There is little difference in the proportion of blacks and Hispanics reporting multiple instances of these three media, and the results generally withstand controls for income and parent education.

Thus, similar to what we find in our examination of extra or add-on media, patterns of multiple media ownership again point to a tendency for African American households to be somewhat more oriented toward visual, "entertainment" media (i.e., television), and white households toward "reality" media (i.e., computers) and music media.

more video games (there is a significant difference in the older sample); (2) among 8- to 18-year-olds, there is no difference due to race or ethnicity in multiple VCR ownership (there is a significant difference in the younger sample).

Media in Young People's Bedrooms

In addition to enumerating the types and number of media available in the home, young people also indicated the media (and associated services) to which they have access in their own bedrooms. The migration of media to children's bedrooms had begun by 1970, when Jack Lyle and Heidi Hoffman (1972a) found that 6 percent of a sample of Southern California sixth graders had televisions in their bedrooms. By 1988, the proportions had more than tripled; Ellen Wartella and her colleagues reported that 19 percent of 6- to 12-year-olds living in Champaign-Urbana had their own TV sets,[8] and that almost two-thirds of them had their own radios (Wartella, Heintz, Aidman, & Mazzarella, 1990). In our study, both the number of children with their "own" media and the array of media they possess have continued to increase at a rapid pace. As we shall see, where once the words "Go to your room" implied the punishment of isolation, for many children today it is little more than a directive to visit a media arcade.

Table 3.2 presents the proportion of children at each age with each of the media in their bedroom. Compared with even a few years ago, the sheer numbers of children and adolescents possessing personal media is remarkable. One-third of 2- to 7-year-olds and two-thirds of 8- to 18-year-olds have their own televisions, and about half of each of these groups claim their own VCRs. Roughly four in 10 younger children and over 85 percent of older youths possess either a radio or a CD or tape player. (Indeed, when these sources of music are combined, 53 percent of 2- to 7-year-olds and 92 percent of 8- to 18-year-olds have a music medium of some kind in their bedroom.) Finally, 45 percent of older youths have their own video game consoles, and 21 percent claim their own computers.

AGE AND BEDROOM MEDIA

Table 3.2 shows that personal ownership of each of these media is strongly and, until the later teen years, positively related to age. In the younger sample, personal ownership of all but VCRs increases significantly between 2 to 4 years and 5 to 7 years. Similarly, in the older sample there are large and statistically significant increases between

---

[8] Indeed, we suspect the number would have been much higher had the proportion reported been based just on 12-year-olds.

Table 3.2. *Media Availability in Children's Bedrooms by Age* (%)[a]

	2–7 years	2–4 years	5–7 years	8–18 years	8–10 years	11–14 years	15–18 years
TV	32	26_a	39_b	65	59_a	70_b	64_a
VCR	16	14	18	36	29_a	39_b	36_b
Radio	43	32_a	53_b	86	72_a	90_b	94_c
Tape/CD player	38	32_a	43_b	88	73_a	92_b	94_b
Video-game console	13	7_a	18_b	45	43_a	49_b	41_a
Computer	6	4_a	9_b	21	22	21	19

[a] For an explanation of the subscripts in the table, see p. 25.

8 to 10 years and 11 to 14 years for all media but computers. The pattern changes only when 11- to 14-year-olds are compared with 15- to 18-year-olds. The small increase with age in possession of a radio is statistically significant, but there are no differences between the two older groups in the proportions that have their own VCRs, tape or CD players, or computers. Moreover, compared with 11- to 14-year-olds, significantly *fewer* of the oldest teens report a TV set or video-game console in their bedrooms. As we see in Chapters 4 and 7, this dovetails with the finding that 11- to 14-year-olds spend more time than 15- to 18-year-olds with both television and video games. Regardless of such decreases in the oldest group, however, a typical U.S. adolescent is almost certain to possess several personal music media and is quite likely to have a TV set. Over a third have a video-game console or a VCR, and there is a one in five chance of them having their own personal computers.

GENDER AND BEDROOM MEDIA

Except for video-game consoles, no gender differences in possession of personal media occur within the younger sample. Among 2- to 7-year-olds, 8 percent of girls and 17 percent of boys have a video-game console in their bedrooms. When we examine older children and adolescents, however, a number of small but statistically significant gender differences emerge. Older girls are significantly more likely than boys to possess their own CD or tape players (90% vs. 86%) and slightly (but not significantly) more likely to have their own radios (88% vs. 85%). Boys, on the other hand, are more likely than girls to have their own televisions (69% vs. 61%) and their own VCRs (38% vs. 33%). Finally, 30 percent of girls and 58 percent of boys claim their own video-game consoles. As we see in chapters below, these results are consistent with evidence that boys spent more time with television (see Chapter 4) and that girls spend more time with music media (see Chapter 5). And clearly, patterns of personal ownership of video-game consoles strongly support claims that video gaming is primarily a male activity, and that the gender difference appears quite early (see Appendix 3.3).

SOCIOECONOMIC STATUS AND BEDROOM MEDIA

The patterns of young people's personal possession of various media in relation to household income and to parent education resemble some of those that emerged for household media ownership, but they are far from identical. Figures 3.8 and 3.9 illustrate children's personal possession of media in relation to household income.

Consider first the personal computer. The substantial increases at each successive level of income that we found when examining *household access* disappears for children's personal computer ownership. There are no meaningful differences in the proportion of youngsters from each income level having their own computers in either sample. Among 2- to 7-year-olds, level of parent education also fails to locate differences in children's personal computer ownership. However, a significant relationship between parent education and the proportion of youths possessing their own computers does appear among 8- to 18-year-olds (see Appendix 3.3). Among older youths, the proportion possessing

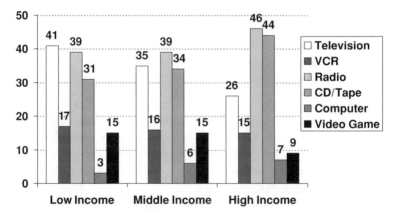

Figure 3.8. Proportion of children with bedroom media by income among 2- to 7-year-olds.

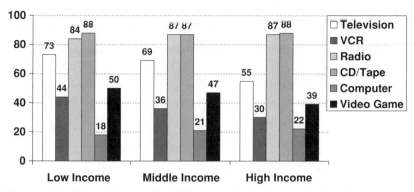

Figure 3.9. Proportion of children with bedroom media by income among 8- to 18-year-olds.

their own computers increases as level of parent education increases from high school (13%) to some college (19%) to college graduate (25%). When results for parent education are further controlled for household income, the overall pattern holds, although the differences are no longer statistically significant for middle-income households. In short, the more education a parent has achieved, the more likely older kids are to have their own computers.

Personal possession of a music medium generally increases with both household income and parent education. Significantly more 2- to 7-year-olds from high-income households than from either middle- or low-income households have their own CD or tape players; a similar difference approaches statistical significance for radios (see Fig. 3.8). In the older sample, personal possession of any of the music media is remarkably high and does not vary as a function of household income. When personal music media are examined as a function of parent education, similar patterns appear. That is, at each successive level of parent education, the proportion of 2- to 7-year-olds possessing a CD or tape player increases substantially; for 8- to 18-year-olds, the increase is significant only as we move from low- to either middle- or high-education households (see Appendix 3.3). Personal possession of a radio is significantly higher for 2- to 7-year-olds whose parents completed college than for those whose parents completed no more than high school. In the 8- to 18-year-old sample, more kids from both middle- and high-education families than from low-education families have their own radios. As with personal computers, then, both indicators of household socioeconomic status are positively related to young people's possession of audio media.

The pattern changes for televisions, VCRs, and video game consoles. Figures 3.8 and 3.9 show that the likelihood of children and adolescents having any of these "fantasy/entertainment" media in their bedrooms is generally negatively related to household income. Possession of a television, a video-game console, and, among older youth, a VCR decreases slightly as we move from low- to middle-income households (the difference is statistically significance only for VCRs in the older sample). There follows a substantial drop in personal possession of these media as we move from middle- to high-income households, however (the differences are statistically significant in all cases). Tables in Appendix 3.3 show that when personal possession of each medium is related to parent education, a similar pattern generally holds. Personal possession is largely the same for the low- and middle-education groups, then decreases substantially from the middle- to high-education group. In other words, compared with kids from low- and middle-income or low- and middle-education families, those whose parents earn more than $40,000 per year or whose parents completed college are substantially less likely personally to possess any of the "fantasy-related" media, reversing the pattern found for computers and audio media.

RACE/ETHNICITY AND BEDROOM MEDIA

Figures 3.10 and 3.11 illustrate that race or ethnicity makes a substantial difference in the likelihood that youths have their own media. Although

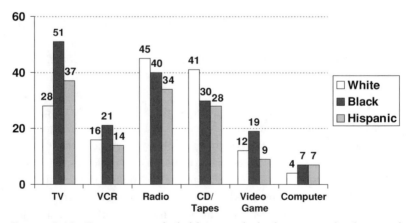

Figure 3.10. Proportion of children with bedroom media by race/ethnicity: proportion of 2- to 7-year-olds personally possessing each of six media.

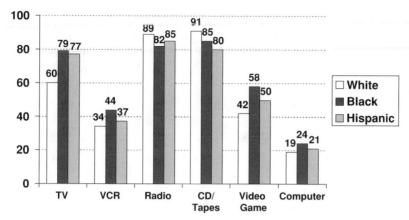

Figure 3.11. Proportion of children with bedroom media by race/ ethnicity: proportion of 8- to 18-year-olds personally possessing each of six media.

there are no differences related to race or ethnicity in the proportion of youngsters possessing their own computer, white youngsters are generally more likely to own personal audio media, while African American kids are more likely to possess personal audiovisual media (a television, a VCR, or a video-game console). The results for Hispanic youth are roughly similar to those for whites, except that Hispanics are more likely than whites to have their own television and, in the younger sample, less likely to possess a radio or CD or tape player.

Looking first at audio media, in both the younger and older samples, significantly fewer Hispanic and African Americans than white youths have their own CD or tape players. In the younger sample, fewer Hispanics than whites have their own radios (with African Americans falling in between); in the older sample, fewer African Americans than whites have their own radios (with Hispanics falling in between). Overall, then, white kids seem a bit more attached than African American or Hispanic kids to audio media.

The most substantial differences related to race or ethnicity emerge for young people's personal possession of televisions and related visual media (see Figs. 3.10 and 3.11). In both the younger and older samples, roughly 20 percent more African American than white youths report having their own TV sets. Among 2- to 7-year-olds, Hispanic children fall in between; significantly more of them than whites (9%) and significantly fewer of them than blacks (14%) have their own televisions. Among 8- to 18-year-olds, there is no difference in the proportion of African American and Hispanic youth with televisions in their bedrooms. This general pattern is repeated for VCRs and video-game consoles. Among 2- to 7-year-olds, race or ethnicity is not re-lated to possession of a VCR, but more young black than either young white or Hispanic children have their own video-game console. Among 8- to 18-year-olds, a higher proportion of African American than white youths claim their own VCRs, and a higher proportion of both African American and Hispanic than white youths possess their own video-game consoles. These relationships generally withstand controls for household income and for parent education. For example, when household income is taken into account, significantly more African American than white youth in the low- and middle-income groups possess their own televi-sions; a similar difference for youngsters from high-income households fails to reach statistical significance (see Appendix 3.3). Overall, then, it appears that African American youths are particularly likely to possess their own televisions and related media, independent of such factors as parent education or household income. This pattern resembles the results for household media.

HOUSEHOLD TELEVISION ORIENTATION

How television is treated within a household – that is, the "household TV orientation" – can serve as a good indicator of how family members relate to television (Comstock & Scharrer, 1999) and, as we shall see, to most other media. In spite of the proliferation of many different media within U.S. households, there is no question that television dominates. Almost all households have television, and it is the medium to which most people devote the most time. Television is also the medium most likely to be used in a family context (Larson, Kubey & Colletti, 1989), and the public nature of a television screen makes it easy for parents to be aware of at least some of the content their children consume. Arguably, it is the medium about which families are most likely to at-tempt to establish some kinds of rules. For all these reasons, we expect that how television is used within a household will tell us something about the family's orientation not just to television but to media in general.

We assess household TV orientation in three ways. The first derives from Elliot Medrich's (1979) time-budget study documenting the myriad activities making up the day-to-day life of young adolescents in the late 1970s (Medrich et al., 1982). Medrich found that in a substantial proportion of households, television plays most of the day regardless of whether anyone is watching. He also reported that children from such "constant television households" typically watched more television than did their counterparts from homes where the television did not provide a constant background. We identified constant TV households on the basis of the following question: "How often is a TV usually on in your home (even if no one is watching)?" Children or parents responding "most of the time" were classed as coming from a constant television household (other response options included "some of the time," "a little bit of the time," and "never").

We also asked whether or not the television was usually on "during meals." On one hand, we assumed that there would be a strong positive correlation between having the television on "most of the time" and having it on during meals. On the other hand, we surmised that the likelihood of family interaction would vary depending on whether or not the television operated during meals, reasoning that when television is on, either conversation is reduced or the topic of conversation is more likely to be "television oriented."

Finally, we asked whether the family had any "rules about watching television." "Rules" might include controls on amount of viewing, on the kinds of content viewed, on when viewing can occur, and so on. Previous research has demonstrated that, depending on the child's age, anywhere from 30 percent to 70 percent of parents attempt to regulate their children's TV viewing in some way (Bower, 1985; Comstock, Chaffee, Katzman, McCombs, & Roberts, 1978; Stanger, 1997). Of course, the likelihood that parents try to establish rules about TV viewing varies with such things as the child's age (Comstock et al., 1978), parent education (Medrich et al., 1982), and level of concern that certain kinds of TV content inappropriately influence children's behavior (Abelman, 1990; Comstock, 1991). In spite of such variations, however, we expect differences in the amount and kinds of TV content consumed in households with and without TV rules. Moreover, we expect the beliefs and attitudes underlying the existence of TV rules to be related to other kinds of media consumption in the home.

Table 3.3 summarizes the overall proportion of children in each of the two samples living in constant TV households, in homes where the television operates during most meals, and in homes with some form of TV rules. About a third of young children live in homes where the television is usually on (a third live where it is on sometimes, and a third where television is seldom or never on when someone is not

Table 3.3. *Household TV Orientation by Age (%)[a]*

	2–7 years	2–4 years	5–7 years	8–18 years	8–10 years	11–14 years	15–18 years
Live with constant TV	35	38$_a$	32$_b$	46	47	47	46
TV on during meals	47	47	46	65	65	64	67
Household TV rules	71	67$_a$	75$_b$	38	52$_a$	41$_b$	24$_c$

[a] See note to Table 3.2.

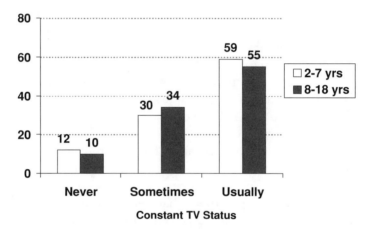

Figure 3.12. Proportion of children who live in homes in which television operates during meals by constant TV status.

watching). For older youths, the picture is quite different. Almost half of them say the television operates "most of the time, even when no one is watching" (just over 16 percent say it is "seldom" or "never" on under these circumstances). Older youths are also more likely to live in homes where the television plays during mealtimes, and less likely to live with rules about TV viewing. Of course, some of the difference between the two samples may be attributable to the fact that parents responded for the younger children. Nevertheless, the overall results for TV rules are consistent with findings from earlier studies that the likelihood of having TV rules decreases after children reach adolescence (Comstock, 1991; Comstock et al., 1978).

Our expectation that constant television would be positively related to mealtime television and absence of household TV rules is borne out. Figures 3.12 and 3.13 illustrate that in constant TV households, the TV

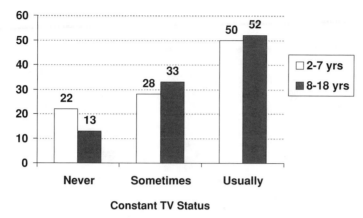

Figure 3.13. Proportion of children with no TV viewing rules by constant TV status.

is more likely to operate during meals and rules regulating TV viewing are less likely to be found. In short, the three questions appear to capture "household television orientation" quite well.

AGE/GENDER AND HOUSEHOLD TV ORIENTATION

With one exception, household TV orientation is unrelated to age or gender. As Table 3.3 shows, the one exception is the relationship be-tween age and the presence of family rules regarding TV viewing. In the younger sample, a higher proportion of 5- to 7-year-olds than 2- to 4-year-olds experience TV rules (75% vs. 67%, respectively), probably because issues of TV control usually do not begin to emerge until the child is 4 to 5 years old and begins to make TV-related requests and de-mands. In the older sample, the pattern is reversed: as youngsters grow older, family TV rules decrease: 52 percent of 8- to 10-year-olds, 41 percent of 11- to 14-year-olds, and 24 percent of 15- to 18-year-olds report family TV rules. This pattern dovetails with a good deal of pre-vious research. (See Appendix 3.4 for additional age-related results for the various measures of household TV orientation).

SOCIOECONOMIC STATUS AND HOUSEHOLD
TV ORIENTATION

Household TV orientation is related to family socioeconomic status. Generally, the higher the level of household income or parent education,

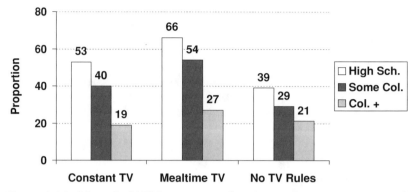

Figure 3.14. Household TV orientation by parent education, as reported by 2- to 7-year-olds.

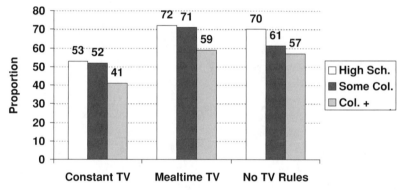

Figure 3.15. Household TV orientation by parent education, as reported by 8- to 18-year-olds.

the lower the likelihood of living in either a constant TV household or one where the television typically operates during meals and the higher the likelihood of there being rules governing TV viewing. Figures 3.14 and 3.15 illustrate the relationships for parent education. Among 2- to 7-year-olds, each successive level of parent education locates substantial decreases in the proportion of children from constant TV households, from households where the television plays during meals, and from households that have *no* rules about TV viewing. Among 8- to 18-year-olds, the pattern changes somewhat. For older youths, decreases in constant TV households and homes where the television plays during meals occur only for families where the parents have completed college. As expected, the relationships are reversed for TV rules. That is, older youths whose parents have no more than a high school education are significantly less likely to report having family rules about watching television than are those whose parents have either at least some college or a college degree.[9]

Household income relates to TV orientation in much the same manner as parent education, although some of the differences between income levels are not as large as those between education levels. Results presented in Appendix 3 demonstrate that the likelihood of finding a constant TV household or a home in which the television typically operates during meals decreases with each successive increase in income. In addition, among 2- to 7-year-olds the probability of there being family rules regulating TV viewing increases with income level.

Because one-parent families tend more than two-parent families to be classified as lower income, we expected the relationship between number of parents and household TV orientation to resemble those found for income, and this was the case. Children and adolescents living with one parent are more likely than those living with two to come from a constant TV household (42% vs. 33% and 50% vs. 45%, for younger and older youths, respectively; the difference is significant only for younger children). Children of single parents are also more likely to live in homes where the television operates during meals (62% vs. 42% and 75% vs. 63% in the younger and older samples, respectively) and to live in homes where there are no rules about TV viewing (63% vs. 74% and 31% vs. 40%).

Interestingly, the differences related to number of parents in the household are not fully accounted for by income. That is, when the relationships between number of parents and the measures of TV orientation are controlled for household income, the differences disappear for lower- and middle-income households, but persist in homes where the annual income exceeds $40,000. In these more well-to-do households, young people in both samples living with one parent experience more constant television, more mealtime television, and fewer TV rules

---

[9] When the relationships between parent education and the three measures of household TV orientation are further controlled for household income, the magnitude of some of the differences is reduced. For example, among 2- to 7-year-olds, the gap between households where parents finished no more than high school and households where they finished some college is no longer statistically significant, but the pattern remains largely the same.

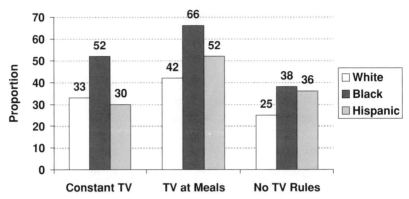

Figure 3.16. Household TV orientation by race/ethnicity, as reported by 2- to 7-year-olds.

than do those living with two parents.[10] At least at higher income levels, then, it appears that single parenthood reduces some of the controls over television that are normally exercised in higher income households. Single parents do not or cannot exert controls over television to the same extent that two parents do. We suspect that this has much to do with the sheer number of demands made on most single parents. Between holding down a paying job, caring for a house, and trying to fulfill basic parenting responsibilities, single parents may lack the energy, the time, or the desire to attempt to control television. Indeed, at times television may even provide a needed escape for parent, child, or both.

RACE/ETHNICITY AND HOUSEHOLD TV ORIENTATION

Race and ethnicity are strongly related to household TV orientation. Figures 3.16 and 3.17 show that African American youths are significantly more likely than either their white or Hispanic counterparts to live where a television is on constantly or during meals. It is also clear from Figure 3.16 that young white children are more likely than African American or Hispanic children to come from families that impose rules

[10] Controls for parent education also affect the relationship. Young children whose parents completed some or all of college are more likely to experience mealtime television if they live with a single parent, and older youths whose parents completed some or all of college experience fewer TV rules if they live with a single parent. Again, it appears that being a single parent overrides some of the controls typically exercised over television among parents with higher education.

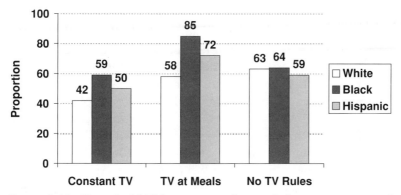

Figure 3.17. Household TV orientation by race/ethnicity, as reported by 8- to 18-year-olds.

about TV viewing, but this difference disappears in the older sample. In both samples, Hispanic youths are more likely than whites to experience television during meals, and in the older sample they are more likely than whites to live with constant television. Although controls for household income and for level of parent education eliminate a few of the differences, particularly for low-income and low-education households, the overall pattern remains. That is, African American households tend to be substantially more "television-oriented" than either white or Hispanic households, regardless of children's age, household income, or level of parent education (see Appendix 3.4).

SUMMING UP THE MEDIA ENVIRONMENT

Several relatively clear patterns begin to emerge from this examination of the media environment in which young people in the United States live. First, and most obvious, it is a rich and varied environment. Regardless of age, socioeconomic status, race or ethnicity – indeed, regardless of any of the demographic variables included in this study – youths in the United States have access to numerous different media. They live in homes with multiple instances of most media; large proportions of them possess their own personal media; and they live in homes where it is not uncommon for the media to be constantly on and seldom controlled.

That said, clear socioeconomic differences in media environments exist. As either household income or level of parent education increases, there tends to be a decrease in possession of and/or attachment to various "fantasy entertainment" media – television, video-game consoles, premium channels, and so forth. At the same time, there is an increase in more "reality-based" media – computers, Internet connections, and so forth. This is also reflected in relationships between socioeconomic status and our measures of TV orientation.

Third, there is general tendency for African American households to be more attached to television and white households to be more attached to computers and audio media. African American youth report more household and personal TV sets and related media (VCRs, cable subscriptions, premium channels, video-game consoles) than do their white or Hispanic counterparts. White youth report more household computers and related media (Internet connections) and more audio media than do their African American or Hispanic counterparts. African Americans are more likely to live in constant TV households, and white youths are more likely to live in households with family rules about TV watching.

As we see in subsequent chapters, these differences in the nature of the media environment experienced by young people from different backgrounds have important implications for the amount of time young people spend with each of the different media, as well as the kinds of media content they seem to prefer.

CHAPTER FOUR

SCREEN MEDIA: TELEVISION, VIDEOS, AND MOVIES

This chapter examines U.S. children's and adolescents' exposure to television, videos, and movies. We label these "noninteractive screen media" because, unlike interactive media, the experience of their content is largely unaffected by viewer response. This is not to say that viewers of television and movies are not cognitively active. Differences in meaning depend on individuals' information-processing activities, and by no means is TV viewing a passive activity (Anderson & Lorch, 1983; Bickman, Wright & Huston, 2001). However, what appears on the television or motion picture screen at any given moment does not depend on what a viewer does. Interactive screen media such as computers and video games, on the other hand, do depend on audience response; where a user clicks or how a game player responds has a direct, immediate effect on which content comes next.[1]

We include television, videos, and movies in the same chapter because there is little reason to differentiate among them. Although on some dimensions the experience of attending a movie in a theater is quite different from watching television in one's own home, at bottom there are more similarities than differences. Audiovisual narratives lie at the core of each medium, and the structure of those narratives is largely the same, with most of the same factors mediating viewer responses to each. For example, it matters little whether a behavior and associated consequences are portrayed on television, a videotape, or in a movie; to the extent that the behavior and associated consequences are clear and salient, the likelihood that viewers will learn is the same

---

[1] Of course, a videotape can be moved forward or backward, but this feature is not a typical part of the viewing process.

across media. In addition, the line between movies and television is further blurred because most movies eventually appear and are watched on television, or at least on a television screen. The experience of watching commercially produced videos is difficult to differentiate from watching television, and when videotape is used to record a television show, the experience is almost identical.[2] For all these reasons, we have grouped "noninteractive" screen media.

AMOUNT OF SCREEN EXPOSURE

In spite of recent speculation in the popular press that the new interactive media may be cutting into the time young people devote to television (Bennahum, 1999; Klein, 2001; Venes, 1999), there is little question that television remains the dominant medium among U.S. children and adolescents. On any given day, 85 percent of young people in the United States watch television. TV exposure averages over 2 hours daily (2:02) among 2- to 7-year-olds and over 3 hours daily (3:08) among 8- to 18-year-olds. When exposure to television, videos, and movies is combined, young children watch almost 3 hours daily (2:55) and older kids see over 4 hours daily (4:07) of screen media content. As we see in Chapter 8, television consistently accounts for over 40 percent of all of young people's media exposure, and when exposure to videotapes and movies is added, the proportion rises to well over 50 percent. Although various demographic and psychosocial variables locate substantial variations in the time kids spend watching television, with the single exception of music media among 15- to 18-year-olds, television never ceases to be the medium to which U.S. young people are most exposed. Indeed, even among frequent users of computers and the Internet, television still accounts for the lion's share of overall media exposure.

Clearly, most U.S. children and adolescents devote substantial time to noninteractive screen media. Nevertheless, a great deal of variation in exposure related to various demographic characteristics remains. To these variations we now turn.

AGE AND SCREEN EXPOSURE

Age is an important predictor of amount of screen exposure. Table 4.1 summarizes mean amount of exposure to television, videos, and movies

[2] Except, of course, that commercials can be skipped.

Table 4.1. *Screen Media Exposure by Age (in years)*[a]

	2–7	2–4	5–7	8–18	8–10	11–14	15–18
Average time spent watching (hr:min)							
TV	2:02	2:02	2:02	3:05	3:19$_a$	3:30$_a$	2:23$_b$
Videos of TV	0:03	0:04	0:03	0:14	0:21$_a$	0:14$_b$	0:10$_b$
Commercial videos	0:27	0:33$_a$	0:21$_b$	0:27	0:25	0:29	0:28
Movies	0:02	0:01	0:02	0:18	0:26$_a$	0:19$_a$	0:09$_b$
Total	2:33	2:40	2:27	4:04	4:31	4:32	3:09
Proportion reporting no exposure the previous day							
TV	16	16	17	15	9$_a$	12$_a$	25$_b$
Videos of TV	94	94	95	76	67$_a$	75$_b$	83$_c$
Commercial videos	62	54$_a$	70$_b$	64	58$_a$	64$_b$	68$_b$
Movies	99	99	99	90	86$_a$	89$_a$	94$_b$
Proportion reporting more than 1 hour and more than 5 hours TV exposure the previous day							
More than 1 hour	60	59	61	69	74$_a$	74$_a$	59$_b$
More than 5 hours	7	7	7	22	24$_a$	28$_a$	14$_b$

Note: In this table, videos of TV programs and commercial videos are separated.
[a] See note to Table 3.2.

for each of five age groups, as well as the proportion of youths who on any given day watched over an hour of television and over 5 hours of television. Three aspects of the results in Table 4.1 are particularly noteworthy:

1. the sheer amount of television exposure that occurs across age;
2. the apparent spike in exposure between 5–7 years and 8–10 years;
3. the steady increase in exposure until 11–13 years, followed by a substantial decline.

We look at each in turn.

First, it is clear that television viewing begins early and quickly reaches several hours per day. Daily TV exposure averages 2 hours as early as 2 to 4 years, and climbs to 3 ½ hours by 11 to 14 years. As we see in Chapter 8, with the exception of music media (radio, CDs, and tapes) during later adolescence, no other medium ever garners even 1 hour per day of exposure. Moreover, depending on age, kids devote another 30 minutes to an hour per day to videos and movies. In addition to mean exposure time, several other indicators of screen media exposure also attest to their dominance. For example, on any given day 85 percent of U.S. youth watch television and over 40 percent watch some kind of videotape. Similarly, on any given day, 60 percent of 2- to 7-year-olds and 69 percent of 8- to 18-year-olds watch more than 1 hour of television, while 7 percent of the younger group and over 20 percent of the older group watch more than 5 hours. In short, screen media exposure is substantial among all age groups.

Turning to the large increase in exposure time that occurs between 5 to 7 years and 8 to 10 years (Table 4.1), the issue is whether the spike in amount of exposure is due solely to increased viewing. We think not. Rather, because we rely on parent reports of young children's media use, there are several reasons to suspect that 2- to 7-year-olds' screen exposure may be underestimated. Much of the difference may be due to social desirability demands. In Chapter 3 we saw that many children possess their own TV sets, and below in this chapter we see that a good deal of children's television viewing occurs when no parent is present. Thus, there is good reason to believe that parents often don't know how much television their children watch. In addition, the debate over how much TV exposure is good for children is almost as old as the medium itself. We suspect that parental awareness of that discussion biases them to underreport their children's TV use in order to appear responsible to the interviewer (or themselves), and that lack of information about their children's TV exposure facilitates that bias. A third factor that may account for some of the difference between these two age groups is our finding that parents of 2- to 7-year-olds reported that their child was in the room "doing something else" an average of 43 minutes daily while they (the parent) watched television. Apparently parents did not include such "in the room" time in estimates of their child's TV exposure. Arguably, if older children were asked a similar question, they very probably might include time spent in a room where the television is on as exposure time, even if it is "their parents' program." It is extremely difficult not to watch under such conditions (Csikszentmihalyi & Kubey, 2002). Our point is that if young children's "in the room" time is counted as exposure, the difference in TV exposure between 5- to 7-year-olds and 8- to 10-year-olds is halved. Regardless of which combination of these factors may have been operating, much of the large difference between 5- to 7-year-olds and 8- to 10-year-olds in television exposure is arguably an artifact of the two different data-gathering methods.

Third, Table 4.1 also reveals that across age, average TV exposure and average total screen exposure (TV, video, and movie exposure combined) form inverted U-shaped curves. Exposure increases steadily until some time during the middle school years, then decreases significantly. Roughly similar patterns hold for exposure to movies and video-taped TV programs. That is, in the early years, children see very few movies (1% of 2- to 7-year-olds watch a movie on any given day) and very little recorded television (6% report such exposure the previous day). Although neither of these media ever account for a large share of young people's overall daily media budget (see Chapter 8), exposure to both increases to over 20 minutes daily in the 8- to 10-year-old group (of whom 15% saw a movie the previous day and 33% watched a recorded video), then declines during the teen years.[3]

George Comstock and his colleagues (1978) noted much the same pattern a quarter-century ago when they combined the results of several small-scale surveys of children's TV use to construct a curve relating average hours of daily TV viewing to age. Comstock reasoned that the new interests, new freedoms, and new school-related time demands that emerge near the beginning of the teen years influence young adolescents to reduce TV exposure. Indeed, they described a similar decrease related to changing demands on time when 5-year-olds make the transition to elementary school. Comparable patterns emerge in our results not only for TV viewing but, as we see in chapters below, for several other media and for overall media exposure.

Fortunately, the size and age range of the current samples enable us to look at TV exposure in one-year increments in order to test whether such a curvilinear relationship emerges in a single study. Figure 4.1 shows that our results generally replicate the patterns described by Comstock and his colleagues. That is, TV exposure increases until about the time children move from kindergarten to elementary school, at which point it decreases. It then increases again until around 12 or 13 years, followed by a substantial decline that roughly coincides with the transition from junior to senior high school. Clearly, available time, which is a function of age-related school and social transitions, plays a major role in young people's TV exposure.

Two additional findings in Table 4.1 warrant comment. First, relative to other screen media, movie attendance is generally quite low. Only 1 percent of young children and 10 percent of older children saw

---

[3] Only commercially produced videotapes break the pattern of increasing then de-creasing exposure. Regardless of age, U.S. youths report about half an hour per day of exposure to prerecorded videos.

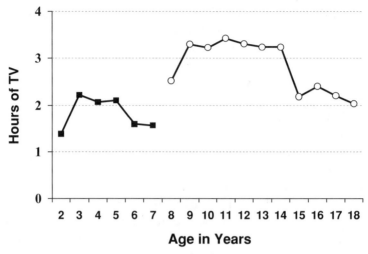

Figure 4.1. Average TV exposure by age.

a movie the preceding day. Movie attendance is at its highest among 8- to 10-year-olds, then declines throughout early and later adolescence. We suspect that both of these findings reflect the importance of video playback systems in the United States, which brings us to our second point. Viewing of commercially produced videos begins very early and remains relatively constant across age. Children and adolescents in both samples report close to 30 minutes daily exposure to these tapes. Substantial exposure to self-recorded videotapes, on the other hand, does not occur until 8 to 10 years, after which it follows the pattern of television and movies, declining through the teen years. Taken together, these patterns suggest that for a substantial portion of U.S. youth, movies are watched in the form of commercially produced videotapes. Videotapes are convenient, are a good deal cheaper than movies, and provide a convenient means for parents to control what young children see. Given the relatively small role played by self-recorded videos, we combine commercially produced and self-recorded videos in subsequent examinations of how screen exposure varies with demographic and social characteristics.

GENDER AND SCREEN EXPOSURE

On an average day, boys watch about 20 minutes more television than do girls. The difference holds for both younger (17 minutes) and older youth (20 minutes), and is largely responsible for the finding that when exposure to all screen media is combined, boys view more than girls (see Appendix 4.1). In the younger sample, the gender difference holds for both 2- to 4-year-olds and 5- to 7-year-olds, but reaches statistical significance only for the latter. In the older sample, 8- to 10-year-old girls actually watch a few minutes more per day than do their male counterparts. Among 11- to 14-year-olds and 15- to 18-year-olds, however, boys watch significantly more than girls. Although there is little difference in the proportion of boys and girls who watch television on any given day, boys are more likely to spend more time once they begin watching. Particularly from 11 to 14 years, when screen media exposure peaks, boys are slightly more likely than girls to report watching more than 1 hour the previous day, and significantly more likely to report viewing more than 5 hours.

Interestingly, gender differences in TV viewing seem to have changed over the years. Early U.S. research (Schramm et al., 1961) found no meaningful gender differences in TV viewing. In the early 1970s, Lyle and Hoffman (1972a) found much the same thing, but noted that in sixth and tenth grade, girls tended to watch a bit more than did boys. By 1990, however, the pattern had reversed. Jane Brown and her colleagues (1990) reported that 12- to 14-year-old boys watched significantly more television than girls, about 2:18 more per week. If we focus on the 11- to 14-year-olds in our sample, the difference has continued to increase. The 34 minutes per day more that boys are exposed than girls multiplies out to just under 4 hours per week.

SOCIOECONOMIC STATUS AND SCREEN EXPOSURE

Consistent with earlier research (Brown et al., 1990; Schramm et al., 1961; Tangney & Feshbach, 1988), as socioeconomic indicators such as household income or parent education increase, children and adolescents spend less time with screen media in general and television in particular. Figure 4.2 shows the relationship between household income and TV exposure. Similar results emerge when the level of parent education is related to TV exposure, and when either income or education is related to total screen exposure (see Appendix 4.1). For the most part, the differences between income and education groups hold for each of the smaller age groupings we have been examining. That is, for all but 8- to 10-year-olds, kids from households earning over $40,000 per year and kids whose parents have completed college watch substantially less television than do those from low-income households or those whose

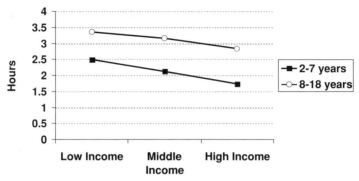

Figure 4.2. Average TV exposure by income.

parents completed no more than high school. Exposure among young-sters from middle-income households varies, sometimes resembling that for low-income youths, sometimes that for high-income youths.

Similar patterns emerge for the other screen media from about 11 years onward, although differences often are not large. Eight- through 10-year-olds are the exception. During these years, children from middle-income households watch more television, more movies, and more overall screen media than either their low- or high-income counterparts. Indeed, for this age group, the difference in TV exposure located by household income is almost 1 hour, and climbs to more than an hour and a half for all screen media combined (see Appendix 4.1).

Socioeconomic differences in screen exposure are further evident in the proportions of youngsters from each income category who watch no television, more than 1 hour of television, and over 5 hours of tele-vision daily. For example, on any given day only 8 percent of 5- to 7-year-old children from low-income households fail to watch television; 21 percent of middle-income children and 18 percent of high income do not watch (see Appendix 4.1). Similarly, almost 20 percent more young children from low-income homes than from high-income homes are exposed to more than an hour of television daily (73% vs. 55%), and 5 percent more watch for more than 5 hours (10% vs. 5%). Turning to the older sample, on any given day twice as many 8- to 10-year-olds from high-income families (15%) than from low- and middle-income families (7% and 6%) fail to watch television. On the other hand, many more middle-income kids (31%) than either low-income (16%) or high-income (20%) kids watch more than 5 hours daily. From 11 years onward, income locates few differences in the proportion of youths who watch no television or who watch more than 1 hour per day. However, among both 11- to 14-year-olds and 15- to 18-year-olds, kids from low-income homes are more likely to watch in excess of 5 hours of television a day. Again, roughly similar patterns appear when the data are examined in relation to parent education (see Appendix 4.1).

When exposure to screen media is examined as a function of whether youngsters live with one or two parents, the picture changes little. Single-parent households tend to fall into the lower income categories, and exposure to screen media tends to be higher in one-parent than two-parent homes. Indeed, for all but 2- to 4-year-olds, both TV and overall screen exposure is significantly greater for children from single-parent homes. It is also noteworthy that for all but 2- to 4-year-olds, from 5 percent to 10 percent more children from single-parent homes than two-parent homes watch in excess of 5 hours of television daily. As was the case for household TV orientation in Chapter 3, however, income does not explain all of the difference in TV exposure between single-parent and two-parent households. When TV exposure is examined holding income level constant, both younger and older kids from single-parent homes tend to watch more television, and many of the differences remain statistically significant. In other words, it appears that beyond income differences, the demands on time and energy placed on single parents may lead to more TV exposure among their children.

RACE/ETHNICITY AND SCREEN EXPOSURE

Race and ethnic background are strongly related to young people's screen exposure. Figure 4.3 shows not only that African American youths are exposed to more television than either Hispanic or white youths, but that the differences are substantial across the entire age range. Typically, Hispanic youths watch more than their white counterparts, but less than African Americans. Among 2- to 7-year-olds, there is little difference in the proportion of children from any of these groups who watch television on a given day (see Appendix 4.1). However, young black children are substantially more likely than their white or Hispanic counterparts to watch more than 1 hour and more than 5 hours of television per day (e.g., 4% of white, 10% of Hispanic, and 15% of black children watch television more than 5 hours on any given day). Among 8- to 18-year-olds, African American kids are more likely than whites to watch television on a given day (91% vs. 81%), more likely to watch for more than 1 hour (79% vs. 65%), and more than twice

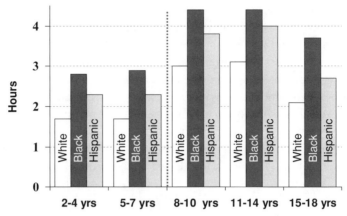

Figure 4.3. Average TV exposure by race/ethnicity.

as likely to report over 5 hours of exposure (36% vs. 17%). Again, the proportions for Hispanics tend to fall in between those for the other two groups, sometimes resembling those for white youths, sometimes those for African Americans.

The remarkable consistency in TV exposure as a function of race and ethnicity displayed Figure 4.3 largely withstands controls for income. Except among 2- to 7-year-old children from middle-income households, African American youth consistently watch more television than white youths and usually watch more than Hispanic youths.[4] Similarly, when race or ethnicity is controlled for level of parent education, results remain the same. For both the younger and older samples, at every level of parent education, white youths are exposed to substantially less television than are African Americans, with exposure levels for Hispanic kids falling between.

This pattern for TV exposure and for overall screen exposure is consistent with the findings in Chapter 3 indicating that television seems to play a particularly central role in African American families. Our results also dovetail with those of earlier studies indicating higher TV exposure among black youths (Brown et al., 1990; McIntyre & Teevan, 1972; Tangney & Feshbach, 1988), and with findings that black adults

---

[4] Unfortunately, when both age and income are controlled, the number of youths in some race by age by income groupings is reduced to the extent that the means are highly suspect. Nevertheless, the pattern of African American youths reporting much higher TV exposure than white youths, and somewhat higher exposure than Hispanic youths, is characteristic of most of the comparisons (see Appendix 4).

express more positive attitudes toward television than do whites (Bower, 1973; Robinson & Godbey, 1997; also see Comstock & Scharrer, 1999, p. 93).

HOUSEHOLD TV ORIENTATION AND SCREEN EXPOSURE

In Chapter 3 we introduced three indicators of what we call household TV orientation: constant television, television during meals, and TV rules. In this section, we add a fourth indicator: whether or not a young person has a television in his or her bedroom. These four measures attempt to capture what Comstock terms "television centrality" (Comstock, 1991; Comstock & Scharrer, 1999), the degree to which television plays an important role within a household. As expected, each of these indicators locates significant differences in children's and adolescents' exposure to screen media. Children from "television oriented" households watch more television and more screen-related media overall.

Not surprisingly, whether or not the television is "usually on even when no one is watching" (i.e., whether the youngster lives in a constant TV household) makes a big difference in amount of TV exposure. Figure 4.4 shows that differences between constant and nonconstant TV households are substantial for every age group, ranging from a high of 1:24 among 5- to 7-year-olds to a low of 55 minutes among 15- to 18-year-olds. Similarly, although the magnitude of the differences is not so great when the samples are divided as a function of whether or not the television is on during meals, or whether or not there are TV rules

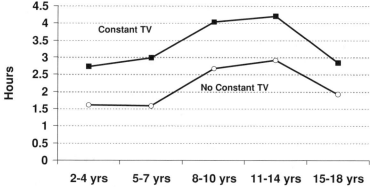

Figure 4.4. Average TV exposure by age and constant television.

in the household, the overall pattern remains the same. That is, in every age group youths from homes where the television usually operates during meals watch more television than do those from homes where the television does not operate, and for all but 15- to 18- year-olds, children from homes with rules about television watch less (see Appendix 4.2).

Finally, an almost identical pattern results when we compare kids with and without a television in their bedroom. Those with a TV set in their bedroom watch substantially more television. The differences range from a low of 35 minutes (among 5- to 7-year-olds) to a high of 1:22 (among 8- to 10-year-olds). When the effect of a television in a child's room is examined in relation to indicators of socioeconomic status, the picture changes a good deal for older youths. Although 2- to 7-year-olds with a TV set in their bedroom consistently watch more than those without one, significant differences emerge only for children from high-income households and for those whose parents completed college. Among 8- to 18-year-olds, however, TV exposure remains higher for youths with a television in their bedroom regardless of household income or parent education. When the effect of presence or absence of a bedroom television is examined as a function of race or ethnicity, even more complex results emerge. Generally, the increase in TV exposure related to the presence of a bedroom television is highly significant for white youths regardless of age. Older African American kids with their own television also watch more than their counterparts without a television, but the difference just reaches conventional levels of statistical significance ($p < .05$). Among younger black children and Hispanic youths in both samples, presence of a bedroom television makes no difference in amount of exposure (see Appendix 4.2).

CONTENT PREFERENCES

Content matters. Most parents would be less concerned about television if their children devoted several hours per day to educational, cultural, or news and public affairs programs rather than to cartoons, action adventure shows, and music videos. It is important to examine the kinds of programming that young people choose to watch.

Information about the kinds of screen media content consumed was gathered in several different ways. Each youngster who watched any television the preceding day completed "television grids" similar to those found in the typical TV guide: one grid each for the morning, afternoon, and evening. The grids contained all programs available during

the relevant hours for the preceding day (or weekend day).[5] We classified all shows into one of 19 predefined genres (see Appendix 2), then
computed the proportion of viewers who watched each genre.[6] Because
a number of program types attracted few young viewers, we combine several genres. For example, news, news magazine, and news commentary
programs are collapsed into a single "news" category, and children's slap-
stick, super hero, mystery, social relations, and variety programs form a
single "children's entertainment category." Finally, we report results only
for the categories of TV programs that, on any given day, are watched
by at least 10 percent of the young people in one of the two samples.

Information about the kinds of videos young people watch was obtained from the parents of 2- to 7-year-olds and from adolescents in
the seventh through twelfth grades ($n = 1,188$; age range 12 through
18 years).[7] Those who watched commercially produced videotapes the
preceding day indicated what they saw from a list of 10 genres: action,
comedy, drama, family/children, fitness, horror, romance, science fiction, music videos, and "something else." Finally, 2- to 7-year-olds and
seventh through twelfth graders who attended a movie the preceding
day indicated what they saw from the same list, minus the music video
and fitness categories.

TV CONTENT

Table 4.2 presents the proportion of viewers in both samples and in
each of the smaller age subgroups who watch each kind of TV show.
The percentages reveal that three content genres dominate most U.S.
2- to 7-year-olds' TV viewing (two if we combine the two children's
categories of entertainment and education), and that humor is king.
Children's programming, most of which relies on humor, draws 80 percent of young viewers; the next closest category is comedy, which attracts
26 percent. No other program genre claims even 10 percent of young

[5] Program grids were constructed to fit each local broadcast area. Respondents were
instructed to circle only one show per half-hour time slot only if they watched
"most" of the show.
[6] Note that most young people who watched television watched several shows during
the course of a day. Thus, the resulting number is the proportion of viewers who
watch each of the various genres on any given day. The proportions, therefore, do
not sum to 100%.
[7] This question was not asked of third- through sixth-grade children in order to
reduce questionnaire length.

Table 4.2. *Television Content Preferences by Age (%)*[a]

Program genre	2–7 years	2–4 years	5–7 years	8–18 years	8–10 years	11–14 years	15–18 years
Comedy	26	19_a	33_b	50	43_a	56_b	48_a
Drama	7	6	8	24	18_a	27_b	24_b
Movies	7	6	8	18	13_a	18_b	21_b
Sports	4	1_a	6_b	17	10_a	21_b	18_c
News/News commentary	3	3	4	12	9_a	10_a	19_b
Reality	4	4	5	12	7_a	15_b	12_b
Talk	1	1	1	10	4_a	10_b	15_c
Entertainment/ variety	2	1	2	12	6_a	13_b	16_b
Music videos	1	–	2	10	7_a	13_b	9_a
Child entertainment	62	33_a	43_b	23	40_a	23_b	8_c
Child educational	68	77_a	60_b	24	43_a	24_b	8_c
(All children's)	80	85	76	36	60_a	34_b	14_c

[a] See note to Table 3.2.

viewers. Humor also dominates older youths' viewing. Comedy draws half of all 8- to 18-year-olds, followed by children's programming, which continues to attract 36 percent. No other genre attracts even a quarter of older viewers; the proportions range from a high of 24 percent for drama to a low of 10 percent for music videos and talk shows. In short, the major attraction of TV programs for U.S. youth is some form of humor.

Age makes a difference in what children and adolescents watch. Several age trends that are related to the three most watched program genres (children's educational, children's entertainment, and comedy programs) are apparent. First, as age increases, fewer youths watch children's educational programming; each successive age increment locates a significant reduction in the proportion of viewers, declining from 77 percent of 2- to 4-year-olds to 8 percent of 15- to 18-year-olds. Second, the proportion viewing children's entertainment programming increases until the middle elementary school years (8 to 10 years), then declines during adolescence. Finally, the proportion of kids who watch comedy steadily increases until middle adolescence (from 19% of 2- to 4-year-olds to 56% of 11- to 14-year-olds), then declines slightly in later adolescence. Within the younger sample, the proportions viewing other, more adult-oriented programs increase slightly with age, but only the 5 percent difference in the proportion watching sports programs is statistically significant. On the other hand, several age-related increases in viewing other kinds of content emerge within the older sample. With the exception of children's programs, the proportion of older kids watching all but news shows increases significantly between 8 to 10 years and 11 to 14 years. From 11 to 14 years to 15 to 18 years, the proportion viewing each of the various genres remains generally the same, with a few notable exceptions. First, relative to 11- to 14-year-olds, significantly higher proportions of 15- to 18-year-olds watch news (10% vs. 19%) and talk shows (10% vs. 15%). Second, lower proportions of the oldest adolescents watch comedy (56% vs. 48%) and music videos (13% vs. 9%).

More interesting than age-related increases and decreases in the proportion of young people viewing specific content genres is the fragmentation of taste that occurs as kids get older. As they move through the elementary school and high school years, the proportion of viewers watching any of the various genres becomes more evenly distributed. In other words, as young people grow older, program preferences spread out across most genres. Comedy remains king, but by 11 to 14 years, each of the 11 genres in our list attracts at least 10 percent of viewers (with the caveat that among 15- to 18-year-olds, the proportion viewing the two types of children's programs and music videos returns to less than 10%.) In general, then, as children grow older, their tastes and interests broaden, a wider variety of content types begin to appeal to them, and they increasingly spread their program selections out over the full array of available choices. We encounter a similar kind of trend in Chapter 5, when examining the evolution of young people's tastes in popular music genres.

Gender is the only other demographic characteristic that locates consistent differences in young people's program choices, and these occur primarily in the older sample. Among 2- to 7-year-olds, higher proportions of boys than girls watch sports and children's entertainment programs; no other gender differences are statistically significant. Among 8- to 18-year-olds, however, the picture changes substantially. Significantly more girls than boys watch comedy, drama, music videos, talk shows, and children's educational programs. Conversely, more boys than girls watch sports and children's entertainment programs. The remaining four genres attract relatively equal proportions of boys and girls (see Appendix 4.3).

Gender differences in TV content preferences among older children also vary with age. For example, from 11 to 14 years, the age when U.S. youths watch the most television, only two noteworthy gender differences occur: more girls than boys watch talk shows and more boys than girls watch sports. However, among 8- to 10-year-olds higher proportions of girls than boys watch comedy, movies, music videos, and children's educational shows. Among 15- to 18-year-olds, too, higher proportions of girls than boys watch talk shows, music videos, and children's educational programs. The oldest boys continue to prefer sports programs, and significantly more of them than girls watch children's entertainment programs. In short, only sports programming produces a consistent gender difference regardless of age, and only talk shows attract more girls than boys during most of adolescence.

The tables in Appendix 4.3 reveal only a few, scattered differences in TV content selection as a function of the other demographic variables we have been considering. For example, substantially higher proportions of 2- to 7-year-old African American children than either white or Hispanic children watch comedy programs, and more Hispanics than African Americans watch children's entertainment programs; the latter group, in turn, watch this genre in greater proportions than do white children. Among older youths, the likelihood of watching drama is higher among children from high-income households, and the likelihood of watching talk shows is lower. These occasional differences, however, do not form any consistent patterns. In other words, once we move beyond age and gender, few generalizations about young people's TV content preferences in relation to demographic characteristics are warranted.

VIDEO CONTENT

The pattern of content choices for videos roughly resembles that for television. Young children gravitate to child- or family-oriented content; 85 percent of 2- to 7-year-olds who watch videos see one of this type. The next closest category, comedy, attracts only 7 percent. On the other hand, comedy and action videos dominate the choices of older viewers (44% and 42%, respectively), followed by drama (17%) and horror (16%). No differences in video content preferences emerge when smaller age subgroups are compared.[8]

[8] No 11-year-olds were in the seventh grade.

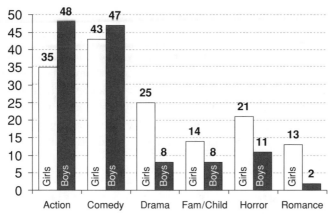

Figure 4.5. Gender differences in video content preferences: proportion of seventh to twelfth grades who reported viewing each six genres of commercial video content.

As was the case for TV content, clear gender differences in video content preferences arise among older children. Only one substantial gender difference appears among 2- to 7-year-olds: a higher proportion of boys (9%) than girls (1%) watch action videos. Among seventh through twelfth graders, however, gender differences occur for five of nine categories. As Figure 4.5 shows, more boys than girls choose action videos, and more girls than boys choose drama, family/children's shows, romance, and (somewhat surprisingly) horror videos.

One other point related to gender deserves comment. Because viewers were asked to indicate *all* videos watched "yesterday," the extent to which the sum of all videos watched exceeds 100 percent indicates viewing of multiple videos on a single day. When the percentage watching each type of video is computed separately for the two genders, girls total 166 percent and boys 134 percent. Since equal proportions of boys and girls watched videos the previous day (18%), the 32 percent difference indicates that girls are more likely than boys to watch multiple videos on any given day. This may partially explain the higher proportion of girls than boys watching in the several categories where gender differences occur.

As was the case for television, the few, scattered differences in video content preferences that emerge in relation to other demographic variables form no consistent patterns.

MOVIE CONTENT

Table 4.1 shows that only 1 percent of 2- to 7-year olds and 10 percent of 8- to 18-year-olds see a movie on any given day, too few to allow for reliable analyses of subgroup differences in content preferences. In general, however, it seems safe to say that older youths prefer action (41%) and comedy (36%) films, the only two genres to attract more than a third of movie attendees. The only other finding of note is that, as was the case for videos, boys are more attracted than girls to action films (54% vs. 28%).

SUMMING UP SCREEN CONTENT PREFERENCES

Age and gender are the only demographic variables consistently related to the kinds of screen content children and adolescents choose to watch. Young children begin with a preference for things humorous – children's programs and comedy. Humor remains a mainstay of screen media content choices among older youth, but comedy becomes far more preferred than children's programming. At the same time, age clearly brings fragmentation of taste. Such content genres as sports, reality and talk programs, action, drama, romance, and horror all begin to receive increased attention. In addition, several gender stereotypes seem to hold. Although there are some variations with age, boys prefer sports and action and girls gravitate to child- and family-oriented content, romance, comedy, and, to our surprise, horror. With the exception of gender, perhaps the most noteworthy finding relevant to other demographic variables is how similar content preferences are across children.

THE CONTEXT OF EXPOSURE

Whether children watch screen media alone, with parents, or with siblings or friends has long been considered an important element in the viewing process (Paik, 2001; Van Evra, 1998). Conversations between coviewers, comments by others about what appears on screen, even incidental modeling of how one watches (e.g., some parents talk back to the TV screen; others frequently ignore it) – any such elements of the viewing context may influence whether and what children view, how they view, and what they learn from what is portrayed (Anderson & Collins, 1988; Hodge & Tripp, 1986; Wartella, 1986). In short, a question deserving of attention is: Who are young people with when they watch television?

Chapter 2 describes how genres of television viewing were measured for each part of the day (morning, afternoon, and evening). The social context within which that viewing took place was assessed through two additional questions also associated with each day part. First, we asked any youth who watched television during any day part to indicate whether watching occurred "mainly alone" or "mainly with someone else." It is important to note that because the question asked whether the child was "mainly" alone or with someone else, we cannot determine the precise amount of time they watched in the company of others. We can assume only that the "mainly alone" classification identifies youths who watched television alone for more than half of the time that they viewed during any day part. Thus, a child who viewed for 2 hours in the morning might have been alone for 2 hours, or 90 minutes, or 61 minutes; another who watched for 15 minutes might have viewed alone from 8 to 15 minutes. Both youngsters are counted as watching mainly alone for that day part. Second, for each of the three day parts, viewers who reported watching mainly with someone else further indicated with whom they were watching from a list including parents, siblings, relatives, friends, teachers, and so forth. We use this information to estimate the proportion of young people who typically watch television in the company of parents and in the company of other youths (siblings and friends) for each day part.[9]

Three generalizations seem warranted when we consider solitary viewing. First, as Figure 4.6 shows, the proportion of young people who watch mainly alone is fairly substantial. Although during the evening hours only about 10 percent of 2- to 7-year-olds are alone when they watch television, 30 percent of them engage in solitary viewing in the morning and 25 percent are mainly alone when they watch in the afternoon. The proportions are much larger for older youths. Over a third of 8- to 18-year-olds view mainly alone in the evening, and in excess of 40 percent watch alone earlier in the day.

Second, day part makes a difference in solitary viewing. Watching alone is at its highest in the morning, declines slightly in the afternoon, and is at its lowest in the evening, a pattern that probably reflects availability of parents and other family members. During mornings and

---

[9] Because children were instructed to indicate all others with whom they mainly watched, the resulting proportions for each coviewer group are not independent. That is, a child may have watched with parents, siblings, and friends at the same time.

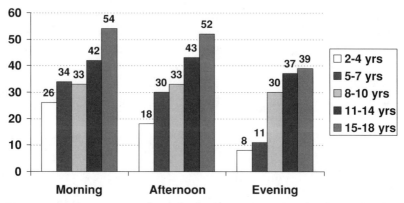

Figure 4.6. Proportion of youth watching TV "mainly alone" by day part.

afternoons, most parents are preparing for work, at work, or engaged in various household activities that reduce time available to watch television. Siblings are also likely to be preparing for or attending school, and thus not available to coview. By evening, however, other members of the family are present to share the TV screen. Thus, although 30 percent of 2- to 7-year-olds view mainly alone in the morning, only 10 percent watch alone in the evening. At the other extreme, the proportion of 15- to 18-year-olds watching alone drops from 54 percent in the morning to 39 percent during the evening hours (see Appendix 4.4).

Third, as U.S. youths grow older, they are more likely to watch alone. The proportion of young people who watch mainly alone during each day part consistently increases with each successive age increment. Several factors probably account for the age differences. First, because adolescents are engaged in establishing independence from their parents and other adolescents, they may well avoid "family" viewing. In addition, differences in child, adolescent, and adult tastes, a wide array of programming choices, and multiple TV sets (see Chapter 3) all may function to reduce coviewing. Parents who are willing to watch a child-oriented show such as *Sesame Street* often rebel at watching something designed to appeal particularly to adolescents (e.g., MTV's *Jackass*). Similarly, teenage girls may not want to view a little brother's favorite action program. And finally, the ability to view alone is certainly facilitated by the proliferation of television sets in U.S. youths' bedrooms, as noted in Chapter 3.

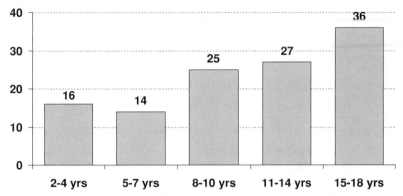

Figure 4.7. Proportion of TV time spent viewing "mainly alone."

Finally, we calculated a rough index of the proportion of youths who do most of their viewing mainly alone *throughout the day*.[10] Figure 4.7 shows the results of this calculation. From 14 percent to 36 percent of youths view mainly alone, and as age increases, there is a steady increase in solitary viewing. By 8 to 10 years, a quarter of U.S. children view mainly alone throughout the entire day, and the proportion rises to over a third by 15- to 18 years.

Although substantial numbers of children and adolescents engage in solitary viewing, it is also evident that even higher proportions watch in the company of others. Table 4.3 shows who some of those others are. More often than not, young people watch television with parents, siblings, friends, or some combination of both. The proportion viewing with parents complements the results for solitary viewing. That is, within each day part, the proportion of youth viewing with parents decreases as age increases, and regardless of age, parental coviewing is highest during the evening hours. Interestingly, from about 8 years onward, a higher proportion of U.S. youth watches television in the presence of other young people – siblings and friends – than in any other social context. The only break in this pattern occurs during the afternoon hours, when kids are more likely to watch with parents. Finally, the likelihood of older youths coviewing with other young people also drops off with increased age, a phenomenon that occurs for all three day parts.

[10] If a youth responded "viewed mainly alone" for each of the day parts during which television was viewed, he or she was classified as "viewed mainly alone" for all of their viewing for that day.

Table 4.3. *Who Children View Television with by Day Part and Age (%)*[a]

	2–7 years	2–4 years	5–7 years	8–18 years	8–10 years	11–14 years	15–18 years
Proportion viewing mainly alone							
Morning	30	26$_a$	34$_b$	41	33$_a$	42$_b$	54$_c$
Afternoon	25	18$_a$	30$_b$	42	33$_a$	43$_b$	52$_c$
Evening	10	8	11	35	30$_a$	37$_b$	39$_b$
Proportion viewing with parents							
Morning	21	27$_a$	14$_b$	8	13$_a$	8$_b$	4$_c$
Afternoon	15	16	13	13	14$_a$	16$_a$	7$_b$
Evening	30	26$_a$	34$_b$	24	28$_a$	27$_a$	19$_b$
Proportion viewing with siblings or friends							
Morning	25	24	26	19	31$_a$	18$_b$	10$_c$
Afternoon	22	18$_a$	26$_b$	26	34$_a$	29$_a$	15$_b$
Evening	25	19$_a$	30$_b$	32	36$_a$	32$_a$	27$_b$
Proportion of viewing "mainly alone" throughout the day							
Full day's viewing	15	16	14	29	25$_a$	27$_a$	36$_b$

[a] See note to Table 3.2.

Our findings for solitary viewing and coviewing with parents receive further support from analysis of the supplementary diary data described in Chapter 2. Each time youngsters who kept the supplemental media diaries recorded use of a medium for any half-hour period of the day, they also indicated with whom, if anyone, they watched. We used these data to calculate yet an estimate of the percentage of all viewing *time* young people spend alone or with parents over the course of a week. This calculation produces proportions for time viewing alone that are highly similar to the proportion of youths viewing alone reported above. However, when half-hour segments of time spent viewing with parents are calculated in this way, the estimates of parent-child coviewing drop dramatically. According to this measure, 2- to 7-year-olds spend about 19 percent of their TV time viewing in the presence of parents. From 8 years onward, kids spend 5 percent or less of their viewing time in the presence of parents.

When the proportion of children who view television mainly alone is examined in relation to most of the other demographic variables we have been examining, very few meaningful relationships emerge. Except that a higher proportion of older boys view alone during the evening, factors such as gender, race or ethnicity, and family socioeconomic status do not differentiate between young people who do and do not watch television mainly alone. However, two additional attributes do differentiate between young viewers who do and do not watch mainly alone. The first is whether or a youngster is an only child; the second is whether or not he or she has a television in his or her bedroom. Obviously, the presence of siblings should reduce the opportunity for solitary viewing, and our results show that is the case. Among 8- to 18-year-olds,[11] for example, 63 percent of only children watch television mainly alone in the morning versus 36 percent of those with siblings. In the afternoon, the proportions are 58 percent for only children versus 37 percent for those with siblings, and in the evenings 45 percent of only children versus 32 percent of those with siblings. Similarly, a TV set in a child's bedroom increases the opportunity to view alone, and U.S. youngsters seize that opportunity. During both the morning and afternoon, 45 percent of youths with a TV set in their bedroom watch alone, versus 32 percent (mornings) and 35 percent (afternoons) of those who do not have their own television. Finally, during the evening, when parents and siblings are most likely to be available for coviewing, 46 percent of kids with their own television watch mainly alone versus 35 percent of those with no TV set in their room (see Appendix 4.4).

Finally, we asked 2- to 7-year-olds who they are mainly with when they watch videos, and seventh- through twelfth-grade youth who they are with when either watching videotapes or attending a movie. The social context for viewing videos is roughly similar for young and older children. Twenty percent of 2- to 7-year-olds who watch videos view them mainly alone, 35 percent watch with a parent, and 50 percent watch with a sibling or friend.[12] Among adolescents who view videos, 30 percent watch mainly alone, 24 percent watch with a parent, and 55 percent watch with a friend or sibling. Although the results for movies are highly tentative since relatively few adolescents attend a movie on any given day, about 16 percent of seventh through twelfth graders see a movie alone, 10 percent with a parent, and 65 percent attend with a

[11] Analysis is limited to the older sample because they are more likely to have siblings.

[12] Recall that these questions are not independent. Because children can watch with parents and siblings at the same time, the proportions sum to more than 100%.

friend or sibling. These results recall Schramm et al.'s (1961) contention that a primary function of movie attendance for adolescents is social. That is, the movie theater is an excellent place to gather with friends. It appears that movies (and, to a slightly lesser extent, videos) continue to serve such a social function.

In general, then, although a substantial portion of U. S. young peo-ple's TV viewing occurs while the child is "mainly alone," most of the time they watch television, they are with someone else. More often than not, however, that someone else is likely to be another young person – a sibling or a friend. Less than a third of all TV viewing occurs mainly in the presence of a parent. To the extent that parental example and comment makes a difference in how young people are influenced by TV content, and the evidence indicates that it does (Van Evra, 1998), these numbers are not encouraging.

ATTITUDES TOWARD TELEVISION

Youths in the older sample indicated whether, when they watch televi-sion, they are entertained, learn interesting things, or are just killing time. Responses for each question ranged from "most of the time" through "some of the time" and "a little of the time" to "never." Figure 4.8 presents responses to each of the three questions for the three

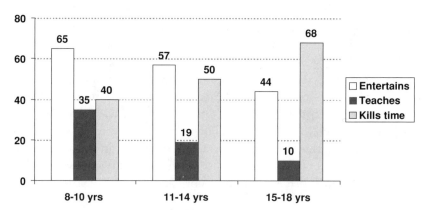

Figure 4.8. Attitudes toward television by age among 8- to 18-year-olds: proportion of youths responding "most of the time" when asked whether television entertains and whether they learn new things, and "most of the time" or "some of the time" when asked whether when they watch television they are killing time.

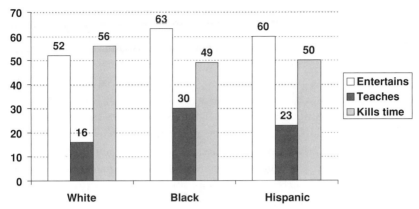

Figure 4.9. Attitudes toward television by race/ethnicity among 8- to 18-year-olds: proportion of youths responding "most of the time" when asked whether television entertains and whether they learn new things, and "most of the time" or "some of the time" when asked whether when they watch television they are killing time.

older age subgroups. Interestingly, perceptions of television as both entertaining and a teacher of interesting things decline as youths grow older. For each successive increase in age, significantly smaller proportions of kids answer that most of the time television entertains or that they learn interesting things from it. Similarly, as children grow older, they are increasingly more likely to say that when they watch television they are killing time.[13] In addition to the differences among age groups, simply the raw percentages tell a story. As the perception that television entertains most of the time drops from almost two-thirds of young viewers to fewer than half of the oldest adolescents, and the perception that television teaches "interesting things" drops from over one-third to just 10 percent, the admission that watching television is frequently a way to kill time climbs from 40 percent to over two-thirds. These strike us as extremely large proportions of youths expressing a kind of low-level dissatisfaction with the medium.

Only one other demographic variable is strongly related to responses on these three questions. When responses are examined in relation to race or ethnicity, as in Figure 4.9, African American and Hispanic

[13] Because relatively few youths indicated they are killing time most of the time they watch, we combined the "most of the time" and "some of the time" responses for this question.

youths are more positive than whites toward the medium. Although the proportions entertained most of the time remain consistently over 50 percent, higher proportions of black and Hispanic than white kids make that claim. Black and Hispanic youths are also more likely to say they learn interesting things from television. Finally, white youths are more apt than black youths to say that when they watch television they are mostly killing time. Although the differences between African American and Hispanic youths are never large enough to be statistically significant, there is nevertheless a slight tendency for the African American kids to be a bit more positive toward the medium. This may be more evidence of the apparent importance or centrality of television in the lives of black youths (see Appendix 4.5).

Summing Up Screen Media Exposure

U.S. children and adolescents devote a substantial portion of their leisure time to screen media, particularly television. Some scholars have argued that no other single leisure time activity claims as much time from young people as does television (e.g., Timmer, Eccles, & O'Brien, 1985), and it is hard to disagree, particularly if one adds video and movie exposure to the total. Depending on age, average screen exposure ranges from 2 ½ to 4 ¼ hours daily. Viewing peaks during the middle school years, then drops off throughout the remainder of adolescence. Screen time is negatively related to various indicators of socioeconomic status. Television seems to be especially central in the leisure time of African American youth.

For the most part, children and young people prefer TV content that includes some kind of humor. Humor also appeals in videos and movies, but so too does action, particularly among older youth. Perhaps the most interesting trend in content preferences is the clear fragmentation of tastes as young people grow older. Where one or two content categories account for most viewing among young children, by the adolescent years preferences spread out over five to seven different genres. Aside from age, gender is the only attribute of young people that consistently differentiates content preferences. Boys gravitate to sports and action; girls prefer comedy, talk, romance, and horror.

When they watch television, about a third of U.S. youth are mainly alone, although the proportions vary substantially depending on age. Another third watch mainly in the presence of parents, and about half coview with siblings or friends. Both amount of viewing and the social context of viewing are somewhat dependent on the environment in which young people find themselves. Children who have a television in their bedroom view more and are more likely to view alone. Children with siblings are more likely than only children to view with others. To the extent that parents conceive of either the amount of viewing or viewing in the absence of adult supervision as important, the results described in this chapter certainly suggest it might be useful to consider removing TV sets from children's and adolescents' bedrooms.

Finally, there is at least tentative evidence that although U.S. youth spend a great deal of time with television, they do not find it to be particularly stimulating (also see Larson, Kubey & Colletti, 1989).

CHAPTER FIVE

AUDIO MEDIA: RADIO, TAPES, AND CDs

This chapter examines young people's use of audio media – radio, tapes, and CDs. It considers how much time kids are exposed to audio media, as well as what they listen to. For the most part, U.S. youth conceive of audio media as music media. There is, of course, some exposure to such radio formats as news and talk, and there is some use of tapes or CDs to listen to stories or for instructional purposes. But typically, when children and especially adolescents talk about listening to the radio or some kind of recording, they are talking about listening to music. For young people in the U.S. today, audio media are, fundamentally, music media.

It is difficult to obtain accurate estimates of time spent listening to radio or recordings. One of audio media's most important distinguishing characteristics is that they so conveniently operate in the background – as a secondary or even tertiary activity. Consider, for example, that young children often play in the family room or living room to the sound of a parent's favorite album or a sibling's portable radio. Or imagine teenagers driving to a football game arguing animatedly about what to do after the game, while a local "alternative" rock station booms from the car radio. Meanwhile, the football team is in the gym, changing from street clothes to football pads to the reverberations of a rapper emanating at maximum volume from the locker room boom-box. And, of course, it is a rare adolescent who does not do homework with some kind of music in the background. Indeed, we suspect that many readers of this paragraph do so accompanied by music. In short, more often than not, people are exposed to audio media while they do something else – drive, work, read, chat with friends, surf the web, and so on.

It is precisely because audio media function so well as a background activity that the time young people spend with radio and recordings is difficult to measure. If the hypothetical youths imagined above were asked what they were doing during the periods described, they would quite probably respond "playing" or "driving" or "doing homework" rather than "listening to. . . ." Indeed, if the kids in the car were pressed to explain what they were doing in addition to driving, they would be more likely to reply "talking" than "listening to music." It follows that many estimates of audio exposure are apt to be underestimates (Christenson & Roberts, 1998; Roberts & Henriksen, 1990). Of course, it can be argued that if audio media fade so far into the background, perhaps such secondary listening should not be considered "legitimate" exposure. After all, it is not as if the music is really being listened to. We think Christenson and Roberts (1998) offer the best response to such an argument: "Simply turn off the 'background' music when adolescents are studying, chatting, or doing chores and observe their responses. They will respond in the clearest of terms that they are 'listening'" (1998, p. 35).

Our measures of audio exposure attempt to account for the background nature of much listening by including a sensitizing phrase (cf. Roberts & Henriksen, 1990). Questions about listening to radio and to CDs or tapes the preceding day were introduced as follows: "People often listen to [radio; CDs or tapes] while doing other things (for example, eating, getting dressed, doing homework, walking or riding in a car or bus). Thinking only about yesterday. . . ." All youngsters in both samples were asked about exposure to CDs or tapes. Parents of 2- to 7-year-olds and seventh through twelfth graders (13 to 18 years) responded to a question about four types of radio broadcast: music, news, talk, and other. Because of time constraints, third through sixth graders answered only a single item about overall radio exposure. For both radio and CDs or tapes, parents of young children were explicitly asked to include exposure with other people: "About how much time did [X] spend listening to [music, news, talk] either on his/her own, or with other people, or with you while you were listening to the radio?" Older children, on the other hand, were simply asked: "About how much time did you spend listening to. . . ." There is, then, some likelihood that estimates of audio exposure for young children contain more "incidental" music exposure than do estimates for older youth.

Amount of Audio Exposure

In the United States, from 75 percent of 2- to 4-year-olds to 96 percent of 15- to 18-year-olds listen to some kind of audio on any given day.

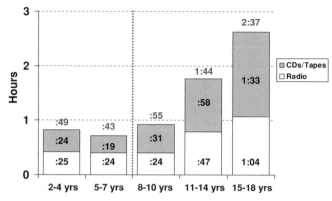

Figure 5.1. Average audio exposure by age.

Average daily exposure time ranges from three-quarters of an hour among 2- to 7-year-olds to over 2½ hours among 15- to 18-year-olds. Figure 5.1 shows that, as was the case for television, audio media exposure begins quite early; 75 percent of 2- to 4-year-olds report some listening, and they hear an average of 49 minutes daily. Unlike television exposure, which drops off in late adolescence, audio exposure increases steadily from 8 to 10 years through 15 to 18 years. Younger children hear a few minutes more of radio than of CDs or tapes each day, but from 8 to 10 years onward, CDs or tapes take the lead, and by 15 to 18 years U.S. kids spend about 30 minutes more per day with recordings than with radio (see Appendix 5.2). We suspect the growing preference for recordings is a sign of adolescents preferring to exercise more independent choice as they grow older; recordings put *them* in charge of what to hear.

Perhaps the most interesting aspect of young people's audio use is that of all the media considered in this study, only exposure to audio increases steadily from 8 to 10 years through 15 to 18 years. Indeed, audio exposure increases to levels that exceed those for TV exposure. Figure 5.2 indicates that there is reason to question several recent studies that estimate U.S. adolescents' TV exposure to be higher than audio exposure (e.g., Brown et al., 1990; Horatio Alger Foundation, 1996; Kubey & Csikszentmihalyi, 1990; Larson & Kubey, 1983). When exposure to the two media is examined in yearly age increments, the steady growth in the importance of audio media becomes clear. Once sensitized to include background listening, by late adolescence U.S. kids say that they devote more time to audio media than to television. The steady increase in exposure to audio media occurs largely because they function

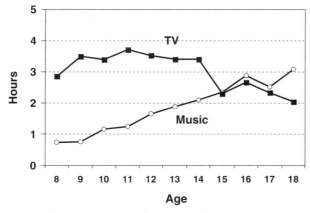

Figure 5.2. Average audio and TV exposure by age.

primarily as a source of music, and for adolescents music is arguably the most important type of media content.

Of course, neither radio nor recordings are exclusively devoted to music. News and public affairs programs, talk shows, religious broadcasts, and sports all contribute to the radio broadcast spectrum. Similarly, recordings include such content as books on tape, nursery rhymes, and various kinds of instructional material. To account for these kinds of content, we explicitly asked about exposure to both music and nonmusic formats: news, talk, books on tape, and other. Not surprisingly, 2- to 7-year-olds are substantially more likely to listen to children's recordings than any other type of recording, a category that includes stories and nursery rhymes as well as children's music. Once beyond "children's music," however, relatively few young children attend to other types of music; rather, they listen to stories and nursery rhymes. Older youths, on the other hand, listen almost exclusively to music when they use CDs or tapes.

Radio listening presents a different story. Both young children and adolescents are exposed to nonmusic radio formats. Parents report that 2- to 7-year-olds hear an average of 2 minutes per day of news, 2 minutes of talk radio, and less than 1 minute of other radio content, a total of 17 percent of all radio exposure time. The averages are somewhat higher for seventh through twelfth grade youth (12 to 18 years). They report daily exposure to 5 minutes of news, 4 minutes of talk radio, and 3 minutes of other content, a total of 20 percent of radio exposure time (which amounts to 9% of all audio time; see Appendix 5.2). We suspect that for both age groups, most nonmusic exposure is largely incidental, consisting of the occasional news break that most music stations program every hour, shows stumbled on as new stations are sought, or something a parent has chosen to listen to in their presence. Whatever the explanation, U.S. kids think of audio media primarily as music media (cf. Christenson & Roberts, 1998).

PREDICTORS OF AUDIO EXPOSURE

Consistent with several earlier studies of young people's use of audio media (Brown et al., 1990; Lyle & Hoffman, 1972a; Roberts & Henriksen, 1990), gender is the only demographic characteristic other than age that consistently relates to amount of audio exposure. Figure 5.3 shows that young boys and girls differ little in how much they listen to the radio or recordings. By 8 to 10 years, however, girls are more likely than boys to listen to either the radio or CDs or tapes, on any given day (see Appendix 5.1), and they spend more time listening to each medium. The difference between girls and boys in audio exposure increases from about $\frac{1}{2}$ hour at 8 to 10 years to just under an hour at 11 to 14 years, then declines to 19 minutes by late adolescence, the only period during which the gender difference is not statistically significant. Interestingly, Roberts and Henriksen (1990) found a similar age-related decrease in the gender gap in audio exposure over a decade ago. In their study, ninth-grade girls (15-year-olds) reported 51 minutes more audio exposure than boys; by eleventh grade (17 years), however, the difference had declined to 21 minutes.

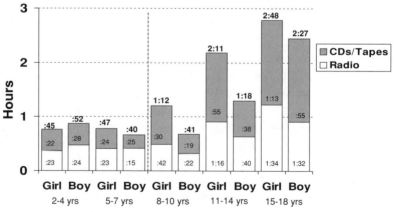

Figure 5.3. Average audio exposure by age and gender.

The reduction in the gender difference in audio exposure during late adolescence occurs largely because older boys substantially increase their use of CDs and tapes, hence their total audio exposure (see Appendix 5.1). That is, the difference between boys and girls in average radio exposure remains constant from 11 to 14 years to 15 to 18 years (17 to 18 minutes), but the difference in exposure to CDs and tapes does not. At 11 to 14 years, girls listen to CDs or tapes 36 minutes more on any given day than do boys (1:16 vs. 0:40), but by 15 to 18 years the difference drops to 2 minutes (1:34 vs. 1:32). Apparently, boys' interest in music increases as they grow older, and it seem that the greater control over music selection offered by CDs or tapes makes recordings their preferred medium. A recent Recording Industry Association of America consumer profile supports this explanation, reporting that 15- to 19-year-olds account for the largest proportion of dollars spent on recordings of any age group in the U.S., while 10- to 14-year-olds account for the lowest proportion[1] (RIAA, 2002).

Exposure to audio media does not differ greatly in relation to most of the other demographic variables we have been considering. As the tables in Appendix 5.1 reveal, except among the youngest children, there is little or no relationship between race/ethnicity and either the likelihood of listening or average time exposed to radio or recordings. This is a bit surprising in light of the few earlier studies that have examined race and radio listening. Jane Brown and her colleagues (Brown et al., 1990) found that 12- to 14-year-old African American youths from the Southeastern United States listen to substantially more radio than their white counterparts. Similarly, Lyle and Hoffman (1972a) found that Mexican American tenth graders engaged in more radio listening than white tenth graders. Radio produces the single statistically significant relationship between race/ethnicity and exposure in our study, but it emerges only for younger children. Among both 2- to 7-year-olds and 8- to 10-year-olds, African American kids listen to more radio than white kids, with Hispanic youths reporting exposure that falls between (and does not differ from either of the other two groups).

Similarly, differences in likelihood and/or amount of exposure related to socioeconomic status that typically emerge for other media (see

---

[1] Actually, the 45+ age category is credited with spending the highest percentage of total dollars spent on recording, but that category includes all years beyond 45, while younger consumers are grouped in 5-year segments.

Chapters 4, 6, and 7) largely disappear when we examine audio media. A few, scattered relationships emerge, but they depend on age and form no consistent pattern. For example, at 8 to 10 years, middle-income kids listen to more radio, at 11 to 14 years low-income kids listen to more, and at 15 to 18 years high-income kids listen to more. Roughly similar findings, albeit this time related to CDs or tapes, hold when audio exposure is examined in relation to parent education. In other words, one of the more striking characteristics of audio media is how very democratic they seem to be, at least in terms of how much they appeal to young people from all backgrounds (see Appendix 5).

Music Content Preferences

MULTIPLE MUSIC GENRES

We have argued that music is the primary attraction of audio media for most young people. However, to say that young people like music, or even "popular music," is to say little. Contemporary popular music is characterized by a wide array of very different genres. For example, Christenson and Roberts (1998) note that *Billboard Magazine*, the primary trade publication for the U.S. music industry, went from "charting" three music categories in 1950 to 20+ categories in the late 1990s. "Popular music" includes numerous kinds of rock (e.g., mainstream, modern, alternative, hard rock, or heavy metal), rap/hip-hop, rhythm and blues, top 40 (or "pop"), "golden oldies," country and western, techno, salsa, and on and on through a list that is both long and constantly changing. In the United States, popular music audiences are similarly highly fragmented – indeed, balkanized. Many followers of one genre tend only reluctantly to listen to others. Hip-hop fans attend little to mainstream rock; alternative devotees cringe at the top-40 sound. And because both the sound and the lyrics characteristic of each genre differ in significant ways (Christenson & Roberts, 1998; Rice, 1980), it is important to examine the kinds of music young people listen to, and which young people listen to which kinds of music.

Young people in this study who reported any audio exposure also indicated the kinds of music they heard the previous day from a list of 17 genres: alternative rock, children's, classic rock, classical, country and western, gospel or Christian, hard rock or metal, jazz or blues, Latin or salsa, rap or hip-hop, rave or techno, reggae, rhythm and blues or soul, ska

Table 5.1. *Proportion of Seventh through Twelfth Grade Adolescents Selecting Each of 11 Music Genres by Age (%)*

	12–14 yrs	15–18 yrs
Alternative rock	38	45
Classic rock	7	16
Country and western	9	18
Gospel/Christian	7	19
Hard rock/heavy metal	15	23
Latin/salsa	4	6
Rap/hip-hop	50	53
Rhythm and blues/soul	13	13
Ska/punk	7	8
Soft rock	10	10
Top 40	10	8

or punk, soft rock, top 40 rock, or something else.[2] A further point about these genres is important. Among many music fans, particularly adolescents, the distinctions among music genres are issues of intense debate, and boundaries – indeed, genres – frequently change. For example, to the uninitiated there might be little difference among the various "rock" labels included in the list. To the fan, however, these are important distinctions. The categories employed here come from various recording industry publications and/or current writing about popular music. Nevertheless, it is possible to combine and recombine music genres, thereby changing the percentages assigned to any given category.

Only two genres attract double-digit proportions of young listeners: 39 percent of 2- to 7-year-olds hear children's content and 10 percent hear gospel or Christian music. There is relatively little dispersion among the remaining categories (see Appendix 5.2), with each of the various popular music genres attracting roughly 1 percent to 9 percent of young listeners. We suspect that much of young children's popular music "listening" results from them being present when parents or older siblings are listening to "their" music. Since so few young children are exposed to the various popular music genres, we examine them no further.

The picture is quite different when we turn to older youth. Table 5.1 presents the proportion of seventh through twelfth graders in each of

[2] Because more than one genre could be indicated, combined proportions total to more than 100%.

Table 5.2. *Proportion of Seventh through Twelfth Grade Adolescents Selecting Each of 11 Music Genres by Race or Ethnicity (%)*

	White	Black	Hispanic
Alternative rock	51	5	39
Classic rock	15	2	5
Country and western	18	3	10
Gospel/Christian	7	19	6
Hard rock/heavy metal	24	2	16
Latin/salsa	-0-	-0-	16
Rap/hip-hop	43	84	65
Rhythm and blues/soul	9	31	18
Ska/punk	10	-0-	5
Soft rock	12	3	11
Top 40	10	-0-	8

two age groups (12 to 14 years and 15 to 18 years) exposed to those music genres that attracted at least 10 percent of one of the major demographic subgroups we have been examining, a list of 11 genres.[3] Two types of music account for the lion's share of listening: rap/hip-hop (52% for both age subgroups combined) and alternative rock (sometimes know as "modern" rock; 42%). Of course, distinctions among the various types of rock are subjective (and often highly fluid), and it is noteworthy that most other "rock" categories also draw double-digit proportions of listeners. If distinctions among the various rock genres are ignored and the proportion of adolescents listening to any kind of rock music is calculated, the resulting more general rock category attracts 56 percent of U.S. adolescents. The only other music genres to garner more than 10 percent of the adolescent audience are country and western (14%) and rhythm and blues (13%).

PREDICTORS OF CONTENT PREFERENCES

The most interesting differences in music preferences emerge in relation to race and ethnicity. Table 5.2 reveals that African American, Hispanic,

[3] Thus, children's music (and rhymes), classical, gospel/Christian, jazz/blues, rave/techno, and reggae all fall off the list. In addition, other than music genres, it should be noted that the proportion of older youths who listen to nonmusic content on CDs or tapes is minimal; less than 1% for books on tape and 4% for comedy.

and white youth have very different tastes in music. Rap/hip-hop is the only music genre highly popular among all three racial/ethnic groups. It is the overwhelming favorite of both African American (84%) and Hispanic (65%) kids, and is the second most listened-to music genre among white youth (43%). Only two other music categories attract more than 10 percent of black adolescents: rhythm and blues/soul (31%) and gospel/Christian (19%). In other words, African American youth focus most of their listening on music genres usually associated with black culture, music that has evolved from a long gospel and blues tradition, usually performed by African American musicians – what the music industry has long labeled "black music" (i.e., rap/hip-hop, R&B, soul, and gospel). White youngsters, on the other hand, spread their listening out over many more music genres, eight of the 11 categories attracting at least 10 percent of listeners, and listen to both "white" (i.e., various types of top 40, rock, and country and western) and "black" music. Alternative rock is most preferred by white adolescents (51%), followed by rap/hip-hop (43%), and then hard rock (24%), country and western (18%), and classic rock (15%), with the remaining rock categories attracting from 5 percent to 12 percent of listeners. Arguably, Hispanic youth display the most ecumenical music tastes. Rap/hip-hop is their most preferred music (65%), followed by alternative rock (39%), rhythm and blues/soul (18%), then by hard rock (16%) and Latin/salsa (16%), the last of which neither white nor black adolescents pay much attention to. When these findings for race and ethnicity are further controlled for either household income or level of parent education, little changes. That is, regardless of income or education level, African American kids focus on "black" music, while white and Hispanic kids tend to sample from a wide array of genres.[4] All in all, a fair summary of the proportions in Table 5.2 is that African American kids listen primarily to "black music," white kids to both "black" and "white" music, and Hispanic kids listen to "black," "white," and "Latin" music (see Appendix 5.3).

Gender also differentiates music tastes. Although the differences are not as large as those found for race and ethnicity, Table 5.3 shows that greater proportions of boys than girls listen to hard rock/heavy metal. Conversely, higher proportions of girls than boys listen to soft rock, country and western, and top 40. These results replicate earlier findings

[4] Conclusions based on these controls are highly tentative, however, because of a substantial reduction in the numbers of African American and Hispanic teenagers who fall into the upper income and upper education classifications.

Table 5.3. *Proportion of Seventh through Twelfth Grade Adolescents Selecting Each of 11 Music Genres by Gender (%)*

	Girls	Boys
Alternative rock	44	39
Classic rock	11	13
Country and western	17	11
Gospel/Christian	11	5
Hard rock/heavy metal	12	27
Latin/salsa	4	1
Rap/hip-hop	52	53
Rhythm and blues/soul	17	8
Ska/punk	7	8
Soft rock	15	5
Top 40	11	6

that girls prefer ballads and "softer" types of music, while boys gravitate to louder, more "hard-edged" genres (cf. Christenson & Peterson, 1988; Christenson & Roberts, 1998). Indeed, at least one researcher has suggested that the music industry could junk its current system of music genres for one that distinguishes simply between music with "male appeal" and "female appeal" (Warner, 1984).

Socioeconomic status also locates several differences in music tastes (see Appendix 5.3). Most notably, teenagers from low-income households and teenagers whose parents completed no more than a high school education are more likely to listen to rap/hip-hop than are those from upper income households or those whose parents have at least some college. Conversely, kids from middle or upper income homes listen to more alternative rock and classic rock, and those whose parents have completed at least some college listen to more classic rock.

FRAGMENTATION OF MUSIC PREFERENCES

There also appears to be a tendency for music tastes to fragment as either household income or level of parent education increases. That is, music choices of kids from both low-income and low parent-education backgrounds tend to cluster around fewer music genres than do those of kids from middle or upper income households or whose parents completed at least some college. Using 10 percent as a marker, only five music genres account for most choices of teenagers from low-income or low-education households, but from seven to nine music types are chosen by kids from middle- and upper income or education households (see Appendix 5.3). Although some might interpret such a pattern in terms of taste cultures that parallel social stratification (Gans, 1967) – arguing, for example, that adolescents from lower socioeconomic backgrounds are less adventuresome, hence less likely to sample a variety of music genres – caution is warranted. Disproportionate numbers of African American youths fall into the low-income and parent-education classifications, and as we have seen, African American kids focus primarily on just three music types. It follows that some of the restriction in music preferences found for youth from low-income and low-education households might be confounded with the substantial differences in music taste located by race noted earlier. Indeed, when the relationship between music genre preferences and either household income or level of parent education is examined only among white youth, the pattern of increased fragmentation of taste at higher socioeconomic levels is much less clear[5] (see Appendix 5.3). In short, our results largely mirror those of several earlier studies in that we find little evidence that socioeconomic status plays a major role in U.S. teenagers' music tastes.

Audio Media: A Coda

Audio media in general and music in particular play an important role in children's and adolescents' media diets. As we see in Chapter 8, audio media account for the second largest proportion of U.S. youth's overall media time. Moreover, audio is the only medium for which amount of exposure increases from 8 to 18 years; indeed, by late adolescence, exposure to audio media surpasses that for any other medium. Throughout most of childhood and early adolescence, girls tend to spend more time than boys listening to radio and recordings, but the difference largely disappears by late adolescence. None of the other demographic variables we have been considering shows much relationship to amount of audio exposure. In short, in terms of overall exposure, audio media are arguably the most democratic of the media; they attract youth from every kind of background equally.

---

[5] Because so few fell into the upper income or education categories, these analyses could not be conducted for African American or Hispanic adolescents.

On the other hand, there is a great deal of differentiation in the types of music that adolescents from different backgrounds prefer. The strongest relationships emerge for race and ethnicity and for gender. African American youth almost exclusively listen to genres typically regarded as "black" music: rap/hip-hop, rhythm and blues and soul, and gospel. No other music type attracts more than 5 percent of African American teenagers. Substantial numbers of white youths listen to rap/hip-hop, but large numbers also choose each of the various types of rock (from alternative/modern to metal to classic rock). Finally, Hispanic youth manifest the most ecumenical taste. They listen to "black" music, to each of the various types of rock, and to Latin and salsa (a category that fails to attract any African American or white teenagers).

"Softer" versus a more "hard edged" sound differentiates adolescent girls' and boys' music tastes. More girls than boys listen to soft rock, top 40, and country and western. More boys than girls gravitate to hard rock/heavy metal. For most other genres, however, gender differences are minimal. Girls are as likely as boys to hear rap/hip-hop; boys are as likely as girls to hear alternative rock.

All in all, then, perhaps the most striking finding to emerge when various predictors of U.S. youth's audio exposure and music taste are how democratic audio media seem to be. Aside from the substantial differences in music taste located by race and ethnicity, most U.S. teenagers from most backgrounds like similar kinds of music and spend roughly the same, relatively large amounts of time listening. As noted earlier, several factors probably combine to make audio media – particularly as they function as music media – the ideal medium for adolescents. By mid-adolescence, a wide variety of activities vie for U. S. teenagers' time, and music is an almost perfect accompaniment to these teenage activities, particularly since music delivery systems have become so portable. In addition, a central attraction of popular music for adolescents is that it is of, by, and for young people (Christenson & Roberts, 1998; Roe, 1987). Many songwriters and performers are young people, and much of their work appeals to teenagers because they sing about many of the issues central to adolescence – friendship, romance, love, sex, independence, rebellion. Small wonder that popular music attracts such a large and committed audience of young people. Small wonder that young people's economic clout does much to keep the music industry afloat.

CHAPTER SIX

PRINT MEDIA: BOOKS, MAGAZINES, AND NEWSPAPERS

Before film, radio, television, or the computer, mass media consisted of print media – books, newspapers, and magazines – and reading was the only media activity available to young people. While there is no question that electronic media, especially television, have come to dominate U.S. youths' media diet, neither is there any doubt that today's kids still read for pleasure. Recreational print use continues to constitute a significant part of children's and adolescents' media diet. On any given day, between 80 percent and 90 percent of U.S. kids spend at least a few minutes with print. Although there are variations with age, between 2 and 18 years they average about 45 minutes per day engaged in recreational reading.

This chapter examines young people's leisure time exposure to books, magazines, and newspapers. This does not, of course, account for all reading. "Reading" is simply too pervasive in kids' lives (indeed, in all of our lives) to be estimated fully. Much of what young people do on the Internet – sending e-mails, visiting chat rooms, surfing the Web – requires reading, and Chapter 7 reports some of this time. In addition, children and adolescents also read billboards, junk mail, cereal boxes, CD liners, and T-shirts; sometimes they even read words on a TV or motion picture screen. Our study captures none of these kinds of reading. We report only time spent on recreational use of books, magazines, and newspapers. "Recreational use" refers to reading that is not engaged in the service of school, homework, or some kind of job – that is, leisure reading. It is also important to note that for our younger sample, "reading" includes being read to. Reading specialists frequently argue that reading begins in the "prereading stage," when adults read to very young children. They contend that when parents hold a book and translate print into

Table 6.1. *Proportion of Youth Reading at Least 5 Minutes and More than 30 Minutes the Previous Day by Age (in years) (%)*

	2–7	2–4	5–7	8–18	8–10	11–14	15–18
Proportion who did not read the previous day							
Magazines	53	56_a	51_b	45	57_a	41_b	41_b
Newspapers	88	90_a	85_b	58	69_a	58_b	49_c
Books	21	16_a	26_b	53	31_a	53_a	72_b
All print	12	11	13	20	20	19	21
Proportion reading more than 30 minutes the previous day							
Magazines	11	12	11	13	15_a	13_{ab}	10_b
Newspapers	1	1	1	4	4	3	4
Books	22	30_a	15_b	18	28_a	17_b	13_c
All print	49	55_a	44_b	42	50_a	42_b	34_c

auditory words, they are modeling the reading process (e.g., Chall, 1983). Thus, parents in this study were asked about both their 2- to 7-year-old's own reading time and time during which an adult read to the child.

We begin this chapter looking at the proportion of youth of different ages who do and do not read, and the amount of leisure time they devote to each of the three primary print media. We then examine the relationship between reading and the other demographic variables that play an important role in media use, as well as the influence of household TV orientation. Finally, we look at what young people read. Much of the statistical information about print exposure appears in Appendix 6.

AMOUNT OF PRINT EXPOSURE

A large majority of U.S. kids – between 80 percent and 90 percent depending on age – spend at least a few minutes each day reading for pleasure, and younger children are a bit more likely than older youths to spend time with print media. As Table 6.1 shows, on any given day younger children are more likely to spend at least a few minutes with books (from 84% of 2- to 4-year-olds to 69% of 8- to 10-year-olds read books at least 5 minutes per day). Adolescents tend to prefer magazines (59% of 11- to 18-year-olds read a magazine at least 5 minutes per day).[1]

---

[1] Table 6.1 displays the proportion of youth who reported no reading the previous day. Since 31% of 8- to 10-year-olds engaged in no reading, we infer that 69%

A similar pattern emerges when we look at the proportion of youths at each age who devote at least 30 minutes daily to print media. Almost half of 2- to 7-year-olds and just over 40 percent of 8- to 18-year-olds read for more than 30 minutes, with books garnering the most attention at every age. We suspect that the high proportion of 2- to 7-year-olds exposed to books (and, for that matter, to magazines) on any given day is largely accounted for by parental reading to children.

Newspapers receive the least attention at all ages. Prior to 10 years, fewer than 15 percent of children even glance at a newspaper on any given day, and as late as 15 to 18 years, only half do so. Contrary to some popular opinion, however, the relatively low proportion of youngsters who report no exposure to newspapers does not appear to be a sign of changing times. Although differences in the way questions about newspaper reading have been asked make comparisons less than perfect, our results differ little from other findings reported since 1960. In 1958–60 in San Francisco, for example, 57 percent of sixth graders and 66 percent of twelfth graders reported "daily" newspaper reading (Schramm et al., 1961). In comparison, 47 percent of sixth graders and 64 percent of twelfth graders in our national sample report at least 5 minutes of newspaper exposure "yesterday." At the beginning of the 1970s, Lyle and Hoffman (1972a) found 47 percent of a sample of Los Angeles tenth graders claiming daily newspaper reading; 49 percent of the tenth graders in our sample say they read a newspaper "yesterday." Finally, according to the Newspaper Advertising Bureau (1978), in 1978, some 21 percent of a national sample of 9- to 11-year-olds read a newspaper the preceding day; the figure for our 9- to 11-year-olds is 33 percent. Similarly, they found 43 percent of 12- to 14-year olds and 46 percent of 15- to 17-year-olds read a newspaper the previous day; comparable proportions for our sample are 45 percent and 51 percent, respectively. In short, if "newspaper reading" is taken to mean at least glancing at some part of the paper for a few minutes, the proportion of U.S. children and adolescents who do so has remained fairly constant over the past 50 years.

Turning to time devoted to each of the three print media, two conclusions seem immediately obvious. First, as Figure 6.1 shows, within each of the two samples, average overall reading time declines as age increases. That is, 2- to 4-year-olds read more than 5- to 7-year-olds, and

spent at least 5 minutes reading books, 5 minutes being the lowest response option greater than 0.

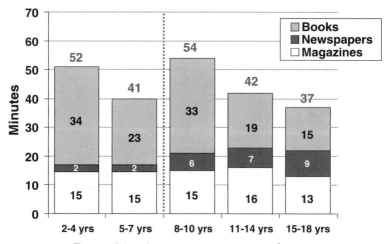

Figure 6.1. Average print exposure by age.

8- to 10-year-olds read more than either 11- to 14- or 15- to 18-year-olds. The pattern is quite similar to that found for TV viewing (see Chapter 4, Fig. 4.1). Second, the decline derives entirely from a drop in time spent with books. Magazine reading stays constant across age, and newspaper reading actually increases in late adolescence.[2] As was the case for TV viewing time (see Chapter 4), we suspect that age-related demands of school probably explain the decline. That is, when young children move into kindergarten (at around 5 years), time formerly spent with parents they now spend with teachers. Similarly, books formerly read to children by parents are now read to them by teachers.[3] These factors probably combine to create the decline in "leisure reading" found among 2- to 7-year-olds. School-related pressures on reading time are somewhat different for older children, but they result in the same outcome. As youngsters move from elementary school into middle and high school, they are typically asked to engage in a good deal more school-related reading than was formerly the case, a factor that probably reduces both desire and time to read outside school. In addition, during late adolescence, myriad additional activities vie for young people's time – sports, extracurricular activities, social events, earning a driver's license,

---

[2] Although the difference is only 2–3 minutes, the difference is statistically significant.

[3] And, of course, since parents were asked not to include in-school reading in their estimates of young children's print exposure, books read by teachers are not included in estimates of recreational reading.

part-time jobs, dating, and so forth. These, too, cut into time available for reading much beyond what is required for school. As seems to be the case for noninteractive screen media, then, leisure time print exposure is also related to available time, and available time is related to age.

Finally, the decline in book reading relative to magazine and newspaper use among older adolescents also makes sense in terms of the time commitment required by and the typical content conveyed by each of the media. Many, if not most, books are either long fictional stories or extended treatments of a particular topic. They require a relatively large commitment of time. Newspapers and magazines, on the other hand, can be consumed in brief time segments. Additionally, magazines and newspapers often present information immediately relevant to the lives of adolescents, ranging from discussions of dating, grooming, or sports found in teen magazines (Evans, Rutberg, Sather, & Turner, 1991; Garner, Sterk, & Adams, 1998; Kaiser Family Foundation & YM Magazine, 1998) to current events information in newspapers, which becomes more and more relevant as adolescents prepare to assume adult responsibilities. In short, it seems quite reasonable for leisure book exposure to decline during late adolescence, while magazine reading holds relatively steady and newspaper reading actually increases.

GENDER AND PRINT EXPOSURE

Among younger children, boys and girls do not differ in time spent reading. However, gender is a strong predictor of amount of print exposure among 8- to 10-year-olds and 11- to 14-year-olds. Once again, as illustrated in Figure 6.2, almost all of the difference is due to time spent with books. Eight- to 10-year-old girls average 12 minutes more per day than boys with books (39 vs. 27 minutes), and 11- to 14-year-old girls read books 6 minutes more than boys per day (22 vs. 16 minutes). In these age groups, neither magazine nor newspaper exposure differentiates between the two genders, even though teenage girls are far more likely than teenage boys (i.e., seventh through twelfth graders) to subscribe to a magazine (73% vs. 58%). Finally, by 15 to 18 years, there is no difference between boys and girls in either book reading or magazine reading. However, boys read newspapers 2 minutes more per day than do girls, a difference which though small, is statistically significant.

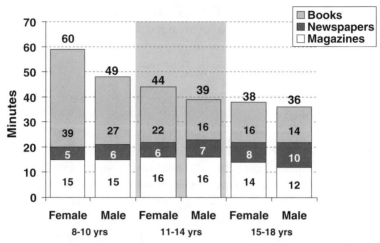

Figure 6.2. Average print exposure by gender.

SOCIOECONOMIC STATUS AND PRINT EXPOSURE

Not surprisingly, given the close association between print and education, level of parent education makes a substantial difference both in
whether or not young people are exposed to print and in the amount of
time they spend reading. As level of parent education increases, young
people's print exposure increases. The effect of parent education begins
to appear quite early. Among 2- to 7-year-olds, three times as many children of parents with no more than a high school education than of those
whose parents completed college report "no reading" on any given day
(18% vs. 6%; see Appendix 6). Conversely, fewer young children of high
school–educated parents than of college-educated parents report more
than 30 minutes of reading on any given day (44% vs. 53%).[4] Books
account for most of the differences in young children's print exposure
associated with parent education. Books are the only print medium for
which the difference in average amount of time spent reading reaches
statistical significance (25 minutes per day among 2- to 7-year-olds with
high school–educated parents vs. 34 minutes per day among those with
college-educated parents), possibly a result of more educated parents

[4] Surprisingly, among young children the likelihood of spending any time with
magazines is inversely related to level of parent education. That is, significantly
fewer 2- to 7-year-old children of high school–educated parents (48%) than of
college-educated parents (59%) reported no previous-day exposure to magazines.

spending more time reading to their young children. In spite of these differences, however, it is important not to lose sight of the fact that even within the lowest parent education classification, over 80 percent of young children report at least 5 minutes daily print exposure.

Parent education is even more strongly related to print exposure among 8- to 18-year-olds. As the tables in Appendix 6 indicate, both overall and for each of the three age subgroupings, the likelihood of no reading on any given day goes down and the likelihood of reading more than 30 minutes per day goes up as level of parent education increases. For example, 26 percent of older kids whose parents completed no more than high school versus 16 percent of those whose parents completed college report no reading the previous day. Conversely, 47 percent of those with college-educated parents spend more than 30 minutes daily reading compared with 31 percent of those with high school–educated parents.

Figure 6.3 shows that parent education is also strongly related to amount of print exposure. When 8- to 18-year-olds are examined as a single group, statistically significant differences related to education emerge for each of the three individual print media. Youths whose parents completed no more than high school spend less time with all print, particularly books. Typically, youths whose parents finished some college behave much like those whose parents completed college. The relationship with parent education is particularly strong for kids from 8 through 14 years (see Appendix 6.1). For example, 8- to 10-year-olds with high school–educated parents report 37 minutes daily print exposure;

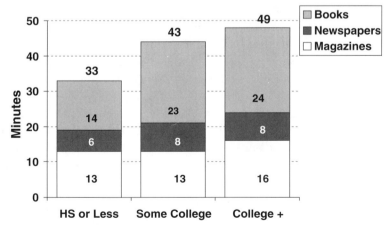

Figure 6.3. Average print exposure by parent education.

those whose parents completed college report 1:04. Most of this overall difference is accounted for by a significant difference in time spent with books, although the means for magazines and newspapers produce a similar pattern. Among 11- to 14-year-olds, those from the lowest parent education group spend significantly less time with both books and newspapers than do their counterparts whose parents completed college. Only among 15- to 18-year-olds does the negative relationship between parent education and print exposure fail to reach statistical significance, although older youths from the lowest education subgroup consistently report the lowest print exposure. It is worth noting that many of these findings echo patterns of print exposure reported by Schramm et al. (1961) more than 40 years ago.

Several factors probably combine to make parental education a more powerful predictor of print exposure among 8- to 14-year-olds than among 15- to 18-year-olds. By the time youths reach late adolescence, competing activities, as well as other media more suited to socializing with peers (see Chapter 7), begin to dominate free time regardless of level of parent education. In addition, as "tweens" become adolescents, peers become more important socialization agents – some argue more important than parents (Harris, 1998). Finally, parent education probably exerts much of its influence via the values parents imbue in children through modeling, by shaping the home environment (i.e., affecting how much print material is available in the home; see Roberts, Bachen, Hornby, & Hernandez-Ramos, 1984), and through behavioral proscription. Each of these sources of influence seems more likely to affect younger than older adolescents. For example, we noted in Chapter 3 that household rules about watching television drop off substantially among 15- to 18-year-olds. In addition, Chaffee, McLeod, and Atkin (1971) demonstrated that parental modeling of newspaper reading (as well as their attention to TV news) influences the news-consumption behavior of junior high school youths but not senior high school youths.

Household income, though correlated with parent education, is not strongly associated with print exposure. Children from 2 through 7 years living in lower income areas spend less time reading and are less likely to read or to be read to on a typical day. Among older youths, however, family income locates few significant differences in print exposure. For 8- to 10-year-olds, the relationship between average amount of print exposure and household income resembles that found for parent education; children from high-income households spend more time reading than do children from low-income households. Among 11- to 14-year-olds and 15- to 18-year-olds, however, time spent with print does not differ as a function of household income.[5] One reason for the relatively weak association between household income and print exposure may derive from imprecision inherent in our method of estimating household income levels on the basis of the median household income in the school district where the child attended school (see Chapter 2).

Finally, and somewhat surprising given the association between number of parents with whom a youngster lives and our other socioeconomic indicators, there is no relationship between either the likelihood of reading or the amount of reading and whether a child lives with one or both parents.

RACE/ETHNICITY AND PRINT EXPOSURE

Race or ethnicity locate relatively few differences in print exposure, and what differences emerge fail to form any consistent pattern. White 2- to 7-year-olds (9%) are significantly less likely than either black (19%) or Hispanic (20%) 2- to 7-year-olds to report no reading the previous day. They are also more likely to report spending more than 30 minutes reading magazines and books, but not more likely to spend more than 30 minutes with print overall. Moreover, race and ethnicity locate no significant differences in average amount of print exposure in the younger sample.

Among 8- to 18-year-olds, fewer white than black or Hispanic youth report no reading the previous day (18% vs. 23% and 24%, respectively). On the other hand, substantially more African American than Hispanic youths report more than 30 minutes of print exposure (47% vs. 35%), with whites falling in between (41%). Finally, Hispanic kids tend to spend the least time with print. They report significantly less newspaper exposure than African Americans, and significantly less book exposure than either African American or white youths. However, the differences in amount of overall print exposure are not statistically significant (see Appendix 6.1).[6]

---

[5] The one exception to this generalization is that 11- to 14-year-olds from high-income households report significantly less book exposure than do their counterparts from middle-income households.

[6] Unfortunately, when analyses of the effect of race and ethnicity on print exposure are controlled for either household income or parent education, the number of

PLACE OF RESIDENCE AND PRINT EXPOSURE

Whether a child lives in an urban, suburban, or rural setting is only weakly associated with print use, particularly when household income or level of parent education is controlled. Among 2- to 7-year-olds, rural children consistently read less than suburban or urban children, but the difference is statistically significant only for book reading. Moreover, when household income is taken into account, that difference largely disappears.

Among older children, the effect of residence locale is a bit stronger. Although the differences are small, rural children, particularly 8- to 10-year-olds, consistently read less than their urban or suburban counterparts (see Appendix 6). Once again, however, statistical significance largely disappears when controls for either household income or level of parent education are applied.[7] The exception to this pattern is for newspaper reading. Urban youths spend more time than rural youths with newspapers regardless of level of income or parent education, probably because of greater newspaper availability in urban as opposed to rural settings.

HOUSEHOLD TV ORIENTATION AND PRINT EXPOSURE

We argued in Chapter 3 that household TV orientation might be an indicator of more than how young people relate to television. There is good reason to expect that both the centrality of television in a household and whether or not parents attempt to impose some kind of controls on the medium's use might be associated with the degree to which other media are used. Arguably, a constantly operating television creates an environment in which it is more difficult to read. Similarly, parents who impose rules on TV watching may be more likely to regulate and/or encourage the use of other kinds of media. Thus, we examined the likelihood and amount of print exposure in relation to

---

youths in some of the categories becomes very small. Nevertheless, results continue to indicate that Hispanic youth read the least. One interesting, albeit highly tentative, result to emerge from these further analyses is that African American youths from either high-income households or whose parents have completed at least a college education tend to read more than other youngsters.

[7] We caution, however, that when such controls are applied, the number of suburban youths in the low-income and low-education cells is small. These findings should be taken as only suggestive.

whether or not a household is classified as a constant TV household, whether or not there are rules about watching television in the household, and whether or not youngsters have their own television in their bedroom.

Among 2- to 7-year-olds there is little relationship between our indicators of household TV orientation and either likelihood or amount of reading (see Appendix 6). The single exception to this generalization is that more young children from constant TV homes (26%) than from nonconstant TV homes (19%) report no reading "yesterday."

Quite a different picture emerges for 8- to 18-year-olds. Older kids living in constant TV households and those with a television in their bedroom are less likely to read and spend less time reading on any given day. Conversely, those from homes in which some kind of rules about watching television are in place are more likely to read and read more. When 8- to 18-year-olds are examined as a group, those from homes in which television does not constantly operate spend significantly more time than those from constant TV homes with newspapers, with books, and with print overall. However, Figure 6.4 shows that the effect of constant television varies with age. Although 8- to 10-year-olds from nonconstant TV households report more exposure to all three print media, none of the differences is statistically significant. Among the two older age subgroups, on the other hand, both book reading and overall print exposure are significantly higher among youths from nonconstant

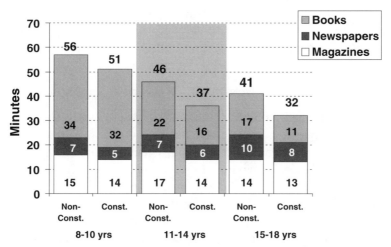

Figure 6.4. Average print exposure in constant and nonconstant TV households.

TV homes. Controls for parent education eliminate some but not all of the differences in amount of book reading and overall print exposure in the two types of household. In particular, in homes where parents have at least some college education and to a lesser extent in homes where parents have completed college, total print exposure is higher when the television is not constantly on.

When print exposure among youths from homes with and without rules about TV watching is compared, those who experience some kind of television regulation spend more time reading magazines, books, and overall print. The differences are particularly large among 11- to 14-year-olds, and for children whose parents completed college. Similar patterns of print exposure also hold for older youths who have a television in their bedroom, although the differences are not as striking. That is, both 11- to 14-year-olds and 15- to 18-year-olds with a TV set in their bedroom spend less time reading books than do their counterparts who do not have their own TV. They also average less overall print exposure, but the differences are not statistically significant. Once again, controls for parent education indicate that most of the difference occurs among youngsters whose parents have completed some college.

In general, then, it is safe to say that in homes where the television plays a central role – where the television constantly operates, where there are no rules about TV watching, and where kids have their own TV set – print exposure tends to be lower. Most of the difference occurs for book reading and for overall print exposure, and the relationship is particularly strong for 11- to 14-year-olds and among children whose parents have completed at least some college.

MAGAZINE SUBSCRIPTIONS AND PRINT EXPOSURE

We also examined likelihood and amount of print exposure in relation to whether or not adolescents subscribe to a magazine, a question asked of all seventh through twelfth grade students in the sample ($n = 1,188$). Logically, having one's own subscription should increase magazine reading if only because of increased availability of that particular print medium. However, the fact that an adolescent subscribes to his or her own magazine probably also indicates a positive orientation toward print in general. Young people who subscribe to (and presumably read) magazines might be more likely than nonsubscribers to read books and newspapers.

As expected, many more magazine subscribers (77%) than nonsubscribers (33%) read magazines on any given day, and more read in excess of 30 minutes per day (39% vs. 31%). Similarly, subscribers average 16 minutes per day reading magazines as opposed to 10 minutes for nonsubscribers. None of this is surprising given that the two groups are defined in terms of magazine availability. However, it is also worth noting that whether or not a young person subscribes to a magazine appears to locate a difference in orientation toward print. Magazine subscribers are also significantly more likely than nonsubscribers to spend a least a few minutes with books and with print materials in general, and they are significantly more likely to devote more than 30 minutes daily to recreational reading. Finally, subscribers spend more time than nonsubscribers reading books (16 minutes vs. 11 minutes) and more time with print overall (40 minutes vs. 31 minutes). Clearly, whether or not young people subscribe to a magazine locates differences in both the physical and psychological environment that influence print exposure.

Content Preferences: What Young People Read

In addition to being asked how much time they spend reading each of the three print media, seventh through twelfth graders in our sample ($n = 1,188$; ages 12 through 18 years) were also asked what they read.[8] On any given day, 80 percent of U.S. seventh to twelfth graders devote at least a few minutes to some kind of print material: 50 percent read newspapers, 33 percent read books, and 59 percent read magazines.

Although amount of time devoted to newspapers is quite low, half of our adolescents look at a newspaper daily, and most sections of the paper receive at least brief attention. Figure 6.5 shows the proportion of youths selecting each of eight categories of newspaper content. Only one – fashion – fails to be selected by at least 10 percent of young readers.[9] Local news, comics, and sports garner the most attention, attracting from about 40 percent to 50 percent of young readers.

Selection of book genres is also highly dispersed. At least 10 percent of young readers select seven of the 12 book genres listed in our questionnaire, and no more than 25 percent choose any one genre (Appendix 6.2). Mysteries and adventures are most chosen; books on religion, self-help, and science/nature receive little attention. Finally,

---

[8] Time constraints precluded asking younger children this question.
[9] By 15 to 18 years, attention to youth/teen news also drops to single digits.

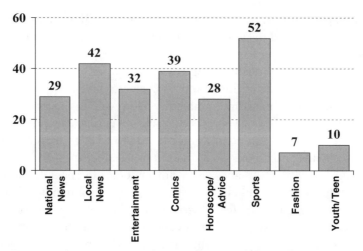

Figure 6.5. Proportion of seventh to twelfth graders reading various parts of the newspaper.

of 11 types of magazines, five are selected by 10 percent or more readers. Teen, sports, and entertainment magazines garner most attention; general interest, men's, and home magazines are largely ignored.

With few exceptions, age and gender are the primary demographic characteristics that locate large differences in reading tastes. Preferences are largely consistent with age and gender stereotypes. For example, Appendix 6.2 indicates that when looking at newspapers, 15- to 18-year-olds are more likely than 12- to 14-year-olds to read local and national news (they are approaching civic participation) and slightly less likely to look at the youth or teen sections of the newspaper (they are leaving "youth" behind). When selecting books, girls are more likely to choose literature, mystery/thrillers, romance, and self-help books; boys opt for adventure, science fiction/fantasy, science/nature, and sports. Finally, Figure 6.6 shows that girls prefer teen, women's, and entertainment magazines, while boys choose magazines devoted to sports and hobbies, findings similar to those reported by Lyle and Hoffman (1972a) over 30 years ago.

SUMMING UP PRINT BEHAVIOR

The American Academy of Pediatrics recommends that young people spend some time reading every day. In that context, our findings provide some good news and some bad news. The good news is that a substantial

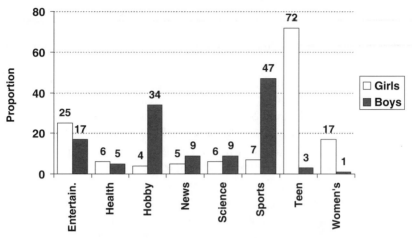

Figure 6.6. Magazine content preferences by gender.

majority of U.S. young people report at least a few minutes of leisure print exposure each day. U.S. children and adolescents read for an average of about 45 minutes daily, outside school. The bad news is that "at least a few minutes" can be a very few minutes indeed, because averages conceal a great deal of information. Although most young people glance at (or listen to) print on a daily basis, from 4 to 7 years onward, no more than 50 percent spend in excess of 30 minutes daily engaged in recreational reading (only a third of 15- to 18- year-olds read that much). Given that average overall print exposure is consistently greater than 30 minutes, it is clear that relatively few young people read a great deal to in order to produce mean times that high. Indeed, just over 20 percent of 8- to 18-year-olds read more than an hour per day (see Chapter 9).

Our overall findings for print exposure indicate that both the physical and social environments are related to young people's likelihood of and amount of reading. However, the social context seems to be the more powerful. On the side of the physical environment, there is a slight positive relationship between print exposure and household income, a variable that, among other things, indexes available resources with which to acquire print materials. Additionally, we found that more reading occurs among children who have greater access to magazines. Seventh through twelfth grade youths who subscribe to magazines read more. This latter result is consistent with earlier findings that as the availability of print materials in the home increases, so too does amount of reading and reading ability (Roberts et al., 1984).

More impressive, however, is the impact of the social environment on print exposure. First, and probably most important, as parent education increases, so too does likelihood and amount of print exposure. Given the close association between education and print (it is probably no accident that "reading" precedes "writing and 'rithmetic" in the old song), this should not be surprising. It replicates the findings of earlier research (e.g., Schramm et al., 1961) and makes a good deal of sense. Arguably, a major result of education is that it makes one value print, and parents who value print are likely to pass similar values along to their children. Second, there is a similar strong relationship between our indexes of household TV orientation and print exposure. Not only does household TV orientation appear to locate attitudes and values that value television, they seem to be negatively related to print use. As television becomes more central to the household, the likelihood and amount of print use declines, and this finding obtains even after parent education is taken into account. In short, the implicit and explicit attitudes toward print that operate within the home appear to exert substantial influence on reading behavior.

Finally, in spite of claims to the contrary (e.g., Postman, 1985; Winn, 1985), there is little evidence that young people's leisure reading has changed much over the past half-century. Work conducted in the 1940s (Lyness, 1952) and 1950s (Schramm et al., 1961; Witty, 1967) estimated U.S. children's leisure book reading to average about 15 minutes daily. More recent work also reports similar levels (Anderson, Hiebert, Scott, & Wilkinson, 1985; Neuman, 1986). If anything, the averages we found are a bit higher that those that seem to have held for some time. Perhaps the increasing number of magazines aimed at children and adolescents and such children's book phenomena as the recent Harry Potter craze may be helping reading to gain a bit.

CHAPTER SEVEN

INTERACTIVE MEDIA

"Clickerati." "Connexity Generation." "Net Generation." "Generation I." Each of these terms has been attached to U.S. youth in recent years (e.g., Foley, 2000; Thompson, 1999) and for good reason. Today's kids have never known a world without video games and personal computers. One recent study finds that only 1 percent of 15- to 17-year-olds have *never* used a computer (Kaiser Family Foundation, 2001). We doubt that the same can be said for people in their 30s or older. Although many of us work and play differently since the introduction of personal computers, for today's kids "different" does not apply. They have always known digital media; they have trouble imagining a world without them – even kids who on most days typically spend little or no time with a mouse or on-line. If we are to understand the implications of growing up digitally, we need to know who is using interactive media and how.

This chapter explores children's use of computers and video games. We emphasize computers because the evidence from both this study and other recent work (Center for Media Education, 2001; Lenhart, Rainie & Lewis, 2001; National Public Radio, Kaiser Family Foundation, & Harvard University Kennedy School of Government, 2000; Wartella, O'Keefe, & Scantlin, 2000) indicates they are moving inexorably to center stage of young people's media experience. For the most part, we focus on "recreational" computer use – interactive activities occurring primarily outside the school (or work) context: computer games, e-mail, chat rooms, surfing the Web. We also attempt to take note of evidence that the digital landscape is rapidly changing. For example, in the brief interval since data for this study were collected, instant messaging has emerged to become a major factor in teenagers' digital experience. Unfortunately, we collected no data on that particular computer activity.

Because the digital landscape is changing so rapidly, we have tried to incorporate findings from some more recent research into our discussion of young people's use of interactive media. In the following pages we begin with a brief discussion of U.S. youths' access to computers. We then examine how often young people use interactive media and how much time they devote to them, followed by a look at the kinds of content and activities that attract most of their attention. Finally, we examine similar findings for video games.

A Further Word about Access

Although Chapter 3 explores computer and video-game console availability in U.S. youths' homes and bedrooms, a further word is necessary. Unlike television or radio, interactive media, especially computers with an Internet connection, have not yet fully penetrated the U.S. population. Thus, factors such as race or ethnicity and socioeconomic status locate differences in computer access that are no longer found for such older media as television. These differences lead us to examine computer use somewhat differently than we have looked at the use of other media.

A good deal of discussion about interactive media concerns the "digital divide," a term that refers primarily to inequities in computer access. Theoretically, in order for a computer (or, for that matter, any medium) to influence young people, access to it is needed. Or is it? Fundamentally, the term "digital divide" suggests that in contemporary society *not having* a computer may have at least as profound an effect as having one. Meyrowitz (1994) observes: "In any given social period, roles are shaped as much by *patterns* of access to social information as by the *content* of information. That is, different cultures and different historical periods are characterized by different role structures not only because of 'who knows what,' but also because of . . . 'who knows what *compared* to whom'" (p. 59). In other words, computers and all they bring with them affect all individuals regardless of whether they have access, and some of the more negative consequences may accrue to those who lack access *because* they lack access. Concerns about the digital divide, then, are fundamentally concerns that kids who lack easy access to computers may miss out on the kind of information necessary to function successfully in today's world.

As we saw in Chapter 3, U.S. young people's in-home computer availability varies with socioeconomic status and with race or ethnicity. Kids from lower income households, kids whose parents completed no more than a high school education, and African American and Hispanic kids are all less likely to live in homes with a computer or an Internet connection. Of course, it can be argued that when all of the many potential access points for computers and the Internet are considered (e.g., home, school, or public libraries), almost all U.S. youths have at least some access to computers, and a very high proportion have access to the Internet (National Center for Education Statistics, 1999; National Public Radio et al., 2000; Sarkar, 2001). Granted, some kids encounter computers everywhere they turn (e.g., home, friend's houses, school, and libraries), while others must exert much more effort to gain access. Nevertheless, although there remains much room for progress, enormous strides have been made toward hooking up America's youth to the new interactive media. In this study, for example, almost as many 8- to 18-year-olds from low-income communities (26%) as from high-income communities (31%) report using a computer in school "yesterday." In addition, new avenues of access to the Internet are rapidly appearing as it becomes more readily available via televisions, cell phones, and personal digital assistants. Since teenagers are typically among the earliest adopters of new kinds of communication technologies (Center for Media Education, 2001), we suspect that relatively soon teens may no longer rely on computers to surf the Web. At that point, concern about a "digital divide" debate may be largely moot.

That said, however, substantial differences in who has easy, in-home access to computers and Internet connections presently remain, and there is little question that access makes a difference. Ease of access affects both the likelihood and duration of computer use. For example, there is no difference in the proportion of 8- to 18-year-olds with and without in-home computer access who use a computer *in school* on any given day (28% vs. 27%). However, as Figure 7.1 makes strikingly clear, at every age youths with in-home access to computers are more than twice as likely than those without access to use a computer. From 8 to 10 years onward, fewer than 30 percent of kids with no in-home access compared with well over half of those with in-home access use a computer on a given day. The overall result is that on any given day, 65 percent of 8- to 18-year-olds with in-home access use a computer (in or out of school) versus 25 percent of those who lack in-home access. Since the likelihood that a youngster has in-home computer access is related to such variables as household income or race and ethnicity, it is not surprising that computer use is also related to those variables. Figure 7.2 shows that although household income is not associated with differences

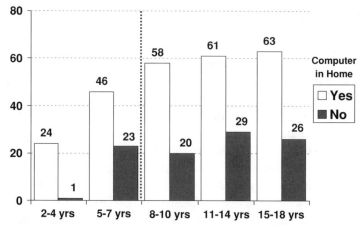

Figure 7.1. Proportion of youth who use a computer by age and presence of computer in the home.

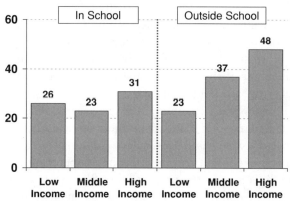

Figure 7.2. Proportion of school children who use a computer.

in the proportion of youths who use a computer *in school*, the proportion who use computers *outside school* increases substantially as household income goes up: 23 percent of low-income, 37 percent of middle-income, and 48 percent of high-income youths use computers outside school. This is convincing evidence that concerns about a digital divide systematically favoring some social groupings over others are justified.

Such differences in access and use prompt us to look at young people's computer use from an additional perspective not employed in earlier chapters. To this point, average exposure times for the various media have included those youths who do not use a particular medium on any given day. For example, the 15 percent of U.S. kids reporting no TV viewing are included in the calculation of average TV exposure. We are describing the behavior of all youth – those who watch and those who do not. We implicitly take for granted that nonviewers could watch if they wanted, and so the average logically should reflect their behavior. Their decision not to view is as integral to the average as is another youngster's decision to watch for 5 hours. From one perspective, the same reasoning applies to computer exposure. That is, if we wish to summarize U.S. youth's computer time, we must include all young people regardless of whether they use a computer on a given day. However, given differences in access, we can't assume that failure to use a computer is a result of a youngster's decision. Many kids simply don't have a computer – a great many. Thus, once we move beyond examination of who uses computers to look at the various kinds of things kids do with them, a more accurate (or at least, very different) picture is provided by focusing only on "computer users."

WHO USES COMPUTERS?

"How many kids use computers or the Internet?" might seem a simple question with which to begin. However, the answer varies substantially depending on a variety of factors, not the least of which is the time span covered by the question. One recent study conducted by a market research firm was summarized by the following headline: "Study Shows Two-Thirds of All Teenagers Now Wired" (Internetnews.com, 1998). The problem is that the "two-thirds" is based on 12- to 19-year-olds who "claim to have used or subscribed to on-line services over the past 12 months." Another study found that when kids who have *ever* used the Internet are combined, 82 percent claim to have gone on-line (National Public Radio et al., 2000).[1] However, that same study also reports that 44 percent use the computer at home *on a daily basis*, a number similar to the 49 percent of 8- to 18-year-olds in this study who use a computer on any given day. We think it's debatable whether a 15-year-old who uses a friend's computer to surf the Web once every couple of months should be classed as "wired" or "a computer user." Rather, although it seems safe to say that most U.S. kids have used a computer, it is also clear

---

[1] The 82% figure includes youths who use the Internet "almost every day," "about once a week," or "less often than that," but *not* those who say they *never* use it.

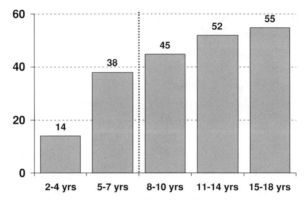

Figure 7.3. Proportion of youth who use a computer by age.

that many fewer use them frequently enough to be classed as "computer users" or "wired." As noted in Chapter 2, in this study we asked young people about the media they used "yesterday." This is an admittedly conservative approach, but one that seems to us to minimize memory and estimation problems among young respondents and to facilitate the comparisons among different media presented in our examination of overall media budgets (see Chapter 8). It is important to keep in mind, however, that focusing on use "yesterday" also results in estimates of computer "users" that are somewhat lower than those reported by some other studies.

Figure 7.3 graphs the proportion of young people in each age subgroup who use a computer, either in or out of school, on any given day. Within both samples, the proportions increase with age, more than doubling from 2 to 4 years to 5 to 7 years, then increasing more slowly in later childhood and adolescence to peak at 55 percent among 15- to 18-year-olds. These percentages are similar to those from an NPR survey (National Public Radio et al., 2000) indicating that 44 percent of U.S. 10- to 17-year-olds use computers at home every day, and that 55 percent use them at school either every day or about once a week. On the other hand, several more recent studies report somewhat higher estimates. Since the data for this study were collected (1998–99), not only have more households acquired personal computers, but the nature of recreational computer use has changed. Rather than "computer use," recent surveys often ask about "going on-line," a term quickly becoming synonymous with recreational computer use (not the case in 1998–99).

Thus, for example, Lenhart et al. (2001) find that 42 percent of 12- to 17-year-olds go on-line daily, and the Kaiser Family Foundation (2001) reports that almost half of 15- to 24-year-olds use the Internet daily and another 29 percent several times per week. These data, although not directly comparable with our own because of different age spans and questions, clearly suggest an increase in frequency of on-line use and, by extension, computer use.

As suggested above, the likelihood of using a computer is strongly related to socioeconomic indicators and to race or ethnicity. Appendix 7.1 presents detailed information on the proportion of different groupings of youths who use computers on a given day, the average time they spend on each of four computer activities, and their overall computer exposure. We briefly summarize only a few examples here. Generally, as either household income or parent education increases, so too does the proportion of youths who use a computer. For example, among young children, 15 percent from low-income versus 26 percent from middle-income and 32 percent from high-income households use computers – a pattern of differences that also characterizes narrower 2- to 4-year-old and 5- to 7-year-old age groupings. The pattern also holds among older youths; 38 percent of low-income, 47 percent of middle-income, and 62 percent of high-income kids use computers, and the differences are replicated within each smaller age grouping (although among 11- to 14-year-olds, the increments are not statistically significant). Finally, Figure 7.4 shows that computer use is similarly associated

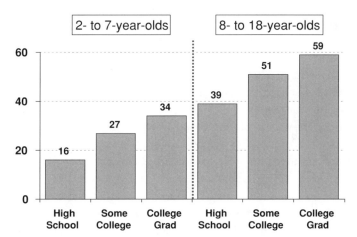

Figure 7.4. Proportion of youth who use a computer by parent education.

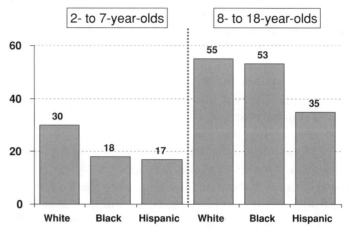

Figure 7.5. Proportion of youth who use a computer by race/ethnicity.

with level of parent education. That is, the likelihood of using a computer goes up significantly with each increase in parent education, both in the full samples and within each age subgroup (although once again, the relationship is not quite so strong among 11- to 14-year-olds; see Appendix 7.1).

Race or ethnicity is also a strong predictor of computer use. Figure 7.5 reveals that during the early years, substantially more white than either black or Hispanic children use computers. By 8 to 18 years there is no difference in the proportion of African American and white youths using computers, but Hispanics continue to lag well behind. The differences located by race or ethnicity generally hold within the smaller age groupings, except that once again among 11- to 14-year-olds they are not statistically significant. It is not clear why differences associated with household income, parent education, race/ethnicity, and even residence locale (significantly more suburban than urban or rural kids use computers, except among 11- to 14-year-olds) do not hold for 11- to 14-year-olds. Perhaps this age cohort is at the leading edge of a generation of computer users that transcends differences formerly associated with sociodemographic characteristics.

Gender is not related to likelihood of computer use. A quarter of young girls and 28 percent of young boys use computers; 51 percent of both older girls and older boys use computers. Similarly, number of parents in the household makes little difference in the likelihood of using a computer. Modest relationships emerge showing that 2- to 7-year-olds and 8- to 10-year-olds who live with two parents as opposed to one are more likely to use computers, but the differences largely disappear when household income is controlled. Finally, suburban 8- to 10-year-olds and 15- to 18-year-olds use computers more than do their urban or rural counterparts, but once again, the differences fade when household income is controlled.

"Computer users" – that is, youths reporting using a computer "yesterday" – tend to be slightly older and come from higher socioeconomic backgrounds. Overall they are slightly more likely to be white than African American or Hispanic, although the white-black difference disappears by the middle elementary school years. Regardless of age, they are least likely to be Hispanic. They include equal proportions of boys and girls, and there are no differences in residence locale once household income is taken into account. Finally, the most important predictor of the likelihood that a young person will use a computer on any given day is access. Kids who have a computer at home are far more likely to spend time logged on than are kids lacking in-home access.

AMOUNT OF COMPUTER USE

When *all* youths in our samples are included in the calculations, 2- to 7-year-olds devote an average of 6 minutes daily to computers, with average time doubling from 4 minutes among 2- to 4-year-olds to 8 minutes among 5- to 7-year-olds. Older youths spend about $\frac{1}{2}$ hour daily with computers. Average daily exposure rises from 23 minutes for 8- to 10-year-olds to 31 minutes for 11- to 14-year-olds, then drops slightly to 26 minutes for 15- to 18-year-olds (continuing the pattern of 11- to 14-year-olds being particularly involved with computers that reappears in many subsequent analyses). These averages, as well as those related to variables such as socioeconomic status, race or ethnicity, and gender, largely recap the patterns produced in our examination of the proportion of young people at each age level who use computers (see Appendix 7.1).

Although about $\frac{1}{2}$ hour per day of computer use is a valid estimate of the average computer time of *all* U.S. 8- to 18-year-olds, many parents whose children have in-home access to a computer may have trouble accepting that figure. In their experience, today's kids seem to spend hour upon hour at the keyboard – playing games, surfing, chatting, instant messaging, and so forth. As noted earlier, the reason for this difference is the large numbers of kids who do not use a computer on any given day (three-quarters of 2- to 7-year-olds and half of 8- to 18-year-olds), who are averaged into the figures. If we are interested in which computer activities most attract young people, and in how much time they spend with each, however, it seems appropriate to focus on kids who spend some time with a computer. Thus, the following estimates of how much time children and adolescents devote to each of four primary computer activities – playing games, visiting chat rooms, visiting Web sites, and using e-mail – include only "computer users," that is, youths who report using a computer the day previous to completing the survey questionnaire.[2]

When calculation of amount of computer exposure is limited to computer users, time spent with computers almost quadruples among 2- to 7-year-olds – from 6 to 23 minutes. Interestingly, 2- to 4-year-olds use computers 9 minutes more daily than do 5- to 7-year-olds (30 minutes vs. 21 minutes). Since almost all of young children's computer time is spent with games (as we see below, educational games), we suspect the difference is largely due to the school-related decrease in time 5- to 7-year-olds experience, in combination with an increased likelihood that some parents spend time in front of a computer screen encouraging a very young child to engage an educational game. An additional possibility is that it simply takes the very youngest children, whose fine motor skills are not yet fully refined, more time to get through a game. We must also note that relatively few 2- to 7-year-olds are classed as computer users, so these age subgroup differences are based on very small numbers, hence are highly tentative. Indeed, lack of sufficient numbers of 2- to 7-year-olds in the "computer user" group prompts us to limit the remainder of our examination of computer users to older youths.

Among 8- to 18-year-olds, "computer users" spend almost double the average time *all* older kids spend with computers – from 27 to 52 minutes per day. Figure 7.6 shows that 11- to 14-year-olds spend the most time with computers (0:58), 15- to 18-year-olds the least (0:47), with 8- to 10-year-olds falling between (0:50). The decrease in overall time 15- to 18-year-olds spend with computers is primarily driven by a decline in playing computer games. That is, the two younger age groups spend much of their computer time playing games, significantly more time than 15- to 18-year olds. Conversely, 8- to 10-year-olds use e-mail and

[2] This procedure admittedly excludes some youngsters who often use computers and probably includes a few who seldom log on. Nevertheless, it has the advantage of probably including most kids who are frequent users, and allows us to examine their characteristics more closely.

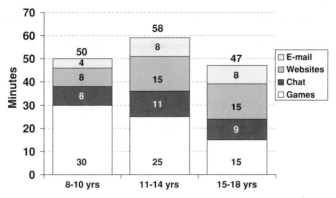

Figure 7.6. Average time computer users spend on computer activities by age.

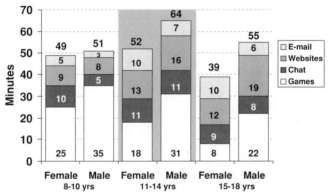

Figure 7.7. Average time computer users spend on computer activities by age and gender.

visit Web sites significantly less than do kids in either of the older groups. All three groups spend about the same amount of time in chat rooms.

Gender locates substantial differences in young people's computer exposure. Boys spend more time than girls with computers (0:58 vs. 0:46). As Appendix 7.1 shows, boys spend more time visiting Web sites and playing computer games, and girls spend more time sending e-mail. There is no gender difference in visiting chat rooms. These overall gender differences also depend on age. Figure 7.7 shows that there is no difference in exposure between boys and girls among 8- to 10-year-olds (0:51 vs. 0:49). However, by 11 to 14 years boys spend 12 minutes more per day with computers (0:64 vs. 0:52), and the gap increases to 16 minutes by 15 to 18 years (0:55 vs. 0:39). In all three age groups, boys spend much more time than girls playing games. Indeed, until 15 to 18 years, computer games dominate boys' but not girls' computer budgets. Young girls spend more time than young boys visiting chat rooms, but from 11 to 14 years onward, both genders spend equal amounts of time chatting. In the two younger age groups, boys and girls spend about the same amount of time using e-mail and visiting Web sites. By 15 to 18 years, however, this changes. The oldest girls spend more time than boys using e-mail; the oldest boys spend more time than girls visiting Web sites. As we see below when we consider the kinds of games and Web sites boys and girls use, most of the gender differences in amount of computer time devoted to different activities appear to be driven by gender-related content preferences.

One of the more interesting differences distinguishing findings for overall computer use (i.e., average exposure based on the entire sample) from findings based just on youths classed as computer users emerges when amount of exposure is examined as a function of race or ethnicity. When the entire sample is considered, there are no differences in the time white (0:28), black (0:26), and Hispanic (0:25) 8- to 18-year-olds spend with computers. This is something of a surprise, since on any given day, many fewer Hispanic (35%) than either white (55%) or African American (53%) youths use a computer. Moreover, as Figure 7.8 shows, it foreshadows a finding that emerges quite clearly when just computer users are examined. That is, among computer users, Hispanic youths spend about 20 minutes more with computers than do either white or black youths, a highly significant difference. Hispanic kids spend

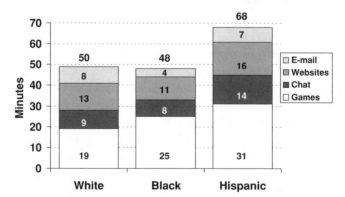

Figure 7.8. Average time computer users spend on computer activities by race/ethnicity.

more time than white kids playing computer games, and more time than black kids with e-mail. Although the differences are not significant, they also spend a bit more time than kids in either of the other two groups visiting chat rooms and Web sites. Clearly, although Hispanic youths are the least likely to use a computer on a given day (largely, we suspect, because they have the lowest in-home access to computers), when they do obtain access, they spend substantially more time using computers than do either white or African American kids. Additionally, while a substantial part of the increased time is spent playing computer games, "computer using" Hispanic kids also devote as much or more time to each of the other computer activities as do white or African American kids.

Differences between the total sample and just "computer users" in how computer time is distributed also emerge when use is related to household income. Among all 8- to 18-year-olds, computer exposure increases at each successively higher level of household income, from 0:21 to 0:28 to 0:30 (for kids from low-, middle-, and high-income households, respectively). When attention is limited just to computer users, however, the pattern is curvilinear. Youths from low-income households use computers for 53 minutes daily and those from middle-income homes for 57 minutes; among kids from high-income households, however, computer time drops off significantly, to 47 minutes. On the other hand, computer exposure remains similarly related to level of parent education regardless of whether the full sample or just computer users are examined. In general, youths whose parents have completed a college education spend substantially more time with computers than do kids whose parents completed no more than high school; kids whose parents have some college fall in between. Neither number of parents living in the household nor residence locale are related to the amount of time young people spend with computers.

In general, then, when we focus on 8- to 18-year-olds who use computers, it seems safe to say that computer use follows a pattern we have noted for several other media, rising to a peak among 11- to 14-year-olds, then dropping off among 15- to 18-year-olds. Boys spend more time than girls using computers, but most of the difference derives from time spend with computer games. Indeed, if we remove computer games from the averages, there is no difference between boys and girls in computer exposure either overall or within each of the three age groups. White and African American computer users spend almost identical amounts of time with computers, but both groups trail far behind Hispanic computer users, a pattern that differs dramatically from the findings for either likelihood of computer use or average exposure when the entire sample of youths is considered. Computer exposure drops off to the lowest levels among computer users from high-income households, but increases to the highest levels among youths whose parents completed a college education.

Much of the research on young people and interactive media published in the brief interval since our data were collected focuses on on-line activities. The findings make it quite clear that kids are social beings and that the new media serve this function particularly well. Adolescents primarily use new technologies such as the Internet to maintain relationships, and sometimes to establish new ones. The number one activity of kids on-line is e-mailing (Cheskin Research & Cyberteen.com, 1999; Kaiser Family Foundation, 2001; Lenhart et al., 2001; Roper Starch Worldwide Inc., 1999), an activity that appears to transcend all demographic and geographical boundaries. One U.S. government study reports that e-mail overwhelmingly represents the most popular types of Internet activity for all kids around the world (National Telecommunications and Information Administration, 1999). Some 78 percent of people who use the Internet use it to send e-mail. Even more recently, instant messaging has become tremendously popular among adolescents. Lenhart et al. (2001) report that three-quarters of 2- to 17-year-olds with on-line access have sent an instant message (compared with 44% of on-line adults). Girls seem to get hooked on instant messaging earlier than boys: 72 percent of on-line 12- to 14-year-old girls send instant messages versus 60 percent of on-line 12- to 14-year-old boys. By late adolescence, however, boys catch up. Ninety percent of instant messengers report using it to keep in touch with friends and family who do not live in their area. Finally, a substantial proportion of 9- to 17-year-olds (32%) report that they often use the Internet to visit chat rooms, still another social activity.

On-line teen expression does not end with e-mail, instant messaging, and chat rooms. One study reports that 43 percent of on-line 13- to 19-year-olds have their own websites (Cheskin Research & Cyberteens.com, 1999), and another that 24 percent of 12- to 17-year-olds have created their own web pages (Lenhart et al., 2001).[3] Regardless

---

[3] The discrepancy between the two studies probably results from several factors: (1) the Web-based sample employed versus a national random telephone sample used by the earlier and later studies, respectively; (2) the difference in timing – the two-year separation probably marks a surge in on-line teens, and it is possible that more technologically savvy teens were on-line prior to 1999; and (3) the slightly older sample used in the first study.

of the differences in the estimates provided by the two studies, the fact
that at least one-quarter of U.S. on-line teens are creating their own
Web sites is certainly consistent with claims that this is the first time in
history that a generation of kids has overtaken their parents in the use
of new technology (Thompson, 1999).

VIDEO GAMES

Video games – interactive games that operate through a TV screen –
have been available to the public since the early 1970s, much longer
than personal computers. Clearly, however, much has changed since
the rudimentary graphics and limited user control of early games such
as Pong and Asteroids. Today's video games offer stunningly lifelike
graphics and special effects, and much more user control than once
thought possible. The very latest generation of video-game consoles
offer even more sophisticated experiences, providing a platform not only
for video games but for connections to the Internet and a way to watch
DVD movies (Center for Media Education, 2001), activities that until
recently were available only to computer users. It will be interesting to
witness the effects of such convergence over the next few years.

Video games are largely the domain of boys, particularly during the
late childhood and early adolescence (8 to 14 years). On any given
day 16 percent of 2- to 7-year-olds play video games, for an average of
8 minutes, and 39 percent of 8- to 18-year-olds play video games for
an average of 26 minutes. Thus, video games claim as much time as
computers; with young children spending 2 minutes more per day with
video games than with computers, and older youths spending 1 minute
more. However, video-game time matches that for computers almost entirely because of the behavior of boys, as illustrated in Figure 7.9, which
shows the proportion of boys and girls at each age who play video games.
Within every age group, substantially higher proportions of boys than
girls play video games. Among girls, the proportion rises to just over a
third between 8 and 10 years, then drops off rapidly throughout adolescence. Among boys, video-game playing begins early, rises substantially
within each successive age group until surpassing 60 percent for 11- to
14-year-olds, then declines to 50 percent for the oldest adolescents.
Tables in Appendix 7.1 show that the same pattern is maintained when
we examine average time spent with video games: boys spend more time
than girls playing within each age group; girls' playing time peaks at
8 to 10 years and boys at 11 to 14 years. The one deviation from result
for proportions occurs among 11- to 14-year-olds. In that age subgroup,

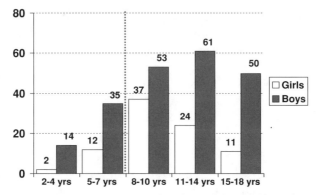

Figure 7.9. Proportion of girls and boys who play
video games by age.

about 2 ½ times more boys than girls play video games; however, boys almost quintuple the amount of time girls spend with video games. Clearly,
video games hold the greatest attraction for middle-school boys – a finding very much in line with claims that the content of most video games
is highly gender-stereotyped, appealing far more to boys than girls (e.g.,
Calvert, 1999; Funk, 1993; Tanaka, 1996).

So few young children play video games that it is not possible to examine the relationship of game playing to indicators of socioeconomic
status or race/ethnicity. Among older youths, however, video-game
playing appears related to race or ethnicity, although we caution that
the numbers on which these estimates are based are relatively small.
African American youths are more likely to play video games on any
given day (46% of black youths vs. 37% of white youths), and black and
Hispanic youths spend 11 to 12 minutes more daily than whites with
video games. Household income is negatively related to both the likelihood of playing and the amount of time spent playing. That is, a higher
proportion of low-income kids than high-income kids play video games
(41% vs. 34%) and they play for a longer period of time (28 minutes vs.
20 minutes). It is worth noting, however, that the negative relationship
is due almost entirely to the behavior of kids between 8 and 14 years,
and that this is probably something of a "medium access" effect. That
is, youths from higher income homes have greater in-home access to
computers and, not surprisingly, are a bit more likely than their lower
income counterparts to play computer games. Low-income youths, who
lack computers at home, spend more time with video games. Among
15- to 18-year-olds, differences related to household income disappear,

primarily because interest in gaming of any kind begins to decline. Finally, video-game playing is unrelated to level of parent education (see Appendix 7.1).

CONTENT PREFERENCES

To say that young people spend a large part of their computer time playing games or that older kids spend a lot of time visiting Web sites is helpful, but still leaves a lot of uncertainty about specific kinds of content accessed. There is a good deal of difference between what kids might take away from educational games designed to teach anything from the alphabet to ecological principles and a "first-person-shooter" game in which the goal is for the player to annihilate as many opponents as possible as quickly as possible. Similarly, we expect Web sites devoted to sports or entertainment, history, the day's news, or any of a number of political or social causes to attract different audiences and engender different consequences. This section, then, presents a brief look at the kinds of content children and adolescents access when playing either computer games or video games and when visiting chat rooms or surfing the Web.

INTERACTIVE GAMES

As noted earlier, 2- to 7-year-olds' computer time is devoted almost exclusively to games. These consist primarily of what we define as educational games, children's games, or arts and crafts games. In other words, most of young children's computer time is spent engaged in activities that most adults would argue are to their benefit, no doubt because of much higher parental supervision of young children's than of older children's computer activities. No 2- to 4-year-olds and only 6 percent of 5- to 7-year-olds who play computer games play action or combat games.

Games also comprise a substantial part of older youths' computer diet, but as the tables in Appendix 7.2 illustrate, their game selection is more varied. Action and combat genres account for 20 percent to 25 percent of older youths' game choices. Sports games also attract high and roughly equal proportions of kids from all three age subgroups (from 16% to 23%). Educational games remain important to 8- to 10-year-olds, with a third still playing them, but their popularity drops off rapidly from 11 years onward. Arts and crafts games follow the same downward trend with age. The attraction of classic and/or gambling games (e.g., chess, solitaire, or black-jack), interactive and role-playing games, and simulation games increases with age. Indeed, classic and gambling games constitute the only category to attract a third or more of the two older age groups. It appears that as young people grow older, more "cognitively oriented" games gain in attraction.

Gender also strongly differentiates computer game preferences, for the most part in ways that are not surprising. Classic and gambling games comprise the only category to attract significantly more girls than boys (36% vs. 23%). Boys dominate the action/combat, adventure, sports, and strategic and simulation categories, consistent with arguments that most such computer games are designed with boys in mind (e.g., Calvert, 1999).

Game choice is also related to race or ethnicity, primarily because Hispanic kids choose games different from white or African American youths, who generally play the same kinds of games. Hispanic kids are more likely than either whites or African Americans to play adventure games, more likely than whites to play arts and crafts games, and less likely than whites to play sports games, although given the relatively small number of Hispanic "computer users," these proportions are highly tentative.

Game choice also relates to socioeconomic status, but few meaningful patterns emerge. Of youths who use computers, over 60 percent from all three income categories play computer games. Kids from high-income households are less likely to play either adventure or arts and crafts games. Fewer kids from middle-income households choose educational games. More low-income youths play classic/gambling games (game genres, it is worth noting, that come pre-loaded on most computers – perhaps another indicator of the importance of access). Similarly, the proportions of kids with parents from each education level who play any kind of games do not differ, but their game choices are highly varied. For example, children of college graduates are most likely to select action/combat games, and least likely to play interactive role-playing games, both findings somewhat at odds with assumptions that young people from lower socioeconomic backgrounds might prefer more violent content and that those from higher socioeconomic backgrounds might prefer more cognitively oriented content.

Video games offer a narrower array of game genres. Children's games, educational games, arts and crafts games, popular culture/lifestyle games – none of these genres appear in the list of video games played. Not surprisingly, then, higher proportions of kids from each of our various demographic categories play more action-oriented games. They, after all, are what is most available. Action and combat games, adventure games, and sports games are far and away the most popular with all age groups, although 15- to 18-year-olds tend to gravitate toward sports games, while 8- to 11-more year-olds prefer adventure games (see Appendix 7.2). Boys are most attracted to action-oriented games, with substantially higher proportions of them selecting from the action/combat, sports/competition, and simulation/strategic categories. Differences in video-game choices related to race or ethnicity are somewhat stronger than those noted for computer games. Although a higher proportion of white than African American youths play video games, higher proportions of African American 8- to 18-year-olds choose games in the action/combat, adventure, and classic/gambling/puzzle categories. However, we again caution that the number of youths on which these estimates are based is relatively small, so they must be viewed as highly tentative. Although the numbers on which our estimates are based are small, youths from all three levels of household income choose action/combat, adventure, and sports/competition games, with the caveat that more kids from low-income homes play sports games. For the most part, level of parent education fails to differentiate video-game preferences.

In general, then, patterns of both computer game and video-game choice fit both age and gender expectations. As young people grow older, they begin to turn away from games based primarily on fighting and killing and more often choose more cognitively oriented games – simulations, interactive role-playing games, and instances of the classic and gambling categories. This trend, however, is much more apparent with computer games than video games, we suspect largely due to differences in the array of choices available. Similarly, and also not surprising, boys are much more likely than girls to choose action/combat, sports, adventure, and strategic/simulation games for both the computer and the video-game console. Less easily explained, however, are game choices in relation to race/ethnicity, household income, or level of parent education. We suspect that the tendency for minority youths to spend more time that whites with action, combat, and adventure games is at least partly due to the fact that lack of access limits their opportunity to spend time with computers, thus giving them more time to spend with video games. And since video-game availability tends to be biased in the direction of offering many more action, combat, adventure, and sports titles than anything else, these are the kinds of games most often selected.

CHAT ROOMS

The most popular chat rooms for all three age groups are those devoted to entertainment and to hobbies. Those devoted to sports draw substantial numbers of 8- to 10-year-olds and 11- to 14-year-olds, but not 15- to 18-year-olds. Visits to chat rooms devoted to relationships and/or lifestyles attract relatively few 8- to 10-year-olds, but increase substantially at each successive age level. This pattern is very much in line with developing adolescent concerns about social relationships and the building of self-identity (Feldman and Elliott, 1990; Kirchler, Palomari, & Pombeni, 1993). Gender locates differences in two kinds of chat rooms, both of which fit gender expectations. Not surprisingly, girls are more than twice as likely as boys to visit chat rooms devoted to discussion of social relationships and lifestyles, while boys are more than twice as likely to seek out sports-related chat rooms.

Unfortunately, when we attempt to relate preference for different chat-room genres to race or ethnicity, household income, or level of parent education, we are handicapped by numbers shrinking to levels that make comparisons highly unstable. We can, however, note the tables in Appendix 7.2 that show African American computer users are least likely (19%) and Hispanic users most likely (34%) to visit chat rooms, with white users (26%) falling between. There is no relationship between likelihood of visiting a chat room and either household income or parent education. One difference emerges when kids who live with one versus two parents are compared. Those from single-parent households are almost twice as likely as those living with two parents to visit entertainment sites. Entertainment sites also appeal to more urban and rural kids than suburban kids.

WEBSITES

The patterns of use of various genres of websites are roughly similar to those found for chat rooms (see Appendix 7.2). Entertainment sites are most popular across all three age subgroups, but particularly among older adolescents. Not surprisingly, websites devoted to interactive gaming are quite popular among 8- to 10-year-olds, but their use drops off dramatically by 15 to 18 years, mirroring the drop-off in the attraction of computer games noted above. Although older kids are not nearly as attracted to websites dealing with relationships and lifestyles as they are to chat rooms devoted to these issues, there is a consistent, age-related increase in their use of search engines and in their visits to websites used for information and research. Finally, among 11- to 14-year-olds, websites devoted to sports are highly popular. Relatively few gender differences in website use emerge. More girls than boys visit sites devoted to entertainment (65% vs. 46%), and more boys than girls visit sites devoted to sports (34% vs. 11%). The only other meaningful gender difference concerns use of search engines; 21% of boys and 11% of girls use search engines – a difference that we are frankly at a loss to explain.

As was the case with chat rooms, small numbers limit our ability to look at use of various website genres in relation to race or ethnicity, except to note that African American computer users (32%) are substantially less likely than Hispanic computer users (53%) to visit websites, with white users (46%) falling between. Neither household income nor level of parent education relates to the likelihood of visiting websites. The same preference for entertainment sites found for kids from single-parent homes when chat rooms are considered also holds for websites. Finally, residence locale makes little difference in what websites kids choose, except that urban youths are more likely than rural kids to visit shopping sites.

Overall, then, few surprises emerge from our examination of the kinds of chat rooms and websites that 8- to 18-year-olds choose to visit. Aside from the strong attraction of gaming sites to 8- to 10-year-olds, U.S. kids generally spend a great deal of their on-line time chatting and visiting websites about entertainment and entertainers, sports, and, particularly as they move through the adolescent years, relationships and lifestyles. A third of girls spend time in chat rooms devoted to entertainment sites and a third in sites devoted to discussions of relationships and lifestyles. Sixty-five percent of girls visit entertainment websites. No other genres attract more than 15 percent. Boys spend time at entertainment and sports sites, as well as with search engines. They also chat about relationships and lifestyles, although in much smaller proportions than girls. We can say little about similarities or differences in the kinds of chat rooms and websites preferred by youths from different racial or ethnic backgrounds, or by those from different socioeconomic groupings, except to note that relatively few African American youths visit chat rooms or websites.

SUMMING UP INTERACTIVE MEDIA USE

In spite of speculation that today's young people are devoting more of their time to computers than to any other medium, including television (e.g., Stanger, 1998), it seems that the new interactive media have not yet claimed center stage. Although in Chapter 9 we argue that the day when interactive media do come to dominate may be drawing near, in terms of both the proportion of kids using interactive media and time devoted to them, it has not yet arrived. Indeed, Chapter 8 shows that even when combined, computers and video games account for a smaller proportion of young people's overall media budget than television, audio media, or even print. To a large extent, interactive media probably lag behind other media because they have not yet fully penetrated the population. Substantial numbers of youths live in homes that do not have a video-game console; even more live in homes lacking a personal computer. Still another factor tending to keep computers from displacing television and print may be that they are not functionally equivalent. Most computers today are not very good substitutes for TV sets; when a youngster wants to watch an audiovisual narrative, television still does the job better. Similarly, when reading for pleasure is the goal, a magazine or a paperback novel remains more convenient than even the smallest of lap-top computers. We suspect that the first real test of functional equivalence may be under way right now: more and more, computers are becoming an important source of music for young people. For example, in 1999, some 76 percent of U.S. kids expressed interest in downloading music on-line (Roper Starch Worldwide Inc., 1999). The ability to stream and/or download music (often at little or no cost), to store vast numbers of popular songs, and to mix, remix, and burn one's own CDs is rapidly transforming computers into a primary music source for adolescents. We fully expect that over the next few years, young people will conceive of computers as music media, little different from either radio or CDs and tapes – and in some ways, superior.

In the interim, there is little doubt that today's young people are enamored of the new interactive media (see Chapter 9), and that they are finding a multitude of new uses for them. One of the most important of the new uses consists of new ways to engage in social interactions. Three-quarters of on-line teens say the Internet is an important connection to their friends (Cheskin Research & Cyberteens.com, 1999). E-mail, instant messaging, joining in chat room conversations, even "lurking" (observing but not participating in chat room exchanges) have all become common activities for growing numbers of adolescents. To some extent these kinds of media activities may be an extension of the "parasocial interaction" that television offers to some viewers (Horton & Wohl, 1956; Perse & Rubin, 1989; Rubin, Perse, & Powell, 1985). Once past "lurking," however, there is little about these interactions to label "para-" or even "virtual" interactions. For today's kids, they are real interactions, and in the minds of young people who grow up with media that make them possible, "social interaction" is quite likely to become an expected function of mass media. Consider, for example, the money and effort currently being expended on attempts to make it possible for people to talk back to their televisions, their newspapers and even their radios.

Most kids who are already are on-line or at least have computers recognize that the on-line world is here to stay. Some 79 percent say that the Internet is where the future is headed and 80 percent describe it as "fun" (Cheskin Research & Cyberteens.com, 1999). And they eagerly look forward to new developments. In 1999, some 78 percent of kids said they are somewhat or very interested in sending and receiving pictures on-line, and 70 percent wanted to have a live video conference with a friend online (Roper Starch Worldwide Inc., 1999). Based on expectations such as these, it seems clear that today's kids will push the envelope on the social applications of the Internet.

CHAPTER EIGHT

Patterns of Overall Media

Consumption

Now that we have examined U.S. young people's exposure to individual media, it is time to turn to overall media use and media diets. How much are children and adolescents exposed to media overall? How does overall media consumption vary with such factors as age, gender, race and ethnicity, or socioeconomic status? What proportion of the total media budget is accounted for by each different medium?

With all of the media options available, it is no surprise that U.S. children and adolescents devote an enormous portion of each day to their use. As we have seen, they watch television, listen to music, play video games, use computers, read books, magazines, or newspapers, watch videos, and go to the movies. Moreover, today's kids often do two or three or more of these things simultaneously. Christenson and Roberts (1998), for example, present evidence that most teenagers' music listening accompanies other activities, quite often other media activities. Similarly, Lenhart et al. (2001) report that today's computer activities almost stereotypically imply multitasking on the part of young people. One 17-year-old girl states, "I get bored if it's not all going on at once, because everything has gaps – waiting for someone to respond to an IM, waiting for a Website to come up, commercials on TV, etc." (p. 13). Another 15-year-old says, "I do so many things at once. . . . I'm always talking to people through instant messenger and then I'll be checking e-mail or doing homework or playing games AND talking on the phone at the same time" (p. 13).

Exposure versus Use

Such parallel processing of media points to an important distinction between media *use* – the amount of time kids spend with media – and media *exposure* – the amount of media content they encounter. For example, if a youth spends 1 hour reading while simultaneously listening to music, she has *used* media for 1 hour but has been *exposed to* 2 hours of media content. Typically, then, estimates of young people's total media exposure are likely to be somewhat higher than estimates of their total media use (i.e., "person-hours" devoted to media) because the former double counts overlapping use.

In line with previous research on children's media consumption, this study has focused primarily on media exposure. That is, youngsters were asked how much time they spend with each individual medium. Simply summing responses to individual exposure questions provides the most direct method of estimating total *media exposure*. However, given that today's kids often use several media at once, it is not a good estimate of how much time they *use* media, irrespective of simultaneous media use. Because real-world time budgets are both interesting and important, and because it is apparent that parallel processing of multiple media has become quite common, in addition to assessing media *exposure*, we also report an estimate of total media *use* that removes the double counting inherent in simply totaling reports of time spent with each individual medium.

We calculate overall leisure media exposure by totaling children's (or parents') reports of the amount of time they use each individual medium for leisure purposes (i.e., not for school or work). We include time spent with each medium examined in earlier chapters: print (magazines, newspapers, and books – excluding books for school but including parental reading to young children), television, taped TV shows, commercially produced videos, video games, movies, radio, CDs and tapes, and computers (including computer games, the World Wide Web, e-mail, and chat rooms, but excluding computer use for school or work). This approach replicates procedures employed by the few prior studies that report children's overall media consumption (e.g., Greenberg et al., 1989; Maccoby, 1951; Schramm et al., 1961). It provides a reasonable estimate of how much media content children are exposed to in units of time, but not of media use – that is, how much time individual children devote to media, ignoring multitasking. We included our supplemental diary sample as a means to estimate media *use*. The diary asked children to indicate whenever they used two or more media concurrently, enabling us to calculate the proportion of exposure time during which several media are used simultaneously. When the sum of reports of time given to each individual medium – that is, media exposure – is reduced by this proportion, an estimate of media use results. Media *use*, then, is a measure of person-hours devoted to media from which simultaneous media use has been removed. The distinction is important when we consider that many young people report in excess of 10 hours daily of media exposure, amounts that may be difficult to take seriously unless one considers the frequency of media multitasking. Although we concentrate primarily on children's media exposure, then, we also report briefly on media use (person-hours of media consumption) in order to provide at least a partial explanation for the high amount of exposure that some youths report.

Data from the supplemental diary samples indicate that, overall, children spend an average of 16 percent of their media time using two or more media simultaneously. Of course, some subgroups of children use multiple media more than others (proportions range from 12% to 20% depending on the subgroup examined), but since most of the differences between groups are not statistically significant, we calculated media use by reducing exposure estimates by 16 percent across the board. Parents report that young children (ages 2 to 7) are exposed to 4 hours and 20 minutes a day of media messages. Youths from 8 to 18 years claim 7 hours and 29 minutes of daily exposure to media messages. These numbers translate to about 3 ½ hours (3:38) of media *use* among the younger children, and 6 ¼ hours (6:17) of media *use* among older youths. In other words, 2- to 7-year-olds use more than one medium simultaneously for 41 minutes daily; 8- to 18-year-olds engage in simultaneous media use for 1:12 daily.

Of course, numerous earlier studies, as well as preceding chapters in this book, show that young people's media consumption varies dramatically with age. Our data for total media exposure are no different. Table 8.1 presents overall media consumption (both exposure and use) for the five age groupings we have been considering throughout this book. It reveals that 2- to 4-year-olds consume slightly more media than 5- to 7-year-olds, and that 11- to 14-year-olds consume significantly more media than either 8- to 10-year-olds or 15- to 18-year-olds. It also indicates that a closer examination of the relationship between media consumption and age is warranted. As in earlier chapters, complete tables and results of statistical tests can be found in Appendix 8.

Table 8.1. *Comparison of Average Media Exposure and Average Media Use by Age (hr:min)*

Age groups	Media exposure	Media use
2–4 years	4:29	3:46
5–7 years	4:11	3:31
8–10 years	7:14	6:04
11–14 years	7:55	6:39
15–18 years	7:11	6:02

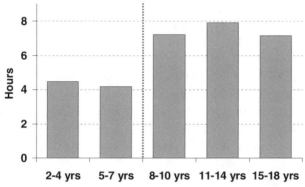

Figure 8.1. Average media exposure by age.

OVERALL MEDIA EXPOSURE

AGE AND MEDIA EXPOSURE

The mean amounts of young people's media exposure summarized in Table 8.1. are pictured in Figure 8.1. The most striking feature of this graph is the magnitude of the difference between the two younger versus the three older age groups. Media consumption appears to increase dramatically between 7 and 8 years. There is little question that some of this difference is real. It probably stems from several factors. For example, parents are more likely to monitor and supervise younger children's media exposure than that of older children; older children have longer days (they sleep less), thus more time to devote to media; and there is arguably more media content appropriate for older viewers available on any given day. In other words, there is good reason to expect children under 8 years to spend substantially less time with media than do their older counterparts. However, we also believe that some part of the difference shown in Figure 8.1 is attributable to parent underestimates of time that young children spend with the various media making up our index. As noted in Chapter 4, these underestimates probably are due both to lack of information (children often use media when parents are not present) and to a tendency for parents to give socially desirable responses about their own children. Thus, we reiterate that we separately analyze responses for 2- through 7-year-olds (based on parent reports) and for 8- through 18-year-olds (self-reports), and remind readers that comparisons between these two age cohorts must be approached with caution.

Although 2- to 4-year-olds are exposed to slightly more media content than 5- to 7-year-olds, the difference is not statistically significant. Among older youths, 11- to 14-year-olds report more media exposure than either 8- to 10-year-olds or 15- to 18-year-olds, but only the latter difference reaches statistical significance. At around 11- to 14 years, children are typically in middle school or junior high school. They still depend on parents or older siblings for transportation, leaving them less freedom of choice in how they spend their time. Children in the 8- to 10-year-old age range are more likely to have rules governing their use of television, and to have less private access to media than older children (see Chapter 3). Both factors probably operate to limit their overall time with media. As noted earlier, the oldest kids (15- to 18-year-olds), who are exposed to about the same amount of media content as the 8- to 10-year-olds, have more demands on their time as they become involved in school-related and social activities. They have more nonmedia opportunities available to them as newfound independence leads them farther from home. As we see below in this chapter, although amount of exposure is almost equal, the media mix differs for these two age groups.

A quarter-century ago George Comstock and his colleagues (Comstock et al., 1978) constructed a graph showing the relationship between age and amount of TV viewing using averages from reports of a number of small-sample studies of TV use. That graph, displayed in Figure 8.2, showed young children's viewing peaking at about 5 years, followed by a substantial dip. Viewing then increased from 8 to 12 years, followed by a steady decline during the teen years. Comstock and colleagues explained this pattern on the basis of available time. That is, as noted in Chapter 4, TV exposure is related to available time which, in turn, depends on school-related demands on children's time.

The current study is unusual in that it offers an opportunity to test directly whether the curve proposed by Comstock and his colleagues

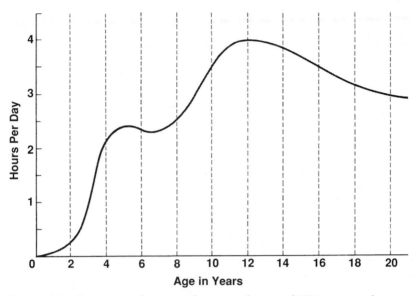

Figure 8.2. Constructed curve of average hours of TV viewing by age (from Comstock et al., 1978).

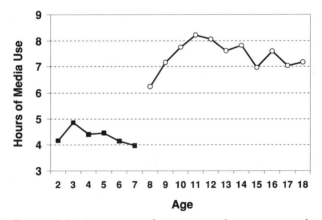

Figure 8.3. Average media exposure by age in yearly increments.

does characterizes U.S. young people's current media behavior. Our re-sults, albeit for total media use as opposed to TV viewing only (see Chapter 4 for examination of TV viewing), are quite consistent with those proposed by Comstock. Figure 8.3 shows young children's media exposure peaking at about 3 years, then steadily declining thereafter.

Among 8- to 18-year-olds, media exposure increases substantially from 8 to 11 years, then also declines throughout the remainder of adolescence. In other words, and quite consistent with the explanation offered by Comstock et al. (1978), overall media exposure increases until about the age at which children typically enter preschool or kindergarten. It then declines as they make the transition from home to a school setting, a transition that leaves less time for recreational media. Similarly, pre-teen children's overall media consumption increases as they grow older and settle into the demands of elementary school (and quite likely as bedtimes are pushed later into the evening). The peak in total media exposure at around age 11 or 12 years occurs just about when they enter middle school or junior high school, another period during which young people typically must adjust to new demands on their time. Finally, by the time they reach senior high school (about age 14 to 15 years), older adolescents probably become more involved in school-related and social activities associated with high school – activities such as organized sports and other extracurricular activities, part-time jobs, and dating. Additionally, teens gain more independence as they grow older; for example, the freedom accompanying a driver's license expands possibilities and leaves less time for media use. Not surprisingly, then, from about 14 years onward, adolescents' overall media consumption tapers off. In short, the patterns shown in both these figures are consistent with the notion that the amount of time spent with media is largely a function of available (free) time, which, in turn, is a function of the age-related demands of school.

GENDER AND MEDIA EXPOSURE

Boys use media slightly more than girls, although none of the differences is statistically reliable (see Appendix 8.1). In both the younger and older samples, boys use media about a quarter-hour per day more than girls. Among older youths, however, the relationship depends on age. Although 11- to 14-year-old boys and 15- to 18-year-old boys spend about $\frac{1}{2}$ hour per day more than their female counterparts using media, among 8- to 10-year-olds, girls report higher levels of daily exposure (21 minutes more). We repeat, however, that none of these differences is statistically significant.

Among 2- to 7-year-olds, the trend toward boys using media slightly more than girls is largely accounted for by boys' tendency to spend more time than girls with television and video games. Among older children, time devoted to those two media and to computers accounts for most of the difference. In general, however, it seems safe to conclude that gender does not play a major role in explaining overall media exposure.

RACE/ETHNICITY AND MEDIA EXPOSURE

In light of the findings for many of the individual media examined earlier in this book, it is not surprising that race or ethnicity is related to overall media exposure. In general, African American youths report the most media exposure, followed by Hispanics, who in turn report slightly more exposure than whites. Looking first at younger children, among 2- to 7-year-olds overall, black kids are exposed to about 5:06 of media, Hispanics to 4:28, and white kids to 4:06 (only the white-black difference is statistically reliable). Figure 8.4 reveals that the overall picture changes little when narrower age groupings are examined. That is, among both 2- to 4-year-olds and 5- to 7-year-olds, media exposure is highest among African American kids, followed by Hispanic, then white children, and again, only the white-black differences are statistically reliable.

Much the similar pattern holds for older youths. When 8- to 18-year-olds are examined as a group, white youths report significantly less media exposure than either black or Hispanic youths (6:56, 9:01, and 8:19 for whites, blacks and Hispanics, respectively), and only the white-black difference reaches statistical significance. Within the smaller age groupings displayed in Figure 8.4, however, there is a slight change in media use. As is the case for younger children, both 8- to 10-year-old and 15- to

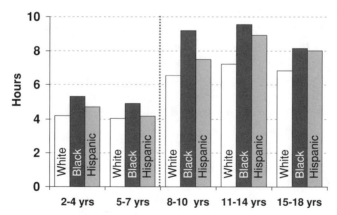

Figure 8.4. Average media exposure by age and race/ethnicity.

18-year-old white youths report significantly less media exposure than African American kids, and Hispanic youths fall in between. Among 11- to 14-year-olds, however, the pattern changes. There continues to be no difference in media exposure between African Americans and Hispanics, but white youngsters report significantly less exposure than in either of those groups. In general, then, at every age level African American youth report the highest levels of media exposure, followed by Hispanic and then by white youth. The only reliable difference, however, is between whites and blacks.

SOCIOECONOMIC STATUS AND MEDIA EXPOSURE

Both indices of socioeconomic status – household income and parent education – are negatively related to overall media exposure. For the most part, however, the relationships are weak, and the differences in total media exposure at each level of household income or parent education are seldom statistically significant.

Overall media exposure decreases slightly as household income increases. In the 2- to 7-year-old sample, children from low- and middle-income homes are exposed to about ½ hour more media per day than children from high-income homes (4:32, 4:31, and 4:04, respectively). A similar pattern holds for 8- to 18-year-olds. That is, older youths from low-income homes report the most total media exposure (8:00), followed by middle-income kids (7:41), then by high-income kids (6:57). However, even thought the difference exceeds an hour daily, it is not statistically significant.[1]

Age also affects the nature and magnitude of the relationship between media exposure and household income. For example, within some age groups the relationship is curvilinear. Figure 8.5 presents media exposure by household income within each of the five age subgroupings we have been examining. Among 5- to 7-year-olds, 11- to 14-year-olds, and 15- to 18-year-olds, the linear negative relationship generally holds (although the mean difference is statistically significant only among 11- to 14-year-olds; see Appendix 8). That is, in these age groups youngsters from the

---

[1] The Pearson correlation coefficient for the relationship between household income and media exposure for 2- to 7-year-olds is $r = -.08$, $p < .05$; for 8- to 18-year-olds, $r = -.09$, $p < .01$. Although significant, these are not strong correlations. Even though the mean differences related to both income and parent education sometimes look large, the variance around those means is also large; hence, the differences are not statistically significant.

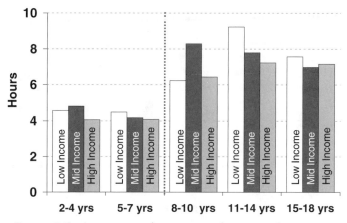

Figure 8.5. Average media exposure by age and income.

low-income homes are most exposed to media, followed by youngsters from middle-income households, with those from high-income households reporting the least media exposure. The pattern changes, however, within the two remaining age groups; both 2- to 4-year-olds and 8- to 10-year-olds produce a curvilinear pattern between media exposure and income level. That is, the highest media exposure occurs among youngsters from middle-income homes, although the difference is reliable only for the 8- to 10-year-olds.

The relatively low association between household income and media exposure, as well as some of the age-related inconsistency just described, probably stems in part from our method of estimating household income. As discussed in Chapter 2, there is a good deal of error inherent in attempting to relate aggregate measures (e.g., household income as indexed by the median income of the zip code in which young people live or go to school) to individual level measures (e.g., media exposure). Some children who live or attend school in high-income communities probably come from moderate or low-income households. Similarly, some children who live or attend school in low-income communities come from moderate or high-income households. Although we cannot directly test this explanation, we suspect that there is enough crossover of this type in our sample to attenuate the relationship between "household income" and media exposure and to help produce some of the inconsistencies that emerge when examining smaller age groups.

Within the younger sample, the negative relationship between parent education and amount of media exposure is somewhat stronger than

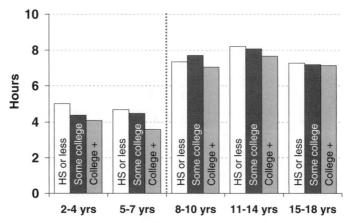

Figure 8.6. Average media exposure by age and parent education.

that for household income. Once again, however, the relationship is relatively trivial among older youths.[2] Children aged 2 to 7 years with parents who completed college are exposed to an hour less media than children whose parents completed no more than high school (3:51 vs. 4:52, a reliable difference); children with parents who completed some college fall between (4:26). Among 8- to 18-year-olds, however, there is no difference in young people's media exposure as a function of parent education. Youths whose parents completed no more than high school and those whose parents completed some college report 7:41 total media exposure; those whose parents completed college report about 20 minutes less (7:20).

Figure 8.6 shows that when the relationship between parent education and media exposure is examined for smaller age groups, the relationship is negative and linear for all but 8- to 10-year-olds. This group shows the same curvilinear pattern found for household income, with kids from "middle education" homes reporting more overall media exposure. Within all three older age groupings, however, none of the mean differences in media exposure is statistically reliable (nor are any of the correlation coefficients). Within the younger sample, the picture changes. Media exposure is significantly lower among 2- to 4-year-olds whose parents completed college than among their counterparts whose parents report no more than a high school education. Similarly, there is

[2] Among 2- to 7-year-olds, the Pearson correlation between parent education and media exposure is $r = -.17$, $p < .01$; among 8- to 18-year-olds, $r = -.04$, n.s.

significantly less media exposure among 5- to 7-year-olds whose parents have college degrees than among youngsters whose parents completed either high school or less or some college.[3]

Several explanations for why parent education should influence young children's media exposure but fail to affect older children's media exposure suggest themselves. First, the data for the younger children come from parent reports. It is not unreasonable to expect that more highly educated parents may be more in touch with the "desirable" response, thus more likely to report less media use. Second, there is evidence from earlier research (Bower, 1973, 1985; Foehr, Rideout, & Miller, 2001; also see Comstock, 1991; Comstock et al., 1978) and this study (Chapter 3) that parental controls on children's TV viewing increase with level of parent education and decrease with the age of the child. Within the younger sample, then, higher income parents and better educated parents are more likely to restrict their children's media exposure and/or more likely to be in touch with the "socially desirable" response. Both factors should operate to produce less media use among younger children as socioeconomic status increases. A negative relationship would not be so strong among older youths because their parents are less likely to control TV viewing (see Chapter 3) and because they are less likely to be aware of the socially desirable response.

Finally, the dearth of strong negative relationships between media exposure and either measure of socioeconomic status, particularly among the older children, can be somewhat misleading. Their absence fails to tell a complete story about the relationship between indicators of socioeconomic status and media exposure. Although kids from homes that differ in income or parent education appear to spend similar amounts of time exposed to all media, we have also seen that youths from different socioeconomic backgrounds do, in fact, manifest very different patterns of media use. Moreover, these patterns often reverse each other. For example, TV viewing and video-game playing both increase as socioeconomic indicators decrease. Conversely, print exposure and computer use are positively related to both income and education. When all of these kinds of media exposure are combined into a single index of overall media exposure, however, these variations in use of individual media appear to offset one another. The result is a dampening of any relationship

[3] For both of the younger age groups, correlations between parent education and media exposure are negative and statistically reliable; 2- to 4-year-olds: $r = -.15$, $p < .01$; 5- to 7-years-olds: $r = -.19$, $p < .01$.

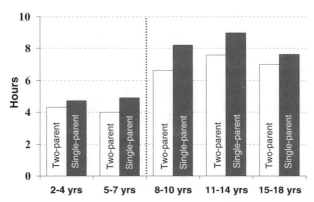

Figure 8.7. Average media exposure by age and family composition.

between media exposure and young people's socioeconomic background, particularly once children are old enough to make independent media decisions.

FAMILY COMPOSITION AND MEDIA EXPOSURE

As illustrated in Figure 8.7, at every age level media exposure is greater among children who live with a single parent than among those from two-parent households, although the differences reach statistical significance only for 5- to 7-, 8- to 10-, and 11- to 14-year-olds. At the tails of the age range, the difference is modest (24 minutes among 2- to 4-year-olds; 39 minutes among 15- to 18-year-olds), but it approaches an hour among 5- to 7-year-olds, and an hour and a half among 8- to 10- and 11- to 14-year-olds.

Several explanations for these patterns suggest themselves. The most obvious is simply that single parents have less time to devote to monitoring their children's media habits. In addition, several factors associated with socioeconomic status probably reinforce the trend. That is, the slight tendency for media exposure to increase as indicators of socioeconomic status decrease is continued, and even intensified, in this analysis. Our data reflect U.S. census bureau findings in that the income and education levels in single-parent households (typically headed by women) substantially trail those in two-parent households. For each age group, when number of parents is examined as a function of either household income or parent education, strong, positive relationships emerge. That is, as the number of parents in the household increases from one to two, so too does household income level. Similarly, the education level of parents is higher in two-parent households than in one-parent households.[4]

Another possible reason for the difference in media exposure is that single-parent households have fewer rules governing television use than do two-parent households (see Chapter 3), and fewer controls may also contribute to increased exposure to other kids of media. However, while it is true that a smaller proportion of single-parent households (31%) than two-parent households (40%) have TV rules, controlling for presence or absence of such rules fails to affect the relationship between number of parents and media exposure. Kids who live with one parent report more media exposure than those who live with two parents whether or not they have rules about watching television. Regardless of the underlying factors contributing to the relationship between media exposure and number of parents, it is clear that children from single-parent households are exposed to substantially more media than their counterparts who live with two parents.

RESIDENCE LOCALE AND MEDIA EXPOSURE

As pervasive as media have become in the United States, it is tempting to assume that residence locale should not influence amount of media exposure. However, as illustrated in Figure 8.8, where one lives seems to make quite a bit of a difference, but not always in predictable ways. Among 2- to 7-year-olds, whether children live in urban, suburban, or rural areas does not seem to influence media exposure substantially (4:29, 4:13, and 4:17, respectively). Among 8- to 18-year-olds, however, kids living in urban settings (8:04) are exposed to over an hour more media than are those living in rural settings (7:00), with suburban residents falling in between (7:20).

Given the sheer size of the differences within the older sample, it is somewhat surprising that a statistically significant difference is found only among the 15- to 18-year-olds. Moreover, for these oldest youths, the pattern of media exposure differs from that found for the larger age range (see Appendix 8). Fifteen- to 18-year-old suburban teens report

---

[4] When number of parents is crossed with household income, among 2- to 7-year-olds, r (Kendall's *tau*) = .15, and among 8- to 18-year-olds, r = .12; p < .001 for both. For the relationship between number of parents and parent education, among 2- to 7-year-olds, r = .24, p < .001, and among 8- to 18-year-olds, r = .11, p < .01.

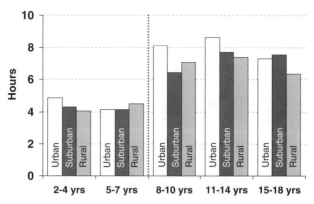

Figure 8.8. Average media exposure by age and residence locale.

over an hour more media exposure than do their rural counterparts, with urban teens falling in the middle. The differences related to locale that emerge in both the two larger age groups, and the five smaller age groupings, are likely a result of fluctuations in time spent with various individual media, an issue we examine more fully below in this chapter.

One might expect that living in cities would afford older kids many alternative, nonmedia opportunities right outside their doorsteps, resulting in less total media exposure. Interestingly, however, it is rural kids who report less media exposure as they get older. Perhaps urban youths' higher rates of media exposure indicate less safe conditions outside the home, in at least some urban settings. Suburban youths, on the other hand, may use more media because they have more media options at their disposal (e.g., they are more likely to live in a household with a computer; see Chapter 3). Another possibility is that younger suburban kids are more likely to be stranded at home (they are not yet old enough to drive and there is little easy access to public transportation). Rural kids are more likely to live in safe areas, with ample activities to engage them outside the home – different and possibly more attractive activities than may be available to urban or suburban kids.

THE MEDIA BUDGET

How do young people apportion their media budget? Although total exposure to media is a useful statistic, it does not provide information about how kids distribute their time across various media. Given all the media that they are exposed to, which claim most of their media time?

Which claim the least? Which kids are using which media? The preceding chapters looked in detail at each individual mass medium, and we
have just described amount of total exposure. Now we turn to how each
individual medium contributes to young people's overall media budget.

The media budget is simply the proportion of total media time
devoted to each medium or type of medium. Media budgets allow us to
examine how children distribute their media time. Budgets highlight
differences that may not be uncovered just by looking at average
exposure to each medium. For example, imagine two children who both
watch 3 hours of television a day. One child uses no other media, while
the other spends an additional 2 hours listening to music, and one more
hour using the computer. Although these hypothetical youngsters spend
identical amounts of time with TV, their media budgets look very different. The first child devoted 100 percent of media time to television; the
second watches the same amount of television, but clearly has a different
kind of media experience. This kind of information gets lost when
looking at overall averages for subgroups of children. Media budgets
were calculated for each child and adolescent in our sample. Average
proportions of total time devoted to each medium were then computed
for the various subgroups of young people we have been examining.

In calculating media budgets, we grouped certain media in order to
create a more meaningful and understandable composite. The media
budget consists of six components:

1. Television: Because television commands such a great deal of time
   from U.S. children and adolescents, it constitutes a separate part of
   the media budget.
2. Other screen media: Other "noninteractive screen media" such as
   prerecorded videos of TV shows, commercial videos of movies or
   other programs, and movies in theaters have been grouped to make
   a second category within the media budget.
3. Video games: Video games also constitute their own segment of the
   media budget primarily because they are prevalent among *certain*
   subgroups, and because they do not fit conveniently within other
   classifications.[5]

---

[5] A case can be made that video games should be grouped with computer games.
From a "functional" point of view, such a grouping makes sense. However, it seems
to us that computer games fit even more logically and conveniently with other
computer activities, particularly in light of the recent trend toward on-line gaming
and the proliferation of websites and chat rooms.

4. Print media: Print media are grouped to represent another piece of the media budget. This category encompasses all nonschool reading of newspapers, magazines, or books.
5. Audio media: Audio media, made up of CDs, tapes, and radio listening, create another category of media use. The preponderance of audio media use consists of music listening, and will typically be referred to as such.
6. Computer: Computer activities, which include games, chat rooms, websites, and e-mail, constitute the final component in the media budget.

In many cases, these budget categories represent fundamentally different kinds of information-processing activities; each mediates information in different ways. Television and other screen media provide engaging multimedia presentations that may include audio, visual, and/or textual representations, but that do not require consciously enactive responses from viewers. Video games and computer activities also use multimedia formats, but differ from TV and other screen media in that they require input from users. On one hand, a screen is a screen is a screen; on the other hand, certain activities inherent in interactive media may produce more powerful effects *because* they require enactive behaviors (see Calvert, 1999). Print media communicate primarily through text (sometimes with pictures supplementing the textual information) and require somewhat deeper or more mindful processing than do pictures (see Salomon, 1979). Audio media communicate primarily through sound. However, with the advent of music videos, this experience is probably not the same as 20 years ago because many listeners now have "precreated" images to attach to a musical experience.

Although these various formats are important factors in how one processes media messages, as technology and creativity advance, the lines between formats are becoming blurred, both technically and psychologically. Technically, audiences now have more power to manipulate the format in which they receive information. For example, on the Web one can choose to read a news story, watch a video clip of an event, see a picture, or just listen to a reporter's voice. Psychologically, even more formats may be available. As exemplified by the audio example in the preceding paragraph, one might listen to music, but instead of creating one's own images of the song's lyrics, simply recall the prefabricated images encountered in a music video. Similarly, one might read a book, but use the images provided by a recent feature film treatment of the

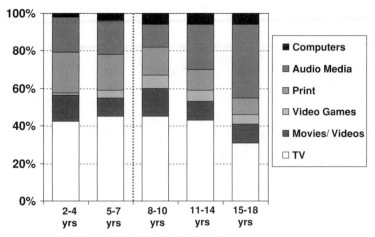

Figure 8.9. Media budget by age groups.

novel. When considering how different subgroups of youth divide their time among different kinds of media, then, it is helpful to keep in mind how the different categories of media present information.

AGE AND MEDIA BUDGETS

In spite of the many different media options available to young people today, and contrary to frequent speculation that they are turning away from "traditional media" in droves to embrace computers and the World Wide Web for information and entertainment, without question television remains the dominant medium among American youth. Figure 8.9 makes clear that television dominates all but the oldest youths' media budget. From 2 to 4 years through 11 to 14 years, television consistently accounts for over 40 percent of media time. Among youth 14 years and younger, no other media category ever consumes as much as 25 percent of the budget. Moreover, if we fold in other screen media (self-recorded and commercial videos and movies), "noninteractive screen media" account for well over half of all but the oldest youths' media time. Clearly, the lure of simply sitting and watching remains very powerful.

Conversely, computers and video games – the "interactive screen media" – account for the smallest part of young people's media budget. The contribution of interactive media to the overall budget is particularly small among 2- to 4- and 5- to 7-year-olds, whose lack of motor skills and reading ability probably limits the degree to which they find the new media engaging. Even among the older groups, however, neither computers nor video games ever account for as much as 10 percent of the total media pie; indeed, the two combined never make up 15 percent. It is also worth noting that from 8 years onward computer use remains a constant 6 percent of the media budget. The proportion of media time given to video games, however, increases until 8 to 10 years, then begins to drop off slightly. As we see below, there are youngsters who devote a substantial portion of their total media budget to these new media. However, they are fewer than reports in the popular press might lead one to expect (e.g., Klein, 2001). In short, when the average media budget for all U.S. kids is examined, interactive media play a fairly minor role across age groups.

Print media also play a relatively minor role in leisure media use, particularly by the middle school years. Among the younger children, leisure reading accounts for about 20 percent of overall media time. Among older youths, leisure reading drops steadily from 15 percent of media time among 8- to 10-year-olds to less than 10 percent among 15- to 18-year-olds. It is important to note that among younger children, leisure print exposure consists primarily of being read to by parents or other adult caretakers. Very few 3- or 4-year-olds read newspapers or magazines by themselves, although many probably do thumb through various children's books. From 8 years onward, however, most leisure reading is probably engaged by kids themselves. These are the years during which children become more capable of reading for meaning (Chall, 1983) and more interested in reading their own books, subscribe to their own children's and teen magazines, and begin to scan at least some sections of the newspaper. Within just a few years, however, school reading assignments begin to mount, and from about middle school onward leisure reading steadily decreases. We suspect that the increasing amount and complexity of reading associated with each successive year of school plays a major role in the steady decrease in the proportion of total media time given to leisure reading. Several hours spent reading for a school assignment probably reduce the probability that an adolescent will opt for leisure reading over TV viewing during free time.

Finally, Figure 8.9 also illustrates how audio media increase in importance from the preteen to the late teen years. According to parent reports, audio media consume about 20 percent of young children's (2 to 7 years) media budget. As described in Chapter 5, 40 percent of young children's audio exposure consists of tapes of children's songs, nursery rhymes, and stories. The remaining 60 percent is spread across all of the remaining music genres – from classical to top 40 to rap – probably because that is what their parents or older siblings are listening to. By

8 to 10 years, however, children begin to control more of their own listening experience. Children's tapes tend to disappear from their audio diet, and music exposure increases from about an eighth (12%) of the media budget among 8- to 10-year-olds to a quarter (24%) among 11- to 14-year-olds to 39 percent among 15- to 18-year-olds. Among this oldest group, music comprises the largest single component of the overall media budget. In other words, as we argued in Chapter 5, by late adolescence music media become as important as television.

Several different factors probably contribute to the shifts in how older youths apportion media budgets. Earlier we noted that one of the most important is teenagers' increasing independence and mobility. As adolescents grow older, they spend less time with the immediate family and more with peer groups, less time at home and more time in school, at work, and in recreational settings. They also have more structured activities available to them than do younger children and preteens (e.g., organized sports, clubs, school social events, and part-time jobs). And, of course, many gain access to automobiles. The move away from home and toward peers and outside activities goes hand in hand with a decrease in overall media exposure. Figure 8.9 also reveals that the decrease is associated with a reapportionment of the overall media budget, particularly a decrease in the proportion of time devoted to television. In line with Larson and Kubey's (1983; Larson, Kubey & Colletti, 1989) evidence that TV viewing tends to be a family-oriented activity, as young people spend less time within the family context, it is not surprising to find that television takes less of their overall media time. Finally, we believe the reason overall media exposure drops no more than it does among the oldest youths is because of the growing importance of music media in adolescent lives (see Christenson & Roberts, 1998), in combination with the fact that more than any other media, audio media are frequently experienced in conjunction with myriad other adolescent activities. For most adolescents, music accompanies homework, socializing, driving, work – even other media activities such as reading and using a computer. Thus, not only does exposure to audio media increase throughout the preteen and teen years, but audio media begin to comprise a larger and larger part of the media budget because music provides the background for so much of adolescent life.

GENDER AND MEDIA BUDGETS

Gender differences in how children and adolescents apportion their media budgets are largely due to differences in time given to video games and

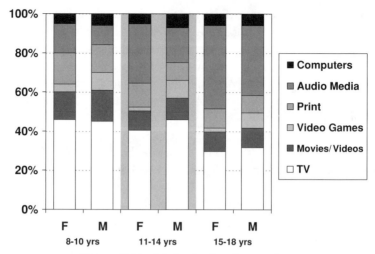

Figure 8.10. Media budget by gender.

audio media. These differences are less apparent among younger children. Among 2- to 4-year-olds, there are no statistically reliable gender differences. Among 5- to 7-year-olds, boys devote a higher proportion of media time to video games (7% vs. 2% among girls), and girls devote a higher proportion of their media time to audio media (20% vs. 16% among boys). Although small in absolute terms, these mean differences are statistically significant.

Figure 8.10 shows that these same patterns emerge even more strongly among older kids. Even though video games continue to represent a relatively small portion of the overall media budget, boys in all three age groups spend significantly more time with them than do girls (from 5% to 7% more). Similarly, as audio media come to claim a large share of adolescents' media budgets, the early trend showing girls spending more of their media time with them continues even more strongly. Among 8- to 10-year-olds, audio media claim 5 percent more of girls' than boys' media time; by 11 to 14 years, girls devote 30 percent of their media budget to music media, almost doubling the proportion given by boys. The difference narrows somewhat among 15- to 18-year-olds, when audio media clearly dominate the media budgets of both genders, and boys begin to catch up. Nevertheless, girls still spend 7 percent more of their media time with music. All of these differences are statistically significant (see Appendix 8.1).

It is tempting to speculate that these gender differences are related to the preponderance of sex-typed content associated with both video games and music. Many, perhaps most, video games follow action scenarios, dominated by violence, aggression, and intense competition (Calvert, 1999). Generally, these are content characteristics more likely to attract boys than girls. Conversely, the fundamental topic of most popular music is romance and love (Carey, 1969; Christenson & Roberts, 1998), content that usually has greater appeal to girls than boys, at least until later adolescence. Such media-specific content differences would seem to explain why boys give more time than girls to video games and why girls give more time than boys to music media.

RACE/ETHNICITY AND MEDIA BUDGETS

Race and ethnicity also locate substantial differences in how young people divide their media time. Figure 8.11 indicates that by far the largest difference in proportioning media time occurs for television. White children spend 40 percent of their media time with television; black and Hispanic children devote just over half of their media time to television (51% and 52%, respectively), a substantial difference. Conversely, white children give 5 percent more of their media budget to reading than do African American or Hispanic children. Young white children also spend more of their media time with computers and other screen media (videotapes and movies) than do black or Hispanic children. The differences are small but reliable. The difference in computer use probably stems from minority children's more limited home access to computers (see Chapter 3). The difference in proportion of media time given to

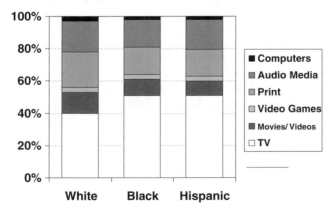

Figure 8.11. Media budget among 2- to 7-year-olds by race/ethnicity.

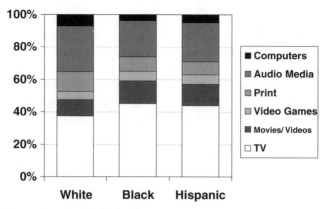

Figure 8.12. Media budget among 8- to 18-year-olds by race/ethnicity.

videotapes and movies is a bit more difficult to explain, especially since the pattern reverses among older youths. That is, among young children, other screen media make up more of white children's than black or Hispanic children's overall media budget, but among older youths the reverse is true. (Media budgets in relation to race or ethnicity within each of the narrower age groupings are similar; see Appendix 8.)

Figure 8.12 shows that 8- to 18-year-olds largely replicate the pattern found for younger children. That is, white preteens and teens continue to devote a significantly smaller proportion of their media time to television (37%) than do black (45%) and Hispanic (44%) preteens and teens, and larger proportions to reading and computer use. Additionally, white youths devote more of their media time to audio media. The single reversal of the pattern found for younger children is that already noted for other screen media; that is, 8- to 18-year-old white youths spend reliably less of their media time with videos and movies than do 8- to 18-year-old black youngsters.

With one major exception, when narrower age groupings are examined, the relationships between race or ethnicity and media budgets are roughly similar to those found for 2- to 7-year-olds and 8- to 18-year olds. The exception is 8- to 10-year-olds, among whom the differences in media budgets located by race or ethnicity seldom reach statistical significance (see Appendix 8).

SOCIOECONOMIC STATUS AND MEDIA BUDGETS

Both household income and level of parent education relate to media budgets much as they do to individual media. Figure 8.13 shows that

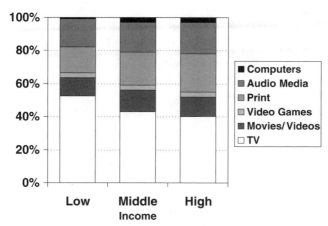

Figure 8.13. Media budget among 2- to 7-year-olds by income.

television commands a significantly larger share of the media budget of 2- to 7-year-olds from low-income homes than of their counterparts from either middle- or high-income homes. It also shows that the relationship is reversed for both reading and computer use. That is, young children from low-income homes spend significantly less of their total media time reading and using computers than do children from middle- or high-income homes. Some of the difference for computers probably is explained by differences in computer penetration as a function of income (see Chapter 3). This pattern holds for both the 2- to 4-year-old and 5- to 7-year-old subgroups, although the differences are statistically reliable only in the latter group (see Appendix 8).

Somewhat surprisingly given the negative relationship between household income and amount of TV viewing described in Chapter 4, among older youths the negative relationship between household income and proportion of media time devoted to television disappears. Figure 8.14 reveals that 8- to 18-year-olds from all three income groups give about 40 percent of their media budget to television, indicating that as they grow older, youths from low-income backgrounds decrease the proportion of media time they spend with the small screen. That is, youths from middle- and high-income households continue to devote about 40 percent of their media budget to television, just as they did during the early school years. Older youths from low-income backgrounds, on the other hand, give substantially less of their media time to television (40%) than do 2- to 7-year-olds from low-income backgrounds (53%). In other words, television's bite out of their media budget

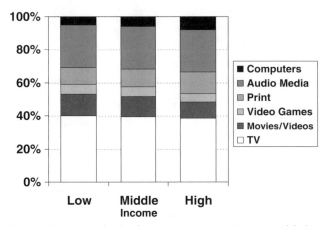

Figure 8.14. Media budget among 8- to 18-year-olds by income.

decreases, resulting in highly similar proportions of TV time across the three income groups.

Similar to the pattern for television, the significantly smaller proportion of media time that younger children from low-income communities devote to print also disappears among 8- to 18-year-olds. In this case, however, the parity in media time devoted to print derives from a somewhat greater drop in the proportion of media time spent with print media among middle- and high-income older children than among low-income children. Moreover, the print media differences take somewhat longer to disappear. Within the 8- to 10-year-old group, low-income children continue to read less than do their counterparts from middle- or high-income homes. It is only from 11 years onward that income-related differences fade away, and reading accounts for about 10 percent of the media budget of kids from all three income groupings.

Finally, even though computer time makes up a relatively small part of the overall media budget, youths from high-income households give significantly more of their media budget to the computer than do youths from low-income households. Again, this appears to be a reasonably straightforward function of the relationship between computer ownership and median community income level (see Chapter 3).

Several other income-related differences that warrant comment emerge when the narrower age groupings within the 8- to 18-year-old sample are examined. First, income locates a number of significant differences within the 8- to 10-year-old subgroup that, for the most part, disappear for 11- to 14-year-olds and 15- to 18-year-olds. For example, low-income 8- to 10-year-olds give more time to video games than do their middle-income counterparts, who in turn give more time to video games than do their high-income counterparts. No such differences occur within the two older age subgroupings. High-income 8- to 10-year-olds read significantly more than middle income 8- to 10-year-olds, but no differences in reading occur within the two older age subgroupings. Middle-income 8- to 10-year-olds give more media time to audio media and to videotapes and movies than do their high-income counterparts. Income locates no such differences among 11- to 14-year-olds; among 15- to 18-year-olds, low-income adolescents use the other screen media significantly more than either middle- or high-income adolescents and give less of their media time to music than do high-income adolescents. Finally, high-income 8- to 10-year-olds devote a greater portion of their media budget to computers than do low-income 8- to 10-year-olds, a pattern that disappears among the 11- to 14-year-old subgroup but reemerges among 15- to 18-year-olds (see Appendix 8).

Clearly, substantial differences in how youngsters apportion their media budgets are located by income level, but these differences occur primarily among younger and preteen children. Patterns that begin to emerge among 2- to 4-year-olds become statistically reliable among 5- to 7-year-olds and are largely continued among 8- to 10-year-olds. By early adolescence, however, most of the differences in media budgets located by income level dissipate or disappear. Again, we suspect that part of the explanation lies in adolescents' growing independence. As teens spend more of their time in settings other than the home, household characteristics related to income probably exert less influence on youths' media behavior.

Relationships between media budgets and level of parent education are roughly similar to those found for household income. In general, television consumes less of the media budget and print and computers more of the media budget as level of parent education increases. Figures 8.15 and 8.16 show that the proportion of time devoted to television accounts for the largest difference, particularly among 2- to 7-year-olds. Young children whose parents' education stopped at high school give significantly more of their media time to television (52%) than do those whose parents attended some college (45%; Fig. 8.15). In turn, children whose parents completed some college spend significantly more of their media budget on television than do those whose parents completed college (36%). Much the same pattern emerges for older youths,

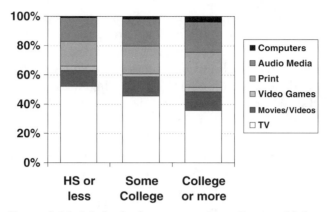

Figure 8.15. Media budget among 2- to 7-year-olds by parent education.

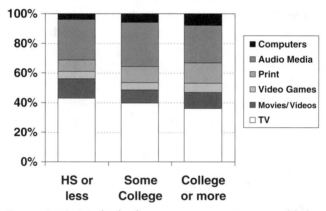

Figure 8.16. Media budget among 8- to 18-year-olds by parent education.

although the differences are not as pronounced (Fig. 8.16). That is, 8- to 18-year-olds whose parents' education stopped with high school give more of their media time to television (43%) than do youths whose parents attended some college (40%). These kids, in turn, devote more time to television than do kids whose parents graduated from college (36%).[6] Turning to print materials and to computers, 2- to 7-year-olds whose parents completed college devote more media time to reading and to using a computer than do either young kids whose parents have

---

[6] This latter difference, however, is not statistically reliable.

a high school education or less or those whose parents completed some college (Fig. 8.15). The pattern holds for 8- to 18-year-olds; the differences among all three education levels are statistically reliable for both media (Fig. 8.16). Finally, young children whose parents completed college spend more time with audio media than do children whose parents stopped with high school, a difference that does not emerge among 8- to 18-year-olds.

The same general patterns of relationships between parent education and media budgets are found within the narrower age groupings. That is, the inverse relationship between level of parent education and proportion of media time devoted to television holds for all five of the narrower age subgroupings, although the magnitude of the differences is somewhat smaller among the three older age groups (see Appendix 8). Similarly, parent education and the proportions of the total media budget given to both reading and computers are positively related within all five age groups. The differences between the low and high education subgroups are statistically reliable for all but the 15- to 18-year-olds' media time given to print (see Appendix 8). Indeed, it appears that the proportion of time kids with less educated parents spend with television is taken primarily from time that kids with more educated parents devote to reading and to computers. That the magnitude of the differences in time devoted to television and print is greater among younger children probably reflects parents' greater control over children's media behaviors during the early years. To the extent that encouragement of reading and/or discouragement of TV viewing is related to parents' education level, as evidence from both this study and previous research indicates (Bower, 1985; Medrich et al., 1982), it is not surprising that the influence of parent education declines as children grow older. Young people's increasing independence goes hand in hand with a decline in parental controls over media behavior regardless of education level, reducing or eliminating some of the differences related to parent education among younger children.

FAMILY COMPOSITION AND MEDIA BUDGETS

Although family composition is related to amount of media exposure, it is not particularly important to children's apportionment of media time. Similarly, even though number of parents is positively related to both household income and parent education, differences in media budgets located by those two indicators of socioeconomic status do not carry over to family composition. Regardless of whether the data are examined for the two larger age groupings or the five narrower age groupings, the only media category for which there is even a slight indication of a difference is media time devoted to computers. Among 5- to 7-year-olds, children living in single-parent households give 2 percent of their media time to computers, and children living in dual-parent households give 3 percent. Among 8- to 18-year-olds, youths from single-parent households give 5 percent of their media budget to computers, and youths from dual-parent households give 7 percent. Although these comprise very small parts of the overall budget, the difference is statistically significant for the younger group and approaches significance for the older group. Once again, we believe that computer penetration and its relationship to socioeconomic status probably explains most of the tiny difference that exists. The most notable result of our examination of media budgets in relation to family composition, then, is how little young people's budgeting of media time is related to whether they live with one parent or two.

RESIDENCE LOCALE AND MEDIA BUDGETS

Whether young people live in urban, suburban, or rural settings also is only modestly related to how they distribute their media time. The single statistically reliable difference occurs for the proportion of the media budget that 2- to 7-year-olds give to television. Within this younger group, suburban children spend substantially less of their media time with television (40%) than do rural children (50%); urban children fall between (46%). Two other differences approach statistical significance among these younger children: rural kids devote a slightly lower portion of media time than do suburban kids to videos and movies, and slightly less than either urban or suburban kids to audio media. We suspect that these findings for younger rural children speak to their lesser access to movie theaters and video rental outlets, and possibly to a smaller array of radio stations. There are no differences in how 8- to 18-year-olds living in different environments apportion their media budgets.

CHAPTER NINE

Media Behavior: A Youth Perspective

The preceding chapters have looked at young people's media behavior from a "mediacentric" perspective. That is, we have focused on each individual medium (and on media overall), exploring their roles in children's and adolescents' lives. Our perspective changes somewhat in this chapter. Rather than beginning with media, we begin with the young people themselves, then explore how their attitudes, abilities, and actions are related to their media behaviors. In the following pages we examine such things as whether and how social adjustment or "contentedness" and academic performance relate to media behavior. We also compare heavy and light media users and examine the degree to which high exposure to one medium relates to amount of exposure to other media. Finally, we report the results of an analysis conducted to determine whether 8- to 18-year-olds can be classified into different "types" of media users.

Personal Contentedness and Media Use

A negative relationship between media consumption and various conceptualizations of social satisfaction or contentedness or "affective equilibrium" has long been noted, to the point that "greater-than-ordinary use of pictorial media such as television arguably has become recognized as a possible symptom of personal maladjustment" (Comstock, 1991, p. 33). Several early studies of young people's TV use found that children and adolescents having difficulties with parents or friends devote more time to television than do better adjusted youngsters (Johnston, 1974; Maccoby, 1954; Schramm et al., 1961; Tangney, 1988). Similar relationships have also been reported for young people's VCR usage

(Morgan, Alexander, Shanahan, & Harris, 1990) and for adolescents' music consumption (Christenson & Roberts, 1998; Lyle & Hoffman, 1972a). Finally, there is evidence that adults and older adolescents use media for mood management – to escape unpleasant emotions and/or maintain satisfying mood states (Kubey, 1986; Kubey & Czikszentmihalyi, 1990; Zillmann, 1988).

To determine whether a relationship between media use and contentedness still holds, we included a small battery of items assessing the degree to which young people or their parents view themselves or their children as well adjusted or contented. Parents of 2- to 7-year-olds indicated how well each of the following four statements characterize their child:

- My child has trouble getting along with other children.
- My child is cooperative and well-behaved.
- My child is usually active and interested in his/her surroundings.
- My child is often sad and unhappy.

Response options included "a lot like," "somewhat like," "not much like," and "not at all like" him or her. Older youths (8 to 18 years) used the same response options to characterize themselves on six items:

- I have a lot of friends.
- I get along well with my parents.
- I am often bored.
- I often feel sad and unhappy.
- I have been happy at school this year.
- I get into trouble a lot.

Items were summed to create an index on which higher scores indicate higher levels of contentment or social adjustment.

Scores on the index for young children are highly skewed toward the positive end (highly contented). On a scale ranging from 4 to 16 with a midpoint of 10, obtained scores ranged from 6 to 16 with a mean of 14.7 and a median of 15. Not surprisingly, given that almost all parents rate their child as happy and well-adjusted, contentedness scores for younger children are unrelated to any of our measures of media. These results serve primarily as testimony to the fact that in any but the most extreme cases, asking parents about their young children's interior feelings and emotions is risky at best.

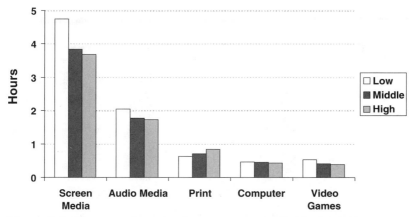

Figure 9.1. Contentedness and exposure to individual media among 8- to 18-year-olds.

Contentedness scores for 8- to 18-year-olds also skew in the positive direction, but to a far lesser degree. The six-item index could range from a low of 6 to a high of 24 with a midpoint of 15; actual scores range from 9 to 24, with a mean of 18.9 and a median of 19.[1] Thus, it is important to keep in mind that the large majority of youths participating in this study rate themselves as generally contented and well adjusted; any differences located by contentedness scores are *relative* differences among generally happy kids. To illustrate the relationships between contentedness scores and media exposure more conveniently, we created a three-level "contentedness index," classifying youths roughly one standard deviation below (19% of respondents) and above (18% of respondents) the mean as low-contented and high-contented, respectively. The remaining 63 percent are classified as moderately contented. This contentedness index grouping (low, middle, high) is used to examine amount of media exposure and several other features of the media environment.[2]

Figure 9.1 illustrates the relationship between level of contentedness and amount of exposure to each of the various media. For all but print, contentedness is inversely related to media exposure. That is, the

---

[1] Appendix 9.1 presents intercorrelations among the six items used in the contentedness index. Chronbach's alpha for the six-item index is .52.

[2] Correlation coefficients presented in Appendix 9.1 summarize relationships between overall contentedness scores and media exposure.

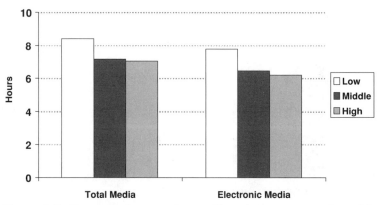

Figure 9.2. Contentedness and overall media use among 8- to 18-year-olds.

least contented youths report more media exposure than those scoring moderate or high on the contentedness index (differences for screen media, audio media, and video games are statistically significant; see Appendix 9.2). The pattern reverses for print media; less contented youth spend significantly less time with print than do either moderately or highly contented youth. The accumulation of all of these differences is striking. Figure 9.2, which presents both total recreational media exposure and total electronic media exposure (that is, total exposure minus print exposure) as a function of the contentedness index, leaves little question that young people's level of contentedness or adjustment is strongly related to media consumption. Youths scoring in the lowest 19 percent on the contentedness index are exposed to 1½ hours per day more of electronic media than are those who scored in the highest 18 percent and to 1¼ hours more than those classed as moderately contented. Conversely, they spend about ¼ hour per day less than highly contented youth with print media (see Appendix 9.2).

Contentedness scores also relate to gender (girls score higher on contentedness than boys), level of parent education (youths whose parents completed at least some college score higher), and family composition (kids who live with two parents are more contented than those who live with one parent). Nevertheless, when these variables are held constant, the overall negative relationship between the contentedness index and media use is largely unaffected. For example, when youths from each level of parent education are examined separately, low-contented kids continue to use media more than moderately contented or

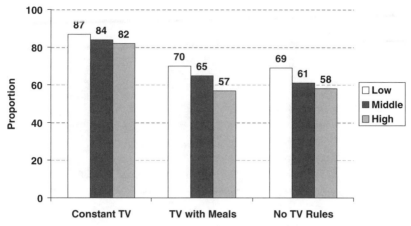

Figure 9.3. Contentedness and household TV orientation among 8- to 18-year-olds.

high-contented kids regardless of level of parent education. Similarly, the findings for contentedness hold when girls and boys are examined separately (see Appendix 9.2).

Contentedness is also related to several measures of household TV orientation (see Chapter 3). Figure 9.3 shows the likelihood of living in a constant TV household declines slightly as contentedness increases, although none of the differences is significant. On the other hand, less contented youths are significantly more likely than either moderate- or high-contented youths to live in homes where the television operates during meals, and significantly less likely to live in homes with rules about TV viewing. In other words, 8- to 18-year-olds scoring in the bottom 19 percent on contentedness are more likely to live in what we have labeled "TV-oriented" households.

Results of these analyses converge with those from earlier work showing a negative relationship between young people's level of satisfaction with life (i.e., "contentedness") and media use. Youngsters who express less contentment use media more than those who express more contentment, with the caveat that most of the youths in our sample produced relatively high contentedness scores. Because these are correlational data, they do not directly address whether less contented youths turn to media to escape their troubles, whether heavy media use engenders higher levels of discontent, or whether some third variable is at work. However, if we conceive of one dimension of escaping from troubles

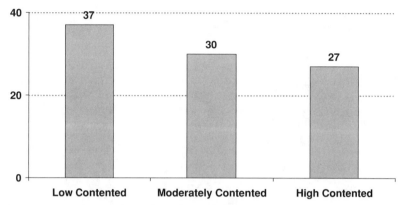

Figure 9.4. Proportion of total TV viewing "mainly alone" by contentedness among 8- to 18-year-olds.

as avoidance of social contact, then there is at least tentative evidence
that unhappiness may engender media use rather than the reverse. That
is, if we assume one of the attractions of media for unhappy kids is that
they facilitate "being alone," then discontented kids should spend more
time than contented kids viewing television alone. Recall that 8- to
18-year-olds indicated both amount of TV exposure and whether or not
they viewed "mainly" alone or with someone else for each of three day
parts. This information enables a rough calculation of both the amount
of solitary TV exposure and the proportion of total exposure accounted
for while viewing alone.[3] Looking first at amount of solitary exposure,
on a typical day, low-contented youths spend significantly more time
watching television alone than do those from either the middle- or
high-contented groups. Low-contented kids average 1:29 daily watching television while alone; those in the middle group watch alone 1:08
daily; and the most contented kids watch alone for 53 minutes daily.
Finally, as Figure 9.4 shows, when these numbers are taken as a proportion of each youngster's total TV exposure, kids in the low-contented
group spend a significantly higher mean proportion of all TV time viewing alone. While not conclusive, results such as these tend to support
the idea that media provide a means of escaping from unhappiness or

[3] These calculations are only rough approximations; any indication that viewing
  during a day part was "mainly alone" resulted in all time for that day part being
  counted as "alone" even though such responses might include anywhere from 51%
  to 100% of time for that day part.

discontent. Whether or not such an escape is functional, of course, is another question. And, of course, it is also possible that being alone for whatever reason independently mediates both lower contentedness scores and more TV viewing.

ACADEMIC PERFORMANCE AND MEDIA USE

Negative relationships between media exposure and various measures of young people's academic performance have been reported for television (cf. Comstock, 1991; Neuman, 1988, 1995; Williams, Haertel, Hartel, & Walberg, 1982), music media (Burk & Grinder, 1966; Larson & Kubey, 1983; also see Christenson & Roberts, 1998), and more recently, for video games and computer games (Harris & Williams, 1985; Lieberman, Chaffee, & Roberts, 1988; Lin & Lepper, 1987). However, Comstock and Scharrer (1999) note that the relationships vary depending on the sample, the measures, and various individual and social characteristics of the youths surveyed (also see Comstock, 1991; Neuman, 1995), and that whether and how media exposure affects scholastic performance is still hotly debated. (On the basis of their extensive review of the research literature, however, Comstock and Scharrer also conclude that there is a distinct, albeit small, negative effect of viewing on scholastic performance.)

Lacking access to official grade-point averages, we asked 8- to 18-year-olds to report what grades they typically earn in school. Response options included "mostly A's," "mostly A's and B's," "mostly B's," "mostly B's and C's," and "mostly D's and F's." Although there is legitimate concern that such self-reports produce inflated grade estimates, earlier work found a substantial positive relationship ($r = .77$) between self-reported grades and actual grade-point average (Dornbusch, Ritter, Liederman, Roberts, & Fraleigh, 1987). Results for this question are, in fact, skewed toward the high end. Of the 1,886 school kids who reported their "typical" grades,[4] 61 percent claimed mostly A's or A's and B's, 32 percent indicated they typically earned mostly B's and mostly B's and C's, and 7 percent said mostly C's and mostly D's and F's. We are relatively confident that the two lower grade categories accurately reflect earned grades, but we suspect that the highest category probably represents considerable grade inflation. Such grade inflation, however,

---

[4] Thirty youths gave no answer and 97 youths attend schools that do not give grades.

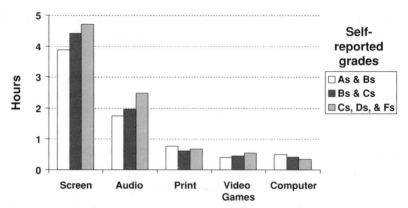

Figure 9.5. Average exposure to five types of media by scholastic performance among 8- to 18-year-olds.

should operate to reduce any differences found among youths in the
three grade classifications. That is, to the extent that media exposure is
negatively related to scholastic performance, differences in exposure between high and low achievement groups will be reduced to the extent
that poor students inflate their grades, placing themselves in a higher
grade category.

Figure 9.5 shows that statistically significant relationships between
academic performance and exposure emerge for all media but video
games. The relationship is negative for television and audio media, with
the weakest students reporting substantially more exposure to both. The
pattern is reversed for print and computer exposure, although the differences are not nearly as large as those for television and audio. That is,
weaker students report using print and computers less than do stronger
students. When exposure to individual media is combined into a measure either of overall leisure media exposure or of electronic media exposure (i.e., print media exposure is not included),[5] the negative relationship between academic performance and media exposure is striking.
Figure 9.6 shows that students reporting mostly A's or mostly A's and B's
spend about an hour and a half less daily with media (all media and just
electronic media) than students reporting mostly C's through mostly D's
and F's.

---

[5] Since, unlike exposure to all other media, print exposure is positively related to
grades, for this analysis it makes sense to look at media exposure with reading time
removed.

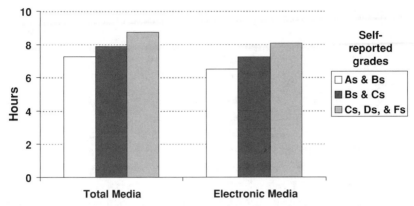

Figure 9.6. Average total media exposure by scholastic performance among 8- to 18-year-olds.

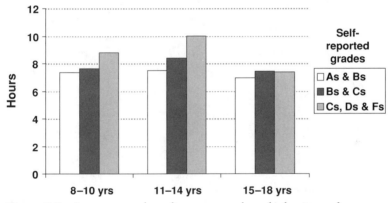

Figure 9.7. Average total media exposure by scholastic performance and age among 8- to 18-year-olds.

As Comstock and Scharrer (1999) have argued, however, the negative relationship between academic performance and media exposure may not be quite so straightforward as it first appears. For example, when we examine media exposure and self-reported grades as a function of age, as is the case in Figure 9.7, the relationship is statistically significant only for 11- to 14-year-olds. Among 8- to 10-year-olds the relationship is negative but not statistically significant; among 15- to 18-year-olds it all but disappears. In other words, the differences that emerge for the total sample are primarily due to 11- to 14-year-olds, among whom the difference in total media exposure between the strongest and weakest students exceeds 2 ½ hours daily. The point is that the relationship between academic performance and media exposure depends on age in ways that are not immediately obvious when the total sample is examined as a group.

Additional analyses looking at the relationship between academic performance and media exposure as a function of other variables also produce mixed results (see Appendix 9.3). Although the general pattern (i.e., lower grades associated with higher media exposure) holds for gender, parent education, and number of parents in the household, controlling for other variables changes the results. For example, holding race or ethnicity constant shows that African American youths who earn the highest grades report the most media exposure, and those with moderate grades the least, and that Hispanic youths with moderate grades use media the least. Holding income constant reveals a curvilinear relationship among youths from high-income homes. That is, B and C students use media over an hour more per day than either those reporting A's and B's or those reporting C's through F's. Similarly, youths from suburban areas who earn mostly B's and C's use media almost an hour a day more than either those who report A's and B's or those who report C's, D's, and F's. At the same time, in both analyses the more typical negative relationship between grades and media exposure holds for low and middle-income youths and for rural and urban youths. Once again, our data do not enable us to examine whether poor academic performance drives young people to use media more, whether heavy media use leads to poor academic performance, or whether some other variable accounts for either or both phenomena. Clearly, however, the frequent observation that children and adolescents who are not doing well in school tend to use screen and audio media more than their counterparts who are earning good grades is supported once again. That said, it is also apparent that the first-order relationship is modified by a number of third variables, including age, race/ethnicity, parent income, and residence locale, providing further evidence for the complexity to which Comstock and Scharrer (1999) point.

HEAVY VERSUS LIGHT MEDIA USERS

Several early studies of the introduction of television in the United States noted that much of the time children gave to the new medium was taken from other media such as movies and radio (Maccoby, 1951;

Schramm et al., 1961).[6] However, Coffin (1955) also found that the decrease in use of other media accounted for no more than 50 percent of the time given to television, and Weiss (1969) concluded that much of the time given to television came from other, nonmedia activities and from simultaneous use of more than one medium. Mutz, Roberts and van Vuuren (1993) trace a long history of "displacement" studies – research examining whether and how TV use "displaces" use of other media as well as nonmedia activities – and conclude that the nature and degree of displacement depends on how the phenomenon is measured. For example, Neuman (1995) states that the introduction of television "shattered" the movie industry because of the ensuing aggregate decline in movie attendance (from 82 million weekly in 1946 to 36 million in 1955). However, she also notes that the teen audience did not decrease all that much, primarily because of the social function movies serve for adolescents but not adults. Mutz and her colleagues (1993) also demonstrate that when individuals are followed over time immediately following the introduction of television, for many of them a substantial portion of the initial decrease in time spent with other media returns to near former levels. This occurs sometimes because audience members discover that "older" media serve functions not addressed by new media (e.g., movie attendance serves a social function for teenagers), sometimes because older media reorganize themselves (e.g., radio formats changed from variety and drama to music and talk), and sometimes because individuals use several media simultaneously (e.g., most teenagers listen to music while reading). For all these reasons, there is something of a sense of déjà vu in recent claims that computers and the Internet are "displacing" older media (e.g., Kane, 2001; Klein, 2001; UCLA, 2000, 2001). We suspect that the continuing evolution of the computer and Internet into a kind of central information/entertainment utility will render the question moot. Internet use will be synonymous with listening to radio, watching television, and/or reading a newspaper or magazine. In the interim, however, the current study provides a unique opportunity to examine how various kinds of media use relate to each other. Do heavy users of one medium ignore others? Is watching a great deal of television synonymous with reading very little, as some critics claim (Postman, 1985; Winn, 1985)? Now that personal computers have been around for some time, have kids

---

[6] Wilbur Schramm (1945) began to shape the question in an early study of college students' reading and radio-listening patterns.

who spend a great deal of time with them turned away from other media?

We address these questions by classifying 8- to 18-year-olds as high, moderate, or low users of print media, of television, and of computers on the basis of the previous day's exposure, then examining their exposure to each of the other media as well as their total media time (excluding time spent with the classification medium). A straightforward displacement hypothesis predicts that youngsters who spend a great deal of time with one medium – for example, computers – will report less time with other, ostensibly competing media, and with the total of all competing media. Conversely, it implies that low users of any of these three media are likely to spend more time with the other media than do their counterparts who are classified as high users.

Ideally, we would define the low- and high-exposure groups as the bottom and top 15 percent of children on amount of previous-day print, TV, and computer exposure (approximately 1 standard deviation above and below the mean). However, both the obtained distributions of exposure time for each medium and the logic of our questions dictated different cut-off points. For example, we use zero exposure to define the low group for computers because 53 percent of youths reported no previous-day use. On the other hand, since prior research indicates that 1 hour per day of TV exposure is relatively low (cf. Comstock, 1991; Comstock & Scharrer, 1999), we define low-TV exposure as 1 hour even though 16 percent of the sample report no previous-day exposure. Table 9.1 presents the number and proportion of youths who fell into each exposure group for each of the three media, as well as the cut-off points (i.e., absolute amount of exposure) used to make the assignments. For example, youths who watched an hour or less of television are classed as low users; those who watched more than 5 hours are high users. Similarly, youths who did not read or use a computer the previous day are low users and those who reported more than 1 hour of reading or computer time are high users.

Figure 9.8 presents total exposure time to all media *excluding* the one used to classify the youths. That is, the first set of bars shows how much time low, moderate, and high readers devote to all *nonprint* media; the second set shows how much time low-, moderate-, and high-TV viewers devote to all media *other than television*; and the third set shows how much time low-, moderate-, and high-computer users spend with all media *other than computers*. We present results for all three media in one figure because much the same story applies to all three. Clearly,

Table 9.1. *Number and Percentage of 8- to 18-Year-Olds in the Low-, Moderate-, and High-Exposure Groups for Print, Television, and Computers*

	Classification	Number	%
Print media			
None (0)	Low	408	20
5 min. to 1 hour	Moderate	1183	59
More than 1 hour	High	422	21
Television			
1 hour or less	Low	657	33
1+ to 5 hours	Moderate	918	45
More than 5 hours	High	439	22
Computer			
None (0)	Low	1148	57
5 min. to 1 hour	Moderate	586	29
More than 1 hour	High	279	14

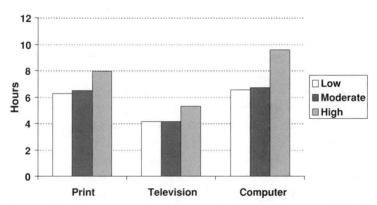

Figure 9.8. Average media exposure by low, moderate and high use of three media among 8- to 18-year-olds. For each average, time spent with the medium on which youths are classified as low, moderate, or high has been omitted. Thus, high-television users spend 5 ½ hours with media excluding television.

high exposure to any one of these three media goes with high exposure to other media. In all three instances, the difference between the low- and high-exposure groups is large and highly significant. Youths in the high-TV group report about 1¼ hours more daily use of other media than do kids in the low-TV group. Those in the high-print group exceed low-print users by almost 1¾ hours, and youths classified as high-computer users spend 3 hours per day more with other media than do those who did not use a computer the previous day. Moreover, with but two exceptions, the overall pattern of high use of one medium going with high use of all other media also holds for each of the individual media. That is, exposure to print does not vary significantly in relation to low-, moderate-, and high-TV exposure; exposure to audio media does not vary significantly in relation to low-, moderate-, and high-print exposure (although the means are still in the right direction). Indeed, only one of the 15 comparisons among individual media tabulated breaks the overall pattern. Youths classified as low-TV users spend more time with radio than do those classed as high in TV exposure (see Appendix 9.4).

Each of these analyses was also conducted controlling for the various demographic variables we have been considering. For the most part, such controls fail to change the overall pattern of results. That is, regardless of age, gender, socioeconomic status, or race and ethnicity, youths classified in the high-exposure categories for each of the three media (print, television, and computers) generally report more exposure to other media than do their low- and moderate-exposure counterparts.

Rather than high use of one medium displacing time spent with other media, then, it appears that media use begets media use. That is, high exposure to print, television, or computers goes hand in hand with more exposure to most other media. On the other hand, it is also important to note that it is unusual for a young person to be classified as a high user of more than one medium. Only 4 percent to 5 percent of 8- to 18-year-olds are high users of two media, and fewer than 2 percent are high users of all three. Thus, although the highest users of print, television, or computers report more exposure to other media relative to low users of each of the three media, very few of the highest users of one medium are also among the highest users of another. This may indicate some validity for a displacement explanation.

It is also interesting to note that if "moderate" exposure is taken as a baseline, youngsters in the high-exposure group account for most of the obtained differences. That is, for all three comparisons, the low and moderate groups differ little in amount of exposure to "other" media; the difference ranges from less than 1 minute between low- and moderate-TV users to 16 minutes between low- and moderate-print users. In other words, low exposure to any of the three comparison media does not go hand in hand with low exposure to other media. Youths in the

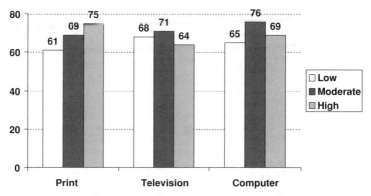

Figure 9.9. Proportion of low, moderate and high 8- to 18-year-old users of three media earning good grades (defined as respondents selecting "mostly A's and B's" or "mostly A's" when asked what their grades are).

low-exposure groups look very much like those who make up the moderate-exposure groups. Rather, the action lies with those kids who define themselves as belonging to a high-exposure group. They are clearly different.

Pursuing this difference theme a bit further, Figure 9.9 graphs the proportion of youths in each of the exposure classifications claiming to earn mostly A's and B's. The pattern for print media exposure makes the most sense. That is, assuming that print is the "academic" medium, it is not surprising that print exposure and academic achievement go hand-in-hand; a substantially higher proportion of high-print than of low-print kids claim to earn mostly A's and B's. The pattern is partially reversed for TV exposure. That is, fewer high-TV kids earn A's and B's, but it is moderate- rather than low-TV kids who report the highest grades. Finally, youths classed as moderate-computer users are more likely than those classed as low-computer users to earn high grades, with high users falling between. In other words, good grades (i.e., mostly A's and B's) are more likely among kids who read a lot, among kids who watch a moderate amount of television, and among those who spend a moderate amount of time with a computer. They are least likely among kids who watch a great deal of television (in excess of 5 hours daily), and among those who spend little or no time reading.

A similar kind of pattern emerges when we examine a young person's classification as a low, moderate, or high user of print, television, or computers in relation to scores on the contentedness index. Overall, 19 percent of the youths in our sample fell into the low group on the contentedness index. However, youths who spend a great deal of time reading are less likely than those who spend no time reading be in the low contented group (15% vs. 25%). Conversely, kids who spend more than 5 hours daily watching television are more likely than those who watch an hour or less to score low in contentment (25% vs. 15%). Finally, fewer moderate-computer users (15%) than high-computer users (23%) fall into the low contentedness group. In other words, high-TV viewers are more likely and high readers are less likely to express discontent about their personal and social lives (see Appendix 9.4).

A TYPOLOGY OF YOUNG PEOPLE'S MEDIA BEHAVIOR

Joe is a preteen media hound. He uses media every spare moment, often several at once, and has access to just about all forms of media – most of them in his bedroom. His home is very promedia, with the television often on in the background and during meals. Joe's a pretty happy guy, has a lot of friends, generally gets along with his parents, and earns pretty good grades. Jill is a teenage girl also has access to most media and lives in a promedia environment with few rules about television and the television often on during meals. Jill, however, spends very little time with media. She is occupied with other activities and interests such as seeing her friends, dating, and playing sports. Do either of these kids sound familiar?

Other chapters in this book explore differences in media use or access based on one or two characteristics at a time. Here, we use a statistical technique called cluster analysis to attempt to make sense of a number of variables at once. Cluster analysis is a procedure that classifies a large number of cases into relatively homogeneous groups (clusters) on the basis of information about whatever variables are of interest – in this case, information about young people's media environments and media exposure. Cluster analysis enables construction of "media types," grouping youths so that the degree of association among classification variables is strong among individuals within the cluster and relatively weak between members of different clusters. The analysis is limited to older children, because by 8 years, media use is more self-directed and usually reflects a youth's active choices and decisions.

We use six media-related variables or indices to create distinct groups of media types. The six include: (1) number of media in the home,

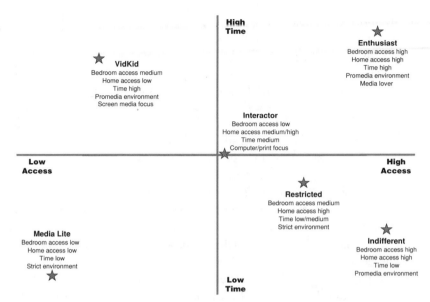

Figure 9.10. Media use Clusters.

(2) number of media the youngster's bedroom, (3) number of televisions in the home, (4) three household TV orientation items (see Chapter 3) and the proportion of time spent watching television alone, (5) number of different media a child uses, and (6) total amount of media exposure. These variables successfully pinpoint differences in media behaviors and environments, and classify youths into six distinct media clusters.[7]

Figure 9.10 plots the six clusters that emerge from our analysis in relation to axes representing amount of media exposure and accessibility provided by the media environment, and displays the "media-type" labels we have attached to each cluster. Thus, for example, the cluster in the upper left quadrant comprises youths with relatively low media access, who live in a "promedia" environment (e.g., no rules about television or constant television), and who spend a lot of time with media, especially screen media. We call them *VidKids*. Those in the center cluster have high access to media in their homes but not in their bedrooms and report an average amount media exposure, particularly time with

[7] While several different cluster solutions were considered, the final solution was chosen for its effectiveness in producing cohesive groups of a reasonable size with meaningful differences. Discriminate analysis shows that 95.6% of the original grouped cases are correctly classified.

print and computers. These we name *Interactors*. Those in the lower right-hand quadrant are high in access but low in media exposure. They are labeled *Indifferents*.

Once youths were assigned to clusters, the clusters were compared on the basis of the various demographic and media-related variables we have been examining throughout this book. For example, we looked at the proportion of each cluster that is male and female, or that is 8 to 10 years versus 11 to 14 years, and so on. Similarly, we looked at the proportion of youths in each cluster who used each medium the preceding day, the average amount of time devoted to each medium, the proportion of youths in each group who live in households with rules about TV viewing, and so on. The characteristics of the youths comprising each cluster were then examined with an eye to developing a "media type" label for each group, and a brief characterization of the youths in that group. All of the comparisons are tabulated in Appendix 9.5.[8] In addition, several of the variables that seem most germane to our discussion of the various clusters because they strongly differentiate one or more media types from the others are presented graphically. Figure 9.11 displays the proportion of youths in each cluster with home and bedroom access to computers and the Internet. Figure 9.12 shows the proportion of youths in each cluster who watch television, movies (in a theater or on videotape), play video games, or use a computer on any given day. Finally, Figure 9.13 illustrates the average amount of time youths in each cluster devote to all media, to television, to computers, and to print. This information provided the basis for the labels attached to and the characterizations of the following six media types: *Media Lite, Interactor, VidKid, Restricted, Indifferent*, and *Enthusiast*.

MEDIA LITE (18% OF 8- TO 18-YEAR-OLDS)

These youths spend the least amount of time with media and are among the least likely to use any one medium on any given day. The time they do devote to media is spent primarily with television, music, and print. Their low media exposure may be explained by their lower access and more restrictive media environments. *Media Lites* are among the least

---

[8] Numbers in the "total" column in the appendix may differ slightly from numbers reported in other chapters for 8- to 18-year-olds because of handling of missing cases.

Home Access to a Computer

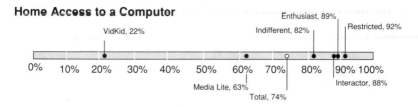

Home Access to the Internet

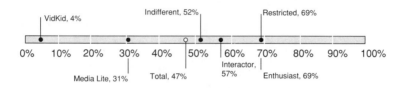

Bedroom Access to a Computer

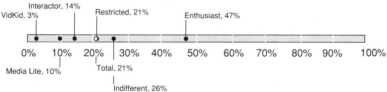

Bedroom Access to the Internet

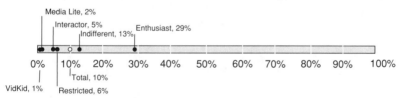

Figure 9.11. Proportion of each media type with home and bedroom access to a computer and the Internet.

likely to have access to various media in their homes or bedrooms; they average 2.2 televisions in the home, compared with the overall average of 3.1. *Media Lite* kids are among the most likely to report household rules about television and the least likely to report having constant television, television during meals, or spending more than half of their TV time alone. Media exposure seems to be a deliberate choice among these kids. They are the most likely to report watching one TV show at a time, rather than channel surfing or switching between two programs.

Watched TV (including prerecorded TV)

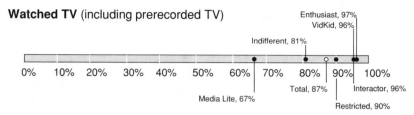

Watched Movies (in theater or on tape)

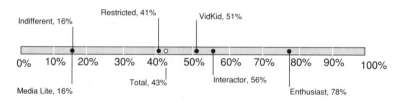

Played Video Games

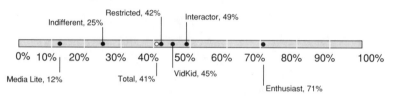

Used a Computer for Enjoyment

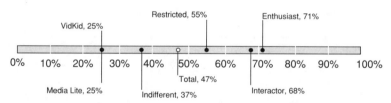

Figure 9.12. Proportion of each media type who watch television or movies, play video games, or use a computer for enjoyment.

They are among the least likely to claim many friends, but are the most likely to report getting along well with parents, being happy at school, and getting good grades.

Media Lite youths tend to be younger, and are slightly more likely to be female; they may be those youngsters on whom parents still keep a close eye. They are slightly more likely to be white and less likely to be African American. On other variables such as parent education

Average Time with Recreational Media

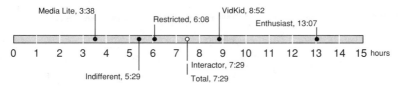

Average Time with TV (including prerecorded TV)

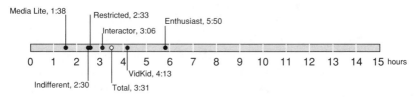

Average Time with Computers for Enjoyment

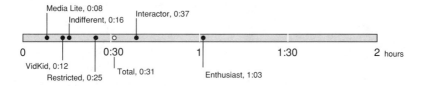

Average Time Reading

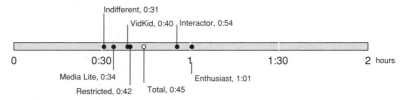

Figure 9.13. Average media exposure for youths of each cluster.

and income, they are relatively representative of kids throughout the nation.

INTERACTOR (16% OF 8- TO 18-YEAR-OLDS)

Interactors embrace computers. They are less likely than most kids to have access to various media in their bedrooms, but they are among the most likely to have computer and Internet access at home. These youths spend an average amount of time with media overall, but they are more avid users of print media and the computer than most. *Interactors* are more likely than other media types to use a computer or read on any given day, and they spend more time with these two media. They are among the most likely to report that computers are entertaining and the least likely to say they use them just to kill time.

Interactors spend about the average time playing video games. Television does not seem to be a strong force in their lives. They are less likely than most to live in a "constant TV household" or to have the television on during meals, but their parents are neither more nor less likely to have rules about television than the average household. Demographically, 51 percent of *Interactors* are boys, and their average age is 12 years 10 months. They are more likely to be white, to go to school in middle or high-income areas, and to have parents with a college education.

VIDKID (15% OF 8- TO 18-YEAR-OLDS)

Other than *Enthusiasts* (see below), *VidKids* spend the most time with media, with television and taped television accounting for nearly half their media exposure. They spend more time than most other types with television, movies, videotapes, video games, and music, but less time than most with computers. They are about average in reading time. *VidKids*, along with *Media Lites*, are least likely to use a computer for recreation on a given day, perhaps because of their low access to a computer at home. While only about two in 10 report in-home access to a computer, 70 percent have a video-game console. Although their bedroom access to most media is average or below average, almost three in four *VidKids* have their own television. Indeed, television is a constant presence in their lives; 91 percent report the television is usually on during meals, and 59 percent say that the television is on "most of the time." Only one in four *VidKids* live in homes that have rules about watching television. They are more likely than most others to find television entertaining and to report learning interesting things from television.

Almost half of *VidKids* are minority youths, with 21 percent Hispanic and 24 percent black. They are slightly more likely to be girls, and moderately more likely to come from single-parent homes. They are less likely than most to earn good grades, and they are the media type most likely to have parents who completed no more than a high school education.

RESTRICTED (15% OF 8- TO 18-YEAR-OLDS)

Restricted kids live in the most controlled media environments of any of the media types. Not surprisingly, they spend a little less than the average amount of time with media. *Restricteds* are the least likely to live in a "constant TV home," the least likely to have the television on during meals, and among the least likely to spend more than half of their TV time alone. They are also the most likely to have rules about television. *Restricteds* have about average access to media in their bedrooms, but high access in their homes. Indeed, they have the highest number of TVs in their homes, averaging 4.2. They are also the most likely of all groups to have a computer at home, and they report above-average access to most other media. Nevertheless, these kids are exposed to almost 1½ hours per day less media content than the average young person, reporting just over 6 hours of exposure. Although they do not spend a great deal of time with media overall, they typically use more than four different kinds of media on any given day, and are more likely than average to use computers and audio media.

Restricteds are more likely to be white, slightly more likely to be boys, and nearly half fall into the 11- to 14-year age category. They are the least likely to be from single-parent homes, and among the most likely to have college-educated parents, live in suburban areas, and to go to school in the wealthiest neighborhoods. They are the most likely of all media types to report good grades.

INDIFFERENT (18% OF 8- TO 18-YEAR-OLDS)

Although they have some of highest, best access to media both in their bedrooms and in their homes and live in some of the least restrictive media environments, *Indifferent* kids spend less time with media than most youths, 2 hours less than the overall average. Nine out of ten *Indifferents* have a television in their bedroom, and over one in four have a computer in their room. Their home access to media is also above average. They are the least likely to have controls on their TV use (only 14% have rules) and are the most likely to report spending more than half of their TV time alone. Additionally, they are among the most likely to report that the television is on "most of the time" and during meals. In spite of all this, they report a total of 5½ hours of media exposure daily, less than any other group except *Media Lites*, and they spend among the least amount of time with each individual medium.

Though spending less time than average, *Indifferents* appear to be most interested in music media; on any given day they are more likely to listen to music than to use any other medium. Television still plays a role in their lives, however. They are almost as likely to watch television as to listen to music, although they spend well below the overall average time watching. Some 83 percent of *Indifferents* are between 11 and 18 years, with a mean age of 13½ years. Given their low interest in media, it is not surprising that this group contains more older adolescents, those kids who spend more of their time engaged in nonmedia activities such as sports, dating, social gatherings, and part-time jobs. *Indifferents* are the most likely to be an only child, are slightly more likely to live in suburban areas, and tend to earn good grades. Not surprisingly, *Indifferents* are the least likely to report learning interesting things from television, and are among the most likely to report having a lot of friends. We suspect that much of their "indifference" to the media is a function of their interest and participation in a wide variety of other, nonmedia activities.

ENTHUSIAST (19% OF 8- TO 18-YEAR-OLDS)

Enthusiasts are avid media users, reporting far and away the most media exposure and living in the richest media environments. They are the most likely to use almost every medium, and they spend more time with almost every medium than any other kids. Enthusiasts report over 13 hours of media exposure daily, with more than half of their media time devoted to television and music media. They have some of the best home access to virtually all media. Nearly all (96%) *Enthusiasts* have a television in their bedroom, and almost half (47%) have their own computer. They are the most likely to report that they live in constant TV households, 76% say that the television is usually on during meals, and just three in 10 report that they have rules about television. *Enthusiasts* are the most likely of all media types to say that television and the computer are entertaining most of the time and that they learn interesting things from television and computers. They are also the most likely to report mainly channel surfing (rather than mainly watching one or two shows at a time) when they watch television. More *Enthusiasts* than youths from the other media types report having a lot of friends and that being sad and unhappy is *not* a good description of them. On the other hand, they are the least likely to report getting along well with their parents or to say that getting into trouble is *not* a good description of them.

Sixty-two percent of *Enthusiasts* are boys, and almost half are between the ages of 11 and 14 years. They are more likely to be black or Hispanic than most other groups and more likely to live in urban areas. They come from homes where the household income is slightly below average, and their parents are slightly more likely than average to have a college education.

Additional differences and similarities among media types are presented in the tables in Appendix 9.4, far too many to enumerate here. What should be clear from these brief descriptions, however, is that media behavior is not fully described in terms of heavy or light exposure, or a preference for one medium over another. Young people in the United States comprise several different, fairly coherent configurations of media types. These groups vary meaningfully in access to media, in household orientation toward media, in amount and type of media exposure, and, of course, across a number of other demographic and background variables. Given the coherence of the clusters that emerge from this analysis, it is interesting to speculate whether there might be the similar variability among groups in terms of how young people respond to media content. For example, might we expect differences in whether and/or how *Enthusiasts*, *Indifferents*, and *Media Lites* learn from a TV program? Or in whether and to what degree a music video might arouse kids from the various media types? Or to what extent different types might persevere in an on-line information search or spend time in a chat room? Although such questions cannot be answered in a survey of the type describe here, they point to some interesting new directions for future research.

CHAPTER TEN

Summary and Conclusions

The sobriquet "Media Generation" clearly fits the current cohort of America's young people as they enter the twenty-first century. Today's youth spend more time with more media than any generation before them, and there is every reason to assume that both their media use and exposure will continue to increase. The environment of today's kids – their homes, their schools, the automobiles they ride in, and, we suspect, most of their other gathering places – is filled with media of all kinds. Their bedrooms contain televisions, print materials, radios and audio systems, game systems, and, increasingly, computers. They choose content from dozens of TV channels and radio stations, hundreds of print publications, thousands of videos, and virtually an unlimited number of websites. More and more they carry miniaturized versions of most media with them wherever they choose to go; more and more they use multiple media simultaneously. It is no exaggeration to say that in the United States today the average junior high student spends more time with media than he or she devotes to any other waking activity. A typical 11- to 14-year-old gives more than $6\frac{1}{2}$ hours per day to media, and because he or she often uses several media simultaneously, encounters almost 8 hours per day of media content.

On the other hand, in addition to illustrating that the average U.S. 12- to 13-year-old is awash in media messages, this study also demonstrates that there is nothing so elusive as "the average kid." Every bit as noteworthy as the substantial amounts of time that some young people devote to media is the remarkable variation among kids in how much and what they are exposed to, and under what conditions. Some kids encounter media a good deal more than 8 hours per day, others a good deal less. Some devote most of their media time to television, others to

print, others to music media. Variations in media behavior are related
to age, race and ethnicity, gender, socioeconomic status, and various
indicators of social and psychological adjustment. Finally, the findings
from this study call into question several stereotypes attached to popular
conceptions of the media behavior of today's children and adolescents.
For example, the idea that today's kids may be giving up the TV screen
in favor of the computer screen does not receive much support, nor does
the claim that television killed reading. In short, this study gives us a
profile of today's young media user with a kind of detail seldom available, and the picture it paints is not always the one that might have
been expected.

In these final few pages, we summarize some of the major findings to
emerge from this survey of the media behavior of American youth, and
offer a few observations concerning what the findings may tell us about
today's young people and the kinds of messages most likely to reach
them.

The Media Environment

America's young people are immersed in media. The typical U.S. youth
enters the twenty-first century living in a household equipped with three
TV sets, two VCRs, three radios, three tape players, two CD players, a
video game system, and a computer. Since most media have reached
saturation levels in most households, such factors as household income
or parental education levels are not related to the likelihood that a
youngster has access to most media. Of the two media that have not yet
penetrated the entire population – computers and video-game systems –
only computer ownership varies systematically with such factors as socioeconomic status and race or ethnicity. Computers are more likely to be
found in households located in communities where the median annual
household income exceeds $40,000 and in white as opposed to minority
households. On the other hand, there is at least tentative evidence
that youngsters from lower income communities and from minority
households have a good deal of access to computers in their schools.

Our results reveal that a remarkable number of children have their
own personal media – that is, media in their bedrooms. Over half possess
televisions, tape players, or CD players in their bedrooms; 70 percent report having their own radios; a third have video-game systems. Although
the likelihood of youngsters having media in their bedrooms increases
as children get older, parents tell us that a substantial percentage of even

the very youngest children have media in their bedrooms. Over a quarter of 2- through 4-year-olds have televisions and well over a third have radios in their bedrooms; by 5 through 7 years, almost 40 percent claim TV sets and more than half have their own audio medium. Whether or not youths have media in their bedrooms also varies in relation to socioeconomic indicators and to race or ethnicity, but the differences are not always in the expected directions. Our admittedly rough indicators of socioeconomic status reveal a tendency for more kids from higher income and higher education households to have computers in their bedrooms. This finding is not surprising given that until very recently computers were substantially more expensive than televisions, and that computers carry an educational cachet more likely to be valued by parents with higher education and higher incomes. On the other hand, just the reverse is true for television. Higher proportions of kids from lower income and lower education households have televisions in their bedrooms. Differences in frequency of bedroom media are also located by race/ethnicity. African American kids are substantially more likely than either Hispanic or white kids to have both a television (indeed, a television with a VCR and cable access) and a video game system in their bedrooms.

Below in this chapter we suggest that availability of these media in young people's bedrooms, and the increase in media exposure in general and unsupervised media exposure in particular that such bedroom access implies, may be something that parents should consider reexamining.

Media Exposure and Media Use

Today's children and adolescents not only inhabit a world saturated with media, they devote a great deal of attention to them. It is a rare child who is unexposed to at least some media messages on any given day. Indeed, most kids actively use at least one or two different media on a daily basis, and many use several media simultaneously. On any given day, only 5 percent of youngsters are exposed to media for an hour or less; almost three-quarters of U.S. youths are exposed for 3 hours or more. The average youngster between 2 and 18 years actively gives $5\frac{1}{2}$ hours per day to media. Moreover, by dint of using several media simultaneously, most kids are typically exposed to at least an additional hour of media messages – $6\frac{1}{2}$ hours of daily exposure to media content. Indeed, it is worth emphasizing that this is one of the few studies ever to attempt to differentiate between children's *media use* (the amount of daily time that kids spend with media) and *media exposure* (the addi-tional hours of media to which kids are exposed because they use several media simultaneously). Our results indicate that, depending on various demographic characteristics, kids encounter from 12 percent to 20 per-cent more additional media content per day (in units of time) because of such overlapping exposure.

Media exposure begins quite early – average daily media exposure among 2- through 4-year-olds is well over 4 hours – and increases rapidly from the preschool years onward. Media *use* peaks at about 6¾ hours daily and *exposure* at just under 8 hours daily around 11 to 14 years, when kids enter middle school or junior high school. Subsequently, as they face the academic and social demands of new school settings, overall media exposure begins to decline a bit, and the mix of media comprising the total media diet changes somewhat.

Television dominates the media budget throughout childhood and adolescence, but its dominance wanes substantially during the later teen years. By 15 to 18 years, TV viewing declines and use of music media increases to the point that audio media account for the biggest share of media exposure. Indeed, were it not for the increased time adolescents devote to music (radio music, CDs, and tapes), the drop-off in total media use beyond 14 years of age would be even more dramatic. That is, high school students not only reduce their time watching television, but they read less, watch videos less, go to movies less, and play video games less. We suspect this, too, has to do with the myriad other demands placed on U.S. teenagers' time and supports the contention that one of the best predictors of media use is available time – time not filled by other, more structured and/or more attractive activities.

Finally, there is no question that over the past decade new media such as computers and video games have begun to vie for and win a significant chunk of young people's media time. Nevertheless, it is quite clear that "traditional media" still claim the lion's share of atten-tion. On any given day about 40 percent of 2- through 18-year-olds report using a computer either at home or at school, and 30 percent report playing video games. On the other hand, 68 percent listen to radio, 82 percent engage in leisure reading, and 83 percent watch tele-vision. In other words, computers and video games constitute about 12 percent of the average 2- to 18-year-old's daily media budget, while television alone accounts for 40 percent of all media exposure time, and videos and movies add another 11 percent. We believe these proportions will change dramatically as computers take on more and more of the functions traditionally served by television and by audio media, but at the end of the twentieth century, interactive media still have a long way to go before they dominate, at least in terms of time.

SUBGROUP DIFFERENCES IN MEDIA CONSUMPTION

On average, African American youth spend about 2 hours and Hispanic youth 1 hour more per day with media than do white youth. Most of the difference is accounted for by TV exposure, although African American youngsters also report more time with taped TV programs, movies, and video games. Television also accounts for about 10 percent more of African American than white kids' overall media budget. Television's attraction for African American kids is also reflected in their responses to several of the attitudinal questions. More black kids than white say they are entertained by television, more say they learn interesting things from television, and fewer say they are just killing time when they watch.

Overall media exposure is inversely related to socioeconomic status. Generally, exposure is highest among youth from low-income households and among those whose parents completed no more than a high school education. It is lowest among youth from high-income households and those whose parents completed college. However, because both measures of socioeconomic status locate a high degree of variability in media exposure time, the overall differences are not statistically significant. Within several of the smaller age groups (e.g., 2- to 4-year-olds, 8- to 10-year-olds, 11- to 14-year-olds), on the other hand, the differences are statistically reliable, and the means for the two remaining groups manifest a negative relationship. Finally, youngsters from single-parent homes spend about an hour more per day with media than do those from two-parent homes, another indication that as household resources increase, media exposure declines.

Several factors may account for children's increased media use as socioeconomic level declines. One concerns the relationship between economic resources and the number and variety of activities available to kids. As noted in relation to age differences in media exposure, one possible explanation for some of the variation is simply number of available alternative activities. That is, as attractive alternatives to media use become available, media use declines. In other words, when youngsters are given something exciting or interesting to do, media take a back seat. A similar mechanism probably operates in relation to socioeconomic status. To the extent that fewer attractive alternatives exist in lower income households (e.g., single-parent households have fewer resources to pay for dance lessons, send kids to camp, or provide other competing activities) or in lower income neighborhoods (where, for example, fewer structured activities are available for kids, or where more dangerous streets may influence kids to remain indoors – with the television), children may turn to media as an easily available alternative.

In this same vein, one of the attributes associated with greater parent education is a child-rearing philosophy that views a wide variety of activities as highly beneficial to children. Not only are well-educated parents more likely to have more economic resources to devote to their children, they tend to place greater importance on devoting those resources to a range of activities for their children, particularly "educational" activities. Earlier studies (e.g., Bower, 1973, 1985) found that as education levels increase, attitudes toward many of the media – particularly screen media – become less positive, implying that parents who have completed college may place more restrictions on at least some kinds of media use. This possibility is supported by results for measures of household TV orientation, which show that television is substantially more likely to play "most of the time" and during meals in homes where parents completed no more than high school than in homes where parents completed college. Similar findings emerge for household income and for number of parents in the household: lower socioeconomic levels are related to more "constant television." In the same vein, households where high school is the highest level of parent education are also least likely to have family rules about TV viewing. In short, both the physical and social environment in lower socioeconomic households operate to increase the likelihood that children will spend more time with media, particularly screen media and games. Some of the same factors, but particularly level of parent education, also increase the likelihood that children spend more time with print media and, to a slight extent, with the computer.

Heavy versus Light Media Use

One of the more interesting findings to emerge from this study is how little it supports the displacement hypothesis. The idea that as children adopt new media, they do so at the expense of old media is simply not borne out. There may be such a shifting in the proportions of time that different media contribute to the overall media budget among children who spend a moderate or small amount of time with media, but no such displacement effect emerges among heavy media users in this study. Among 8- through 18-year-olds, kids classified as heavy users of television, the computer, or print also use most other media a great deal. For example, the 22 percent of older youths who watch television more than 5 hours daily use other media almost $1\frac{1}{2}$ hours more per day than kids who watch small or moderate amount of television. Similarly, the 21 percent of 8- through 18-year-olds who read more than an hour per day use other media almost $1\frac{1}{2}$ hours per day more than do those who read less or not at all. And perhaps most remarkable, kids who spend more than an hour per day on the computer use other media almost 3 hours per day more than those who use the computer less or not at all. It seems that there is a small, but by no means trivial, cohort of kids who are simply "into" media, a group well worth further examination.

New Media versus Old

The personal computer, of course, is one of the newer and arguably most important additions to the large array of media available to American youth. As such, it receives a great deal of attention and comment – some might even say "hype." Images in the popular press of kids devoting hour upon hour to interactive games, surfing the Web (often, it is claimed, to visit violent or sexually explicit sites), jabbering away in teenage chat rooms, or "instant messaging" are common. Also familiar are predictions that because the computer and its link to the Internet offers today's youth fingertip access to more information than any generation before them has even dreamed of, it is revolutionizing most young people's media behavior. There probably is some truth to each of these conceptualizations of how today's youth use the computer, but as noted earlier, it seems as though it will be a while before the computer and the linkages it enables constitute the heart and soul of young people's media experience. Given that just over 40 percent of 8- to 18-year-olds use computers on any given day, it is not surprising U.S. youths average less than $\frac{1}{2}$ hour per day with the new medium, substantially less time than they spend with television and slightly less than they spend with radio, CDs or tapes, or print.

On the other hand, young people who use computers tend to use them a great deal. Those 8- through 18-year-olds who use a computer on any given day spend more time with it than any other medium but television and CDs or tapes. They average over 50 minutes per day with a computer for recreational purposes (that is, omitting school-related use), compared with 45 minutes with print media or radio, and just over an hour with CDs or tapes. Somewhat surprisingly, when we look at all kids, large differences in the amount of time spent with a computer do not emerge as a function of socioeconomic variables or race/ethnicity in the overall sample. On the other hand, on any given day about 15 percent more white than black or Hispanic youths use a computer at home. Still, if we focus just on kids who used computers the previous day, Hispanic youth claim a full half hour more computer time than either African American or white youngsters, and there is no difference in the computer time claimed by black and white kids. We believe this testifies to the importance of programs designed to make computers available in schools, where slightly more minority than white youth use computers on any given day. When access is made available, kids without comput- ers at home spend as much (or more) time using them as do kids who can log on within their own households.

GENDER DIFFERENCES

Most of the gender differences revealed in this study seem to have more to do with taste for different kinds of content than for different me- dia. The exception to this generalization is the large gender difference in taste for action/adventure content, although even this difference is not as dramatic as we had originally expected. Girls listen to about 20 minutes more audio media daily than do boys. They watch about 20 minutes less daily television than boys, a change from the early 1970s when Lyle and Hoffman (1972a) found girls watching slightly more. They also spend less time with video games and with computers, but the latter difference warrants further comment. Among all 2- to 18-year-olds, boys spend 10 minutes more per day than girls with the computer, and if we limit attention to just the subsample of computer users, boys spend about 20 minutes more per day than girls. However, most of the time differential in computer use associated with gender can be accounted for by time devoted to games – boys play a lot, girls don't. Indeed, when computer games are removed from consideration, there is no gender difference in time spent with computers.

On the other hand, boys and girls often select different kinds of media content. The two genders largely choose the same kinds of TV programs. The major exception is sports programming, which is four times more likely to be watched by boys than by girls. There are no large gender differences in movie selection. Paralleling the findings for interactive games, on the other hand, boys are a bit more likely than girls to choose action/adventure videos, while from the seventh grade onward, girls are much more likely than boys to watch videos in the drama, horror, family/children, and romance categories. Girls are also slightly less likely than boys to choose music with a hard edge; they are not as likely as boys to listen to hard rock or rap and they are slightly more likely to listen to soft rock or rhythm and blues. Some of the largest gender differences occur in choice of reading material. Among seventh through twelfth graders, many boys and very few girls read sports magazines or hobby magazines. Conversely, most girls read teen magazines and most boys do not, and many more girls than boys read entertainment and popular culture magazines and women's magazines. In general, then, there are more similarities than differences in the kinds of content the two genders select, but when those differences do appear, they tend to relate to boy's preference for material with more action and a harder edge.

Music Tastes

The only other striking differences in terms of content preferences emerge for older children's tastes in music in relation to race or ethnicity. Although most teenagers consume large amounts of popular music, and although two genres – rap/hip-hop and alternative rock – dominate their listening, kids from different racial or ethnic backgrounds exhibit quite different music preferences. African American teens immerse themselves almost exclusively in "black" music. Rap and hip-hop are the overwhelming favorites among African American teenagers (84% listen to this genre), but substantial percentages also listen to rhythm and blues and to gospel. No other music genre attracts more than 5 percent of black kids. White adolescents, on the other hand, spread their listening over several different genres, including some associated with black culture. Rap/hip-hop is the second most preferred genre among white adolescents, second only to alternative rock. In addition, almost a quarter of white kids spend time listening to hard rock and heavy metal, and 10 percent or more of them of them listen to country and western, classic rock, soft rock, and ska or punk. Finally, Hispanic teenagers are the most cosmopolitan of all in terms of the cultural roots of the music they listen to. Rap/hip-hop ranks as their favorite, followed by alternative rock (the top choices of black and white, youth respectively), but over 15 percent of them also listen to Latin/salsa and to hard rock or heavy metal. In addition, 10 percent or more of Hispanic teenagers listen to country and western, rhythm and blues, and soft rock.

In general, then, black kids confine most of their listening to black music. A great many white kids listen to black music, but they also flock to various types of "white" music (e.g., the various subgenres of rock). Hispanic kids manifest the most culturally diverse tastes, including black, white, and Latin music.

Absence of Adults

A worrisome finding that emerges from this study concerns the substantial amount of young people's media exposure that occurs when adults are absent. In light of recent public concern about youth and media voiced everywhere from local PTA meetings to the mass media to the halls of Congress, it is somewhat surprising to discover not only how many youngsters have their own personal media but how many spend much of their media time either alone or with other children, rather than with adults.

Given that half of all youths and two-thirds of 8- to 18-year-olds have their own televisions, not to mention the almost complete saturation of music media in older children's bedrooms, it should not be surprising that kids spend a great deal of their media time in their own rooms. Half of their reading, a fifth of their TV viewing, and a third of their music listening and video-game playing occurs in their bedrooms. Small wonder that so much of youngsters' media exposure is solitary. Almost 15 percent of the youngest and a full third of the oldest youngsters watch television "mainly alone." The numbers for solitary use of other media are even larger. Among junior and senior high school students, over 60 percent of all computer time is spent mainly alone; so too is more than a quarter of the time they spend watching videos.

Moreover, when young people are not using media alone, they are far more likely to be with other kids (siblings or peers) than with their parents. During the evening hours, when parents are most available, only 2- through 7-year-olds are more likely to watch television with a parent than with siblings or peers. From 15 percent to 20 percent more older kids watch television in the evening with other kids than watch with a parent. And again, the differences increase substantially for other media. For example, 11 percent of seventh through twelfth graders go to the movies with parents, while 60 percent attend motion pictures with siblings or peers. Responses to the one other question that taps into parental controls on children's media use – about whether there are rules about TV viewing in the household – also converge with this picture of the unsupervised media behavior of a large proportion of kids. Over 70 percent of parents of the 2- through 7-year-olds state that there are rules about TV viewing in their households. However, this figure declines rapidly as children get older. Some 52 percent of 8- to 10-year-olds say they experience such controls in their homes; 41 percent of 11- to 14-year-olds and 24 percent of 15- to 18-year-olds have such rules. The likelihood of there being rules about viewing television in a family also declines as the household income goes down, as the level of parent education goes down, and as the number of parents in the household goes down – all factors associated with increased media exposure. But regardless of socioeconomic level or any other demographic characteristic, only half of U.S. households have such rules, and by the time children enter the third grade, the likelihood of there being family TV viewing rules drops off rapidly.

Several factors probably contribute to the increasing "ghettoization" of young people's media use. Perhaps it is because the media have become such a ubiquitous part of our environment. Perhaps it is because many parents do not really believe that media messages make all that much difference in their children's lives (maybe in some other children's lives, but not *their* children's lives). Perhaps it is simply because the demands placed on most of today's parents make monitoring their children's media behavior too difficult a task. But whatever the reason, it appears that more and more children spend more and more time exposed to media messages absent adult supervision, adult oversight, adult presence, or an adult "game plan." And while it may be difficult to change some of the structural and social factors influencing media availability to youngsters, the evidence is that some kind of family media policy can be articulated and is likely to be beneficial.

ATTITUDES TOWARD MEDIA

Clearly, the great attraction of most media for most young people is entertainment. Kids simply want to be diverted and have fun. A majority of youngsters say that this is precisely what television and computers do for them; 50 percent or more say that when they watch television or use a computer they are entertained "most of the time" (fewer than 10% say they are *never* entertained by television and fewer than 20% say this about computers). On the other hand, kids also realize that a substantial part of their media use occurs simply to "kill time," although that kind of a response is more associated with television than with computers. In other words, a substantial proportion of youngsters is quite aware that the same media can serve several different functions, some of which are perhaps more positive than others.

PSYCHOLOGICAL AND SOCIAL ADJUSTMENT

Finally, some of the more intriguing findings from this study have to do with the relationship between media behavior and kids' scores on what we have called a "contentedness index." This measure is based on several items assessing young people's social and psychological contentment and/or adjustment. Although even those youths who scored lowest on our contentedness index seem to be relatively contented (i.e., they are not particularly unhappy), when their media behavior is compared with those classified as moderately or highly contented, several interesting differences are revealed.

First and most important, less contented youths spend more time with almost all media than do those who are more contented. The differences in contentedness or adjustment are not great, but the differences in media exposure time are. The contentedness index also produces a finding that we believe is relevant to our previous comments about lack of parental oversight of children's media behavior. Substantially more kids who score high on the index than kids who score lower on the index come from families where there are controls on watching television. Similarly, kids from the high-contentedness group tend to be less likely to inhabit "constant TV households" – that is, households where the television is on during meals or where it is on most of the time even when no one is watching. In short, there is a fairly strong and consistent negative relationship between a measure of happiness or contentedness and amount of media exposure.

Of course, the fact that kids in the lowest group on the contentedness index were not all that discontented leaves some unanswered questions. For example, we cannot say whether the negative trend would continue with kids who are extremely discontented. (A reasonable theoretical case can be made that very unhappy kids might consume very little media content, cutting themselves off from as many forms of social communication as possible.) Moreover, it is not possible to make any kind of causal inference on the basis of these results. We cannot say whether less happy kids are motivated to use more media, whether increased media use decreases kids' happiness, or both, or whether some third factor leads quite independently to both outcomes. On the other hand, causality may be largely irrelevant. Evidence is beginning to emerge in both communication research and psychological research that people sometimes seek media messages that converge with current emotional states, regardless of the origin of that emotional state (see, e.g., Christenson & Roberts, 1998). The concern is that when emotional states and media messages converge, amplification of the original state may occur. Thus, a troubled youth – whether simply momentarily unhappy or chronically angry or alienated – may seek and find media content that reinforces and amplifies the original mood or state, as when, for example, a chronically angry, adolescent boy uses angry heavy metal music to put himself in a mood to "go and beat the crap out of someone" (Arnett, 1991, p. 84).

THE NEED TO PAY ATTENTION

In light of the central role that media play in the lives of today's young people, central at least in terms of the time devoted to media messages encountered, our findings point to a critically important issue that warrants further exploration. Anything strongly related to the psychological and social adjustment of children deserves attention. Similarly, anything that impinges on them for half of their waking hours deserves attention. When the two come together in the form of results showing that scores on a measure of children's contentedness or psychological or social adjustment are strongly and inversely related to amount of media exposure and to at least some common aspects of kids' media environment, alarms should sound.

Similarly, what looks to us to be a kind of parental abdication of oversight over children's media behavior noted several times throughout this book should also trigger alarms. It is fairly clear that furnishing youngsters' bedrooms with various media increases overall media exposure, particularly exposure that occurs without an adult presence. And yet over half our children have a television, a radio, a tape player, and a CD player in their bedroom. There is also evidence that having television constantly available in a household is associated with increased media exposure. And yet over 40 percent of our children say they live in households where "the TV is on most of the time even if no one is watching," and almost 60 percent say it is on during most meals. There is also at least tentative evidence that family rules governing TV viewing are associated with less media exposure. And yet half of our children say no such rules operate in their homes. The point is, these are all conditions that concerned parents can control. Parents can decide whether or not TV viewing or computer use is to be a family activity; they can determine whether media are located in private or common areas of the household. Parents (and children) can resolve to reduce use of media for background purposes, for example, turning the TV set off when no one is watching – or, even better, turning it on only when there is some particular program that someone wants to watch (less watching television, more watching TV programs). Finally, parents and children can negotiate some ground rules governing family media use, guidelines that cover *all* media (not just television). These need not be draconian (the question in this study asked only, "Are there any rules . . . ?"). Simply the fact that guidelines are articulated may be enough to increase both parents' and children's attention to their media behavior, increasing awareness that media and how we use them are important.

For most kids, most of the time, most media are a diversion – mostly entertaining, sometimes little more than a way to kill time, sometimes a source of new and interesting information, often a background activity that functions more like wallpaper than something kids actively "do." Nevertheless, for most kids most of the time, media are ubiquitous. American youth spend more time with media than with any single activity other than sleeping. Substantial numbers spend the bulk of their media time without adult presence; almost all spend at least some of their media time alone; many spend more media time with other kids than with parents.

Nothing that plays this much of a role in the lives of our children can be dismissed as simply a pastime or a diversion. Anything that plays this much of a role in the lives of children deserves our attention.

Appendixes to Chapter 2:
Methods

Appendix 2.1: Sampling Details

CREATING THE IN-SCHOOL SAMPLE

Harris Interactive, Inc., who conducted the sampling and administered the survey, has developed a sampling process and survey methodology for surveying representative samples of U.S. school students. All interviewing is conducted in the classroom.

The Harris national probability samples of schools and students are based on a highly stratified two-stage sampling design. This design employs features similar to sample designs used in various national surveys of students and schools conducted by the National Center for Educational Statistics. In the first stage, a sample of schools is selected from a list of all schools. In the second stage, a class is randomly selected to participate from within the chosen school.

The school sample is drawn from a list of approximately 80,000 public, private, parochial schools in the United States. It is selected to account for differences in grade enrollment, region, and the size of the municipality where schools are located and is designed to ensure that the sampling process adequately represents the full range of schools over the entire nation. A random selection of schools is drawn on the basis of the number of students in each cell proportionate to the number of students in the universe, creating a cross-section of young people in a set of designated grades (in this study, grades three through 12). The sample design also permits oversampling by a variety of criteria (e.g., location, urbanicity, grade level, school type, or race/ethnicity). This study includes an oversample of schools in areas with a high proportion of African American and Hispanic students.

Once schools were selected as part of the sample, a letter was sent to principals soliciting their participation. Harris Interactive then contacted the principal by telephone to request his or her participation in the survey. A number of steps were included in the consent procedure in order to maximize participation. An alert letter contained a brief description of the survey process and some background information on the Harris organization. In addition, a letter from the Kaiser Family Foundation describing the importance and scope of the project was included. Schools were also offered a small incentive to participate. In addition, at a principal's request, calls were made to local school boards or district offices to gain approval from appropriate officials. If necessary, copies of the introductory letters and other materials were mailed or sent via fax to the principal and/or other school official. If a particular school could not participate, it was replaced by a school with similar demographic characteristics in an effort to preserve the integrity of the primary selection. Another randomly drawn school was chosen within the same region, with similar grade enrollment and size of municipality, and in the same or the nearest zip code to the original school. The response rate for schools initially sampled was 37 percent.

Once the principal agreed to participate, a random selection process was used to select a particular class to complete the survey. The principal was asked to alphabetize all classes for the grade assigned; using a random number selection grid, an interviewer for the Harris organization identified an individual class. For junior and senior high schools, where students attend different classes for each subject, only English classes were used to make the selection. Since all U.S. students in all grades must enroll in English classes, this ensures a more representative sample of students by academic track and level of achievement.

WEIGHTING THE DATA

As with all school-based surveys, a two-stage weighting process is used to ensure a representative sample of students. These weights are based on data from the National Center for Education Statistics and the U.S. Bureau of the Census. They control the distribution of students by grade, region, size of place, gender, and race/ethnicity.

Table A.2.1.1 provides a comparison of the demographic profile of the weighted and unweighted samples in this study to U.S. National Census data.

Table A.2.1.1. *Distribution of Sample of 8- to 18-Year-Olds: Weighted, Unweighted, and National Census Data (%)*

Base	Weighted 2,065	Unweighted 2,065	National
Age			
8–10 years	27	27	30
11–13 years	29	29	30
14–18 years	41	41	40
Gender			
Male	51	47	51
Female	49	53	49
Race/ethnicity			
White/other	72	69	72
African American	15	16	15

MARGIN OF ERROR

The results for sample surveys are subject to sampling error – the potential difference between results obtained from the sample and those that would have been obtained had the entire population been interviewed. The size of the potential sampling error varies with both the size of the sample and with the percentage giving a particular answer. For this sample, the overall margin of sampling error is +/− 3 percent. For smaller subgroups of the sample, the margin of error is larger.

THE IN-HOME SAMPLE

Proxy interviews were conducted with 1,090 parents or caregivers of children ages 2 through 7 years. The sample is designed to be representative of a national sample of 2- to 7 year-olds, and included oversamples of African American and Hispanic children.

The sample was drawn from a U.S. Census list of more than 225,000 block groups in the continental United States. In an urban area, a segment can be one block or a group of blocks. In a rural area, a segment is a geographical area of land with identifiable boundaries such as streams, rivers, roads, or civil boundaries. The sample is stratified by region, state, county, census tract, and block group. A random selection of block groups is drawn based on the number of households within each block group. Oversamples were drawn from a list of block groups in the continental United States with a density of at least 20 percent African American residents and from a list of block groups with a density of at least 20 percent Hispanic residents. The sample consisted of 90 block groups, or primary sample units (PSUs), in the cross-section and 30 PSUs in the oversample.

The study used an area probability sample. Area probability samples for a national survey are designed to give each housing unit or household in the country a known chance of being interviewed. The final stage in this type of sample is to list systematically all or a portion of the housing units in the specified block or area. This is usually performed by the interviewer in the field at the time of the survey. Using a map and specially designed listing sheets, the interviewer goes to a designated point in the area and begins to list housing units. The number of units to be listed and the definition of the proper respondent within each housing unit vary from study to study. These listed households then become the interviewer's assignment. In this type of sample, few or no substitutions are allowed, and numerous callbacks may be required to complete all of the assigned interviews.

Some area probability samples, such as the current study's sample, may require that a short screening interview be conducted to determine whether or not the household qualifies for the survey. Interviews are completed only for those households found eligible for the survey. To qualify for the current survey, a household had to have a child aged 2 to 7 years and his/her parent or caregiver in residence. The response rate for this sample was 45.6 percent.

WEIGHTING THE DATA

The completed interviews were weighted to the latest population parameters of the Current Population Survey on age, gender, race or ethnicity, and region. The weighting adjusted these key variables where necessary to their actual proportions in the population. An additional weight was applied to respondents from the oversampled PSUs. Table A.2.1.2 provides a comparison of the demographic profile of the weighted and unweighted samples to U.S. National Census data.

MARGIN OF ERROR

The overall margin of error for this sample is +/− 5 percent. For smaller subgroups of the in-home sample, the margins of error are larger.

Table A.2.1.2. *Distribution of Sample of 2- to 7-Year-Olds: Weighted, Unweighted, and National Census Data (%)*

	Weighted	Unweighted	
Base	1,090	1,090	National
Age			
2–4 years	49	46	49
5–7 years	51	54	51
Gender			
Male	51	51	51
Female	48	47	49
Race/ethnicity			
White	68	58	69
African American	16	19	15
Hispanic	16	22	16

APPENDIX 2.2

CONTENT GENRES FOR EACH MEDIUM

Television
Children's educational
Children's entertainment
Comedy
Documentary
Drama
Entertainment/variety
Foreign language (Spanish)
Foreign language
   (Non-Spanish)
Game shows
Infomercials
Movies
Music videos
News
News magazines
Reality programs
Soap operas
Sports
Talk shows
Other

Movies
Action
Comedy
Drama
Family or children's
Horror
Romance
Science fiction

Videos
Action
Comedy
Drama
Family or children
Fitness
Horror

Music videos
Romance
Science fiction

Video Games
Action or combat
Adventure
Classic games/gambling/
  puzzles and logic
Reflex
Role playing/interactive
  fiction/fantasy
Simulation/strategic/strategic
  planning
Sports or competition

Books
Adventure
Arts and music/hobbies
History/current events
Humor
Literature
Mystery/thriller
Religious
Romance
Science fiction/fantasy
Science/nature
Self-help

Magazines
Entertainment/popular culture
General interest
Health
Hobby/travel
Home
Men's
News
Science/nature
Sports
Teen
Women's

Newspaper
Comics
Entertainment
Fashion
Horoscope or advice columns
Local news
National news
Sports
Youth or teens

Computer Games
Action or combat
Adventure
Arts and crafts
Classic games/gambling/
  puzzles and logic
Educational
Kids
Popular culture/lifestyles
Reflex
Role playing/interactive
  fiction/fantasy
Simulation or strategic
  planning
Sports or competition

Internet Chat Rooms
Entertainment
Family/children
Gaming
Hobbies or groups
News
Relationships/lifestyles
Shopping
Sports

Internet Websites
Entertainment
Family/children
Gaming
News

Relationships/lifestyles
Research/information/
    computer support
Search engines
Shopping

Music
Alternative rock
Children's songs/nursery
    rhymes
Classic rock
Classical

Country and western
Gospel or Christian
Hard rock/heavy metal
Jazz or blues
Latin or salsa
Rap or hip-hop
Rave or techno rock
Reggae
Rhythm and blues/soul
Ska or punk
Soft rock Top 40
Top 40

APPENDIXES TO CHAPTER 3:

THE MEDIA ENVIRONMENT:

RESULTS AND STATISTICAL

TESTS

APPENDIX 3.1: HOUSEHOLDS CONTAINING ONE OR MORE OF EACH MEDIUM

Table A.3.1.1. *Proportion of Homes Containing One or More of Each Medium by Age (in years)*

	2–7	2–4	5–7	8–18	8–10	11–14	15–18
TV	100	99	100	99	99	99	99
VCR	96	95	97	98	97	98	99
Radio	98	98	98	97	95	97	99
CDs/tapes	94	94	95	99	97	99	99
Video-game player	52	44$_a$	60$_b$	81	80	84	80
Computer	62	58$_a$	66$_b$	73	67$_a$	73$_b$	79$_c$
Cable/satellite	73	73	73	74	72	76	73
Premium cable	40	42	39	45	49$_a$	47$_a$	39$_b$
Internet access	40	39	42	47	39$_a$	48$_b$	54$_b$

Table A.3.1.2. Proportion of Homes Containing One or More of Each Medium by Gender and Age

	2–7 years		2–4 years		5–7 years	
	Female	Male	Female	Male	Female	Male
TV	100	100	100	99	99	100
VCR	96	96	96	94	95	98
Radio	98	98	99	97	97	99
CDs/tapes	92	96	93	95	92$_a$	97$_b$
Video-game player	47$_a$	57$_b$	44	44	50$_a$	68$_b$
Computer	63	61	63$_a$	53$_b$	64	67
Cable/satellite	73	73	74	72	72	74
Premium cable	40	41	40	43	39	39
Internet access	42	39	41	36	42	42

	8–18 years		8–10 years		11–14 years		15–18 years	
	Female	Male	Female	Male	Female	Male	Female	Male
TV	99	99	98	99	99	98	99	99
VCR	98	98	96	97	99	97	99	99
Radio	97	97	94	95	97	97	99	98
CDs/tapes	99	98	98	97	99	99	100	99
Video-game player	74$_a$	88$_b$	73$_a$	85$_b$	77$_a$	90$_b$	71$_a$	89$_b$
Computer	75$_a$	71$_b$	70	65	75	70	79	79
Cable/satellite	72$_a$	76$_b$	73	71	74	77	67$_a$	78$_b$
Premium cable	46	45	52	47	49	46	37	41
Internet access	45	49	40	38	46	51	49$_a$	58$_b$

Table A.3.1.3. *Proportion of Homes Containing One or More of Each Medium by Race and Age*

	2–7 years			2–4 years			5–7 years		
	White	Black	Hispanic	White	Black	Hispanic	White	Black	Hispanic
TV	99	100	100	99	100	100	100	100	100
VCR	98	92	93	97	92	93	98	92	94
Radio	98	98	98	98	98	98	98	99	99
CDs/tapes	96$_a$	91$_b$	92$_b$	96$_a$	88$_b$	92$_{ab}$	95	93	92
Video-game player	56$_a$	52$_{bc}$	43$_b$	48$_a$	42$_{ab}$	36$_b$	64$_a$	62$_{ab}$	51$_b$
Computer	71$_a$	45$_b$	40$_b$	69$_a$	42$_b$	31$_b$	73$_a$	49$_b$	49$_b$
Cable/satellite	76$_a$	69$_{ab}$	65$_b$	73$_a$	63$_b$	63$_b$	75	74	66
Premium cable	40	44	39	42	39	42	38$_a$	50$_b$	35$_a$
Internet access	51$_a$	19$_b$	19$_b$	52$_a$	15$_b$	14$_b$	50$_a$	22$_b$	26$_b$

	8–18 years			8–10 years			11–14 years			15–18 years		
	White	Black	Hispanic	White	Black	Hispanic	White	Black	Hispanic	White	Black	Hispanic
TV	99	99	99	98	100	99	99	100	99	99	100	100
VCR	98	98	98	98	97	96	98	96	98	98	100	100
Radio	97	97	98	97	92	94	97	99	98	98	100	100
CDs/tapes	99	99	99	98	96	99	99	99	98	99	100	100
Video-game player	79$_a$	87$_b$	84$_{ab}$	75	85	83	83	89	84	78	86	84
Computer	82$_a$	61$_b$	55$_b$	82$_a$	65$_b$	42$_c$	81$_a$	56$_b$	53$_b$	83$_a$	63$_b$	67$_b$
Cable/satellite	75	76	71	71	80	65	79	79	68	72	69	80
Premium cable	42$_a$	62$_b$	44$_a$	42$_a$	67$_b$	44$_a$	46$_a$	63$_b$	46$_a$	37$_a$	55$_b$	41$_{ab}$
Internet access	57$_a$	34$_b$	28$_b$	51$_a$	43$_a$	11$_b$	58$_a$	29$_b$	29$_b$	59$_a$	31$_b$	40$_b$

Table A.3.1.4. *Proportion of Homes Containing One or More of Each Medium by Household Income[a] and Age*

	2–7 years			2–4 years			5–7 years		
	Low	Middle	High	Low	Middle	High	Low	Middle	High
TV	100	99	100	100	100	100	100	100	100
VCR	90_a	96_b	99_b	88_a	96_b	99_b	93_a	96_{ab}	99_b
Radio	99	97	98	98	97	97	99	96	99
CDs/tapes	88_a	94_b	97_b	84_a	94_b	97_b	92	93	97
Video-game player	51	53	53	45	47	44	57	60	60
Computer	42_a	57_b	75_c	39_a	54_b	69_c	45_a	60_b	78_c
Cable/satellite	62_a	73_b	75_b	55_a	78_b	76_b	68_a	67_a	81_b
Premium cable	37_{ab}	45_a	38_b	33_a	49_b	40_{ab}	41	41	37
Internet access	22_a	35_b	52_c	19_a	35_b	49_c	23_a	34_a	54_b

	8–18 years			8–10 years			11–14 years			15–18 years		
	Low	Middle	High	Low	Middle	High	Low	Middle	High	Low	Middle	High
TV	99	99	98	100	98	99	99	100	97	99	100	98
VCR	96_a	99_b	98_b	93	97	97	96	99	98	97	100	99
Radio	96	97	97	91	94	96	98	98	95	97	99	100
CDs/tapes	98	99	98	94	98	98	98	100	98	100	100	98
Video-game player	83_a	84_a	77_b	75_{ab}	85_a	76_b	88_a	87_a	76_b	81	81	78
Computer	52_a	72_b	86_c	45_a	59_b	85_c	53_a	73_b	85_c	56_a	82_b	90_c
Cable/satellite	75	72	76	75	68	74	72	75	79	79	72	70
Premium cable	53_a	44_b	42_b	59_a	52_a	43_b	53	45	48	50_a	37_b	35_b
Internet access	24_a	47_b	62_c	15_a	28_b	58_c	25_a	51_b	59_b	27_a	55_b	69_c

[a] "Low" indicates an income under $25,000 per year; "Middle," $25,000 to $40,000; and "High," over $40,000.

Table A.3.1.5. *Proportion of Homes Containing One or More of Each Medium by Parent Education and Age*

	2–7 years			2–4 years			5–7 years		
	HS or less	Some college	College or more	HS or less	Some college	College or more	HS or less	Some college	College or more
TV	98	100	99	100	100	99	99	100	100
VCR	91	98	99	90	96	99	91	98	99
Radio	97	98	98	97	99	97	97	97	100
CDs/tapes	88$_a$	95$_b$	98$_b$	87$_a$	95$_b$	99$_b$	90$_a$	95$_{ab}$	98$_b$
Video-game player	59$_a$	57$_a$	44$_b$	54$_a$	50$_a$	33$_b$	65	63	55
Computer	35$_a$	57$_b$	87$_c$	33$_a$	51$_b$	83$_c$	37$_a$	61$_b$	91$_c$
Cable/satellite	64$_a$	74$_b$	79$_b$	64$_a$	75$_b$	78$_b$	65$_a$	73$_{ab}$	79$_b$
Premium cable	40	42	40	43	41	41	36	42	39
Internet access	15$_a$	31$_b$	67$_c$	12$_a$	33$_b$	64$_c$	17$_a$	29$_b$	71$_c$

	8–18 years			8–10 years			11–14 years			15–18 years		
	HS or less	Some college	College or more	HS or less	Some college	College or more	HS or less	Some college	College or more	HS or less	Some college	College or more
TV	99	100	98	97	100	99	99	99	98	99	100	98
VCR	98	98	98	95	95	98	98	97	98	99	100	98
Radio	98	99	96	98	98	94	97	99	97	99	100	98
CDs/tapes	98	99	99	97	97	98	99	99	99	98	100	99
Video-game player	81	85	81	84$_{ab}$	90$_a$	77$_b$	83	89	82	76	78	82
Computer	55$_a$	73$_b$	85$_c$	48$_a$	68$_b$	79$_b$	59$_a$	68$_a$	83$_b$	55$_a$	82$_b$	92$_c$
Cable/satellite	71	77	76	70	69	75	71	78	79	73	80	73
Premium cable	49$_a$	47$_{ab}$	43$_b$	56	42	48	52$_a$	52$_{ab}$	43$_b$	42	41	38
Internet access	29$_a$	41$_b$	63$_c$	27$_a$	27$_a$	52$_b$	30$_a$	44$_b$	63$_c$	29$_a$	45$_b$	72$_c$

Table A.3.1.6. *Proportion of Homes Containing One or More of Each Medium by Family Composition and Age*

	2–7 years		2–4 years		5–7 years	
	Two-parent	Single-parent	Two-parent	Single-parent	Two-parent	Single-parent
TV	99	100	100	99	99	100
VCR	91[a]	97[b]	90	97	91	98
Radio	96	99	98	98	95	99
CDs/tapes	84[a]	97[b]	81[a]	98[b]	87[a]	96[b]
Video-game player	46[a]	53[b]	31[a]	46[b]	56	60
Computer	41[a]	68[b]	36[a]	61[b]	45[a]	74[b]
Cable/satellite	59[a]	76[b]	57[a]	76[b]	60[a]	76[b]
Premium cable	32[a]	43[b]	32	44	32	42
Internet access	19[a]	47[b]	18[a]	43[b]	20[a]	50[b]

	8–18 years		8–10 years		11–14 years		15–18 years	
	Two-parent	Single-parent	Two-parent	Single-parent	Two-parent	Single-parent	Two-parent	Single-parent
TV	99	99	100	99	98	99	98	99
VCR	98	98	98	96	98	98	100	99
Radio	98	97	95	95	99	97	100	99
CDs/tapes	99	99	99	97	97	99	100	99
Video-game player	80	81	77	79	83	83	78	80
Computer	78[a]	62[b]	61	70	53[a]	78[b]	71[a]	83[b]
Cable/satellite	65[a]	76[b]	63	73	68	76	62[a]	77[b]
Premium cable	41	45	43	47	48	46	32[a]	42[b]
Internet access	36[a]	52[b]	34	42	33[a]	54[b]	41[a]	58[b]

Table A.3.1.7. Proportion of Homes Containing One or More of Each Medium by Residence Locale and Age

	2–7 years			2–4 years			5–7 years		
	Urban	Suburban	Rural	Urban	Suburban	Rural	Urban	Suburban	Rural
TV	99	99	100	100	99	100	100	100	100
VCR	95	97	97	94	96	96	96	97	98
Radio	98	99	96	97	99	95	99	99	98
CDs/tapes	94$_{ab}$	96$_a$	90$_b$	93	96	88	94	96	92
Video-game player	48	55	54	40	46	49	56	64	58
Computer	59$_a$	67$_b$	56$_a$	57	60	57	61$_a$	72$_b$	56$_a$
Cable/satellite	70	74	78	68	75	75	71	72	83
Premium cable	41	38	46	43	40	45	39	36	48
Internet access	35$_a$	46$_b$	36$_a$	36	42	37	34$_a$	49$_b$	36$_a$

	8–18 years			8–10 years			11–14 years			15–18 years		
	Urban	Suburban	Rural	Urban	Suburban	Rural	Urban	Suburban	Rural	Urban	Suburban	Rural
TV	99	98	99	98	99	99	100	97	99	99	99	99
VCR	97	99	98	95	98	97	97	98	98	99	100	97
Radio	96	98	97	92	97	94	96	96	99	99	100	93
CDs/tapes	98	98	99	96	98	97	99	98	100	100	99	100
Video-game player	82	80	82	81	76	83	84$_{ab}$	80$_a$	88$_b$	81$_{ab}$	83$_a$	74$_b$
Computer	71$_a$	80$_b$	66$_c$	65$_a$	81$_b$	52$_c$	71	76	69	77$_{ab}$	83$_a$	74$_b$
Cable/satellite	74$_{ab}$	71$_a$	79$_b$	71	73	72	75	74	79	75$_a$	65$_b$	84$_c$
Premium cable	48	40	49	56$_a$	37$_b$	57$_a$	47	44	52	43	38	36
Internet access	45$_a$	55$_b$	40$_a$	35$_a$	53$_b$	24$_c$	46$_{ab}$	54$_a$	44$_b$	51$_{ab}$	58$_a$	43$_b$

Appendix 3.2: Households Containing Three or More of Each Medium

Table A.3.2.1. *Proportion of Homes Containing Three or More of Each Medium by Age (in years)*

	2–7	2–4	5–7	8–18	8–10	11–14	15–18
TV	45	38_a	50_b	70	62_a	75_b	70_b
VCR	12	11	12	26	19_a	27_b	28_b
Radio	48	42_a	54_b	73	54_a	78_b	83_c
CDs/tapes	57	53_a	60_b	90	82_a	92_b	94_b
Video-game player	5	3_a	7_b	24	27_a	25_a	20_b
Computer[a]	16	13_a	19_b	25	23	24	26

[a] For this Table and Tables A.3.3.2–A.3.3.7, the proportion for computers represents homes containing *two* or more computers.

Table A.3.2.2. Proportion of Homes Containing Three or More of Each Medium by Gender and Age

	2–7 years		2–4 years		5–7 years	
	Female	Male	Female	Male	Female	Male
TV	43	46	38	38	48	52
VCR	13	11	13	9	12	12
Radio	48	49	47	38	50	58
CDs/tapes	57	49	55	50	59	61
Video-game player	5	5	3	3	6	7
Computer[a]	17	15	16[a]	10[b]	19	20

	8–18 years		8–10 years		11–14 years		15–18 years	
	Female	Male	Female	Male	Female	Male	Female	Male
TV	70	70	63	61	74	75	70	71
VCR	26	26	18	21	29	26	28	29
Radio	74	72	53	54	79	77	84	81
CDs/tapes	90	89	84	80	92	91	93	94
Video-game player	17[a]	30[b]	22[a]	31[b]	19[a]	30[b]	12[a]	29[b]
Computer[a]	27[a]	22[b]	31[a]	16[b]	25	23	28	27

[a] See Table A.3.2.1.

Table A.3.2.3. Proportion of Homes Containing Three or More of Each Medium by Race and Age

	2–7 years			2–4 years			5–7 years		
	White	Black	Hispanic	White	Black	Hispanic	White	Black	Hispanic
TV	47_a	56_b	27_c	41_a	48_a	23	52_a	63_a	31_b
VCR	13_a	12_a	5	13	11	6	14_a	14_{ab}	4_b
Radio	56_a	42_b	27	49_a	42_a	20_b	62_a	42_b	35_b
CDs/tapes	63_a	48_b	41_b	61_a	41_b	37_b	66_a	54_{ab}	47_b
Video-game player	5	7	2	4	5	1	7	9	4
Computer[a]	19_a	8_b	9_b	16_a	8_{ab}	5_b	22_a	8_b	13_{ab}

	8–18 years			8–10 years			11–14 years			15–18 years		
	White	Black	Hispanic	White	Black	Hispanic	White	Black	Hispanic	White	Black	Hispanic
TV	69_a	80_b	69_a	62_{ab}	74_a	55_b	74	81	76	68_a	85_b	70_a
VCR	26_{ab}	29_b	21_a	16	33	17	28	28	22	29	28	25
Radio	81_a	63_b	60_b	61_a	47_b	46_b	87_a	65_b	63_b	90_a	75_b	68_b
CDs/tapes	93_a	86_b	82_b	85	81	75	96_a	87_b	81_b	94	90	91
Video-game player	23_a	34_b	25_a	27_a	41_b	30_{ab}	23_a	35_b	26_{ab}	20	26	16
Computer[a]	29_a	17_b	16_b	28_a	28_a	13_b	28_a	13_b	16_b	29_a	13_b	20_{ab}

[a] See Table A.3.2.1.

Table A.3.2.4. *Proportion of Homes Containing Three or More of Each Medium by Household Income[a] and Age*

	2–7 years			2–4 years			5–7 years		
	Low	Middle	High	Low	Middle	High	Low	Middle	High
TV	43	45	46	33	42	36	51	49	55
VCR	6_a	14_b	12_b	5_a	15_b	7_a	6_a	12_{ab}	16_b
Radio	33_a	49_b	55_b	25_a	46_b	44_b	39_a	52_a	65_b
CDs/tapes	44_a	55_b	65_c	41_a	52_{ab}	57_b	46_a	60_b	70_c
Video-game player	6	6	4	2	4	4	11_a	9_a	4_b
Computer[a]	6_a	12_b	24_c	7_a	10_{ab}	16_b	5_a	14_b	30_c

	8–18 years			8–10 years			11–14 years			15–18 years		
	Low	Middle	High	Low	Middle	High	Low	Middle	High	Low	Middle	High
TV	66	72	70	52	63	65	70	76	76	68	73	68
VCR	22	25	28	16	20	20	21_a	28_{ab}	32_b	28	26	32
Radio	60_a	72_b	81_c	40_a	47_a	65_b	61_a	78_b	88_c	70_a	84_b	90_b
CDs/tapes	83_a	90_b	93_b	70_a	81_{ab}	87_b	83_a	92_b	96_b	87_a	95_b	95_b
Video-game player	26	25	22	23	30	26	32_a	24_{ab}	21_b	21	22	18
Computer[a]	9_a	24_b	34_c	14_a	18_a	31_b	8_a	25_b	33_c	9_a	29_b	38_c

[a] See note to Table A.3.1.4.
[b] See note to Table A.3.2.1.

Table A.3.2.5. Proportion of Homes Containing Three or More of Each Medium by Parent Education and Age

	2–7 years			2–4 years			5–7 years		
	HS or less	Some college	College or more	HS or less	Some college	College or more	HS or less	Some college	College or more
TV	40	48	46	32	43	40	48	52	52
VCR	9	13	14	10	11	13	8	13	14
Radio	33_a	47_b	61_c	30_a	38_a	55_b	35_a	55_b	68_c
CDs/tapes	42_a	57_b	68_c	39_a	52_b	65_c	46_a	61_b	71_c
Video-game player	6_a	7_a	3_b	5	5	1	7	9	5
Computer[a]	5_a	10_b	28_c	5_a	7_a	23_b	6_a	12_a	34_b

	8–18 years			8–10 years			11–14 years			15–18 years		
	HS or less	Some college	College or more	HS or less	Some college	College or more	HS or less	Some college	College or more	HS or less	Some college	College or more
TV	70_{ab}	77_a	68_b	65	61	62	74_a	86_b	72_a	69	74	70
VCR	23	23	29	23	17	19	23_a	23_a	33_b	23_a	27_{ab}	34_b
Radio	68_a	76_b	77_b	54	50	56	68_a	81_b	83_b	76_a	84_{ab}	87_b
CDs/tapes	86	91	92	84	80	82	92	91	92	93	94	94
Video-game player	22	26	24	28	37	25	23	30	24	16	16	22
Computer[a]	12_a	19_b	35_c	17	26	27	9_a	17_b	35_c	13_a	18_a	41_b

[a] See note to Table A.3.2.1.

Table A.3.2.6. Proportion of Homes Containing Three or More of Each Medium by Family Composition and Age

	2–7 years		2–4 years		5–7 years	
	Two-parent	Single-parent	Two-parent	Single-parent	Two-parent	Single-parent
TV	46_a	28_b	39_a	20_b	53_a	35_b
VCR	13_a	5_b	13_a	4_b	13_a	5_b
Radio	54_a	28_b	49_a	19_b	59_a	35_b
CDs/tapes	60_a	42_b	57_a	33_b	63_a	49_b
Video-game player	5	2	4	–	7	4
Computer[a]	19_a	5_b	14	8	24_a	4_b

	8–18 years		8–10 years		11–14 years		15–18 years	
	Two-parent	Single-parent	Two-parent	Single-parent	Two-parent	Single-parent	Two-parent	Single-parent
TV	71_a	65_b	63	57	76	67	71	67
VCR	28_a	18_b	19	17	30_a	15_b	32_a	22_b
Radio	75_a	66_b	55	51	81_a	63_b	85	79
CDs/tapes	90	89	82	78	94_a	84_b	94	93
Video-game player	23	27	26	33	25	23	18_a	26_t
Computer[a]	26_a	21_b	21_a	34_b	25_a	15_b	32_a	18_t

[a] See note to Table A.3.2.1.

Table A.3.2.7. *Proportion of Homes Containing Three or More of Each Medium by Residence Locale and Age*

	2–7 years			2–4 years			5–7 years		
	Urban	Suburban	Rural	Urban	Suburban	Rural	Urban	Suburban	Rural
TV	44	46	42	41	35	42	48	55	42
VCR	13	12	9	14	8	13	11$_{ab}$	16$_a$	4$_b$
Radio	45$_a$	52$_b$	44$_{ab}$	43	43	36	47$_a$	60$_b$	52$_{ab}$
CDs/tapes	52$_a$	64$_b$	48$_a$	49	57	49	54$_a$	70$_b$	46$_a$
Video-game player	5	4	7	4	2	5	7	6	8
Computer[a]	13$_a$	20$_b$	12$_a$	12	14	11	14$_a$	25$_b$	13$_a$

	8–18 years			8–10 years			11–14 years			15–18 years		
	Urban	Suburban	Rural	Urban	Suburban	Rural	Urban	Suburban	Rural	Urban	Suburban	Rural
TV	71$_a$	73$_a$	64$_b$	63	65	58	72	78	72	77$_a$	73$_a$	56
VCR	27	26	23	24	15	18	28	29	25	28	31	24
Radio	69$_a$	80$_b$	68$_a$	47$_a$	67$_b$	45$_a$	73$_a$	83$_b$	77$_{ab}$	84$_a$	85$_a$	76$_b$
CDs/tapes	87$_a$	92$_b$	90$_{ab}$	77$_a$	89$_a$	79$_a$	86$_a$	94$_b$	95	96	92	93
Video-game player	24	24	24	27	26	28	25	24	26	20	22	17
Computer[a]	24$_a$	30$_a$	18$_c$	22	28$_a$	17$_a$	22$_a$	31$_a$	16$_a$	28	30	22

[a] See note to Table A.3.2.1.

224

APPENDIX 3.3: YOUTHS WITH EACH MEDIUM IN THEIR BEDROOMS

Table A.3.3.1. *Proportion of Youths with Each Medium in Their Bedrooms by Gender and Age*

	2–7 years		2–4 years		5–7 years	
	Female	Male	Female	Male	Female	Male
TV	31	34	27	25	35	41
VCR	15	17	15	14	16	20
Radio	41	44	34	30	48	57
CDs/tapes	38	38	34	30	41	45
Video-game player	8[a]	17[b]	5	3	8	9
Computer	7	6	6	9	10[a]	24[b]

	8–18 years		8–10 years		11–14 years		15–18 years	
	Female	Male	Female	Male	Female	Male	Female	Male
TV	61[a]	69[b]	59	58	63[a]	76	60[a]	69[b]
VCR	33[a]	38[b]	26	32	36	42	34	38
Radio	88	85	72	71	91	88	96	92
CDs/tapes	90[a]	86[b]	76	70	93	91	96	93
Video-game player	30[a]	58[b]	34[a]	50[b]	34[a]	64[b]	23[a]	59[b]
Computer	21	21	30[a]	16[b]	21	21	13[a]	25[b]

Table A.3.3.2. Proportion of Youths with Each Medium in Their Bedrooms by Race and Age

	2–7 years			2–4 years			5–7 years		
	White	Black	Hispanic	White	Black	Hispanic	White	Black	Hispanic
TV	28_a	51_b	37_c	21_a	39_b	31_{ab}	34_a	61_b	44_a
VCR	16	21	14	14	19	12	19	23	17
Radio	45_a	40_{ab}	34_b	31	42	28	58_a	39_b	42_b
CDs/tapes	41_a	30_b	28_b	35	26	25	47_a	35_b	31_b
Video-game player	2_a	19_b	9_a	7	10	7	18	27	12
Computer	6	8	5	4	5	2	7	11	8

	8–18 years			8–10 years			11–14 years			15–18 years		
	White	Black	Hispanic	White	Black	Hispanic	White	Black	Hispanic	White	Black	Hispanic
TV	60_a	79_b	77_b	51_a	76_b	55	65_a	77_b	68	61_a	85_b	64_{ab}
VCR	34_a	44_b	37_{ab}	25_a	46_b	24_a	36	43	38	38	41	32
Radio	89_a	82_b	85_{ab}	75	66	70	93_a	86_b	84_b	93	93	99
CDs/tapes	91_a	85_b	80_b	78_a	66_b	67	95_a	94_a	80_b	95	93	90
Video-game player	42_a	58	50_b	36_a	60_b	40_a	46_a	62_b	55_{ab}	40	49	50
Computer	19	24	21	22	33	18	19	22	25	18	17	18

Table A.3.3.3. Proportion of Youths with Each Medium in Their Bedrooms by Household Income[a] and Age

	2–7 years			2–4 years			5–7 years		
	Low	Middle	High	Low	Middle	High	Low	Middle	High
TV	41_a	35_a	26_b	32_a	29_a	20_b	49_a	43_a	32_b
VCR	17	16	15	12	14	14	21	19	17
Radio	39	39	46	27	30	36	50	50	55
CDs/tapes	31_a	34_a	44_b	24_a	32_{ab}	36_b	38_a	37_a	51_b
Video-game player	16_a	15_a	9_b	8_{ab}	11_a	4_b	23_a	20_{ab}	13_b
Computer	3	6	7	2	4	4	5	9	9

	8–18 years			8–10 years			11–14 years			15–18 years		
	Low	Middle	High	Low	Middle	High	Low	Middle	High	Low	Middle	High
TV	73_a	69_a	55_b	59_a	68_a	49_b	80_a	72_a	59_b	72_a	66_a	57_b
VCR	44_a	36_b	30_c	33_{ab}	34_a	24_b	49_a	39_a	34_b	44_a	36_{ab}	31_b
Radio	84	87	87	63	73	74	88	90	91	91	95	95
CDs/tapes	88	87	88	73	70	76	90	92	93	93	96	94
Video-game player	50_a	48_a	39_b	46_{ab}	48_a	37_b	60_a	52_a	37_b	40	39	43
Computer	17	21	22	21	20	25	19	23	19	13_a	20_{ab}	24_b

[a] See note to Table A.3.1.4.

Table A.3.3.4. *Proportion of Youths with Each Medium in Their Bedrooms by Parent Education and Age*

	2–7 years			2–4 years			5–7 years		
	HS or less	Some college	College or more	HS or less	Some college	College or more	HS or less	Some college	College or more
TV	42_a	40_a	20_b	35_a	27_a	18_b	49_a	50_a	22_b
VCR	17	18	13	15	13	14	21_a	23_a	13_b
Radio	38_a	41_a	49_b	29	32	35	48_a	49_{ab}	59_b
CDs/tapes	26_a	35_b	48_c	21_a	31_b	42_c	32_a	39_a	55_b
Video-game player	17_a	17_a	6_b	11	6	5	24_a	25_a	7_b
Computer	4	7	7	2	5	5	7	9	10

	8–18 years			8–10 years			11–14 years			15–18 years		
	HS or less	Some college	College or more	HS or less	Some college	College or more	HS or less	Some college	College or more	HS or less	Some college	College or more
TV	71_a	76_a	59_b	70_a	77_a	54_b	74_a	78_a	64_b	68	74	59
VCR	34	40	36	28	31	31	39	38	40	32_a	46_b	36_{ab}
Radio	83_a	90_b	88_b	66_a	73_{ab}	76_b	85_a	93_b	91_b	92	95	94
CDs/tapes	85_a	90_b	91_b	69	74	78	88_a	93_{ab}	95_b	91_a	95_{ab}	96_b
Video-game player	44_a	52_b	42_a	36_a	58_b	43_a	50_{ab}	56_a	45_b	43	46	39
Computer	13_a	19_b	25_c	13_a	22_{ab}	28_b	15	21	22	11_a	15_a	25_b

Table A.3.3.5. Proportion of Youths with Each Medium in Their Bedrooms by Family Composition and Age

	2–7 years		2–4 years		5–7 years	
	Two-parent	Single-parent	Two-parent	Single-parent	Two-parent	Single-parent
TV	29[a]	41[b]	22	31	36[a]	49[b]
VCR	15	17	13	13	18	20
Radio	44[a]	36[b]	34	23	55	46
CDs/tapes	41[a]	28[b]	36[a]	19[b]	46	37
Video-game player	11[a]	17[b]	7	5	14[a]	26[b]
Computer	6	8	3	5	8	10

	8–18 years		8–10 years		11–14 years		15–18 years	
	Two-parent	Single-parent	Two-parent	Single-parent	Two-parent	Single-parent	Two-parent	Single-parent
TV	63[a]	70[b]	57	59	69	71	61[a]	77[b]
VCR	35	38	29	30	38	39	35	42
Radio	88[a]	83[b]	73	71	91	82	95	92
CDs/tapes	89[a]	84[b]	74	68	94[a]	87[b]	95	91
Video-game player	44	43	42	40	49	45	39	44
Computer	20	21	20	28	22	15	18	23

Table A.3.3.6. Proportion of Youths with Each Medium in Their Bedrooms by Residence Locale and Age

	2–7 years			2–4 years			5–7 years		
	Urban	Suburban	Rural	Urban	Suburban	Rural	Urban	Suburban	Rural
TV	37_a	29_b	33_{ab}	31_a	20_b	29_a	43	36	37
VCR	17	16	15	16	12	13	19	19	16
Radio	40	46	38	31	33	30	49	57	47
CDs/tapes	37_a	42_a	28_b	31	35	24	43_a	48_a	30_b
Video-game player	14	11	14	7_{ab}	5_a	14_b	21	17	15
Computer	9_a	6_a	1_b	6	3	—	11_a	9_a	1_b

	8–18 years			8–10 years			11–14 years			15–18 years		
	Urban	Suburban	Rural	Urban	Suburban	Rural	Urban	Suburban	Rural	Urban	Suburban	Rural
TV	66	63	65	67_a	49_b	62_a	71	67	72	61_a	70_b	59_a
VCR	36	36	35	37_a	22_b	30_{ab}	41	38	39	30_a	43_b	33_a
Radio	85	88	86	70	75	70	87_a	88_a	94_b	94_{ab}	96_a	90_b
CDs/tapes	85	89	89	70	77	72	89_a	91_a	96_b	94	94	94
Video-game player	44	46	44	48_a	36_b	45_{ab}	48	47	53	34_a	52_b	30_a
Computer	23_a	23_a	15_b	28_a	21_{ab}	17_b	21_{ab}	27_a	15_b	21	21	14

APPENDIX 3.4: HOUSEHOLD TV ORIENTATION

Table A.3.4.1. Household TV Orientation by Gender and Age[a]

	2–7 years		2–4 years		5–7 years	
	Female	Male	Female	Male	Female	Male
Constant TV	35	36	37	39	32	33
TV during meals	46	48	47	47	45	48
No TV rules	28	29	31	35	25	25

	8–18 years		8–10 years		11–14 years		15–18 years	
	Female	Male	Female	Male	Female	Male	Female	Male
Constant TV	52	55	50	44	47	46	49	43
TV during means	64	66	65	65	63	65	65	69
No TV rules	38	38	50	53	43	40	25	24

[a] For this table and Tables A.3.4.2–A.3.4.6, proportion of youths indicating (1) that in their household the television is on most of the time even when no one is watching; (2) that the television is usually on during meals; and (3) that there are no household rules about TV viewing.

231

Table A.3.4.2. *Household TV Orientation by Race and Age*[a]

	2–7 years			2–4 years			5–7 years		
	White	Black	Hispanic	White	Black	Hispanic	White	Black	Hispanic
Constant TV	33_a	52_b	30_a	35_a	52_b	38_a	31_a	51_b	21_a
TV during meals	42_a	66_b	52_c	42_a	67_b	54_b	42_a	65_b	48_a
No TV rules	25_a	38_b	36_b	29_a	45_b	40_b	22	31	30

	8–18 years			8–10 years			11–14 years			15–18 years		
	White	Black	Hispanic	White	Black	Hispanic	White	Black	Hispanic	White	Black	Hispanic
Constant TV	42_a	59_b	50_c	44	54	42	45	54	47	39_a	71_b	42_{ab}
TV during meals	42_a	66_b	52_c	56_a	82_b	71_b	58_a	84_b	68_c	61_a	91_b	79_b
No TV rules	63	64	59	50	54	41	40	44	39	74	83	72

[a] See note to Table A.3.4.1.

Table A.3.4.3. *Household TV Orientation by Household Income[a] and Age[b]*

	2–7 years			2–4 years			5–7 years		
	Low	Middle	High	Low	Middle	High	Low	Middle	High
Constant TV	50_a	38_b	27_c	54_a	42_a	28_b	46_a	34_{ab}	26_b
TV during meals	62_a	53_a	34_b	64_a	55_a	34_b	61_a	52_{ab}	34_b
No TV rules	37_a	31_a	23_b	42_a	36_a	25_b	33_a	25_{ab}	22_b

	8–18 years			8–10 years			11–14 years			15–18 years		
	Low	Middle	High	Low	Middle	High	Low	Middle	High	Low	Middle	High
Constant TV	51_a	47	43_b	57	45	45	50_a	49_a	40_b	49	47	42
TV during meals	75_a	67_b	57_c	76_a	73_a	52_b	71_a	65_a	57_b	80_a	65_b	62_b
No TV rules	66	60	62	44_{ab}	44_a	55_b	60	59	57	85_a	73_b	73_b

[a] See note to Table A.3.1.4.
[b] See note to Table A.3.4.1.

Table A.3.4.4. Household TV Orientation by Parent Education and Age[a]

	2–7 years			2–4 years			5–7 years		
	HS or less	Some college	College or more	HS or less	Some college	College or more	HS or less	Some college	College or more
Constant TV	53$_a$	40$_b$	19$_c$	56$_a$	45$_a$	20$_b$	49$_a$	36$_b$	17$_c$
TV during meals	66$_a$	54$_b$	27$_c$	68$_a$	52$_b$	28$_c$	64$_a$	55$_a$	26$_b$
No TV rules	39$_a$	29$_b$	21$_c$	43$_a$	27$_b$	28$_b$	35$_a$	29$_a$	13$_b$

	8–18 years			8–10 years			11–14 years			15–18 years		
	HS or less	Some college	College or more	HS or less	Some college	College or more	HS or less	Some college	College or more	HS or less	Some college	College or more
Constant TV	53$_a$	52$_a$	41$_b$	59$_a$	44$_{ab}$	44$_b$	50	50	43	54$_a$	58$_a$	35$_b$
TV during meals	72$_a$	71$_a$	58$_b$	73$_a$	69$_{ab}$	57$_b$	68$_a$	73$_a$	57$_b$	76$_a$	71$_a$	59$_b$
No TV rules	30$_a$	39$_b$	42$_b$	54	45	47	66$_a$	56$_{ab}$	56$_b$	86$_a$	74$_b$	68$_b$

[a] See note to Table A.3.4.1.

Table A.3.4.5. Household TV Orientation by Family Composition and Age[a]

	2–7 years		2–4 years		5–7 years	
	Two-parent	Single-parent	Two-parent	Single-parent	Two-parent	Single-parent
Constant TV	33_a	42_b	35	43	31	40
TV during meals	42_a	62_b	42_a	62_b	41_a	62_b
No TV rules	26_a	37_b	31	33	22_a	39_b

	8–18 years		8–10 years		11–14 years		15–18 years	
	Two-parent	Single-parent	Two-parent	Single-parent	Two-parent	Single-parent	Two-parent	Single-parent
Constant TV	45	50	48	45	45	55	43	52
TV during meals	63_a	75_b	63	68	62_a	76_b	64_a	80_b
No TV rules	40_a	30_b	50	40	55_a	73_b	74_a	86_b

[a] See note to Table A.3.4.1.

Table A.3.4.6. *Household TV Orientation by Residence Locale and Age*[a]

	2–7 years			2–4 years			5–7 years		
	Urban	Suburban	Rural	Urban	Suburban	Rural	Urban	Suburban	Rural
Constant TV	34$_a$	32$_a$	49$_b$	39$_{ab}$	33$_a$	52$_b$	30$_a$	31$_a$	45$_b$
TV during meals	51$_a$	42$_b$	52$_a$	51	42	54	51	42	49
No TV rules	34$_a$	25$_b$	25$_b$	39	29	30	29	23	21

	8–18 years			8–10 years			11–14 years			15–18 years		
	Urban	Suburban	Rural	Urban	Suburban	Rural	Urban	Suburban	Rural	Urban	Suburban	Rural
Constant TV	47	47	46	43	48	51	47	44	50	49	50	36
TV during meals	67$_a$	62$_b$	68$_a$	68$_a$	56$_b$	73$_a$	64	60	68	70	68	63
No TV rules	61	62	62	50$_a$	55$_a$	38$_b$	59	55	64	71	76	81

[a] See note to Table A.3.4.1.

APPENDIXES TO CHAPTER 4:
SCREEN MEDIA: RESULTS AND
STATISTICAL TESTS

APPENDIX 4.1: AMOUNT OF SCREEN MEDIA EXPOSURE

Table A.4.1.1. *Screen Media Exposure by Gender (2–7 years)*

	2–7 years		2–4 years		5–7 years	
	Female	Male	Female	Male	Female	Male
Average time spent watching (hr:min)						
TV	$1:53_a$	$2:10_b$	1:53	2:09	$1:52_a$	$2:11_b$
Videotapes	0:30	0:30	0:35	0:39	0:25	0:22
Movies	0:02	0:01	0:02	0:01	0:02	0:01
Total	$2:25_a$	$2:41_b$	2:30	2:49	2:19	2:35
Proportion reporting no exposure the previous day						
TV	17	15	15	17	19	14
Videotapes	59	58	54	47	64	68
Movies	98	99	99	99	98	99
Proportion reporting more than 1 hour and more than 5 hours TV exposure the previous day						
More than 1 hour	58	63	60	59	57_a	66_b
More than 5 hours	6	8	5	9	6	8

Table A.4.1.2. *Screen Media Exposure by Gender (8–18 years)*

	8–18 years		8–10 years		11–14 years		15–18 years	
	Female	Male	Female	Male	Female	Male	Female	Male
Average time spent watching (hr:min)								
TV	$2:55_a$	$3:15_b$	3:24	3:15	$3:13_a$	$3:47_b$	$2:12_a$	$2:34_b$
Videotapes	0:40	0:44	0:42	0:49	0:41	0:45	0:37	0:37
Movies	0:16	0:19	0:25	0:27	0:17	0:22	0:09	0:09
Total	$3:51_a$	$4:18_b$	4:30	4:31	$4:10_a$	$4:54_b$	$2:58_a$	$3:21_b$
Proportion reporting no exposure the previous day								
TV	17_a	14_b	25_a	25_b	14	10	25	25
Videotapes	55	56	47	50	55	55	60	62
Movies	91	89	86	86	91	88	94	94
Proportion reporting more than 1 hour and more than 5 hours TV exposure the previous day								
More than 1 hour	67_a	72_b	74	74	71	78	56_a	62_b
More than 5 hours	20_a	24_b	26	23	23_a	32_b	13	15

Table A.4.1.3. Screen Media Exposure by Race/Ethnicity (2–7 years).

	2–7 years			2–4 years			5–7 years		
	White	Black	Hispanic	White	Black	Hispanic	White	Black	Hispanic
Average time spent watching (hr:min)									
TV	1:45$_a$	2:49$_b$	2:23$_b$	1:44$_a$	2:47$_b$	2:25$_b$	1:45	2:51	2:20
Videotapes	0:32	0:30	0:24	0:36	0:43	0:32	0:28$_a$	0:17$_{ab}$	0:13$_b$
Movies	0:01	0:04	0:01	0:01	0:04	0:00	0:01	0:04	0:02
Total	2:18$_a$	3:23$_b$	2:47$_c$	2:21$_a$	3:34$_b$	2:57$_b$	2:14$_a$	3:13$_b$	2:35$_{ab}$
Proportion reporting no exposure the previous day									
TV	18	15	12	17	16	11	18	14	13
Videotapes	54$_a$	69$_b$	69$_b$	46	58	63	61$_a$	78$_b$	76$_b$
Movies	99	96	99	99	96	100	99	97	99
Proportion reporting more than 1 hour and more than 5 hours TV exposure the previous day									
More than 1 hour	55$_a$	73$_b$	68$_b$	53$_a$	75$_b$	67$_b$	57$_a$	71$_b$	70$_b$
More than 5 hours	4$_a$	15$_b$	10$_b$	4$_a$	15$_b$	14$_b$	5$_a$	15$_b$	6$_b$

239

Table A.4.1.4. Screen Media Exposure by Race/Ethnicity (8–18 years)

	8–18 years			8–10 years			11–14 years			15–18 years		
	White	Black	Hispanic	White	Black	Hispanic	White	Black	Hispanic	White	Black	Hispanic
Average time spent watching (hr:min)												
TV	2:42$_a$	4:12$_b$	3:34$_c$	3:01$_a$	4:22$_b$	3:49$_{ab}$	3:06$_a$	4:27$_b$	4:00$_b$	2:04$_a$	3:44$_b$	2:41$_a$
Videotapes	0:38$_a$	0:55$_b$	0:43$_{ab}$	0:43	0:58	0:42	0:36$_a$	1:07$_b$	0:46$_a$	0:38	0:38	0:40
Movies	0:11$_a$	0:25$_b$	0:31$_b$	0:20	0:28	0:30	0:11$_a$	0:30$_b$	0:40$_b$	0:06$_a$	0:16$_{ab}$	0:18$_b$
Total	3:32$_a$	5:33$_b$	4:49$_c$	4:04$_a$	5:48$_b$	5:00$_{ab}$	3:53$_a$	6:05$_b$	5:26$_b$	2:47$_a$	4:38$_b$	3:39$_b$
Proportion reporting no exposure the previous day												
TV	19$_a$	9$_b$	12$_b$	13$_a$	3$_b$	3$_b$	14	9	8	27	15	24
Videotapes	59$_a$	44$_b$	49$_b$	54$_a$	31$_b$	44	60$_a$	39$_b$	48$_b$	62	63	54
Movies	93$_a$	87$_b$	85$_b$	89	86	84	93$_a$	84$_b$	81$_b$	96	91	91
Proportion reporting more than 1 hour and more than 5 hours TV exposure the previous day												
More than 1 hour	65$_a$	79$_b$	76$_b$	72	83	80	70$_a$	80$_b$	83$_b$	56	72	63
More than 5 hours	17$_a$	36$_b$	28$_c$	19$_a$	39$_b$	30$_{ab}$	22$_a$	41$_b$	31$_b$	10$_a$	27$_b$	18$_b$

Table A.4.1.5. *Screen Media Exposure by Income*[a] *(2–7 years)*

	2–7 years			2–4 years			5–7 years		
	Low	Middle	High	Low	Middle	High	Low	Middle	High
Average time spent watching (hr:min)									
TV	2:30$_a$	2:08$_a$	1:44$_b$	2:20$_a$	2:15$_a$	1:43$_b$	2:38$_a$	1:59$_b$	1:45$_b$
Videotapes	0:29	0:32	0:29	0:43	0:39	0:31	0:16	0:25	0:27
Movies	0:02	0:00	0:03	0:02	0:00	0:03	0:02	0:01	0:02
Total	2:60$_a$	2:40$_a$	2:15$_b$	3:05$_a$	2:54$_a$	2:17$_b$	2:55$_a$	2:25$_{ab}$	2:14$_b$
Proportion reporting no exposure the previous day									
TV	14	16	17	19	12	16	8$_a$	21$_b$	18$_b$
Videotapes	68$_a$	53$_b$	59$_c$	59$_a$	46$_b$	53$_{ab}$	76$_a$	61$_b$	64$_b$
Movies	99	100	98	98	100	97	99	99	99
Proportion reporting more than 1 hour and more than 5 hours TV exposure the previous day									
More than 1 hour	73$_a$	61$_b$	55$_b$	65	64	54	79$_a$	57$_b$	55$_b$
More than 5 hours	10$_a$	8$_a$	5$_b$	11	8	5	9	8	6

[a] See note to Table A.3.1.4.

Table A.4.1.6. *Screen Media Exposure by Income (8–18 years)*

	8–18 years			8–10 years			11–14 years			15–18 years		
	Low	Middle	High	Low	Middle	High	Low	Middle	High	Low	Middle	High
Average time spent watching (hr:min)												
TV	3:21$_a$	3:09$_{ab}$	2:51$_b$	2:52$_a$	3:51$_b$	2:55$_a$	4:07$_a$	3:22$_b$	3:20$_b$	2:45	2:18	2:15
Videotapes	0:50$_a$	0:42$_{ab}$	0:37$_b$	0:46$_{ab}$	0:59$_a$	0:33$_b$	0:55$_a$	0:39$_b$	0:41$_{ab}$	0:46	0:33	0:36
Movies	0:22$_a$	0:20$_a$	0:12$_b$	0:11$_a$	0:38$_b$	0:18$_a$	0:32$_a$	0:20$_{ab}$	0:10$_b$	0:16	0:07	0:08
Total	4:32$_a$	4:12$_a$	3:39$_b$	3:50$_a$	5:28$_b$	3:46$_a$	5:34$_a$	4:20$_b$	4:10$_b$	3:47$_a$	2:58$_b$	2:59$_b$
Proportion reporting no exposure the previous day												
TV	16	14	17	7$_a$	6$_a$	15$_b$	13	12	12	24	25	25
Videotapes	50$_a$	54$_a$	59$_b$	50$_a$	37$_b$	60$_a$	45$_a$	57$_b$	57$_b$	57	64	60
Movies	90$_{ab}$	88$_a$	93$_b$	96$_a$	79$_b$	91$_a$	85	89	92	92	95	95
Proportion reporting more than 1 hour and more than 5 hours TV exposure the previous day												
More than 1 hour	70	71	67	72	79	70	77	73	75	62	61	55
More than 5 hours	24	23	19	16$_a$	31$_b$	20$_a$	34$_a$	27$_{ab}$	24$_b$	17	12	14

Note: See Table A.4.1.5.

Table A.4.1.7. *Screen Media Exposure by Parent Education (2–7 years)*

	2–7 years			2–4 years			5–7 years		
	HS or less	Some college	College or more	HS or less	Some college	College or more	HS or less	Some college	College or more
Average time spent watching (hr:min)									
TV	$2\!:\!36_a$	$2\!:\!10_b$	$1\!:\!29_c$	$2\!:\!38_a$	$1\!:\!56_b$	$1\!:\!36_b$	$2\!:\!34_a$	$2\!:\!22_a$	$1\!:\!22_b$
Videotapes	$0\!:\!31$	$0\!:\!32$	$0\!:\!27$	$0\!:\!37$	$0\!:\!41$	$0\!:\!33$	$0\!:\!25$	$0\!:\!26$	$0\!:\!21$
Movies	$0\!:\!01$	$0\!:\!02$	$0\!:\!02$	$0\!:\!01$	$0\!:\!01$	$0\!:\!02$	$0\!:\!01$	$0\!:\!02$	$0\!:\!02$
Total	$3\!:\!09_a$	$2\!:\!44_b$	$1\!:\!58_c$	$3\!:\!17_a$	$2\!:\!37_b$	$2\!:\!11_b$	$3\!:\!00_a$	$2\!:\!49_a$	$1\!:\!45_b$
Proportion reporting no exposure the previous day									
TV	12_a	16_{ab}	20_b	12	18	18	11_a	14_a	23_b
Videotapes	62	56	57	57	45	48	68	63	67
Movies	99	99	98	99	98	98	99	98	98
Proportion reporting more than 1 hour and more than 5 hours TV exposure the previous day									
More than 1 hour	71_a	66_a	48_b	69_a	60_{ab}	51_b	73_a	71_a	45_b
More than 5 hours	13_a	8_b	2_c	16_a	5_b	2_b	11_a	10_a	2_b

Table A.4.1.8. *Screen Media Exposure by Parent Education (8–18 years)*

	8–18 years			8–10 years			11–14 years			15–18 years		
	HS or less	Some college	College or more	HS or less	Some college	College or more	HS or less	Some college	College or more	HS or less	Some college	College or more
Average time spent watching (hr:min)												
TV	3:20$_a$	3:13$_{ab}$	2:50$_b$	3:29$_{ab}$	3:55$_a$	2:56$_b$	3:52$_a$	3:46$_{ab}$	3:15$_b$	2:37	2:13	2:16
Videotapes	0:48$_a$	0:38$_{ab}$	0:39$_b$	1:01$_a$	0:56$_a$	0:39$_b$	0:51$_a$	0:33$_b$	0:38$_b$	0:36	0:35	0:39
Movies	0:21$_a$	0:10$_b$	0:17$_{ab}$	0:35	0:20	0:24	0:24	0:11	0:19	0:09	0:04	0:09
Total	4:29$_a$	4:02$_{ab}$	3:46$_b$	5:05$_a$	5:11$_a$	3:59$_b$	5:07$_a$	4:30$_{ab}$	4:12$_b$	3:22	2:53	3:04
Proportion reporting no exposure the previous day												
TV	14	15	17	6	5	12	9	9	14	25	27	25
Videotapes	53	57	57	36$_a$	38$_a$	58$_b$	52	61	56	65	63	58
Movies	89	95	90	82	90	87	89	94	89	95	98	93
Proportion reporting more than 1 hour and more than 5 hours TV exposure the previous day												
More than 1 hour	73	69	67	80$_a$	84$_a$	69$_b$	78	78	71	62	50	60
More than 5 hours	24$_a$	26$_a$	18$_b$	23	34	19	31	31	25	17$_a$	16$_{ab}$	10$_b$

Table A.4.1.9. *Screen Media Exposure by Family Composition (2–7 years)*

	2–7 years		2–4 years		5–7 years	
	Two-parent	Single-parent	Two-parent	Single-parent	Two-parent	Single-parent
Average time spent watching (hr:min)						
TV	1:52$_a$	2:24$_b$	1:54	2:09	1:51$_a$	2:35$_b$
Videotapes	0:29	0:34	0:34	0:46	0:24	0:24
Movies	0:02	0:03	0:01	0:04	0:02	0:02
Total	2:23$_a$	3:00$_b$	2:29	2:60	2:17$_a$	3:01$_b$
Proportion reporting no exposure the previous day						
TV	16	17	15	20	17	16
Videotapes	57	62	49	56	65	66
Movies	99	98	99$_a$	96$_b$	99	99
Proportion reporting more than 1 hour and more than 5 hours TV exposure the previous day						
More than 1 hour	58$_a$	68$_b$	57	61	58$_a$	73$_b$
More than 5 hours	6	9	6	8	5$_a$	11$_b$

Table A.4.1.10. Screen Media Exposure by Family Composition (8–18 years)

	8–18 years		8–10 years		11–14 years		15–18 years	
	Two-parent	Single-parent	Two-parent	Single-parent	Two-parent	Single-parent	Two-parent	Single-parent
Average time spent watching (hr:min)								
TV	$2{:}55_a$	$3{:}38_b$	$3{:}03_a$	$3{:}42_b$	$3{:}20_a$	$4{:}11_b$	$2{:}16_a$	$3{:}00_b$
Videotapes	0:40	0:48	0:43	0:53	0:41	0:49	0:37	0:44
Movies	0:15	0:22	$0{:}22_a$	$0{:}38_b$	0:16	0:24	0:08	0:08
Total	$3{:}50_a$	$4{:}47_b$	$4{:}08_a$	$5{:}13_b$	$4{:}18_a$	$5{:}24_b$	$3{:}01_a$	$3{:}52_b$
Proportion reporting no exposure the previous day								
TV	15	14	9	10	13	8	24	23
Videotapes	57_a	49_b	53_a	40_b	57_a	47_b	61	56
Movies	92_a	88_b	89_a	76_b	91	88	95	96
Proportion reporting more than 1 hour and more than 5 hours TV exposure the previous day								
More than 1 hour	69	72	72	78	73	81	61	59
More than 5 hours	19_a	30_b	20_a	30_b	25_a	38_b	12_a	21_b

Table A.4.1.11. Screen Media Exposure by Residence Locale (2–7 years)

	2–7 years			2–4 years			5–7 years		
	Urban	Suburban	Rural	Urban	Suburban	Rural	Urban	Suburban	Rural
Average time spent watching (hr:min)									
TV	$2:13_a$	$1:48_b$	$2:18_a$	$2:18_a$	$1:46_b$	$2:09_{ab}$	$2:08_{ab}$	$1:49_a$	$2:26_b$
Videotapes	0:28	0:32	0:26	0:39	0:37	0:27	$0:17_a$	$0:28_b$	$0:25_{ab}$
Movies	0:02	0:02	0:00	0:02	0:02	0:00	0:02	0:02	0:00
Total	$2:43_a$	$2:22_b$	$2:44_a$	$2:59_a$	$2:25_b$	$2:36_{ab}$	2:27	2:19	2:51
Proportion reporting no exposure the previous day									
TV	16	17	16	14	16	21	18	17	10
Videotapes	62	56	58	51	49	53	73	62	64
Movies	98	99	100	99	98	100	98	99	100
Proportion reporting more than 1 hour and more than 5 hours TV exposure the previous day									
More than 1 hour	63_a	56_b	69_a	64	55	60	60_a	57_a	79_c
More than 5 hours	9_a	5_b	8_{ab}	9	5	9	9	5	7

Table A.4.1.12. *Screen Media Exposure by Residence Locale (8–18 years)*

	8–18 years			8–10 years			11–14 years			15–18 years		
	Urban	Suburban	Rural	Urban	Suburban	Rural	Urban	Suburban	Rural	Urban	Suburban	Rural
Average time spent watching (hr:min)												
TV	3:20$_a$	3:00$_{ab}$	2:54$_b$	3:36	3:00	3:24	4:01$_a$	3:25$_b$	3:04$_b$	2:18	2:33	2:13
Videotapes	0:41	0:41	0:43	0:45	0:36	1:00	0:44	0:46	0:38	0:35	0:40	0:35
Movies	0:26$_a$	0:13$_b$	0:14$_b$	0:38$_a$	0:14$_b$	0:26$_a$	0:24	0:17	0:16	0:17$_a$	0:07$_b$	0:01$_b$
Total	4:27$_a$	3:54$_b$	3:52$_b$	4:59$_a$	3:50$_b$	4:49$_a$	5:09$_a$	4:28$_{ab}$	3:57$_b$	3:10	3:20	2:49
Proportion who did not watch the previous day												
TV	15	16	15	6$_a$	14$_b$	8$_{ab}$	11	12	14	29	23	23
Videotapes	52$_a$	60$_b$	53$_a$	41$_a$	64$_b$	39$_a$	53	56	55	60	61	63
Movies	86$_a$	92$_b$	92$_b$	80$_a$	92$_b$	85$_a$	87	90	91	90$_a$	94$_a$	99$_b$
Proportion reporting more than 1 hour and more than 5 hours TV exposure the previous day												
More than 1 hour	71	68	68	80	70	72	76	75	71	57	59	61
More than 5 hours	24	23	19	25	24	23	33	27	23	13$_{ab}$	17$_a$	9$_b$

Appendix 4.2: Household TV Environment

Table A.4.2.1. *Household TV Environment and TV Exposure by Age (in years) (average time spent watching, hr:min)*

	2–7	2–4	5–7	8–18	8–10	11–14	15–18
Constant TV							
Yes	$2:51_a$	$2:44_a$	$2:59_a$	$3:43_a$	$4:02_a$	$4:12_a$	$2:50_a$
No	$1:36_b$	$1:37_b$	$1:35_b$	$2:31_b$	$2:41_b$	$2:55_b$	$1:55_b$
TV during meals							
Yes	$2:35_a$	$2:32_a$	$2:39_a$	$3:25_a$	$3:43_a$	$3:50_a$	$2:41_a$
No	$1:33_b$	$1:37_b$	$1:30_b$	$2:29_b$	$2:35_b$	$2:56_b$	$1:46_b$
TV rules							
Yes	$1:53_a$	$1:54_a$	$1:52_a$	2:57	$3:00_a$	$3:14_a$	2:17
No	$2:24_b$	$2:19_b$	$2:31_b$	3:11	$3:41_b$	$3:43_b$	2:25
TV in bedroom							
Yes	$2:25_a$	2:28	$2:23_a$	$2:20_a$	$3:53_a$	$3:53_a$	$2:41_a$
No	$1:50_b$	1:53	$1:48_b$	$3:29_b$	$2:31_b$	$2:38_b$	$1:50_b$

Note: Significance tests refer to pairs within columns.

Table A.4.2.2. *Household TV Environment and TV Exposure by Gender (average time spent watching, hr:min)*

	2–7 years		8–18 years	
	Female	Male	Female	Male
Constant TV				
Yes	$2:37_a$	$3:02_a$	$3:30_a$	$3:56_a$
No	$1:30_b$	$1:42_b$	$2:22_b$	$2:40_b$
TV during meals				
Yes	$2:25_a$	$2:43_a$	$3:17_a$	$3:32_a$
No	$1:26_b$	$1:41_b$	$2:14_b$	$2:43_b$
TV rules				
Yes	$1:45_a$	$2:02_a$	$2:39_a$	3:14
No	$2:16_b$	$2:30_b$	$3:05_b$	3:17
TV in bedroom				
Yes	$2:17_a$	$2:31_a$	$3:26_a$	$3:32_a$
No	$1:41_b$	$2:00_b$	$2:05_b$	$2:37_b$

Table A.4.2.3. *Household TV Environment and TV Exposure by Race/Ethnicity (average time spent watching, hr:min)*

	2–7 years			8–18 years		
	White	Black	Hispanic	White	Black	Hispanic
Constant TV						
Yes	$2:30_a$	$3:24_a$	$3:18_a$	$3:26_a$	4:23	3:55
No	$1:23_b$	$2:13_b$	$1:59_b$	$2:08_b$	3:55	3:15
TV during meals						
Yes	$2:17_a$	$3:06_a$	$2:56_a$	$3:03_a$	4:17	3:36
No	$1:23_b$	$2:17_b$	$1:47_b$	$2:14_b$	3:46	3:31
TV rules						
Yes	$1:40_a$	2:35	2:18	$2:27_a$	4:23	3:35
No	$2:02_b$	3:12	2:32	$2:52_b$	4:07	3:34
TV in bedroom						
Yes	$2:08_a$	2:59	2:28	$3:08_a$	$4:23_a$	3:39
No	$1:36_b$	2:40	2:19	$2:03_b$	$3:30_b$	3:19

Table A.4.2.4. *Household TV Environment and TV Exposure by Income[a] (average time spent watching, hr:min)*

	2–7 years			8–18 years		
	Low	Middle	High	Low	Middle	High
Constant TV						
Yes	$3:00_a$	$2:54_a$	$2:52_a$	3:38	$3:49_a$	$3:38_a$
No	$1:59_b$	$1:40_b$	$1:24_b$	3:04	$2:34_b$	$2:13_b$
TV during meals						
Yes	$2:52_a$	$2:29_a$	$2:32_a$	3:23	$3:34_a$	$3:13_a$
No	$1:53_b$	$1:44_b$	$1:20_b$	3:16	$2:20_b$	$2:23_b$
TV rules						
Yes	2:29	2:03	$1:31_a$	3:47	3:06	$2:20_a$
No	2:31	2:17	$2:30_b$	3:10	3:11	$3:11_b$
TV in bedroom						
Yes	$2:49_a$	2:13	$2:25_a$	$3:39_a$	$3:30_a$	$3:22_a$
No	$2:16_b$	2:05	$1:29_b$	$2:32_b$	$2:23_b$	$2:13_b$

[a] See note to Table A.3.1.4.

Table A.4.2.5. *Household TV Environment and TV Exposure by Parent Education (average time spent watching, hr:min)*

	2–7 years			8–18 years		
	HS or more	Some college	College or more	HS or more	Some college	College or more
Constant TV						
Yes	$3{:}06_a$	$2{:}49_a$	$2{:}21_a$	$3{:}53_a$	$3{:}22$	$3{:}41_a$
No	$2{:}05_b$	$1{:}45_b$	$1{:}18_b$	$2{:}44_b$	$3{:}04$	$2{:}13_b$
TV during meals						
Yes	$2{:}49_a$	$2{:}34_a$	$2{:}14_a$	$3{:}32_a$	$3{:}21$	$3{:}17_a$
No	$2{:}16_b$	$1{:}43_b$	$1{:}14_b$	$2{:}50_b$	$2{:}54$	$2{:}13_b$
TV rules						
Yes	$2{:}28$	$2{:}10$	$1{:}22_a$	$3{:}25$	$3{:}24$	$2{:}35_a$
No	$2{:}50$	$2{:}09$	$1{:}59_b$	$3{:}20$	$3{:}06$	$3{:}03_b$
TV in bedroom						
Yes	$2{:}51$	$2{:}12$	$2{:}01_a$	$3{:}35_a$	$3{:}33_a$	$3{:}22_a$
No	$2{:}26$	$2{:}09$	$1{:}21_b$	$2{:}45_b$	$2{:}09_b$	$2{:}04_b$

Table A.4.2.6. *Household TV Environment and TV Exposure by Family Composition (average time spent watching, hr:min)*

	2–7 years		8–18 years	
	Two-parent	One-parent	Two-parent	One-parent
Constant TV				
Yes	$2{:}38_a$	$3{:}06_a$	$3{:}35_a$	$4{:}09_a$
No	$1{:}31_b$	$1{:}55_b$	$2{:}22_b$	$3{:}02_b$
TV during meals				
Yes	$2{:}29_a$	$2{:}46_a$	$3{:}14_a$	$4{:}02_a$
No	$1{:}28_b$	$1{:}49_b$	$2{:}24_b$	$2{:}31_b$
TV rules				
Yes	$1{:}46_a$	$2{:}40$	$2{:}50$	$3{:}31$
No	$2{:}13_b$	$2{:}37$	$2{:}59$	$3{:}45$
TV in bedroom				
Yes	$2{:}17_a$	$2{:}41$	$3{:}22_a$	$3{:}52_a$
No	$1{:}43_b$	$2{:}11$	$2{:}10_b$	$3{:}05_b$

Table A.4.2.7. *Household TV Environment and TV Exposure by Residence Locale (average time spent watching, hr:min)*

	2–7 years			8–18 years		
	Urban	Suburban	Rural	Urban	Suburban	Rural
Constant TV						
Yes	$3:14_a$	$2:31_a$	$2:50_a$	$3:59_a$	$3:41_a$	$3:26_a$
No	$1:41_b$	$1:29_b$	$1:48_b$	$2:44_b$	$2:22_b$	$2:29_b$
TV during meals						
Yes	$2:50_a$	$2:22_a$	2:34	$3:34_a$	$3:26_a$	$3:39_a$
No	$1:35_b$	$1:23_b$	2:01	$2:51_b$	$2:20_b$	$2:16_b$
TV rules						
Yes	$1:59_a$	$1:41_a$	2:16	3:16	$2:38_a$	2:59
No	$2:39_b$	$2:09_b$	2:22	3:22	$3:16_b$	2:53
TV in bedroom						
Yes	$2:38_a$	$2:10_a$	2:29	$3:47_a$	$3:22_a$	$3:19_a$
No	$1:58_b$	$1:39_b$	2:13	$2:25_b$	$2:23_b$	$2:08_b$

APPENDIX 4.3: SCREEN GENRES

Table A.4.3.1. *TV Genres Watched by Gender (%)*

	2–7 years		8–18 years	
	Female	Male	Female	Male
Comedy	27	26	54_a	46_b
Drama	7	7	26_a	21_b
Movies	8	6	18	17
Sports	2_a	5_b	6_a	27_b
News/news commentary	4	3	12	12
Reality	3	5	10	13
Talk	1	1	13_a	7_b
Entertainment/variety	2	2	12	11
Music videos	1	1	13_a	8_b
Child entertainment	35_a	42_b	20_a	27_b
Child educational	69	67	26_a	23_b
(All children's)	79	81	34	37

Table A.4.3.2. *TV Genres Watched by Race/Ethnicity (%)*

	2–7 years			8–18 years		
	White	Black	Hispanic	White	Black	Hispanic
Comedy	25_a	40_b	24_a	50	53	49
Drama	7	8	7	26_a	20_{ab}	16_b
Movies	7	7	5	18	18	20
Sports	3	6	3	18	14	17
News/news commentary	3	5	3	13	16	10
Reality	4_{ab}	8_a	0_b	12	15	8
Talk	1	2	1	9_a	19_b	8_a
Entertainment/ variety	2	1	1	12	15	10
Music videos	1_a	4_b	0_{ab}	9_a	14_b	12_{ab}
Child entertainment	34_a	46_b	52_b	21	24	27
Child educational	66	73	73	22_a	28_b	28_{ab}
(All children's)	79	83	83	32_a	39_b	42_b

Table A.4.3.3. *TV Genres Watched by Income (%)*

	2–7 years			8–18 years		
	Low	Middle	High	Low	Middle	High
Comedy	36_a	27_b	19_c	46	52	49
Drama	6	9	5	17_a	22_a	29_b
Movies	7	8	5	23_a	17_{ab}	16_b
Sports	5	3	4	20	17	15
News/news commentary	3	5	3	12	14	11
Reality	7	4	5	10	11	13
Talk	1	1	1	14_a	10_{ab}	7_b

(*continued*)

Table A.4.3.3 (*continued*)

	2–7 years			8–18 years		
	Low	Middle	High	Low	Middle	High
Entertainment/ variety	3	2	1	8	12	13
Music videos	1	1	1	13_a	9_b	10_{ab}
Child entertainment	44	39	34	22	25	23
Child educational	68	68	68	26	25	22
(All children's)	76	87	78	37	37	34

Table A.4.3.4. *TV Genres Watched by Parent Education*

	2–7 years			8–18 years		
	HS or less	Some college	College or more	HS or less	Some college	College or more
Comedy	34_a	27_a	19_b	47	54	50
Drama	6_a	9_{ab}	5_b	25	23	23
Movies	6	9	6	22_a	16_a	16_b
Sports	3	6	3	21	19	16
News/news commentary	5	4	2	12	14	12
Reality	6_a	5_{ab}	2_b	14_a	16_a	9_b
Talk	2	1	1	12_a	11_{ab}	8_b
Entertainment/ variety	2	1	2	13	15	10
Music videos	1_{ab}	3_a	0_b	10	14	10
Child entertainment	43_a	45_a	31_b	17_a	25_{ab}	25_b
Child educational	65	71	68	23	22	25
(All children's)	76_a	87_b	78_a	31	36	36

Table A.4.3.5. *TV Genres Watched by Family Compositon*

| | 2–7 years | | 8–18 years | |
	Two-parent	Single-parent	Two-parent	Single-parent
Comedy	23_a	41_b	51	48
Drama	6	8	23	23
Movies	7	7	16	18
Sports	4	4	17	15
News/news commentary	3	5	11	16
Reality	3_a	8_b	12	11
Talk	$-_a$	4_b	8_a	16_b
Entertainment/ variety	2	1	12	11
Music videos	1	1	10	11
Child entertainment	38	46	24	23
Child educational	69	64	23	26
(All children's)	81	79	35	37

Table A.4.3.6. *TV Genres Watched by Residence Locale (%)*

| | 2–7 years | | | 8–18 years | | |
	Urban	Suburban	Rural	Urban	Suburban	Rural
Comedy	24_a	25_a	35_b	50	51	47
Drama	7	5	11	19_a	26_{ab}	24_b
Movies	9_a	5_b	9_{ab}	23	17	16
Sports	4	4	4	16	16	20
News/news commentary	2	5	2	11_{ab}	14_a	12_b
Reality	5	4	6	13	12	8
Talk	1	1	1	10	10	11
Entertainment/ variety	$-_a$	1_a	6_b	13	12	9
Music videos	2	–	0	12	9	10
Child entertainment	40	36	43	27_{ab}	24_a	18_b
Child educational	71	66	66	28_a	23_a	23_a
(All children's)	81	80	77	40_a	35_a	32_b

Table A.4.3.7. *Video Genres Watched by Age (in years) (%)*

	2–7	2–4	5–7	All 7th–12th graders	12–14	15–18
Action	5	4	7	42	43	41
Comedy	7	5	10	44	44	45
Drama	1	–	2	17	13	20
Family or children	85	86	82	11	15	8
Fitness	–	0	1	1	1	2
Horror	–	–	1	16	12	19
Romance	0	0	0	7	8	7
Science fiction	1	2	1	5	3	6
Music videos	0	0	0	4	6	2
Something else	4	5	2	2	2	2
Don't know	0	0	0	0	0	0
No answer	2	3	0	6	8	4
Skipped	0	0	0	0	0	0

Table A.4.3.8. *Video Genres Watched by Gender (%)*

	2–7 years		All 7th–12th graders	
	Female	Male	Female	Male
Action	1_a	9_b	35_a	48_b
Comedy	6	7	43	47
Drama	1	1	25_a	8_b
Family or children	88	81	14_a	8_b
Fitness	1	0	3_a	0_b
Horror	1	0	21_a	11_b
Romance	0	0	13_a	2_b
Science fiction	1	2	4	6
Music videos	0	0	6	2
Something else	3	5	2	2
Don't know	0	0	0	0
No answer	2	1	4	8
Skipped	0	0	0	0

Table A.4.3.9. *Video Genres Watched by Race/Ethnicity* (%)

	2–7 years			All 7th–12th graders		
	White	Black	Hispanic	White	Black	Hispanic
Action	5	6	3	39_a	39_{ab}	58_b
Comedy	8	4	6	48_a	59_a	24_b
Drama	2	0	0	17	18	8
Family or children	85	92	85	10	13	8
Fitness	0	0	3	1	5	0
Horror	–	0	3	14	18	24
Romance	0	0	0	8	2	13
Science fiction	1	0	3	4	5	5
Music Videos	0	0	0	3	2	3
Something else	3	0	9	2	4	3
Don't know	0	0	0	0	0	0
No answer	1	0	3	5	9	5
Skipped	0	0	0	0	0	0

Table A.4.3.10. *Video Genres Watched by Income[a]* (%)

	2–7 years			All 7th–12th graders		
	Low	Middle	High	Low	Middle	High
Action	5	5	4	50	36	41
Comedy	7	7	7	47	45	45
Drama	0	2	1	8_a	18_{ab}	20_b
Family or children	83	83	88	7	16	8
Fitness	0	1	0	2	2	1
Horror	0	1	1	24_a	12_b	14_{ab}
Romance	0	0	0	7	7	8
Science fiction	2	2	1	5	5	4
Music videos	0	0	0	2	5	4
Something else	7	2	6	2	1	3
Don't know	0	0	0	0	0	0
No answer	2	2	0	9	3	7
Skipped	0	0	0	0	0	0

[a] See note to Table A.3.1.4.

Table A.4.3.11. *Video Genres Watched by Parent Education (%)*

	2–7 years			All 7th–12th graders		
	HS or less	Some college	College or more	HS or less	Some college	College or more
Action	10_a	5_{ab}	2_b	44	44	38
Comedy	11	8	3	43	44	46
Drama	2	1	1	14_{ab}	7_a	21_b
Family or children	79	83	89	9	11	13
Fitness	0	1	0	2	2	1
Horror	1	0	1	28_a	11_b	11_b
Romance	0	0	0	10	4	7
Science fiction	3	2	1	5	2	5
Music videos	0	0	0	4	7	3
Something else	4	5	3	1	4	2
Don't know	0	0	0	0	0	0
No answer	4	0	2	8	4	4
Skipped	0	0	0	0	0	0

Table A.4.3.12. *Video Genres Watched by Family Composition (%)*

	2–7 years		All 7th–12th graders	
	Two-parent	Single-parent	Two-parent	Single-parent
Action	6	5	43	33
Comedy	7	11	43_a	57_b
Drama	1	2	17	17
Family or children	85	77	12	9
Fitness	0_a	2_b	2	1
Horror	1	0	14_a	23_b
Romance	0	0	7	10
Science fiction	1	3	5	4
Music videos	0	0	4	1
Something else	4	6	1_a	6_b
Don't know	0	0	0	0
No answer	2	2	4	7
Skipped	0	0	0	0

Table A.4.3.13. *Video Genres Watched by Residence Locale (%)*

	2–7 years			All 7th–12th graders		
	Urban	Suburban	Rural	Urban	Suburban	Rural
Action	8	4	2	43	38	44
Comedy	11	5	3	43	48	44
Drama	1	1	2	15	20	12
Family or children	82	86	84	12	5	17
Fitness	1	0	0	0	1	4
Horror	1	–	0	11	19	16
Romance	0	0	0	7	7	8
Science fiction	1	1	2	6	5	3
Music videos	0	0	0	6	4	1
Something else	5	3	5	2	3	1
Don't know	0	0	0	0	0	0
No answer	1	1	5	9	6	2
Skipped	0	0	0	0	0	0

APPENDIX 4.4: SCREEN VIEWING CONTEXT

Table A.4.4.1. *Social Context of TV Viewing by Day Part and Gender (%)*

	2–7 years		8–18 years	
	Girls	Boys	Girls	Boys
Proportion mainly alone				
Morning	32	28	35$_a$	46$_b$
Afternoon	28	22	40	44
Evening	9	11	30$_a$	41$_b$
Proportion mainly with parents				
Morning	19	22	8	8
Afternoon	13	17	14	12
Evening	31	29	28$_a$	21$_b$
Proportion mainly with siblings or friends				
Morning	25	26	19	18
Afternoon	17$_a$	26$_b$	28	24
Evening	25	25	34$_a$	29$_b$

Table A.4.4.2. *Social Context of TV Viewing by Day Part and Race/Ethnicity (%)*

	2–7 years			8–18 years		
	White	Black	Hispanic	White	Black	Hispanic
Proportion mainly alone						
Morning	30	32	25	39_a	42_{ab}	53_b
Afternoon	26	29	19	45	36	42
Evening	10	11	10	36	38	37
Proportion mainly with parents						
Morning	19	23	23	8	8	8
Afternoon	13	18	18	12	17	14
Evening	29	33	30	27_a	21_{ab}	19_b
Proportion mainly with siblings or friends						
Morning	26_a	18_b	30_a	17	17	20
Afternoon	21	19	27	22_a	32_b	33_b
Evening	24	27	27	31	32	31

Table A.4.4.3. *Social Context of TV Viewing by Day Part and Income[a] (%)*

	2–7 years			8–18 years		
	Low	Middle	High	Low	Middle	High
Proportion mainly alone						
Morning	32	33	25	40	43	40
Afternoon	28	21	25	37_a	42_{ab}	47_b
Evening	9	7	14	35	35	36
Proportion mainly with parents						
Morning	23	21	19	11	8	7
Afternoon	18_a	16_a	11_b	16_a	14_a	10_b
Evening	35_a	34_a	22_b	20_a	24_a	28_b
Proportion mainly with siblings or friends						
Morning	20	26	28	18	19	18
Afternoon	21	23	21	30_a	26_{ab}	23_b
Evening	26	27	22	34	33	29

[a] See note to Table A.3.1.4.

Table A.4.4.4. *Social Context of TV Viewing by Day Part and Parent Education (%)*

	2–7 years			8–18 years		
	HS or less	Some college	College or more	HS or less	Some college	College or more
Proportion mainly alone						
Morning	31	32	27	39	44	41
Afternoon	25	29	21	44	40	43
Evening	9	11	10	35	37	35
Proportion mainly with parents						
Morning	24$_a$	22$_{ab}$	17$_b$	10	9	7
Afternoon	19$_a$	18$_a$	9$_b$	15$_a$	16$_a$	11$_b$
Evening	37$_a$	33$_a$	23$_b$	22	29	25
Proportion mainly with siblings or friends						
Morning	24	24	27	21	18	18
Afternoon	24	21	21	27	27	24
Evening	28	26	21	32	32	32

Table A.4.4.5. *Social Context of TV Viewing by Day Part and Family Composition (%)*

	2–7 years		8–18 years	
	Two-parent	One-parent	Two-parent	One-parent
Proportion mainly alone				
Morning	28	33	40$_a$	49$_b$
Afternoon	23	32	42	45
Evening	11	9	34	40
Proportion mainly with parents				
Morning	22	18	9	7
Afternoon	14	17	14	11
Evening	29	36	27$_a$	18$_b$
Proportion mainly with siblings or friends				
Morning	27	21	19	16
Afternoon	23	19	27	24
Evening	24	25	32	34

Table A.4.4.6. *Social Context of TV Viewing by Day Part and Residence Local* (%)

	2–7 years			8–18 years		
	Urban	Suburban	Rural	Urban	Suburban	Rural
Proportion mainly alone						
Morning	27	32	31	45_a	43_a	35_b
Afternoon	21	28	24	41	46	39
Evening	7	10	14	36	36	34
Proportion mainly with parents						
Morning	22	19	21	9_a	6_b	11_a
Afternoon	15	12	23	13	12	15
Evening	27	29	39	22	25	26
Proportion mainly with siblings or friends						
Morning	24	27	25	19	17	21
Afternoon	25_a	19_b	22_{ab}	29	24	26
Evening	28	23	23	33	30	33

Table A.4.4.7. *Social Context of TV Viewing by Day Part for Children With and Without Siblings* (%)

	2–7 years		8–18 years	
	Only child	Has siblings	Only child	Has siblings
Proportion mainly alone				
Morning	51_a	22_b	62_a	36_b
Afternoon	41_a	19_b	58_a	38_b
Evening	17_a	7_b	45_a	32_b
Proportion mainly with parents				
Morning	26_a	19_b	5_a	23_b
Afternoon	19_a	13_b	12	13
Evening	36_a	28_b	23	25
Proportion mainly with siblings or friends				
Morning	2_a	33_b	5_a	23_b
Afternoon	4_a	28_b	10_a	31_b
Evening	2_a	33_b	16_a	37_b

Table A.4.4.8. *Social Context of TV Viewing by Day Part and Absence or Presence of Television in Bedroom (%)*

	2–7 years		8–18 years	
	No TV in bedroom	TV in bedroom	No TV in bedroom	TV in bedroom
Proportion mainly alone				
Morning	26_a	39_b	32_a	45_b
Afternoon	25	25	35_a	46_b
Evening	8	13	25_a	40_b
Proportion mainly with parents				
Morning	21	20	7	9
Afternoon	14	16	11	14
Evening	28_a	34_b	25	24
Proportion mainly with siblings or friends				
Morning	27_a	21_b	20	18
Afternoon	21	22	27	25
Evening	23	29	36_a	30_b

APPENDIX 4.5: ATTITUDES TOWARD TELEVISION

Table A.4.5.1. *Attitudes toward Television by Age (in years)(%)*[a]

	8–18	8–10	11–14	15–18
TV entertains	55	65	57_b	44_c
Learn from TV	20	35_a	19_b	10_c
Watch TV to kill time	53	40_a	50_b	68_c

[a] Proportion of youths responding "most of the time" when asked how often they are entertained, and how often they learn interesting things, and "most of the time" or "some of the time" when asked how often they are just killing time when they watch TV.

Table A.4.5.2. Attitudes toward Television by Gender (%)[a]

	8–18 years		8–10 years		11–14 years		15–18 years	
	Female	Male	Female	Male	Female	Male	Female	Male
TV entertains	54	56	64	65	55	61	45	43
Learn from TV	20	21	36	35	21	17	6_a	14_b
Watch TV to kill time	55	52	39	40	50	50	71	65

[a] See note to Table A.4.5.1.

Table A.4.5.3. *Attitudes toward Television by Race/Ethnicity (%)*[a]

	8–18 years			8–10 years			11–14 years			15–18 years		
	White	Black	Hispanic	White	Black	Hispanic	White	Black	Hispanic	White	Black	Hispanic
TV entertains	52_a	63_b	60_b	67	66	66	55	63	64	39_a	59_b	51_{ab}
Learn from TV	16_a	30_b	23_b	32	46	34	14_a	28_b	23_b	8_a	17_b	14_b
Watch TV to kill time	56_a	49_b	50_b	41_a	28_b	47_b	51	55	42	70	62	66

[a] See note to Table A.4.5.1.

Table A.4.5.4. Attitudes toward Television by Income[a] (%)[b]

	8–18 years			8–10 years			11–14 years			15–18 years		
	Low	Middle	High	Low	Middle	High	Low	Middle	High	Low	Middle	High
TV entertains	52	56	55	59	64	68	60	60	53	41	46	45
Learn from TV	23$_a$	23$_a$	16$_b$	33$_a$	43$_b$	29$_{ab}$	24$_a$	22$_a$	13$_b$	16$_a$	8$_b$	9$_{ab}$
Watch TV to kill time	52	53	55	35	42	39	44	49	55	69	66	70

[a] See note to Table A.3.1.4.
[b] See note to Table A.4.5.1.

Table A.4.5.5. Attitudes toward Television by Parent Education (%)^a

	8–18 years			8–10 years			11–14 years			15–18 years		
	HS or less	Some college	College or more	HS or less	Some college	College or more	HS or less	Some college	College or more	HS or less	Some college	College or more
TV entertains	54	59	53	56	71	64	59	65	55	48	46	42
Learn from TV	19	17	21	41	33	35	18	13	20	6	13	11
Watch TV to kill time	57	51	53	44	32	39	55	47	49	68	66	70

^{a} See note to Table A.4.5.1.

Table A.4.5.6. *Attitudes toward Television by Family Compositon* (%)[a]

	8–18 years		8–10 years		11–14 years		15–18 years	
	Two-parent	Single-parent	Two-parent	Single-parent	Two-parent	Single-parent	Two-parent	Single-parent
TV entertains	55	56	64	70	59	56	44	40
Learn from TV	19	21	34	40	18	21	9	11
Watch TV to kill time	53	54	41	31	50	50	66	73

[a] See note to Table A.4.5.1.

Table A.4.5.7. Attitudes toward Television by Residence Locale (%)[a]

	8–18 years			8–10 years			11–14 years			15–18 years		
	Urban	Suburban	Rural	Urban	Suburban	Rural	Urban	Suburban	Rural	Urban	Suburban	Rural
TV entertains	57	55	52	64	70	59	63	54	57	45	47	39
Learn from TV	22	20	20	36	30	43	21	22	14	12	10	9
Watch TV to kill time	50	56	54	36	39	44	47	55	47	64	69	72

[a] See note to Table A.4.5.1.

269

Appendixes to Chapter 5:
Audio Media: Results and
Statistical Tables

Appendix 5.1: Amount of Audio Exposure

Table A.5.1.1. *Audio Media Exposure by Age (in years)*

	2–7	2–4	5–7	8–18	8–10	11–14	15–18
Average time spent listening (hr:min)							
Radio	0:25	0:25	0:24	0:46	0:24$_a$	0:46$_b$	1:04$_c$
CDs and tapes	0:21	0:24$_a$	0:19$_b$	1:02	0:31$_a$	0:58$_b$	1:33$_c$
Total	0:46	0:49	0:43	1:48	0:55$_a$	1:44$_b$	2:37$_c$
Proportion reporting no exposure the previous day							
Radio	40	41	39	24	45$_a$	21$_b$	12$_c$
CDs and tapes	61	60$_a$	63$_b$	27	45$_a$	21$_b$	17$_b$
Any music	25	25	26	14	30$_a$	11$_b$	4$_c$

Table A.5.1.2. *Audio Media Exposure by Gender*

	2–7 years		2–4 years		5–7 years	
	Female	Male	Female	Male	Female	Male
Average time spent listening (hr:min)						
Radio	0:23	0:26	0:22	0:28	0:24	0:25
CDs and tapes	0:23	0:19	0:23	0:24	0:23	0:15
Total	0:46	0:45	0:45	0:52	0:47	0:40
Proportion reporting no exposure the previous day						
Radio	42	39	45	39	39	39
CDs and tapes	59	63	60	61	59	66
Any music	25	25	26	24	23	27

	8–18 years		8–10 years		11–14 years		15–18 years	
	Female	Male	Female	Male	Female	Male	Female	Male
Average time spent listening (hr:min)								
Radio	0:55$_a$	0:38$_b$	0:30$_a$	0:19$_b$	0:55$_a$	0:38$_b$	1:13$_a$	0:55$_b$
CDs and tapes	1:14$_a$	0:51$_b$	0:42$_a$	0:22$_b$	1:16$_a$	0:40$_b$	1:34	1:32
Total	2:08$_a$	1:30$_b$	1:12$_a$	0:41$_b$	2:11$_a$	1:18$_b$	2:48	2:27
Proportion reporting no exposure the previous day								
Radio	19$_a$	29$_b$	38$_a$	51$_b$	17$_a$	24$_b$	8$_a$	15$_a$
CDs and tapes	22$_a$	30$_b$	36$_a$	53$_b$	17$_a$	26$_b$	19	16
Any music	10$_a$	17$_b$	22$_a$	36$_b$	8$_a$	13$_b$	3	5

Table A.5.1.3. *Audio Media Exposure by Race/Ethnicity*

	2–7 years			2–4 years			5–7 years		
	White	Black	Hispanic	White	Black	Hispanic	White	Black	Hispanic
Average time spent listening (hr:min)									
Radio	0:22[a]	0:33[b]	0:25[ab]	0:22[a]	0:40[b]	0:26[a]	0:23	0:27	0:24
CDs and tapes	0:22	0:15	0:23	0:25	0:12	0:28	0:20	0:17	0:17
Total	0:44	0:48	0:48	0:47	0:52	0:54	0:42	0:43	0:41
Proportion reporting no exposure the previous day									
Radio	42[a]	30[b]	42[a]	44[a]	26[b]	39[ab]	40	34	45
CDs and tapes	58[a]	74[b]	65[ab]	55[a]	79[b]	63[a]	55	79	63
Any music	25	23	29[*]	26	20	24[*]	24	27	34

	8–18 years			8–10 years			11–14 years			15–18 years		
	White	Black	Hispanic	White	Black	Hispanic	White	Black	Hispanic	White	Black	Hispanic
Average time spent listening (hr:min)												
Radio	0:46	0:45	0:55	0:20[a]	0:33[b]	0:24[ab]	0:45	0:44	0:56	1:03	0:58	1:21
CDs and tapes	1:06	0:59	1:03	0:28	0:39	0:37	1:00	0:59	0:53	1:38	1:20	1:40
Total	1:52	1:44	1:58	0:49	1:12	1:01	1:45	1:43	1:49	2:40	2:18	3:02
Proportion reporting no exposure the previous day												
Radio	23	22	27	45	35	47	19	17	26	12	15	13
CDs and tapes	24	26	26	43	41	42	22	13	23	15	27	17
Any music	12	13	16	28	25	32	9	6	15	4	7	5

Table A.5.1.4. Audio Media Exposure by Income[a]

	2–7 years			2–4 years			5–7 years		
	Low	Middle	High	Low	Middle	High	Low	Middle	High
Average time spent listening (hr:min)									
Radio	0:26	0:24	0:26	0:30	0:25	0:24	0:21	0:23	0:27
CDs and tapes	0:19	0:23	0:19	0:18	0:25	0:21	0:19	0:20	0:18
Total	0:44	0:47	0:45	0:49	0:50	0:45	0:40	0:43	0:44
Proportion reporting no exposure the previous day									
Radio	43	43	37	42	44	38	44	41	36
CDs and tapes	71	59	59	69	56	61	72	62	58
Any music	31	25	23	30	24	25	31	26	23

	8–18 years			8–10 years			11–14 years			15–18 years		
	Low	Middle	High	Low	Middle	High	Low	Middle	High	Low	Middle	High
Average time spent listening (hr:min)												
Radio	0:52	0:46	0:43	0:19$_{ab}$	0:30$_a$	0:19$_b$	0:57$_a$	0:46$_{ab}$	0:40$_b$	1:03	1:01	1:09
CDs and tapes	1:04	1:03	1:01	0:29	0:38	0:25	0:57	0:58	0:57	1:31	1:30	1:38
Total	1:56	1:49	1:43	0:48	1:08	0:45	1:55	1:43	1:37	2:34	2:31	2:47
Proportion reporting no exposure the previous day												
Radio	24	23	26	48	39	50.	19	21	20	18$_a$	13$_{ab}$	8$_b$
CDs and tapes	23	27	28	42	45	46	16	21	25	20	19	13
Any music	13	13	15	28	26	33	10	11	11	8$_a$	4$_{ab}$	3$_b$

[a] See note to Table A.3.1.4.

Table A.5.1.5. *Audio Media Exposure by Parent Education*

	2–7 years			2–4 years			5–7 years		
	HS or less	Some college	College or more	HS or less	Some college	College or more	HS or less	Some college	College or more
Average time spent listening (hr:min)									
Radio	0:25ab	0:28a	0:22b	0:27ab	0:32a	0:20b	0:24	0:25	0:23
CDs and tapes	0:18a	0:18a	0:26b	0:21ab	0:17a	0:29b	0:15	0:18	0:22
Total	0:44	0:46	0:47	0:48	0:49	0:49	0:39	0:43	0:45
Proportion reporting no exposure the previous day									
Radio	44a	35b	42ab	42ab	33a	46b	46	36	38
CDs and tapes	69a	66a	52b	66a	66a	51b	72a	67a	53b
Any music	31a	23ab	23b	29	21	24	34a	25ab	21b

	8–18 years			8–10 years			11–14 years			15–18 years		
	HS or less	Some college	College or more	HS or less	Some college	College or more	HS or less	Some college	College or more	HS or less	Some college	College or more
Average time spent listening (hr:min)												
Radio	0:50	0:52	0:44	0:26	0:23	0:25	0:51	0:51	0:42	1:05	1:09	1:03
CDs and tapes	1:05ab	1:17a	0:59b	0:29	0:37	0:32	0:55a	1:17b	0:52a	1:41	1:37	1:31
Total	1:55ab	2:09a	1:43b	0:55	1:00	0:57	1:46ab	2:08a	1:33b	2:46	2:45	2:34
Proportion reporting no exposure the previous day												
Radio	21	21	24	36	47	45	20	16	20	12	14	12
CDs and tapes	25	21	26	42	36	43	25	15	20	16	21	17
Any music	11	10	14	23	27	29	11	6	11	4	6	4

Table A.5.1.6. *Audio Media Exposure by Family Composition*

	2–7 years		2–4 years		5–7 years	
	Two-parent	Single-parent	Two-parent	Single-parent	Two-parent	Single-parent
Average time spent listening (hr:min)						
Radio	0:23$_a$	0:33$_b$	0:24$_a$	0:35$_b$	0:23$_a$	0:31$_b$
CDs and tapes	0:22	0:20	0:26	0:17	0:19	0:22
Total	0:46	0:53	0:50	0:52	0:41$_a$	0:53$_b$
Proportion reporting no exposure the previous day						
Radio	40	38	41	41	40	36
CDs and tapes	59	65	56$_a$	72$_b$	62	59
Any music	24	27	24	30	25	24

	8–18 years		8–10 years		11–14 years		15–18 years	
	Two-parent	Single-parent	Two-parent	Single-parent	Two-parent	Single-parent	Two-parent	Single-parent
Average time spent listening (hr:min)								
Radio	0:43$_a$	0:53$_b$	0:22	0:32	0:43$_a$	0:56$_b$	1:02	1:02
CDs and tapes	0:60	1:00	0:28	0:34	0:55	1:02	1:32$_a$	1:15$_b$
Total	1:43	1:54	0:50	1:06	1:38	1:59	2:34	2:34
Proportion reporting no exposure the previous day								
Radio	23	26	44	46	19	26	12	13
CDs and tapes	27	29	45	50	22	23	18	22
Any music	13$_a$	17$_b$	28	37	10	13	3$_a$	9$_b$

Table A.5.1.7. *Audio Media Exposure by Residence Locale*

	2–7 years			2–4 years			5–7 years		
	Urban	Suburban	Rural	Urban	Suburban	Rural	Urban	Suburban	Rural
Average time spent listening (hr:min)									
Radio	0:25	0:25	0:21	0:30$_a$	0:23$_{ab}$	0:20$_b$	0:21	0:27	0:21
CDs and tapes	0:24	0:21	0:17	0:27	0:24	0:14	0:20	0:17	0:21
Total	0:49	0:46	0:38	0:57$_a$	0:47$_{ab}$	0:34$_b$	0:40	0:44	0:42
Proportion reporting no exposure the previous day									
Radio	43	36	46	39	40	51	48$_a$	33$_b$	41$_{ab}$
CDs and tapes	60	59	69	56$_a$	58$_a$	74$_b$	65	61	64
Any music	29$_a$	20$_b$	32$_a$	25$_{ab}$	21$_a$	37$_b$	33$_a$	20$_b$	28$_{ab}$

	8–18 years			8–10 years			11–14 years			15–18 years		
	Urban	Suburban	Rural	Urban	Suburban	Rural	Urban	Suburban	Rural	Urban	Suburban	Rural
Average time spent listening (hr:min)												
Radio	0:50	0:45	0:43	0:29	0:20	0:22	0:52$_a$	0:38$_b$	0:50$_{ab}$	1:05$_{ab}$	1:10$_a$	0:52$_b$
CDs and tapes	1:03	1:04	1:00	0:39	0:26	0:30	0:53	0:57	1:03	1:34	1:38	1:23
Total	1:53	1:49	1:43	1:08$_a$	0:46$_b$	0:52$_{ab}$	1:45	1:36	1:53	2:40	2:48	2:16
Proportion reporting no exposure the previous day												
Radio	22	25	27	41	46	49	18	25	18*	10$_a$	10$_a$	20$_b$
CDs and tapes	24	28	27	45	43	47	17$_a$	27$_b$	19$_{ab}$	16	17	20
Any music	13	14	14	29	30	31	8$_a$	14$_b$	9$_{ab}$	4	4	6

APPENDIX 5.2: TYPE OF AUDIO EXPOSURE

Table A.5.2.1. *Amount and Proportion of Time 2- to 7-year-olds and 7th–12th Graders Listen to Each Type of Radio Content*

	2–7 years		7th–12th graders	
	Time	%	Time	%
Music	0:20	83	0:47	79
News	0:02	9	0:79	8
Talk	0:02	6	0:04	8
Other	0:01	2	0:03	5
Total radio	0:25	100	1:00	100

APPENDIX 5.3: AUDIO GENRES

Table A.5.3.1. *Audio Genres Listened to by Age (%)*

	2–7 years	All 7th–12th graders	12–14 years	15–18 years
Alternative rock	8	42	38_a	45_b
Books on tape	3	–	0	–
Children's	39	1	1	1
Classic rock	7	12	7_a	16_b
Classical	9	4	2	5
Comedy	–	4	5	4
Country and western	9	14	9_a	18_b
Gospel or Christian	10	8	7	9
Hard rock or metal	1	20	15_a	23_b
Jazz or blues	5	5	2_a	7_b
Latin or salsa	5	5	4	6
Rap or hip hop	7	52	50	53
Rave or techno rock	–	6	6	6
Reggae	3	4	2_a	5_b
Rhythm and blues or soul	6	13	13	13
Ska or punk	1	8	7	8
Soft rock	8	10	10	10
Top 40	9	9	10	8
Something else	5	–	0	1

Table A.5.3.2. *Audio Genres Listened to by Gender (%)*

	All 7th–12th graders	
	Female	Male
Alternative rock	44	39
Books on tape	–	–
Children's	1	1
Classic rock	11	13
Classical	4	3
Comedy	3_a	5_b
Country and western	17_a	11_b
Gospel or Christian	11_a	5_b
Hard rock or metal	12_a	27_b
Jazz or blues	4	6
Latin or salsa	4_a	1_b
Rap or hip hop	52	53
Rave or techno rock	7	5
Reggae	3_a	5_b
Rhythm and blues or soul	17_a	8_b
Ska or punk	7	8
Soft rock	15_a	5_b
Top 40	11_a	6_b
Something else	–	–

Table A.5.3.3. *Audio Genres Listened to by Race/Ethnicity (%)*

	All 7th–12th graders		
	White	Black	Hispanic
Alternative rock	51_a	5_b	39_a
Books on tape	–	0	0
Children's	1	2	0
Classic rock	15_a	2_b	5_b
Classical	4	3	1
Comedy	6_a	0_b	1_{ab}
Country and western	18_a	3_b	10_{ab}
Gospel or Christian	7_a	19_b	6_a
Hard rock or metal	24_a	2_b	16_a
Jazz or blues	5	8	2

	All 7th–12th graders		
	White	Black	Hispanic
Latin or salsa	–	0_a	16_b
Rap or hip hop	43_a	84_b	65_c
Rave or techno rock	5_{ab}	2_a	10_b
Reggae	3	3	7
Rhythm and blues or soul	9_a	31_b	18_b
Ska or punk	10_a	0_b	5_{ab}
Soft rock	12_a	3_b	11_a
Top 40	10_a	0_b	8_a
Something else	–	0	0

Table A.5.3.4. *Audio Genres Listened to by Income^a* (%)

	All 7th–12th graders		
	Low	Middle	High
Alternative rock	30_a	44_b	47_b
Books on tape	–	0	0
Children's	0	1	0
Classic rock	5_a	15_b	13_b
Classical	1	4	4
Comedy	1	5	5
Country and western	13	15	14
Gospel or Christian	6_a	12_b	5_a
Hard rock or metal	18	19	20
Jazz or blues	4	6	5
Latin or salsa	6_a	1_b	2_b
Rap or hip hop	69_a	49_b	47_b
Rave or techno rock	4	6	6
Reggae	3	3	4
Rhythm and blues or soul	16	12	12
Ska or punk	4	8	9
Soft rock	8	11	10
Top 40	6	10	9
Something else	0	1	–

^{a} See note to Table A.3.1.4.

Table A.5.3.5. *Audio Genres Listened to by Parent Education* (%)

	All 7th–12th graders		
	HS or less	Some college	College or more
Alternative rock	39	46	44
Books on tape	0	1	–
Children's	0	1	1
Classic rock	8_a	13_{ab}	15_b
Classical	3	2	4
Comedy	3	3	5
Country and western	15	15	14
Gospel or Christian	7	10	8
Hard rock or metal	20	23	18
Jazz or blues	4	3	6
Latin or salsa	2	4	2
Rap or hip hop	62_a	56_a	44_b
Rave or techno rock	9	5	5
Reggae	4	4	3
Rhythm and blues or soul	13	16	10
Ska or punk	4_a	8_{ab}	9_b
Soft rock	6_a	14_b	11_b
Top 40	5_a	10_{ab}	11_b
Something else	0	0	1
Don't Know	0	0	1

Table A.5.3.6. *Audio Genres Listened to by Family Composition* (%)

	All 7th–12th graders	
	Two-parent	Single-parent
Alternative rock	42	41
Books on tape	–	1
Children's	1	1
Classic rock	12	10
Classical	3	5
Comedy	5	1
Country and western	13	19

	All 7th–12th graders	
	Two-parent	Single-parent
Gospel or Christian	8	7
Hard rock or metal	19	17
Jazz or blues	4	6
Latin or salsa	3	2
Rap or hip hop	50	58
Rave or techno rock	6	5
Reggae	4	4
Rhythm and blues or soul	11$_a$	20$_b$
Ska or punk	8	6
Soft rock	11	8
Top 40	8	10
Something else	–	0

Table A.5.3.7. *Audio Genres Listened to by Residence Locale (%)*

	All 7th–12th graders		
	Urban	Suburban	Rural
Alternative rock	40	43	43
Books on tape	1	0	0
Children's	0	0	2
Classic rock	8$_a$	14$_b$	14$_b$
Classical	3	3	4
Comedy	3	5	4
Country and western	11	15	17
Gospel or Christian	10	8	7
Hard rock or metal	14$_a$	21$_b$	23$_b$
Jazz or blues	4	6	5
Latin or salsa	6$_a$	1$_b$	0$_b$
Rap or hip hop	58$_a$	48$_b$	52$_{ab}$
Rave or techno rock	7	6	4
Reggae	3	5	2
Rhythm and blues or soul	14	12	12
Ska or punk	9	8	5
Soft rock	12	8	11
Top 40	9	8	10
Something else	–	1	0

APPENDIXES TO CHAPTER 6:

PRINT MEDIA: RESULTS AND

STATISTICAL TESTS

APPENDIX 6.1: AMOUNT OF PRINT MEDIA EXPOSURE

Table A.6.1.1. *Print Media Exposure by Age (in years)*

	2–7	2–4	5–7	8–18	8–10	11–14	15–18
Average time spent reading (hr:min)							
Magazines	0:15	0:15	0:15	0:15	0:15	0:16	0:13
Newspapers	0:02	0:02	0:02	0:07	$0:06_a$	$0:07_a$	$0:09_b$
Books	0:29	$0:34_a$	$0:23_b$	0:21	$0:33_a$	$0:19_b$	$0:15_b$
All print	0:46	$0:52_a$	$0:41_b$	0:43	$0:54_a$	$0:42_b$	$0:37_b$
Proportion who did not read the previous day							
Magazines	53	56_a	51_b	45	57_a	41_b	41_b
Newspapers	88	90_a	85_b	58	69_a	58_b	49_c
Books	21	16_a	26_b	53	31_a	53_a	72_b
All print	12	11	13	20	20	19	21
Proportion who read more than 30 minutes the previous day							
Magazines	11	12	11	13	15_a	13_{ab}	10_b
Newspapers	1	1	1	4	4	3	4
Books	22	30_a	15_b	18	28_a	17_b	13_c
All print	49	55_a	44_b	42	50_a	42_b	34_c

Table A.6.1.2. *Print Media Exposure by Gender (2–7 years)*

	2–7 years		2–4 years		5–7 years	
	Female	Male	Female	Male	Female	Male
Average time spent reading (hr:min)						
Magazines	0:16	0:15	0:16	0:15	0:17	0:15
Newspapers	0:02	0:02	0:02	0:02	0:03	0:02
Books	0:30	0:28	0:36	0:34	0:25	0:22
All print	0:49	0:44	0:54	0:50	0:45	0:39
Proportion who did not read the previous day						
Magazines	55	51	57	55	53	48
Newspapers	87	89	89	91	84	86
Books	20	21	17	15	24	27
All print	13	11	10	12	15	11
Proportion who read more than 30 minutes the previous day						
Magazines	13	10	13	9	12	11
Newspapers	1	1	1	1	1	1
Books	25_a	20_b	33	28	18	13
All print	53_a	46_b	57	53	48	41

Table A.6.1.3. *Print Media Exposure by Gender (8–18 years)*

	8–18 years		8–10 years		11–14 years		15–18 years	
	Female	Male	Female	Male	Female	Male	Female	Male
Average time spent reading (hr:min)								
Magazines	0:15	0:14	0:15	0:15	0:16	0:16	0:14	0:12
Newspapers	0:06$_a$	0:08$_b$	0:05	0:06	0:06	0:07	0:08$_a$	0:10$_b$
Books	0:24$_a$	0:19$_b$	0:39$_a$	0:27$_b$	0:22$_a$	0:16$_b$	0:16	0:14
All print	0:46$_a$	0:41$_b$	0:60	0:49	0:44	0:39	0:38	0:36
Proportion who did not read the previous day								
Magazines	47$_a$	43$_b$	59	56	42	39	45$_a$	37$_b$
Newspapers	62$_a$	54$_b$	72	67	62	54	54$_a$	43$_b$
Books	50$_a$	57$_b$	26$_a$	36$_b$	48$_a$	57$_b$	69	75
All print	19	20	16	22	18	21	23	19
Proportion who read more than 30 minutes the previous day								
Magazines	14	11	15	15	14	12	13$_a$	7$_b$
Newspapers	3	4	4	4	4	3	3	5
Books	21$_a$	16$_b$	35$_a$	21$_b$	20$_a$	14$_b$	13	13
All print	43	41	52	48	45$_a$	40$_b$	34	35

Table A.6.1.4. Print Media Exposure by Race/Ethnicity (2–7 years)

	2–7 years			2–4 years			5–7 years		
	White	Black	Hispanic	White	Black	Hispanic	White	Black	Hispanic
Average time spent reading (hr:min)									
Magazines	0:16	0:13	0:14	0:16	0:11	0:17	0:17	0:15	0:10
Newspapers	0:02	0:04	0:01	0:02	0:05	0:01	0:02	0:03	0:01
Books	$0:31_a$	$0:26_{ab}$	$0:24_b$	0:37	0:33	0:28	0:25	0:20	0:19
All print	0:49	0:44	0:39	0:54	0:49	0:46	$0:44_a$	$0:38_{ab}$	$0:31_b$
Proportion who did not read the previous day									
Magazines	53	55	52	56	61	53	51	49	52
Newspapers	89	84	88	92	87	85	86	81	92
Books	18_a	27_b	29_b	12_a	21_{ab}	25_b	23_a	32_{ab}	35_b
All print	9_a	19_b	20_b	7_a	19_b	19_b	10_a	20_b	22_b
Proportion who read more than 30 minutes the previous day									
Magazines	13_a	7_b	8_{ab}	12	8	11	14	7	5
Newspapers	1	2	1	1	4	0	1	0	3
Books	24	18	18*	32	27	25	17	10	10
All print	50	50	43	57	54	49	44	47	35

Table A.6.1.5. *Print Media Exposure by Race/Ethnicity (8–18 years)*

	8–18 years			8–10 years			11–14 years			15–18 years		
	White	Black	Hispanic	White	Black	Hispanic	White	Black	Hispanic	White	Black	Hispanic
Average time spent reading (hr:min)												
Magazines	0:14	0:14	0:14	0:14	0:15	0:13	0:16	0:13	0:17	0:13	0:14	0:11
Newspapers	$0:07_{ab}$	$0:09_a$	$0:05_b$	0:05	0:08	0:05	0:06	0:09	0:05	0:09	0:09	0:06
Books	$0:21_a$	$0:22_{ab}$	$0:14_b$	0:34	0:38	0:25	0:19	0:17	0:15	0:16	0:12	0:05
All print	0:43	0:45	0:34	0:53	1:01	0:43	0:41	0:39	0:37	$0:38_a$	$0:35_{ab}$	$0:22_b$
Proportion who did not read the previous day												
Magazines	42_a	51_b	49_{ab}	56	58	56	37_a	52_b	42_{ab}	39	41	54
Newspapers	56_a	55_a	65_b	71	63	71	57	56	62	46_a	47_a	63_b
Books	56	50	56	32	30	26	54	55	57	74	63	83
All print	18_a	23_{ab}	24_b	18	19	18	18	25	21	19_a	24_{ab}	33_b
Proportion who read more than 30 minutes the previous day												
Magazines	10_a	14_b	15_b	10	18	17	11	11	18	8	16	11
Newspapers	3_{ab}	6_a	2_b	3	5	5	3_a	8_b	1_a	4	3	1
Books	19_a	20_a	11_b	30	31	22	16	19	10	14	11	5
All print	41_{ab}	47_a	35_b	51	58	42	42	42	40	34_a	40_a	21_b

Table A.6.1.6. Print Media Exposure by Income[a] (2–7 years)

	2–7 years			2–4 years			5–7 years		
	Low	Middle	High	Low	Middle	High	Low	Middle	High
Average time spent reading (hr:min)									
Magazines	0:13	0:15	0:16	0:12	0:15	0:16	0:15	0:15	0:16
Newspapers	0:02	0:02	0:02	0:01	0:02	0:03	0:03	0:03	0:02
Books	$0:22_a$	$0:30_b$	$0:30_b$	$0:25_a$	$0:37_b$	$0:34_{ab}$	$0:19_a$	$0:23_{ab}$	$0:26_b$
All print	$0:37_a$	$0:48_b$	$0:49_b$	$0:38_a$	$0:54_b$	$0:54_b$	0:36	0:41	0:44
Proportion who did not read the previous day									
Magazines	51	52	57	53	56	59	50	46	55
Newspapers	86	87	89	88	90	91	83	84	88
Books	30_a	19_b	19_b	22	15	15	37_a	23_b	22_b
All print	19_a	10_b	12_b	17	10	11	20_a	10_b	13_{ab}
Proportion who read more than 30 minutes the previous day									
Magazines	9	10	13	7	9	14	10	11	13
Newspapers	1	1	1	0	1	2	2	2	0
Books	13_a	23_b	25_b	16_a	31_b	32_a	10	14	19
All print	42	50	50	47	54	57	39	47	45

[a] See note to Table A.3.1.4.

287

Table A.6.1.7. *Print Media Exposure by Income* [a] *(8–18 years)*

	8–18 years			8–10 years			11–14 years			15–18 years		
	Low	Middle	High	Low	Middle	High	Low	Middle	High	Low	Middle	High
Average time spent reading (hr:min)												
Magazines	0:15	0:15	0:15	0:12	0:13	0:18	0:18	0:16	0:15	0:14	0:13	0:13
Newspapers	0:08	0:07	0:07	0:06	0:06	0:06	0:08	0:06	0:06	0:09	0:10	0:08
Books	0:20	0:21	0:22	0:27$_a$	0:27$_a$	0:41$_b$	0:19$_{ab}$	0:22$_a$	0:15$_b$	0:17	0:15	0:13
All print	0:43	0:43	0:44	0:45$_{ab}$	0:46$_a$	1:04$_b$	0:45	0:44	0:36	0:40	0:39	0:33
Proportion who did not read the previous day												
Magazines	46	47	43	65	61	50	42	42	39	40	42	42
Newspapers	57	57	59	69	68	71	58	59	56	51	45	51
Books	55	51	55	30	34	30	51$_{ab}$	49$_a$	60$_b$	73	69	75
All print	22	19	19	24	22	15	20	18	20	24	18	22
Proportion who read more than 30 minutes the previous day												
Magazines	13	13	11	11	16	15	17$_a$	14$_{ab}$	9$_b$	10	10	10
Newspapers	4	4	3	5	3	4	5	3	3	4	5	3
Books	17	18	20	23$_{ab}$	22$_a$	36$_b$	17	18	14	13	14	11
All print	38	42	44	43$_{ab}$	42$_a$	61$_b$	42	44	40	32	38	32

[a] See note to Table A.3.1.4.

Table A.6.1.8. *Print Media Exposure by Parent Education (2–7 years)*

	2–7 years			2–4 years			5–7 years		
	HS or less	Some college	College or more	HS or less	Some college	College or more	HS or less	Some college	College or more
Average time spent reading (hr:min)									
Magazines	0:18	0:16	0:14	0:17	0:17	0:13	0:18	0:15	0:14
Newspapers	0:02	0:02	0:02	0:02	0:01	0:03	0:03	0:02	0:02
Books	$0:25_a$	$0:27_a$	$0:34_b$	$0:28_a$	$0:33_{ab}$	$0:40_b$	0:20	0:22	0:27
All print	0:44	0:44	0:50	0:47	0:51	0:56	0:41	0:39	0:43
Proportion who did not read the previous day									
Magazines	48_a	50_a	59_b	51_a	51_a	63_b	44	50	56
Newspapers	89	87	87	91	92	88	88	84	85
Books	31_a	22_b	13_c	27_a	15_b	9_b	35_a	27_a	17_b
All print	18_a	14_a	6_b	17_a	14_a	5_b	19_a	15_a	7_b
Proportion who read more than 30 minutes the previous day									
Magazines	14	11	10	14	10	10	13	13	9
Newspapers	1	1	1	1	1	1	1	1	0
Books	17_a	21_{ab}	27_b	21_a	29_{ab}	37_b	13	15	18
All print	44_a	51_{ab}	53_b	46_a	59_b	60_b	42	44	46

Table A.6.1.9. *Print Media Exposure by Parent Education (8–18 years)*

	8–18 years			8–10 years			11–14 years			15–18 years		
	HS or less	Some college	College or more	HS or less	Some college	College or more	HS or less	Some college	College or more	HS or less	Some college	College or more
Average time spent reading (hr:min)												
Magazines	0:13$_a$	0:13$_a$	0:16$_b$	0:12	0:14	0:16	0:14	0:12	0:18	0:12	0:14	0:14
Newspapers	0:06$_a$	0:08$_{ab}$	0:08$_b$	0:04	0:07	0:07	0:05$_a$	0:07$_{ab}$	0:08$_b$	0:08	0:09	0:10
Books	0:14$_a$	0:23$_b$	0:24$_b$	0:21$_a$	0:26$_a$	0:41$_b$	0:13$_a$	0:22$_b$	0:21$_b$	0:11	0:22	0:14
All print	0:33$_a$	0:43$_b$	0:49$_b$	0:37$_a$	0:48$_{ab}$	1:04$_b$	0:32$_a$	0:41$_{ab}$	0:47$_b$	0:31$_a$	0:45$_b$	0:38$_{ab}$
Proportion who did not read the previous day												
Magazines	48	45	44	59	66	56	46	41	38	43	39	40
Newspapers	60	57	54	73	78	64$_*$	64$_a$	55$_{ab}$	52$_b$	47	50	48
Books	63$_a$	56$_b$	50$_b$	43$_a$	42$_{ab}$	25$_b$	59	51	49	79$_a$	68$_b$	71$_{ab}$
All print	26$_a$	18$_b$	16$_b$	29$_a$	26$_a$	14$_b$	26$_a$	15$_b$	15$_b$	24	19	19
Proportion who read more than 30 minutes the previous day												
Magazines	12	13	12	13	19	13	13	8	14	9	15	9
Newspapers	2	3	5	3	2	5	2	2	4	2	5	5
Books	12$_a$	20$_b$	21$_b$	17$_a$	30$_{ab}$	34$_b$	10$_a$	20$_b$	19$_b$	10	16	13
All print	31$_a$	41$_b$	48$_c$	36$_a$	47$_{ab}$	59$_b$	31$_a$	43$_b$	49$_b$	28$_a$	37$_{ab}$	38$_b$

Table A.6.1.10. *Print Media Exposure by Family Composition (2–7 years)*

	2–7 years		2–4 years		5–7 years	
	Two-parent	Single-parent	Two-parent	Single-parent	Two-parent	Single-parent
Average time spent reading (hr:min)						
Magazines	0:15	0:16	0:15	0:14	0:14	0:19
Newspapers	0:02	0:02	0:02	0:01	0:02	0:04
Books	0:29	0:26	0:34	0:32	0:24	0:22
All print	0:46	0:45	0:51	0:46	0:40	0:44
Proportion who did not read the previous day						
Magazines	54	54	55	65	52	45
Newspapers	88	87	90	91	86	84
Books	19[a]	26[b]	14	21	23	30
All print	10[a]	18[b]	9	16	12	19
Proportion who read more than 30 minutes the previous day						
Magazines	10	14	11	13	10	14
Newspapers	1	2	1	0	0[a]	3[b]
Books	23	18	31	28	16	11
All print	50	47	58	48	43	47

Table A.6.1.11. Print Media Exposure by Family Composition (8–18 years)

	8–18 years		8–10 years		11–14 years		15–18 years	
	Two-parent	Single-parent	Two-parent	Single-parent	Two-parent	Single-parent	Two-parent	Single-parent
Average time spent reading (hr:min)								
Magazines	0:15	0:14	0:14	0:15	0:16	0:14	0:13	0:14
Newspapers	0:07	0:08	0:05	0:05	0:07	0:06	0:09	0:11
Books	0:21	0:21	0:31	0:42	0:20	0:16	0:15	0:12
All print	0:43	0:43	0:49	1:01	0:43	0:36	0:37	0:38
Proportion who did not read the previous day								
Magazines	47	41	60	57	41	43	43$_a$	28$_b$
Newspapers	58	59	70	73	57	65	49	43
Books	55	51	34	23	53	51	74	69
All print	20	17	22	13	19	23	22$_a$	12$_b$
Proportion who read more than 30 minutes the previous day								
Magazines	13	11	13	18	14	10	11	8
Newspapers	3	3	2	2	3	4	4	3
Books	18	17	27	32	18	12	12	13
All print	41	41	45	58	44$_a$	35$_b$	34	36

Table A.6.1.12. *Print Media Exposure by Residence Locale (2–7 years)*

	2–7 years			2–4 years			5–7 years		
	Urban	Suburban	Rural	Urban	Suburban	Rural	Urban	Suburban	Rural
Average time spent reading (hr:min)									
Magazines	0:14	0:17	0:15	0:13	0:17	0:16	0:15	0:16	0:15
Newspapers	0:02	0:02	0:02	0:02	0:02	0:01	0:02	0:02	0:03
Books	$0:28_{ab}$	$0:31_a$	$0:24_b$	$0:34_{ab}$	$0:38_a$	$0:26_b$	0:23	0:24	0:21
All print	0:45	0:49	0:41	0:49	0:57	0:43	0:40	0:43	0:39
Proportion who did not read the previous day									
Magazines	53_a	56_a	46_b	54	60	47	52	52	44
Newspapers	86	89	86	89	90	92	84	88	80
Books	22	21	19	15	16	20	29	26	18
All print	14	12	11	12	11	12	15	13	10
Proportion who read more than 30 minutes the previous day									
Magazines	10	13	9	7_a	15_b	11_{ab}	13	12	6
Newspapers	1	1	0	1	1	0	1	0	0
Books	22_{ab}	25_a	15_b	28_{ab}	34_a	19_b	15	17	11
All print	51	49	48	57	56	49	45	42	47

293

Table A.6.1.13. *Print Media Exposure by Residence Locale (8–18 years)*

	8–18 years			8–10 years			11–14 years			15–18 years		
	Urban	Suburban	Rural	Urban	Suburban	Rural	Urban	Suburban	Rural	Urban	Suburban	Rural
Average time spent reading (hr:min)												
Magazines	0:16a	0:15ab	0:13b	0:17	0:15	0:12	0:18	0:17	0:14	0:13	0:14	0:12
Newspapers	0:09a	0:07b	0:06b	0:08a	0:05ab	0:04b	0:09a	0:06b	0:05b	0:09	0:09	0:09
Books	0:21	0:23	0:19	0:33a	0:41a	0:21b	0:16	0:23	0:18	0:16	0:11	0:20
All print	0:46a	0:45a	0:38b	0:59a	1:01a	0:37b	0:43	0:45	0:36	0:39	0:34	0:40
Proportion who did not read the previous day												
Magazines	45	43	48	52a	54a	67b	41	41	40	45	38	42
Newspapers	56	57	61	65	70	73	53	58	64	53	47	45
Books	54	53	55	31ab	27a	37b	57	49	53	69	74	73
All print	19	19	22	16a	15a	29b	19	19	20	21	22	18
Proportion who read more than 30 minutes the previous day												
Magazines	15a	13ab	10b	20a	12b	13ab	17	13	10	10ab	13a	6b
Newspapers	5a	3b	3	6	3	2	4	3	3	6	2	5
Books	17	21	17ab	24a	37b	21a	14	20	15	14	10	15
All print	42a	46a	35b	50a	60a	37b	43ab	46a	37b	35	37	29

Appendix 6.2: Print Genres

Table A.6.2.1. *Print Genres Read by Age (7th–12th Graders)(%)*

	12–14 years	15–18 years	All 7th–12th graders
Of those who read magazines, the proportion who read:			
Entertainment/pop culture	20	22	21
General interest	0_a	2_b	1
Health	2_a	8_b	5
Hobby/travel	17	21	19
Home	2_a	5_b	4
Men's	0_a	3_b	2
News	4_a	9_b	7
Science/nature	7	8	7
Sports	26	26	26
Teens	48_a	30_b	38
Women's	7_a	12_b	10
Of those who read the newspaper, the proportion who read:			
National news	27	30	29
Local news	26_a	53_b	42
Entertainment	32	31	32
Comics	39	39	39
Horoscope/advice	24	30	28
Sports	48_a	56_b	52
Fashion	8	6	7
Youth or teen	11	9	10
Of those who read books, the proportion who read:			
Adventure	24	19	22
Arts and music/hobbies	8	10	9
History/current events	10	12	11
Humor	12	10	11
Literature	6_a	12_b	9
Mystery/thriller	28	21	25
Religious	2	1	1
Romance	10	14	11
Science fiction/fantasy	13	11	12
Science/nature	6	3	5
Self-help	5	5	5
Sports	13_a	7_b	10

Table A.6.2.2. *Print Genres Read by Gender (7th–12th graders)*

	Female	Male
Of those who read magazines, the proportion who read:		
Entertainment/pop culture	25_a	17_b
General interest	1	2
Health	6	5
Hobby/travel	4_a	34_b
Home	5_a	3_b
Men's	0_a	4_a
News	5	9
Science/nature	6	9
Sports	7_a	47_b
Teen	72_a	3_b
Women's	17_a	1_b
Of those who read the newspaper, the proportion who read:		
National news	26	32
Local news	46	40
Entertainment	33	30
Comics	39	39
Horoscope/advice	47_a	13_b
Sports	31_a	71_b
Fashion	13_a	2_b
Youth or teen	15_a	6_b
Of those who read books, the proportion who read:		
Adventure	16_a	29_b
Arts and music/hobbies	9	9
History/current events	10	12
Humor	13	10
Literature	12_a	5_b
Mystery/thriller	29_a	18_b
Religious	–	2
Romance	19_a	2_b
Science fiction/fantasy	8_a	15_b
Science/nature	2_a	8_b
Self-help	6_a	2_b
Sports	4_a	20_b

Table A.6.2.3. *Print Genres Read by Race/Ethnicity* (7th–12th graders)

	White	Black	Hispanic
Of those who read magazines, the proportion who read:			
Entertainment/pop culture	21	28	25
General interest	2	1	2
Health	5	9	4
Hobby/travel	19	18	13
Home	4	2	0
Men's	2	1	2
News	7	5	5
Science/nature	7	2	5
Sports	28	29	23
Teen	37_{ab}	28_a	49_b
Women's	9	14	11
Of those who read the newspaper, the proportion who read:			
National news	32_a	23_{ab}	12_b
Local news	43	50	29
Entertainment	28_a	41_b	46_b
Comics	38	39	37
Horoscope/advice	25_a	39_b	29_{ab}
Sports	55	44	57
Fashion	6_a	8_{ab}	17_b
Youth or teen	7_a	19_b	17_{ab}
Of those who read books, the proportion who read:			
Adventure	22	26	24
Arts and music/hobbies	7	10	14
History/current events	11	14	14
Humor	11	17	4
Literature	9	7	4
Mystery/thriller	25	22	21
Religious	1	0	0
Romance	11	14	14
Science fiction/fantasy	13	3	14
Science/nature	4	7	0
Self-help	3	7	3
Sports	10	17	7

Table A.6.2.4. *Print Genres Read by Income[a] (7th–12th graders)*

	Low	Middle	High
Of those who read magazines, the proportion who read . . .			
Entertainment/pop culture	23	23	18
General interest	1	2	1
Health	9_a	5_{ab}	3_b
Hobby/travel	16	20	20
Home	3	2	5
Men's	3_{ab}	$*_a$	3_b
News	6	8	7
Science/nature	6	9	5
Sports	29	23	29
Teen	33	40	38
Women's	10	13	6
Of those who read the newspaper, the proportion who read:			
National news	25	33	27
Local news	41_{ab}	50_a	35_b
Entertainment	30_{ab}	38_a	25_b
Comics	31	42	40*
Horoscope/advice	31	34	20*
Sports	55	53	53
Fashion	9	7	6
Youth or teen	12	12	7
Of those who read books, the proportion who read:			
Adventure	28	19	21
Arts and music/hobbies	12	7	8
History/current events	10	13	8
Humor	9	14	12
Literature	5	10	10
Mystery/thriller	21	24	27
Religious	1	1	2
Romance	13	14	9
Science fiction/fantasy	8_{ab}	8_a	18_b
Science/nature	2	4	6
Self-help	5	5	3
Sports	10	11	11

[a] See note to Table A.3.1.4.

Table A.6.2.5. *Print Genres Read by Parent Education*
(7th–12th graders)

	HS or less	Some college	College or more
Of those who read magazines, the proportion who read:			
Entertainment/pop culture	20	25	20
General interest	2	1	2
Health	4	5	5
Hobby/travel	13_a	21_{ab}	21_b
Home	7_a	2_b	3_b
Men's	3	1	2
News	5	7	8
Science/nature	6	4	9
Sports	26	23	29
Teen	42	39	36
Women's	9	7	9
Of those who read the newspaper, the proportion who read:			
National news	21_a	29_{ab}	33_b
Local news	44	43	41
Entertainment	34	36	42
Comics	53	58	53
Horoscope/advice	35_a	26_{ab}	23_b
Sports	53	58	53
Fashion	9_a	2_b	8_a
Youth or teen	12	6	10
Of those who read books, the proportion who read:			
Adventure	16	20	25
Arts and music/hobbies	16_a	8_{ab}	6_b
History/current events	4	12	12
Humor	13	12	12
Literature	5	6	11
Mystery/thriller	27	23	24
Religious	2	0	1
Romance	14	7	13
Science fiction/fantasy	6	13	14
Science/nature	3	1	6
Self-help	1	5	6[*]
Sports	12	14	8

Table A.6.2.6. *Print Genres Read by Family Composition*
(7th–12th graders)

	Two-Parent	Single-Parent
Of those who read magazines, the proportion who read:		
Entertainment/pop culture	21	20
General interest	2	2
Health	4_a	8_b
Hobby/travel	21	13
Home	4	4
Men's	2_a	1_b
News	7	8
Science/nature	9	5
Sports	28	23
Teen	38	37
Women's	8	9
Of those who read the newspaper, the proportion who read:		
National news	31	28
Local news	40_a	55_b
Entertainment	33	30
Comics	39	44
Horoscope/advice	26_a	40_b
Sports	54_a	44_b
Fashion	7	8
Youth or teen	9	13
Of those who read books, the proportion who read:		
Adventure	23	17
Arts and music/hobbies	8	12
History/current events	11	8
Humor	11	16
Literature	10	5
Mystery/thriller	24	24
Religious	1	0
Romance	10	16
Science fiction/fantasy	13	7
Science/nature	4	5
Self-help	5	4
Sports	10	8

Table A.6.2.7. *Print Genres Read by Residence Locale*
(*7th–12th graders*)

	Urban	Suburban	Rural
Of those who read magazines, the proportion who read:			
Entertainment/pop culture	25	20	18
General interest	2	1	2
Health	6	4	5
Hobby/travel	13_a	22_b	22_b
Home	3	5	2
Men's	2	3	1
News	10	5	5
Science/nature	6	6	10
Sports	23	29	28
Teen	42	33	39
Women's	13	8	8
Of those who read the newspaper, the proportion who read:			
National news	33	27	26
Local news	43	44	39
Entertainment	40_a	29_b	24_b
Comics	40	42	34
Horoscope/advice	32	24	29
Sports	56	53	50
Fashion	9	6	6
Youth or teen	11	9	10
Of those who read books, the proportion who read:			
Adventure	16	24	24
Arts and music/hobbies	7	9	10
History/current events	11	12	10
Humor	7	15	13
Literature	9	10	9
Mystery/thriller	20	24	28
Religious	0	2	2
Romance	12_{ab}	5_a	19_b
Science fiction/fantasy	9	14	11
Science/nature	3	6	4
Self-help	9_a	2_b	2_b
Sports	9	14	10

APPENDIXES TO CHAPTER 7:

INTERACTIVE MEDIA: RESULTS

AND STATISTICAL TESTS

APPENDIX 7.1: AMOUNT OF INTERACTIVE MEDIA USE

Table A.7.1.1. *Interactive Media Exposure by Age (in years)*

	2–7	2–4	5–7	8–18	8–10	11–14	15–18
Average time spent using (hr:min)							
Computer games	0:06	0:04$_a$	0:07$_b$	0:12	0:14$_a$	0:13$_a$	0:08$_b$
Chat	0:00	0:00	0:00	0:05	0:04	0:06	0:05
Websites	0:00	0:00	0:00	0:07	0:04$_a$	0:08$_b$	0:09$_b$
E-mail	0:00	0:00	0:00	0:04	0:02$_a$	0:04$_b$	0:04$_b$
Video games	0:08	0:04$_a$	0:13$_b$	0:26	0:31$_a$	0:26$_{ab}$	0:21$_b$
Total computer use	0:06	0:04$_a$	0:08$_b$	0:27	0:23$_a$	0:31$_b$	0:26$_{ab}$
Proportion reporting no exposure the previous day							
Computers	74	86$_a$	62$_b$	49	55$_a$	48$_b$	45$_b$
Computer games	83	88$_a$	78$_b$	68	61$_a$	65$_a$	77$_b$
Video games	84	92$_a$	76$_b$	61	54$_a$	57$_a$	70$_b$
Proportion reporting more than 1 hour interactive media exposure the previous day							
Computers	1	1	1	14	10$_a$	16$_b$	14$_b$
Computer games	1	1	1	2	3	3	2
Video games	3	1$_a$	4$_b$	10	12	11	8

Note: Figures for video-game usage are not included in the "total computer use" figure.

Table A.7.1.2. *Interactive Media Exposure by Gender (2–7 years)*

	2–7 years		2–4 years		5–7 years	
	Female	Male	Female	Male	Female	Male
Average time spent using (hr:min)						
Computer games	0:06	0:06	0:05	0:03	0:07	0:08
Chat	0:00	0:00	0:00	0:00	0:00	0:00
Websites	0:00	0:00	0:00	0:00	0:00	0:01
E-mail	0:00	0:00	0:00	0:00	0:00	0:00
Video games	$0:03_a$	$0:13_b$	$0:01_a$	$0:07_b$	$0:05_a$	$0:19_b$
Total computer use	0:07	0:06	0:05	0:03	0:08	0:09
Proportion reporting no exposure the previous day						
Computers	75	72	85	85	65	60
Computer games	83	83	88	89	78	77
Video games	93_a	75_b	98_a	86_b	88_a	65_b
Proportion reporting more than 1 hour interactive media exposure the previous day						
Computers	1	*	1	0	0	1
Computer games	1	*	1	0	0	1
Video games	1_a	5_b	0_a	3_b	2_a	6_b

Table A.7.1.3. *Interactive Media Exposure by Gender (8–18 years)*

	8–18 years		8–10 years		11–14 years		15–18 years	
	Female	Male	Female	Male	Female	Male	Female	Male
Average time spent using (hr:min)								
Computer games	$0:08_a$	$0:15_b$	$0:12$	$0:16$	$0:09_a$	$0:17_b$	$0:05_a$	$0:12_b$
Chat	$0:05$	$0:04$	$0:05_a$	$0:02_b$	$0:05$	$0:06$	$0:05$	$0:04$
Websites	$0:06_a$	$0:08_b$	$0:04$	$0:03$	$0:07_a$	$0:09_b$	$0:07_a$	$0:10_b$
E-mail	$0:05_a$	$0:03_b$	$0:03$	$0:02$	$0:05$	$0:04$	$0:05_a$	$0:03_b$
Video games	$0:11_a$	$0:39_b$	$0:20_a$	$0:40_b$	$0:09_a$	$0:43_b$	$0:07_a$	$0:34_b$
Total computer use	$0:24_a$	$0:30_b$	$0:23$	$0:23$	$0:26_a$	$0:36_b$	$0:22_a$	$0:30_b$
Proportion reporting no exposure the previous day								
Computers	49	49	54	56	51	46	44	47
Computer games	72_a	64_b	61	61	71_a	60_b	81_a	72_b
Video games	77_a	45_b	63_a	47_b	76_a	39_b	89_a	50_b
Proportion reporting more than 1 hour interactive media exposure the previous day								
Computers	12	15	12	9	13	18	12	17
Computer games	1_a	4_b	1_a	4_b	2_a	4_b	0_a	3_b
Video games	4_a	17_b	5_a	17_b	3_a	19_b	3_a	13_b

Table A.7.1.4. *Interactive Media Exposure by Race/Ethnicity (2–7 years)*

	2–7 years			2–4 years			5–7 years		
	White	Black	Hispanic	White	Black	Hispanic	White	Black	Hispanic
Average time spent using (hr:min)									
Computer games	$0:07_a$	$0:03_b$	$0:04_{ab}$	$0:05_a$	$0:00_b$	$0:02_{ab}$	0:08	0:05	0:07
Chat	0:00	0:00	0:00	0:00	0:00	0:00	0:00	0:00	0:00
Websites	0:00	0:00	0:00	0:00	0:00	0:00	0:00	0:00	0:00
E-mail	0:00	0:00	0:00	0:00	0:00	0:00	0:00	0:00	0:00
Video games	0:08	0:08	0:09	0:04	0:03	0:04	0:12	0:13	0:14
Total computer use	$0:07_a$	$0:04_b$	$0:05_{ab}$	$0:06_a$	$0:01_b$	$0:02_{ab}$	0:09	0:06	0:07
Proportion reporting no exposure the previous day									
Computers	70_a	82_b	83_b	81_a	98_b	94_b	60	69	70
Computer games	80_a	91_{ab}	88_b	84_a	99_b	94_b	76	83	81
Video games	84	81	84	92	94	91	77	69	75
Proportion reporting more than 1 hour interactive media exposure the previous day									
Computers	1	0	1	1	0	0	1	0	1
Computer games	1	0	1	1	0	0	1	0	1
Video games	3	2	5	1	0	2	4	3	8

Table A.7.1.5. *Interactive Media Exposure by Race/Ethnicity (8–18 years)*

	8–18 years			8–10 years			11–14 years			15–18 years		
	White	Black	Hispanic	White	Black	Hispanic	White	Black	Hispanic	White	Black	Hispanic
Average time spent using (hr:min)												
Computer games	0:11	0:14	0:11	0:14$_{ab}$	0:17$_a$	0:07$_b$	0:12	0:16	0:15	0:07	0:07	0:10
Chat	0:05	0:05	0:05	0:04	0:05	0:02	0:05	0:07	0:07	0:06	0:02	0:05
Websites	0:07	0:06	0:06	0:04$_{ab}$	0:07$_a$	0:01$_b$	0:09$_a$	0:04$_b$	0:10$_{ab}$	0:08	0:07	0:04
E-mail	0:04$_a$	0:02$_b$	0:03$_b$	0:03	0:02	0:00	0:05	0:02	0:05	0:05$_a$	0:02$_b$	0:02$_b$
Video games	0:22$_a$	0:34$_b$	0:33$_b$	0:23$_a$	0:40$_b$	0:36$_{ab}$	0:24$_a$	0:38$_b$	0:28$_{ab}$	0:18$_a$	0:21$_{ab}$	0:38$_b$
Total computer use	0:28	0:26	0:25	0:25$_a$	0:31$_a$	0:11$_b$	0:31	0:29	0:36	0:27	0:18	0:20
Proportion reporting no exposure the previous day												
Computers	45$_a$	47$_a$	65$_b$	50$_a$	49$_a$	76$_b$	46	46	55	42$_a$	44$_a$	71$_b$
Computer games	68$_a$	62$_a$	74$_b$	56$_a$	58$_a$	77$_b$	66	57	68	77	72	81
Video games	63$_a$	54$_b$	57$_{ab}$	59	46	52	59$_a$	47$_b$	55$_{ab}$	70	70	66
Proportion reporting more than 1 hour interactive media exposure the previous day												
Computers	14	13	16	9$_a$	18$_b$	6$_{ab}$	15	12	22	15	10	13
Computer games	2	3	2	1	4	3	2	5	2	1	0	1
Video games	8$_a$	14$_b$	13$_b$	8	15	12	10$_a$	19$_b$	13$_{ab}$	7	9	14

Table A.7.1.6. Interactive Media Exposure by Income[a] (2–7 years)

	2–7 years			2–4 years			5–7 years		
	Low	Middle	High	Low	Middle	High	Low	Middle	High
Average time spent using (hr:min)									
Computer games	$0:02_a$	$0:06_b$	$0:07_b$	$0:00_a$	$0:05_b$	$0:05_b$	$0:03_a$	$0:07_b$	$0:10_b$
Chat	0:00	0:00	0:00	0:00	0:00	0:00	0:00	0:00	0:00
Websites	0:00	0:00	0:00	0:00	0:00	0:01	0:00	0:01	0:00
E-mail	0:00	0:00	0:00	0:00	0:00	0:00	0:00	0:00	0:00
Video games	0:08	0:10	0:07	$0:02_{ab}$	$0:07_a$	$0:01_b$	0:14	0:13	0:12
Total computer use	$0:02_a$	$0:07_b$	$0:08_b$	$0:00_a$	$0:05_b$	$0:05_b$	$0:03_a$	$0:08_b$	$0:10_b$
Proportion reporting no exposure the previous day									
Computers	85_a	74_b	68_b	98_a	82_b	83_b	74_a	64_{ab}	55_b
Computer games	94_a	81_b	79_b	98_a	85_b	87_b	91_a	76_b	73_b
Video games	81	83	84	93_{ab}	88_a	95_b	71	77	75
Proportion reporting more than 1 hour interactive media exposure the previous day									
Computers	0	*	1	0	*	2	0	1	1
Computer games	0	*	1	0	*	1	0	1	1
Video games	2	4	2	0_{ab}	3_a	0_b	4	4	4

[a] See note to Table A.3.1.4.

Table A.7.1.7. *Interactive Media Exposure by Income*[a] *(8–18 years)*

	8–18 years			8–10 years			11–14 years			15–18 years		
	Low	Middle	High	Low	Middle	High	Low	Middle	High	Low	Middle	High
Average time spent using (hr:min)												
Computer games	0:10$_a$	0:12$_{ab}$	0:13$_b$	0:07$_a$	0:13$_{ab}$	0:18$_b$	0:15	0:13	0:12	0:05	0:09	0:09
Chat	0:04	0:05	0:06	0:01$_a$	0:02$_a$	0:06$_b$	0:04	0:07	0:05	0:05	0:03	0:07
Websites	0:06	0:08	0:07	0:02	0:04	0:04	0:08	0:08	0:07	0:05$_a$	0:10$_b$	0:09$_b$
E-mail	0:02$_a$	0:04$_b$	0:04$_b$	0:01$_a$	0:01$_a$	0:03$_b$	0:03	0:05	0:05	0:02$_a$	0:05$_b$	0:05$_b$
Video games	0:28$_a$	0:29$_a$	0:20$_b$	0:41$_a$	0:37$_a$	0:21$_b$	0:33$_a$	0:27$_{ab}$	0:21$_b$	0:16	0:24	0:20
Total computer use	0:21$_a$	0:28$_b$	0:30$_b$	0:10$_a$	0:20$_a$	0:31$_b$	0:30	0:33	0:29	0:16$_a$	0:27$_b$	0:31$_b$
Proportion reporting no exposure the previous day												
Computers	62$_a$	53$_b$	38$_c$	76$_a$	65$_a$	38$_b$	48	50	46	71$_a$	46$_b$	28$_c$
Computer games	75$_a$	69$_b$	62$_c$	80$_a$	71$_a$	44$_b$	63	65	67	87$_a$	74$_b$	74$_b$
Video games	59$_a$	57$_a$	66$_b$	52$_{ab}$	48$_a$	62$_b$	49$_a$	56$_a$	66$_b$	73	66	71
Proportion reporting more than 1 hour interactive media exposure the previous day												
Computers	10$_a$	16$_b$	14$_{ab}$	4$_a$	10$_{ab}$	14$_b$	16$_{ab}$	18$_a$	12$_b$	7$_a$	17$_b$	16$_b$
Computer games	2	3	2	1	4	2	2	4	2	1	2	2
Video games	12$_{ab}$	12$_a$	8$_b$	17$_a$	13$_{ab}$	8$_b$	14	12	8	5	10	8

[a] See note to Table A.3.1.4.

Table A.7.1.8. *Interactive Media Exposure by Parent Education (2–7 years)*

	2–7 years			2–4 years			5–7 years		
	HS or less	Some college	College or more	HS or less	Some college	College or more	HS or less	Some college	College or more
Average time spent using (hr:min)									
Computer games	$0:03_a$	$0:05_a$	$0:08_b$	$0:02_a$	$0:02_a$	$0:06_b$	$0:04_a$	$0:07_a$	$0:10_b$
Chat	0:00	0:00	0:00	0:00	0:00	0:00	0:00	0:00	0:00
Websites	0:00	0:00	0:01	0:00	0:00	0:00	0:00	0:00	0:01
E-mail	0:00	0:00	0:00	0:00	0:00	0:00	0:00	0:00	0:00
Video games	0:11	0:07	0:07	$0:08_a$	$0:02_b$	$0:01_b$	0:15	0:10	0:12
Total computer use	$0:04_a$	$0:05_a$	$0:09_b$	$0:02_a$	$0:03_a$	$0:07_b$	$0:05_a$	$0:07_{ab}$	$0:11_t$
Proportion reporting no exposure the previous day									
Computers	84_a	73_b	66_c	93_a	88_a	78_b	75_a	62_b	53_t
Computer games	90_a	83_b	77_b	94_a	89_{ab}	83_b	86_a	77_{ab}	71_t
Video games	83	83	84	86_a	93_{ab}	96_b	79	75	73
Proportion reporting more than 1 hour interactive media exposure the previous day									
Computers	*	*	1	0	0	2	1	1	*
Computer games	*	*	1	0	0	1	99	99	100
Video games	4	2	2	2	1	0	7	3	4

Table A.7.1.9. Interactive Media Exposure by Parent Education (8–18 years)

	8–18 years			8–10 years			11–14 years			15–18 years		
	HS or less	Some college	College or more	HS or less	Some college	College or more	HS or less	Some college	College or more	HS or less	Some college	College or more
Average time spent using (hr:min)												
Computer games	$0:08_a$	$0:12_b$	$0:14_b$	$0:08_a$	$0:14_{ab}$	$0:17_b$	$0:10_a$	$0:13_{ab}$	$0:16_b$	$0:05_a$	$0:10_{ab}$	$0:09_b$
Chat	$0:03_a$	$0:04_{ab}$	$0:06_b$	0:02	0:03	0:04	$0:03_a$	$0:03_a$	$0:08_b$	0:03	0:06	0:06
Websites	$0:05_a$	$0:06_a$	$0:09_b$	0:03	0:05	0:05	$0:06_a$	$0:06_{ab}$	$0:10_b$	$0:04_a$	$0:05_a$	$0:13_b$
E-mail	$0:03_a$	$0:02_a$	$0:05_b$	0:01	0:00	0:03	$0:03_a$	$0:03_{ab}$	$0:06_b$	$0:03_a$	$0:02_a$	$0:06_b$
Video games	0:25	0:22	0:27	0:30	0:23	0:35	0:24	0:20	0:29	0:22	0:25	0:18
Total computer use	$0:18_a$	$0:24_a$	$0:35_b$	$0:14_a$	$0:22_{ab}$	$0:29_b$	$0:22_a$	$0:25_a$	$0:40_b$	$0:15_a$	$0:24_{ab}$	$0:34_b$
Proportion reporting no exposure the previous day												
Computers	61_a	49_b	41_c	73_a	61_a	44_b	55_a	46_{ab}	43_b	61_a	48_b	35_c
Computer games	83_a	83_b	84_b	80_a	61_b	49_b	71_a	64_{ab}	61_b	83_a	69_b	76_{ab}
Video games	62	63	60	53	53	55	58	62	55	72	69	69
Proportion reporting more than 1 hour interactive media exposure the previous day												
Computers	8_a	12_a	18_b	5_a	11_{ab}	13_b	10_a	13_a	21_b	7_a	11_a	20_b
Computer games	1_a	3_{ab}	3_b	2	3	3	1	3	4	0	2	2
Video games	10	8	11	13	5	14	11	8	13	7	11	8

Table A.7.1.10. *Interactive Media Exposure by Family Composition*
(2–7 years)

	2–7 years		2–4 years		5–7 years	
	Two-parent	Single-parent	Two-parent	Single-parent	Two-parent	Single-parent
Average time spent using (hr:min)						
Computer games	$0:07_a$	$0:03_b$	$0:05_a$	$0:01_b$	$0:09_a$	$0:05_b$
Chat	0:00	0:00	0:00	0:00	0:00	0:00
Websites	0:00	0:00	$0:00_a$	$0:00_b$	0:00	0:01
E-mail	0:00	0:00	0:00	0:01	0:00	0:00
Video games	0:08	0:07	0:04	0:04	0:13	0:09
Total computer use	$0:07_a$	$0:04_b$	$0:05_a$	$0:01_b$	0:09	0:06
Proportion reporting no exposure the previous day						
Computers	72_a	79_b	85	93	60	69
Computer games	81_a	90_b	87_a	97_b	75	84
Video games	83	86	91	92	74	80
Proportion reporting more than 1 hour interactive media exposure the previous day						
Computers	1	1	1	0	*	1
Computer games	1	1	1	0	*	1
Video games	3	3	1	3	4	3

Table A.7.1.11. *Interactive Media Exposure by Family Composition (8–18 years)*

	8–18 years		8–10 years		11–14 years		15–18 years	
	Two-parent	Single-parent	Two-parent	Single-parent	Two-parent	Single-parent	Two-parent	Single-parent
Average time spent using (hr:min)								
Computer games	0:11	0:13	0:14	0:11	0:13	0:15	0:07	0:12
Chat	0:05	0:05	0:03	0:06	0:06	0:07	0:05	0:04
Websites	0:07	0:07	0:04	0:04	0:08	0:07	0:09	0:07
E-mail	0:04	0:03	$0:03_a$	$0:00_b$	0:05	0:05	0:05	0:03
Video games	0:24	0:27	0:28	0:33	0:25	0:27	0:20	0:24
Total computer use	0:28	0:28	0:24	0:21	0:31	0:34	0:26	0:26
Proportion reporting no exposure the previous day								
Computers	47	52	52_a	67_b	47	50	45	45
Computer games	67	71	58	70	65	67	65	67
Video games	61	61	56	50	58	60	70	70
Proportion reporting more than 1 hour interactive media exposure the previous day								
Computers	14	15	10	11	16	18	15	14
Computer games	2	3	2	2	3	3	1	4
Video games	10	12	11	11	11	12	7	12

Table A.7.1.12. *Interactive Media Exposure by Residence Locale (2–7 years)*

	2–7 years			2–4 years			5–7 years		
	Urban	Suburban	Rural	Urban	Suburban	Rural	Urban	Suburban	Rural
Average time spent using (hr:min)									
Computer games	$0:05_{ab}$	$0:07_a$	$0:03_b$	$0:03_{ab}$	$0:06_a$	$0:01_b$	0:07	0:09	0:05
Chat	0:00	0:00	0:00	0:00	0:00	0:00	0:00	0:00	0:00
Websites	$0:00_a$	$0:00_a$	$0:01_b$	0:00	0:00	0:01	$0:00_a$	$0:00_a$	$0:01_b$
E-mail	0:00	0:00	0:00	0:00	0:00	0:00	0:00	0:00	0:00
Video games	0:07	0:09	0:09	0:03	0:04	0:06	0:12	0:13	0:11
Total computer use	0:06	0:07	0:05	0:03	0:06	0:03	0:08	0:09	0:07
Proportion reporting no exposure the previous day									
Computers	75	71	79	87	83	92	63	61	65
Computer games	83	81	88	89	86	94	78	76	82
Video games	84	84	82	92	93	90	77	75	74
Proportion reporting more than 1 hour interactive media exposure the previous day									
Computers	*	1	1	0	1	1	1	1	0
Computer games	$*_{ab}$	1_a	0_b	0	1	0	1	1	0
Video games	3	3	2	*	2	1	5	4	3

313

Table A.7.1.13. *Interactive Media Exposure by Residence Locale (8–18 years)*

	8–18 years			8–10 years			11–14 years			15–18 years		
	Urban	Suburban	Rural	Urban	Suburban	Rural	Urban	Suburban	Rural	Urban	Suburban	Rural
Average time spent using (hr:min)												
Computer games	$0:12_{ab}$	$0:13_a$	$0:10_b$	$0:16_a$	$0:16_a$	$0:09_b$	0:14	0:14	0:12	0:07	0:10	0:06
Chat	0:05	0:06	0:04	$0:03_{ab}$	$0:05_a$	$0:01_b$	0:05	0:06	0:06	0:05	0:06	0:03
Websites	0:07	0:07	0:07	0:03	0:05	0:03	0:08	0:07	0:08	0:08	0:09	0:10
E-mail	0:04	0:04	0:03	$0:01_{ab}$	$0:04_a$	$0:01_b$	0:06	0:04	0:04	0:05	0:04	0:05
Video games	$0:31_a$	$0:22_b$	$0:24_{ab}$	$0:38_a$	$0:22_b$	$0:33_{ab}$	0:29	0:23	0:27	$0:26_a$	$0:21_{ab}$	$0:12_b$
Total computer use	0:27	0:29	0:24	$0:24_{ab}$	$0:29_a$	$0:14_b$	0:33	0:30	0:30	0:24	0:29	0:24
Proportion reporting no exposure the previous day												
Computers	52_a	43_b	55_a	59_a	42_b	69_a	46	51	47	52_a	34_b	55_a
Computer games	70_a	64_b	71_a	65_a	48_b	73_a	65	66	64	80	73	79
Video games	58_a	64_b	59_{ab}	46_b	64_b	52_a	56	61	54	69	68	73
Proportion reporting more than 1 hour interactive media exposure the previous day												
Computers	14	14	13	12_a	14_a	3_b	18	13	17	12	16	15
Computer games	3	2	2	4	2	1	4	2	3	0	2	1
Video games	12	10	10	14	9	13	12	11	11	11_a	9_{ab}	4_b

314

Appendix 7.2: Interactive Media Genres

Table A.7.2.1. *Interactive Media Genre Use by Age (in years) (%)*

	2–4	5–7	8–10	11–14	15–18
Games					
Proportion using games	81	59	87	66	42
Action/combat	0	6	22	20	25
Adventure	2	7	16	13	16
Arts and crafts	10	14	10_{ab}	13_a	3_b
Classic/gambling	5	12	13_a	35_b	38_b
Educational	55	52	34_a	15_b	6_c
Kids	39	24	8_a	8_a	1_b
Popular culture/lifestyle	0	2	7	3	2
Reflex	0	2	5	8	8
Role play/interactive	0	2	5_a	8_{ab}	14_b
Simulation/strategic	0	2	9_a	16_b	14_{ab}
Sports	2	4	18	23	16
Chat rooms					
Proportion using chat rooms	3	3	21	30	22
Entertainment	–	–	33	32	28
Family/children	–	–	14	9	7
Gaming	–	–	18	15	9
Hobbies/groups	–	–	19	11	16
News	–	–	6	4	4
Relationships/lifestyles	–	–	8_a	22_b	43_c
Shopping	–	–	8_{ab}	18_a	4_b
Sports	–	–	24_a	25_a	9_b
Websites					
Proportion using websites	3	6	28	49	48
Entertainment	–	–	46_a	51_{ab}	62_b
Family/children	–	–	6	5	3
Gaming	–	–	43_a	28_a	9_b
News	–	–	3	8	13
Relationships/lifestyles	–	–	4	6	8
Research/information/support	–	–	6_a	13_{ab}	21_b
Search engines	–	–	9_a	13_a	23_b
Shopping	–	–	15	10	15
Sports	–	–	18_{ab}	31_a	17_b

(continued)

Table A.7.2.1 (continued)

	2–4	5–7	8–10	11–14	15–18
E-mail					
Proportion using e-mail	5	6	17	39	46
Video games					
Action/combat	–	32	44	49	42
Adventure	–	34	36_{ab}	39_a	29_b
Classic/gambling/puzzles	–	8	4_a	9_b	10_b
Reflex	–	10	2_a	9_b	1_a
Role play/interactive	–	3	13_a	18_{ab}	22_b
Simulation/strategic	–	4	6	9	12
Sports/competition	–	31	37	47	50

Note: Genre use proportions are percentages of the proportion of subjects who indicated interactive media usage.

Table A.7.2.2. *Interactive Media Genre Use by Gender (8–18 years) (%)*

	Female	Male
Games		
Proportion using games	55	69
Action/combat	11_a	31_b
Adventure	11_a	18_b
Arts and crafts	12	8
Classic/gambling	36_a	23_b
Educational	21	18
Kids	8	5
Popular culture/lifestyle	4	5
Reflex	7	7
Role play/interactive	4_a	12_b
Simulation/strategic	7_a	18_b
Sports	11_a	26_b
Chat rooms		
Proportion using chat rooms	26	25
Entertainment	36	26
Family/children	6	12
Gaming	9	18
Hobbies/groups	14	14

	Female	Male
News	3	5
Relationships/lifestyles	34a	18b
Shopping	13	9
Sports	12a	26b
Websites		
Proportion using websites	41	47
Entertainment	65a	46b
Family/children	5a	4b
Gaming	11	33
News	8	10
Relationships/lifestyles	6	7
Research/information/support	19	12
Search engines	11a	21b
Shopping	15	10
Sports	11a	34b
E-mail		
Proportion using e-mail	41	32
Video games		
Action/combat	32a	51b
Adventure	39	34
Classic/gambling/puzzles	10	7
Reflex	6	4
Role play/interactive	17	18
Simulation/strategic	3a	12b
Sports/competition	36a	49b

Note: See note to Table A.7.2.1.

Table A.7.2.3. *Interactive Media Genre Use by Race/Ethnicity* *(8–18 years) (%)*

	White	Black	Hispanic
Games			
Proportion using games	58	70	72
Action/combat	22	18	29
Adventure	14_a	13_a	35_b
Arts and crafts	7_a	12_{ab}	19_b
Classic/gambling	29	29	26
Educational	19	23	19
Kids	6	6	9
Popular culture/lifestyle	5	3	5
Reflex	8	3	7
Role play/interactive	10	8	7
Simulation/strategic	14_a	6_b	14_{ab}
Sports	23_a	19_{ab}	10_b
Chat rooms			
Proportion using chat rooms	26_{ab}	19_a	34_b
Websites			
Proportion using websites	46_a	32_b	53_a
E-mail			
Proportion using e-mail	42	16	32
Video games			
Action/combat	43_a	55_b	45_a
Adventure	32_a	42_b	46_b
Classic/gambling/puzzles	5_a	19_b	1_a
Reflex	3_a	6_{ab}	11_b
Role play/interactive	21_a	10_b	9_b
Simulation/strategic	11_a	4_b	6_{ab}
Sports/competition	45	51	36

Note: See note to Table A.7.2.1.

Table A.7.2.4. *Interactive Media Genre Use by Income*[a]
(8–18 years) (%)[b]

	Low	Middle	High
Games			
Proportion using games	64	64	61
Action/combat	22	22	22
Adventure	17$_{ab}$	18$_a$	11$_b$
Arts and crafts	14$_a$	12$_a$	5$_b$
Classic/gambling	40$_a$	28$_b$	25$_b$
Educational	22$_a$	10$_b$	28$_a$
Kids	4	8	5
Popular culture/lifestyle	4	3	6
Reflex	7	7	7
Role play/interactive	5	7	11
Simulation/strategic	10	12	16
Sports	19	19	20
Chat rooms			
Proportion using chat rooms	24	28	23
Websites			
Proportion using websites	46	48	39
E-mail			
Proportion using e-mail	24	41	36
Video games			
Action/combat	48	44	48
Adventure	34	39	32
Classic/gambling/puzzles	8	9	5
Reflex	8$_a$	5$_a$	1$_b$
Role play/interactive	8$_a$	16$_b$	26$_c$
Simulation/strategic	6	8	12
Sports/competition	55$_a$	42$_b$	43$_b$

[a] See note to Table A.3.1.4.
[b] See note to Table A.7.2.1.

Table A.7.2.5. *Interactive Media Genre Use by Parent Education (8–18 years) (%)*

	HS or less	Some college	College or beyond
Games			
Proportion using games	58	68	62
Action/combat	19$_{ab}$	14$_a$	25$_b$
Adventure	11	18	16
Arts and crafts	13	10	9
Classic/gambling	36	35	26
Educational	10$_a$	16$_{ab}$	22$_b$
Kids	4	4	7
Popular culture/lifestyle	2	2	7
Reflex	3	7	9
Role play/interactive	8	6	10
Simulation/strategic	7$_a$	13$_{ab}$	17$_b$
Sports	19	20	20
Chat rooms			
Proportion using chat rooms	25	26	26
Websites			
Proportion using websites	40	40	48
E-mail			
Proportion using e-mail	31	30	42
Video games			
Action/combat	42	46	47
Adventure	38	31	38
Classic/gambling/puzzles	10$_a$	10$_{ab}$	5$_b$
Reflex	3	8	4
Role play/interactive	14	20	21
Simulation/strategic	7	7	11
Sports/competition	49	48	43

Note: See note to Table A.7.2.1.

Table A.7.2.6. *Interactive Media Genre Use by Family Composition* (8–18 years) (%)

	Two-parent	Single-parent
Games		
Proportion using games	62	61
Action/combat	21	23
Adventure	15	18
Arts and crafts	10	7
Classic/gambling	27	39
Educational	21_a	16_b
Kids	6	6
Popular culture/lifestyle	4	5
Reflex	7	7
Role play/interactive	8	11
Simulation/strategic	13	19
Sports	19	20
Chat rooms		
Proportion using chat rooms	25	23
Entertainment	28_a	50_b
Family/children	10	8
Gaming	13	26
Hobbies/groups	14	10
News	5	3
Relationships/lifestyles	27	23
Shopping	11	15
Sports	18	30
Websites		
Proportion using websites	45	45
Entertainment	52_a	69_b
Family/children	5	1
Gaming	24	23
News	9	12
Relationships/lifestyles	7	7
Research/information/support	15	17
Search engines	18	11
Shopping	12	15
Sports	24	17

(continued)

Table A.7.2.6 (*continued*)

	Two-parent	Single-parent
E-mail		
Proportion using e-mail	40	30
Video games		
Action/combat	45	47
Adventure	36	32
Classic/gambling/puzzles	7	8
Reflex	5	4
Role play/interactive	18	19
Simulation/strategic	9	11
Sports/competition	45	38

Note: See note to Table A.7.2.1.

Table A.7.2.7. *Interactive Media Genre Use by Residence Locale (8–18 years) (%)*

	Urban	Suburban	Rural
Games			
Proportion using games	61	63	64
Action/combat	25	22	19
Adventure	16	14	15
Arts and crafts	6	11	11
Classic/gambling	30_{ab}	24_a	35_b
Educational	18_{ab}	24_a	11_b
Kids	5	7	6
Popular culture/lifestyle	4	6	3
Reflex	7	6	9
Role play/interactive	7_{ab}	12_a	4_b
Simulation/strategic	13	15	9
Sports	16	21	21
Chat rooms			
Proportion using chat rooms	26	25	24
Entertainment	40	21	37
Family/children	10	12	2
Gaming	17	12	12
Hobbies/groups	12	17	13
News	5	3	5

	Urban	Suburban	Rural
Relationships/lifestyles	28	26	23
Shopping	17	7	12
Sports	23	15	22
Websites			
Proportion using websites	45	42	45
Entertainment	54	55	55
Family/children	4	7	1
Gaming	24	23	21
News	13	6	10
Relationships/lifestyles	6	6	7
Research/information/support	17	12	18
Search engines	17	15	17
Shopping	18	12	7
Sports	22	26	21
E-mail			
Proportion using e-mail	37	34	39
Video games			
Action/combat	47	48	41
Adventure	36	39	30
Classic/gambling/puzzles	7	9	7
Reflex	6	4	4
Role play/interactive	15	23	12
Simulation/strategic	6_a	12_b	9_a
Sports/competition	42	47	47

Note: See note to Table A.7.2.1.

Appendix 8.1: Amount of Total Exposure and
Proportion of Time Devoted to Each Medium

Table A.8.1.1. *Total Media Exposure by Age (in years)*

	2–7	2–4	5–7	8–18	8–10	11–14	15–18
Average exposure time (hr:min)							
Television	2:02	2:02	2:02	3:05	$3:19_a$	$3:30_a$	$2:23_b$
Videos of TV	0:03	0:04	0:03	0:14	$0:21_a$	$0:14_b$	$0:10_b$
Commercial videos	0:27	$0:33_a$	$0:21_b$	0:27	0:25	0:29	0:28
Movies (in theaters)	0:02	0:01	0:02	0:18	$0:26_a$	$0:19_a$	$0:09_b$
Video games	0:08	$0:04_a$	$0:13_b$	0:26	$0:31_a$	$0:26_{ab}$	$0:21_b$
Print media	0:46	$0:52_a$	$0:41_b$	0:43	$0:54_a$	$0:42_b$	$0:37_b$
Radio	0:25	0:25	0:24	0:46	$0:24_a$	$0:46_b$	$1:04_c$
CDs and tapes	0:21	0:24	0:19	1:02	$0:31_a$	$0:58_b$	$1:33_c$
Computer	0:06	$0:04_a$	$0:08_b$	0:27	$0:23_a$	$0:31_b$	$0:26_{ab}$
Total media exposure	4:20	4:29	4:11	7:29	$7:13_{ab}$	$7:55_a$	$7:11_b$
Proportion of total media time that is devoted to:							
Television	44	43	45	40	45_a	43_a	31_b
Other screen media	12	14_a	10_b	11	15_a	10_b	10_b
Video games	3	1_a	4_b	6	7	6	5
Reading	21	22	19	12	15_a	11_b	9_b
Audio media	18	19	18	26	12_a	24_b	39_c
Computer	3	2_a	4_b	6	6	6	6

Table A.8.1.2. *Total Media Use by Gender and Age (2–7 years)*

	2–7 years		2–4 years		5–7 years	
	Female	Male	Female	Male	Female	Male
Average exposure time (hr:min)						
Television	1:53$_a$	2:10$_b$	1:53	2:09	1:52	2:11
Videos of TV	0:03	0:03	0:03	0:04	0:04	0:02
Commercial videos	0:26	0:27	0:31	0:34	0:21	0:20
Movies (in theaters)	0:02	0:01	0:02	0:01	0:02	0:01
Video games	0:03$_a$	0:13$_b$	0:01$_a$	0:07$_b$	0:05$_a$	0:19$_b$
Print media	0:49	0:44	0:54	0:50	0:45	0:39
Radio	0:23	0:26	0:22	0:28	0:24	0:25
CDs and tapes	0:23	0:19	0:23	0:24	0:23$_a$	0:15$_b$
Computer	0:07	0:06	0:05	0:03	0:08	0:09
Total media exposure	4:10	4:31	4:15	4:42	4:04	4:20
Proportion of total media time that is devoted to:						
Television	43	44	43	41	43	46
Other screen media	12	12	13	15	11	9
Video games	1$_a$	4$_b$	0$_a$	2$_b$	2$_a$	7$_b$
Reading	22	20	22	21	21	18
Audio media	20	18	19	20	20$_a$	16$_b$
Computer	3	2	2	1	3	3

Table A.8.1.3. *Total Media Exposure by Gender and Age (8–18 years)*

	8–18 years		8–10 years		11–14 years		15–18 years	
	Female	Male	Female	Male	Female	Male	Female	Male
Average exposure time (hr:min)								
Television	2:55$_a$	3:15$_b$	3:24	3:15	3:13$_a$	3:47$_b$	2:12$_a$	2:34$_b$
Videos of TV	0:13	0:15	0:19	0:22	0:13	0:15	0:09	0:11
Commercial videos	0:27	0:28	0:23	0:28	0:28	0:30	0:28	0:27
Movies (in theaters)	0:16	0:19	0:25	0:27	0:17	0:22	0:09	0:09
Video games	0:11$_a$	0:39$_b$	0:20$_a$	0:40$_b$	0:09$_a$	0:43$_b$	0:07$_a$	0:34$_b$
Print media	0:46$_a$	0:41$_b$	1:00	0:49	0:44	0:39	0:38	0:36
Radio	0:55$_a$	0:38$_b$	0:30$_a$	0:19$_b$	0:55$_a$	0:38$_b$	1:13$_a$	0:55$_b$
CDs and tapes	1:14$_a$	0:51$_b$	0:42$_a$	0:22$_b$	1:16$_a$	0:40$_b$	1:36	1:32
Computer	0:24$_a$	0:30$_b$	0:23	0:23	0:26$_a$	0:36$_b$	0:22$_a$	0:30$_b$
Total media exposure	7:21	7:37	7:25	7:03	7:41	8:09	6:53	7:29
Proportion of total media time that is devoted to:								
Television	38$_a$	41$_b$	46	45	40$_a$	46$_b$	30	32
Other screen media	11	12	14	16	10	11	10	10
Video games	2$_a$	9$_b$	4$_a$	9$_b$	2$_a$	9$_b$	2$_a$	8$_b$
Reading	12$_a$	11$_b$	16	14	12$_a$	9$_b$	10	9
Audio media	31$_a$	21$_b$	15$_a$	10$_b$	30$_a$	18$_b$	43$_a$	36$_b$
Computer	6$_a$	7$_b$	5	6	5$_a$	7$_b$	6	6

Table A.8.1.4. *Total Media Exposure by Race/Ethnicity and Age (2–7 years)*

	2–7 years			2–4 years			5–7 years		
	White	Black	Hispanic	White	Black	Hispanic	White	Black	Hispanic
Average exposure time (hr:min)									
Television	1:45$_a$	2:49$_b$	2:23$_b$	1:44$_a$	2:47$_b$	2:25$_b$	1:45$_a$	2:51$_b$	2:20$_b$
Videos of TV	0:04$_a$	0:02$_{ab}$	0:02$_b$	0:04	0:04	0:03	0:04$_a$	0:01$_b$	0:01$_b$
Commercial videos	0:28	0:27	0:22	0:31	0:39	0:29	0:24$_a$	0:16$_{ab}$	0:13$_b$
Movies (in theaters)	0:01	0:04	0:01	0:01	0:04	0:00	0:01	0:04	0:02
Video games	0:08	0:08	0:09	0:04	0:03	0:04	0:12	0:13	0:14
Print media	0:49	0:44	0:39	0:54	0:49	0:46	0:44$_a$	0:38$_{ab}$	0:31$_b$
Radio	0:22$_a$	0:33$_b$	0:25$_{ab}$	0:22$_a$	0:40$_b$	0:26$_a$	0:23	0:27	0:24
CDs and tapes	0:22	0:15	0:23	0:25	0:12	0:28	0:20	0:17	0:17
Computer	0:07$_a$	0:04$_b$	0:05$_{ab}$	0:06$_a$	0:01$_b$	0:02$_{ab}$	0:09	0:06	0:07
Total media exposure	4:06$_a$	5:06$_b$	4:28$_{ab}$	4:12$_a$	5:19$_b$	4:43$_{ab}$	4:01$_a$	4:54$_b$	4:09$_{ab}$
Proportion of total media time that is devoted to:									
Television	40$_a$	51$_b$	52$_b$	39$_a$	48$_{ab}$	50$_b$	41$_a$	54$_b$	54$_b$
Other screen media	13$_a$	10$_{ab}$	9$_b$	15$_a$	14$_{ab}$	10$_b$	12$_a$	7$_b$	7$_b$
Video games	3	3	3	1	1	1	4	4	5
Reading	22$_a$	17$_b$	17$_b$	24$_a$	19$_b$	17$_b$	21$_a$	15$_b$	16$_{ab}$
Audio media	19	17	19	19	18	21	18	17	15
Computer	3$_a$	2$_b$	2$_b$	2$_a$	0$_b$	1$_b$	4	3	3

Table A.8.1.5. *Total Media Exposure by Race/Ethnicity and Age (8–18 years)*

	8–18 years			8–10 years			11–14 years			15–18 years		
	White	Black	Hispanic	White	Black	Hispanic	White	Black	Hispanic	White	Black	Hispanic
Average exposure time (hr:min)												
Television	$2{:}42_a$	$4{:}12_b$	$3{:}34_c$	$3{:}01_a$	$4{:}22_b$	$3{:}49_{ab}$	$3{:}06_a$	$4{:}27_b$	$4{:}00_b$	$2{:}04_a$	$3{:}44_b$	$2{:}41_a$
Videos of TV	$0{:}11_a$	$0{:}26_b$	$0{:}14_a$	$0{:}18_a$	$0{:}28_b$	$0{:}17_a$	$0{:}09_a$	$0{:}34_b$	$0{:}17_c$	$0{:}09$	$0{:}13$	$0{:}09$
Commercial videos	$0{:}27$	$0{:}30$	$0{:}29$	$0{:}25$	$0{:}30$	$0{:}25$	$0{:}28$	$0{:}33$	$0{:}30$	$0{:}28$	$0{:}25$	$0{:}31$
Movies (in theaters)	$0{:}11_a$	$0{:}25_b$	$0{:}31_b$	$0{:}20$	$0{:}28$	$0{:}30$	$0{:}11_a$	$0{:}30_b$	$0{:}40_b$	$0{:}06_a$	$0{:}16_{ab}$	$0{:}18_b$
Video games	$0{:}22_a$	$0{:}34_b$	$0{:}33_b$	$0{:}23_a$	$0{:}40_b$	$0{:}36_{ab}$	$0{:}24_a$	$0{:}38_b$	$0{:}28_{ab}$	$0{:}18_a$	$0{:}21_{ab}$	$0{:}38_b$
Print media	$0{:}43$	$0{:}45$	$0{:}34$	$0{:}53$	$1{:}01$	$0{:}43$	$0{:}41$	$0{:}39$	$0{:}37$	$0{:}38_a$	$0{:}35_{ab}$	$0{:}22_b$
Radio	$0{:}46$	$0{:}45$	$0{:}55$	$0{:}20_a$	$0{:}33_b$	$0{:}24_{ab}$	$0{:}45$	$0{:}44$	$0{:}56$	$1{:}03$	$0{:}58$	$1{:}21$
CDs and tapes	$1{:}06$	$0{:}59$	$1{:}03$	$0{:}28$	$0{:}39$	$0{:}37$	$1{:}00$	$0{:}59$	$0{:}53$	$1{:}38$	$1{:}20$	$1{:}40$
Computer	$0{:}28$	$0{:}26$	$0{:}25$	$0{:}25_a$	$0{:}31_a$	$0{:}11_b$	$0{:}31$	$0{:}29$	$0{:}36$	$0{:}27$	$0{:}18$	$0{:}20$
Total media exposure	$6{:}56_a$	$9{:}01_b$	$8{:}19_b$	$6{:}33_a$	$9{:}11_b$	$7{:}31_{ab}$	$7{:}14_a$	$9{:}34_b$	$8{:}55_b$	$6{:}51_a$	$8{:}10_b$	$8{:}02_{ab}$
Proportion of total media time that is devoted to:												
Television	37_a	45_b	44_b	44	48	52	41	44	47	29_a	43_b	33_a
Other screen media	10_a	14_b	13_{ab}	14	15	15	8_a	16_b	12_{ab}	9	10	12
Video games	5	6	6	5	7	8	6	7	6	5	5	6
Reading	12_a	9_b	8_b	17	13	12	12_a	8_{ab}	8_b	10_a	7_b	5_b
Audio media	28_a	22_b	24_{ab}	12	13	12	26_a	21_{ab}	20_b	41_a	33_b	40_{ab}
Computer	7_a	4_b	5_b	7_a	5_a	2_b	7_a	5_b	7_a	6_a	3_b	4_{ab}

Table A.8.1.6. *Total Media Exposure by Income[a] and Age (2–7 years)*

	2–7 years			2–4 years			5–7 years		
	Low	Middle	High	Low	Middle	High	Low	Middle	High
Average exposure time (hr:min)									
Television	2:30$_a$	2:08$_{ab}$	1:44$_b$	2:20$_a$	2:15$_a$	1:43$_b$	2:38$_a$	1:59$_b$	1:45$_b$
Videos of TV	0:03	0:03	0:03	0:02	0:04	0:03	0:03	0:03	0:02
Commercial videos	0:26	0:29	0:26	0:41	0:35	0:28	0:13$_a$	0:22$_b$	0:25$_b$
Movies (in theaters)	0:02	0:00	0:03	0:02	0:00	0:03	0:02	0:01	0:02
Video games	0:08	0:10	0:07	0:02$_a$	0:07$_b$	0:01$_a$	0:14	0:13	0:12
Print media	0:37$_a$	0:48$_b$	0:49$_b$	0:38$_a$	0:54$_b$	0:54$_b$	0:36	0:41	0:44
Radio	0:26	0:24	0:26	0:30	0:25	0:24	0:21	0:23	0:27
CDs and tapes	0:19	0:23	0:19	0:18	0:25	0:21	0:19	0:20	0:18
Computer	0:02$_a$	0:07$_b$	0:08$_b$	0:00$_a$	0:05$_b$	0:05$_b$	0:03$_a$	0:08$_b$	0:10$_b$
Total media exposure	4:32	4:31	4:04	4:34$_{ab}$	4:49$_a$	4:02$_b$	4:29	4:10	4:05
Proportion of total media time that is devoted to:									
Television	53$_a$	43$_b$	40$_b$	49	44	39	56$_a$	42$_b$	40$_b$
Other screen media	11	13	12	15	14	14	7$_a$	12$_b$	11$_b$
Video games	3	3	3	1$_{ab}$	2$_a$	0$_b$	5	4	5
Reading	16$_a$	20$_b$	23$_b$	18	20	24	14$_a$	20$_b$	21$_b$
Audio media	17	18	19	17	19	20	17	18	19
Computer	1$_a$	3$_b$	3$_b$	0$_a$	2$_b$	2$_b$	1$_a$	4$_b$	4$_b$

[a] See note to Table A.3.1.4.

Table A.8.1.7. *Total Media Exposure by Income[a] and Age (8–18 years)*

	8–18 years			8–10 years			11–14 years			15–18 years		
	Low	Middle	High	Low	Middle	High	Low	Middle	High	Low	Middle	High
Average exposure time (hr:min)												
Television	$3:21_a$	$3:09_{ab}$	$2:51_b$	$2:52_b$	$3:51_b$	$2:55_a$	$4:07_a$	$3:22_b$	$3:20_b$	$2:45$	$2:18$	$2:15$
Videos of TV	$0:19_a$	$0:16_a$	$0:10_b$	$0:18_{ab}$	$0:29_a$	$0:13_b$	$0:24_a$	$0:13_{ab}$	$0:08_b$	$0:15$	$0:08$	$0:08$
Commercial videos	$0:30$	$0:27$	$0:27$	$0:28$	$0:30$	$0:20$	$0:31$	$0:26$	$0:32$	$0:31$	$0:25$	$0:28$
Movies (in theaters)	$0:22_a$	$0:20_a$	$0:12_b$	$0:11_a$	$0:38_b$	$0:18_a$	$0:32_a$	$0:20_{ab}$	$0:10_b$	$0:16$	$0:07$	$0:08$
Video games	$0:28_a$	$0:29_a$	$0:20_b$	$0:41_a$	$0:37_a$	$0:21_b$	$0:33_a$	$0:27_{ab}$	$0:21_b$	$0:16$	$0:24$	$0:20$
Print media	$0:43$	$0:43$	$0:44$	$0:45_a$	$0:46_a$	$1:04_b$	$0:45$	$0:44$	$0:36$	$0:40$	$0:39$	$0:33$
Radio	$0:52$	$0:46$	$0:43$	$0:19_{ab}$	$0:30_b$	$0:19_a$	$0:57_a$	$0:46_{ab}$	$0:40_b$	$1:03$	$1:01$	$1:09$
CDs and tapes	$1:04$	$1:03$	$1:01$	$0:29$	$0:38$	$0:25$	$0:57$	$0:58$	$0:57$	$1:31$	$1:30$	$1:38$
Computer	$0:21_a$	$0:28_b$	$0:30_b$	$0:10_a$	$0:20_a$	$0:31_b$	$0:30$	$0:33$	$0:29$	$0:16_a$	$0:27_b$	$0:31_b$
Total media exposure	$8:00$	$7:41$	$6:57$	$6:14_a$	$8:18_b$	$6:26_{ab}$	$9:16_a$	$7:48_{ab}$	$7:13_b$	$7:34$	$6:60$	$7:10$
Proportion of total media time that is devoted to:												
Television	40	40	39	48	46	44	43	42	45	33	32	29
Other screen media	13_a	12_{ab}	10_b	13_{ab}	19_a	11_b	12	10	9	13_a	9_b	9_b
Video games	6_a	6_a	5_b	10_a	7_b	4_c	6	7	5	3	5	5
Reading	10	11	13	13_{ab}	10_b	22_a	10	11	11	10	10	8
Audio media	26	26	26	12_{ab}	14_a	11_b	23	24	24	36_a	39_{ab}	42_b
Computer	5_a	6_{ab}	8_b	3_a	4_{ab}	8_b	6	6	7	4_a	6_{ab}	8_b

[a] See note to Table A.3.1.4.

Table A.8.1.8. Total Media Exposure by Parent Education and Age (2–7 years)

	2–7 years			2–4 years			5–7 years		
	HS or less	Some college	College or more	HS or less	Some college	College or more	HS or less	Some college	College or more
Average exposure time (hr:min)									
Television	$2:36_a$	$2:10_b$	$1:29_c$	$2:38_a$	$1:56_b$	$1:36_b$	$2:34_a$	$2:22_a$	$1:22_b$
Videos of TV	0:04	0:03	0:03	0:05	0:02	0:04	0:03	0:04	0:02
Commercial videos	0:27	0:29	0:24	0:32	0:38	0:29	0:22	0:21	0:19
Movies (in theaters)	0:01	0:02	0:02	0:01	0:01	0:02	0:01	0:02	0:02
Video games	0:11	0:07	0:07	$0:08_a$	$0:02_b$	$0:01_b$	0:15	0:10	0:12
Print media	0:44	0:44	0:50	0:47	0:51	0:56	0:41	0:39	0:43
Radio	$0:25_{ab}$	$0:28_a$	$0:22_b$	$0:27_{ab}$	$0:32_a$	$0:20_b$	0:24	0:25	0:25
CDs and tapes	$0:18_a$	$0:18_a$	$0:26_b$	$0:21_{ab}$	$0:17_a$	$0:29_b$	0:15	0:18	0:22
Computer	$0:04_a$	$0:05_a$	$0:09_b$	$0:02_a$	$0:03_a$	$0:07_b$	$0:05_a$	$0:07_{ab}$	$0:11_b$
Total media exposure	$4:52_a$	$4:26_a$	$3:51_b$	$5:02_a$	$4:23_{ab}$	$4:05_b$	$4:41_a$	$4:29_a$	$3:36_b$
Proportion of total media time that is devoted to:									
Television	52_a	45_b	36_c	51_a	41_b	37_b	53_a	49_a	35_b
Other screen media	11	13	13	12	16	15	9	11	10
Video games	3	2	3	2_a	1_b	0_b	4	4	5
Reading	17_a	19_a	24_b	18_a	21_{ab}	25_b	16_a	17_a	23_b
Audio media	16_a	18_{ab}	21_b	17	21	20	16_a	16_a	21_b
Computer	1_a	2_a	4_b	1_a	1_a	3_b	2_a	3_a	5_b

Table A.8.1.9. *Total Media Exposure by Parent Education and Age (8–18 years)*

	8–18 years			8–10 years			11–14 years			15–18 years		
	HS or less	Some college	College or more	HS or less	Some college	College or more	HS or less	Some college	College or more	HS or less	Some college	College or more
Average exposure time (hr:min)												
Television	$3{:}20_a$	$3{:}13_{ab}$	$2{:}50_b$	$3{:}29_{ab}$	$3{:}55_a$	$2{:}56_b$	$3{:}52_a$	$3{:}46_{ab}$	$3{:}15_b$	2:37	2:13	2:16
Videos of TV	$0{:}17_a$	$0{:}11_b$	$0{:}13_{ab}$	$0{:}30_a$	$0{:}18_{ab}$	$0{:}18_b$	0:15	0:13	0:12	$0{:}10_a$	$0{:}04_b$	$0{:}11_a$
Commercial videos	0:31	0:28	0:25	$0{:}31_a$	$0{:}37_a$	$0{:}21_b$	$0{:}36_a$	$0{:}20_b$	$0{:}26_{ab}$	0:26	0:31	0:28
Movies (in theaters)	$0{:}21_a$	$0{:}10_b$	$0{:}17_{ab}$	0:35	0:20	0:24	0:24	0:11	0:19	0:09	0:04	0:09
Video games	0:25	0:22	0:27	0:30	0:23	0:35	0:24	0:20	0:29	0:22	0:25	0:18
Print media	$0{:}33_a$	$0{:}44_b$	$0{:}49_b$	$0{:}37_a$	$0{:}48_{ab}$	$1{:}04_b$	$0{:}32_a$	$0{:}41_{ab}$	$0{:}47_b$	$0{:}31_a$	$0{:}45_b$	$0{:}38_b$
Radio	0:50	0:52	0:44	0:26	0:23	0:25	0:51	0:51	0:42	1:05	1:09	1:03
CDs and tapes	$1{:}05_{ab}$	$1{:}17_a$	$0{:}59_b$	0:29	0:37	0:32	$0{:}55_a$	$1{:}17_b$	$0{:}52_a$	1:41	1:37	1:32
Computer	$0{:}18_a$	$0{:}24_a$	$0{:}35_b$	$0{:}14_a$	$0{:}22_{ab}$	$0{:}29_b$	$0{:}22_a$	$0{:}25_a$	$0{:}40_b$	$0{:}15_a$	$0{:}24_{ab}$	$0{:}34_b$
Total media exposure	7:41	7:41	7:19	7:21	7:44	7:04	8:12	8:05	7:40	7:18	7:12	7:08
Proportion of total media time that is devoted to:												
Television	43_a	40_b	36_b	48_a	52_a	41_b	47_a	46_{ab}	40_b	35_a	27_b	29_{ab}
Other screen media	13_a	9_b	11_{ab}	20_a	15_{ab}	13_b	11_a	7_b	10_a	10	7	10
Video games	5	5	6	7	6	7	5	5	6	4	6	5
Reading	8_a	11_b	14_c	9_a	11_a	20_b	8_a	11_b	13_b	8	11	10
Audio media	27	30	25	13	11	12	24	26	23	41	43	38
Computer	4_a	6_b	8_c	3_a	5_{ab}	7_b	5_a	6_a	8_b	3_a	6_b	8_b

Table A.8.1.10. *Total Media Exposure by Family Composition and Age (2–7 years)*

	2–7 years		2–4 years		5–7 years	
	Two-parent	Single-parent	Two-parent	Single-parent	Two-parent	Single-parent
Average exposure time (hr:min)						
Television	$1:52_a$	$2:24_b$	1:54	2:09	$1:51_a$	$2:35_b$
Videos of TV	0:03	0:02	0:04	0:02	0:03	0:01
Commercial videos	0:25	0:32	0:30	0:44	0:21	0:23
Movies (in theaters)	0:02	0:03	0:01	0:04	0:02	0:02
Video games	0:08	0:07	0:04	0:04	0:13	0:09
Print media	0:46	0:45	0:51	0:46	0:40	0:44
Radio	$0:23_a$	$0:33_b$	$0:24_a$	$0:35_b$	$0:23_a$	$0:31_b$
CDs and tapes	0:22	0:20	0:26	0:17	0:19	0:22
Computer	$0:07_a$	$0:04_b$	$0:05_a$	$0:01_b$	0:09	0:06
Total media exposure	$4:09_a$	$4:49_b$	4:19	4:43	$3:60_a$	$4:54_b$
Proportion of total media time that is devoted to:						
Television	42	47	42	44	43	49
Other screen media	12	12	14	15	11	9
Video games	3	2	1	1	5	3
Reading	21	18	23	19	20	17
Audio media	19	19	20	20	18	19
Computer	3_a	2_b	2	1	4	2

Table A.8.1.11. *Total Media Exposure by Family Composition and Age (8–18 years)*

	8–18 years		8–10 years		11–14 years		15–18 years	
	Two-parent	Single-parent	Two-parent	Single-parent	Two-parent	Single-parent	Two-parent	Single-parent
Average exposure time (hr:min)								
Television	$2:55_a$	$3:38_b$	$3:03_a$	$3:42_b$	$3:20_a$	$4:11_b$	$2:16_a$	$3:00_b$
Videos of TV	$0:13_a$	$0:18_b$	0:19	0:27	$0:11_a$	$0:21_b$	0:10	0:10
Commercial videos	0:27	0:29	0:24	0:25	0:30	0:27	0:27	0:34
Movies (in theaters)	0:15	0:22	$0:22_a$	$0:38_b$	0:16	0:24	0:08	0:08
Video games	0:24	0:27	0:28	0:33	0:25	0:27	0:20	0:24
Print media	0:43	0:43	0:49	1:01	0:43	0:36	0:37	0:38
Radio	$0:43_a$	$0:53_b$	0:22	0:32	$0:43_a$	$0:56_b$	1:02	1:02
CDs and tapes	1:00	1:00	0:28	0:34	0:55	1:02	$1:32_a$	$1:15_b$
Computer	0:28	0:28	0:24	0:21	0:31	0:34	0:26	0:26
Total media exposure	$7:08_a$	$8:19_b$	$6:38_a$	$8:14_b$	$7:34_a$	$9:00_b$	6:59	7:38
Proportion of total media time that is devoted to:								
Television	39	42	46	44	42	47	30	35
Other screen media	11	12	14	18	10	10	9	11
Video games	6	6	7	6	6	6	4	6
Reading	12	11	15	18	12_a	8_b	9	10
Audio media	26	24	12	11	24	23	40	33
Computer	7	5	6_a	4_b	7	6	6	5

Table A.8.1.12. *Total Media Exposure by Residence Locale and Age (2–7 years)*

	2–7 years			2–4 years			5–7 years		
	Urban	Suburban	Rural	Urban	Suburban	Rural	Urban	Suburban	Rural
Average exposure time (hr:min)									
Television	2:13$_{ab}$	1:48$_b$	2:18$_a$	2:18$_a$	1:46$_b$	2:09$_{ab}$	2:08$_{ab}$	1:49$_a$	2:26$_b$
Videos of TV	0:03	0:03	0:05	0:03	0:04	0:05	0:02	0:03	0:05
Commercial videos	0:25	0:29	0:21	0:36	0:34	0:22	0:15$_a$	0:26$_b$	0:2C$_{ab}$
Movies (in theaters)	0:02	0:02	0:00	0:02	0:02	0:00	0:02	0:02	0:0C
Video games	0:07	0:09	0:09	0:03	0:04	0:06	0:12	0:13	0:11
Print media	0:45	0:49	0:41	0:49	0:57	0:43	0:40	0:43	0:39
Radio	0:25	0:25	0:21	0:30$_a$	0:23$_{ab}$	0:20$_b$	0:21	0:27	0:21
CDs and tapes	0:24	0:21	0:17	0:27	0:24	0:14	0:20	0:17	0:2?
Computer	0:06	0:07	0:05	0:03	0:06	0:03	0:08	0:09	0:07
Total media exposure	4:29	4:13	4:17	4:51	4:19	4:03	4:08	4:08	4:31
Proportion of total media time that is devoted to:									
Television	46$_{ab}$	40$_a$	50$_b$	44	39	48	47$_{ab}$	41$_a$	51$_b$
Other screen media	11	13	10	13	15	12	9	12	3
Video games	2	3	2	1	1	1	4	5	4
Reading	20	21	21	20	23	24	20	19	18
Audio media	19	19	15	21$_a$	19$_{ab}$	15$_b$	16	20	16
Computer	2	3	2	1	2	1	4	4	3

Table A.8.1.13. *Total Media Exposure by Residence Locale and Age (8–18 years)*

	8–18 years			8–10 years			11–14 years			15–18 years		
	Urban	Suburban	Rural	Urban	Suburban	Rural	Urban	Suburban	Rural	Urban	Suburban	Rural
Average exposure time (hr:min)												
Television	3:20$_a$	3:00$_{ab}$	2:54$_b$	3:36	3:00	3:24	4:01$_a$	3:25$_{ab}$	3:04$_b$	2:18	2:33	2:13
Videos of TV	0:16	0:13	0:15	0:21	0:17	0:25	0:17	0:12	0:13	0:10	0:10	0:09
Commercial videos	0:26	0:29	0:28	0:24$_a$	0:19$_a$	0:35$_b$	0:27	0:33	0:25	0:25	0:31	0:26
Movies (in theaters)	0:26$_a$	0:13$_b$	0:14$_{ab}$	0:38$_a$	0:14$_b$	0:26$_a$	0:24	0:17	0:16	0:17$_a$	0:07$_b$	0:01$_b$
Video games	0:31$_a$	0:22$_b$	0:24$_{ab}$	0:38$_a$	0:22$_b$	0:33$_{ab}$	0:29	0:23	0:27	0:26$_a$	0:21$_{ab}$	0:12$_b$
Print media	0:46$_a$	0:45$_a$	0:38$_b$	0:59$_a$	1:01$_a$	0:37$_b$	0:43	0:45	0:36	0:39	0:34	0:40
Radio	0:50	0:45	0:43	0:29	0:20	0:22	0:52$_a$	0:38$_b$	0:50$_{ab}$	1:05$_{ab}$	1:10$_a$	0:52$_b$
CDs and tapes	1:03	1:04	1:00	0:39	0:26	0:30	0:53	0:57	1:03	1:34	1:38	1:23
Computer	0:27	0:29	0:24	0:24$_{ab}$	0:29$_a$	0:14$_b$	0:33	0:30	0:30	0:24	0:29	0:24
Total media exposure	8:04$_a$	7:20$_{ab}$	7:00$_b$	8:08	6:28	7:05	8:39	7:43	7:23	7:20$_{ab}$	7:33$_a$	6:22$_b$
Proportion of total media time that is devoted to:												
Television	39	40	40	46	44	46	43	45	41	29$_a$	31$_{ab}$	34$_b$
Other screen media	12	10	12	16$_a$	10$_b$	19$_a$	11	10	9	11	9	9
Video games	6	5	6	8$_a$	4$_b$	8$_a$	6	6	7	5$_{ab}$	5$_a$	3$_b$
Reading	11	13	10	13$_{ab}$	21$_a$	10$_b$	10	12	10	10	8	11
Audio media	26	26	25	12	12	13	25$_{ab}$	21$_a$	26$_b$	39	41	37
Computer	6	7	6	5	8	4	6	6	7	6	6	6

APPENDIXES TO CHAPTER 9:

YOUTH PERSPECTIVE ON MEDIA

BEHAVIOR

APPENDIX 9.1: CONTENTEDNESS INDEX CORRELATIONS

Table A.9.1.1. *Intercorrelations among Six Items Comprising Contentedness Index (8–18 years)*

	Item A	Item B	Item C	Item D	Item E	Item F
A. ... has a lot of friends	–	.130*	.110*	.145*	.175*	.035
B. ... gets along with parents		–	.094*	.128*	.204*	.246*
C. ... often bored (rev)			–	.324*	.121*	.105*
D. ... often sad and unhappy (rev)				–	.178*	.136*
E. ... happy at school ...					–	.165*
F. ... gets into trouble a lot (rev)						–

Note: Scoring for items C, D, and F was reversed. Coefficients noted with * are significant at $p < .01$ (two-tailed).

Table A.9.1.2. *Correlations between Contentedness Index Scores and Amount of Media Exposure (8–18 years)*

Amount of exposure to:	Contentedness
Screen media	$-.097^*$
Audio media	$-.038$
Print media	$.063^*$
Computers	$-.044$
Total media exposure	$-.080^*$

Note: Higher scores on the contentedness index indicate higher levels of contentedness. Coefficients noted with [*] are significant at $p < .01$ (two-tailed).

APPENDIX 9.2: AMOUNT OF TOTAL MEDIA EXPOSURE BY CONTENTEDNESS

Table A.9.2.1. *Average Total Media Exposure by Level of Contentedness and Demographic Variables (hr:min)*

	Level of contentedness		
	Low	Middle	High
Full sample			
8–18 years	$8{:}24_a$	$7{:}11_b$	$7{:}04_b$
Age			
8–10 years	7:35	6:35	6:38
11–14 years	$9{:}14_a$	$7{:}29_b$	$7{:}40_b$
15–18 years	$8{:}01_a$	$7{:}01_b$	$6{:}43_b$
Gender			
Girls	$8{:}10_a$	$7{:}06_b$	$6{:}43_b$
Boys	$8{:}37_a$	$7{:}15_b$	$7{:}32_{ab}$
Race/ethnicity			
White	$8{:}31_a$	$6{:}33_b$	$6{:}25_b$
Black	8:58	8:40	9:34
Hispanic	8:08	8:20	8:41
Income			
$25,000 or less	8:05	7:52	7:39
$25,000–$40,000	$8{:}48_a$	$7{:}21_b$	$7{:}22_b$
Over $40,000	$8{:}07_a$	$6{:}39_b$	$6{:}19_b$
Parent education			
High school	$8{:}30_a$	$7{:}10_b$	$7{:}51_{ab}$
Some college	8:12	7:34	7:23
College +	$8{:}41_a$	$7{:}04_b$	$6{:}38_b$

	Level of contentedness		
	Low	Middle	High
Family composition			
Two-parent	8:11$_a$	6:50$_b$	6:56$_b$
Single-parent	8:56$_a$	8:21$_a$	6:29$_b$
Residence locale			
Urban	8:46	7:37	7:58
Suburban	8:44$_a$	7:10$_b$	6:32$_b$
Rural	7:33	6:41	6:43

Note: Significance tests between means for each level of each variable; read across each row.

Table A.9.2.2. *Household TV Orientation by Level of Contentedness (8–18 years)(%)*

	Level of contentedness		
	Low	Moderate	High
Live in "constant TV" household	87	84	82
TV on during meals	70$_a$	65$_a$	57$_b$
Have household TV rules	31$_a$	39$_b$	42$_b$

APPENDIX 9.3: AMOUNT OF TOTAL MEDIA EXPOSURE BY ACADEMIC ACHIEVEMENT

Table A.9.3.1. *Average Media Exposure by School Grades (hr:min)[a]*

	A's & B's	B's & C's	C's or below
Screen media	3:53$_a$	4:25$_b$	4:43$_b$
Audio media	1:44$_a$	1:58$_b$	2:28$_b$
Print	0:46$_a$	0:37$_b$	0:40$_{ab}$
Computer	0:29	0:25	0:20
Video games	0:25	0:27	0:32
Total media	7:17$_a$	7:52$_b$	8:44$_{ab}$
Electronic media	6:31$_a$	7:15$_b$	8:04$_b$

[a] Self-reported grades. A's & B's: "Mostly A's" and "mostly A's and B's"; B's & C's: "mostly B's" and "mostly B's and C's"; C's or below: "mostly C's" or anything lower.

Table A.9.3.2. Average Media Exposure by School Grades and Age (hr:min)[a]

	8–10 years			11–14 years			15–18 years		
	A's & B's	B's & C's	C's or below	A's & B's	B's & C's	C's or below	A's & B's	B's & C's	C's or below
Screen media	4:44	5:01	5:22	$2:52_a$	$3:36_b$	$3:05_{ab}$	$4:09_a$	$4:53_b$	$5:55_b$
Audio media	0:52	0:59	1:23	2:35	2:37	3:01	$1:38_a$	$1:53_{ab}$	$2:35_b$
Print	0:52	0:43	1:03	$0:41_a$	$0:31_b$	$0:32_{ab}$	0:44	0:39	0:35
Computer	0:22	0:23	0:23	$0:29_a$	$0:23_{ab}$	$0:13_b$	0:34	0:28	0:25
Video games	0:31	0:34	0:37	0:19	0:20	0:32	0:24	0:29	0:31
Total media	7:22	7:38	8:47	6:58	7:27	7:23	$7:29_a$	$8:23_{ab}$	$10:01_b$
Electronic media	6:30	6:55	7:44	6:16	6:56	6:52	$6:44_a$	$7:43_b$	$9:26_c$

[a] See note to Table A.9.3.1.

Table A.9.3.3. *Average Media Exposure by School Grades and Gender (hr:min)*[a]

	Girls			Boys		
	A's & B's	B's & C's	C's or below	A's & B's	B's & C's	C's or below
Screen media	3:40$_a$	4:10$_{ab}$	4:58$_b$	4:07	4:37	4:32
Audio media	2:08	2:17	2:52	1:20$_a$	1:44$_b$	2:10$_b$
Print	0:46	0:41	0:35	0:45$_a$	0:34$_b$	0:44$_{ab}$
Computer	0:26	0:21	0:13	0:32	0:28	0:25
Video games	0:10$_a$	0:11$_a$	0:23$_b$	0:40	0:39	0:40
Total media	7:10$_a$	7:40$_{ab}$	9:02$_b$	7:23	8:01	8:31
Electronic media	6:25$_a$	6:59$_{ab}$	8:26$_b$	6:38$_a$	7:28$_b$	7:46$_{ab}$

[a] See note to Table A.9.3.1.

Table A.9.3.4. *Average Media Exposure by School Grades and Race/Ethnicity (hr:min)*[a]

	White			Black			Hispanic		
	A's & B's	B's & C's	C's or below	A's & B's	B's & C's	C's or below	A's & B's	B's & C's	C's or below
Screen media	3:17$_a$	4:08	3:52	5:50	5:17	5:04	4:53	4:28	5:59
Audio media	1:47$_a$	2:08	2:42	1:45	1:53	1:54	1:59	1:47	2:38
Print	0:43	0:38	0:37	0:49	0:37	0:53	0:41$_a$	0:25$_b$	0:22$_{ab}$
Computer	0:29	0:25	0:18	0:23	0:31	0:28	0:29	0:22	0:20
Video games	0:20	0:26	0:29	0:31	0:35	0:44	0:41	0:23	0:51
Total media	6:37	7:45	7:58	9:17	8:53	9:03	8:44	7:26	9:50
Electronic media	5:54	7:07	7:35	8:28	8:16	8:10	8:04	7:01	9:46

[a] See note to Table A.9.3.1.

Table A.9.3.5. *Average Media Exposure by School Grades and Income[a] (hr:min)[b]*

	Low			Middle			High		
	A's & B's	B's & C's	C's or below	A's & B's	B's & C's	C's or below	A's & B's	B's & C's	C's or below
Screen media	$4{:}29_{ab}$	$4{:}16_a$	$6{:}05_b$	$3{:}49_a$	$4{:}35_b$	$5{:}36_b$	$3{:}40_{ab}$	$4{:}18_a$	$2{:}54_b$
Audio media	1:49	1:59	2:24	1:52	1:47	2:07	$1{:}33_a$	$2{:}16_b$	$2{:}50_a$
Print	0:47	0:38	0:47	0:46	0:38	0:46	0:44	0:34	0:30
Computer	0:21	0:21	0:22	0:30	0:25	0:24	0:32	0:29	0:16
Video games	0:31	0:23	0:34	0:27	0:30	0:35	0:18	0:25	0:30
Total media	$7{:}56_a$	$7{:}37_a$	$10{:}12_b$	$7{:}23_a$	$7{:}53_{ab}$	$9{:}28_b$	$6{:}47_a$	$8{:}03_b$	$7{:}00_{ab}$
Electronic media	$7{:}09_a$	$6{:}59_a$	$9{:}25_b$	$6{:}37_a$	$7{:}14_{ab}$	$8{:}41_b$	$6{:}03_a$	$7{:}29_b$	$6{:}30_{ab}$

[a] See note to Table A.3.1.4.
[b] See note to Table A.9.3.1.

343

Table A.9.3.6. *Average Media Exposure by School Grades and Parent Education (hr:min)*[a]

	High school			Some college			College grad		
	A's & B's	B's & C's	C's or below	A's & B's	B's & C's	C's or below	A's & B's	B's & C's	C's or or below
Screen media	4:14	4:48	4:35	4:01	4:04	4:47	$3:33_a$	$4:13_b$	$5:10_b$
Audio media	2:00	1:44	2:30	2:00	2:16	3:11	$1:39_a$	$2:07_b$	$2:05_{ab}$
Print	0:35	0:32	0:33	0:47	0:35	1:01	0:48	0:39	0:58
Computer	0:19	0:18	0:12	0:25	0:21	0:41	0:35	0:34	0:26
Video games	0:29	0:18	0:35	0:22	0:23	0:20	$0:23_a$	$0:37_b$	$0:40_{ab}$
Total media	7:37	7:41	8:25	7:35	7:40	10:01	$6:59_a$	$8:08_b$	$9:19_b$
Electronic media	7:02	7:08	7:52	6:47	7:04	9:01	$6:11_a$	$7:29_b$	$8:22_b$

[a] See note to Table A.9.3.1.

Table A.9.3.7. Average Media Exposure by School Grades and Family Composition (hr:min)[a]

	Two-parent			Single-parent		
	A's & B's	B's & C's	C's or below	A's & B's	B's & C's	C's or below
Screen media	3:40$_a$	4:16$_b$	4:39$_b$	4:16	5:11	5:59
Audio media	1:42$_a$	1:55$_{ab}$	2:16$_b$	1:54	1:50	2:29
Print	0:43	0:38	0:42	0:46	0:37	0:38
Computer	0:29	0:27	0:19	0:35	0:22	0:21
Video games	0:23	0:25	0:37	0:25	0:31	0:35
Total media	6:56$_a$	7:39$_b$	8:32$_b$	7:55	8:32	10:02
Electronic media	6:13$_a$	7:02$_b$	7:51$_b$	7:08	7:55	9:23

[a] See note to Table A.9.3.1.

Table A.9.3.8. *Average Media Exposure by School Grades and Residence Locale (hr:min)*[a]

	Urban			Suburban			Rural		
	A's & B's	B's & C's	C's or below	A's & B's	B's & C's	C's or below	A's & B's	B's & C's	C's or below
Screen media	4:06$_a$	4:39$_a$	6:27$_b$	3:50$_a$	4:38$_b$	3:05$_a$	3:40$_a$	3:52$_a$	5:26$_b$
Audio media	1:47	2:02	2:27	1:43$_a$	2:10$_b$	2:49$_b$	1:43	1:38	2:04
Print	0:49	0:41	0:37	0:47$_a$	0:36$_b$	0:38$_{ab}$	0:38	0:34	0:46
Computer	0:28	0:26	0:31	0:31	0:29	0:18	0:28$_a$	0:17$_b$	0:16$_{ab}$
Video games	0:29	0:29	0:35	0:22	0:27	0:31	0:23	0:23	0:33
Total media	7:40$_a$	8:16$_{ab}$	10:37$_b$	7:14$_a$	8:19$_b$	7:20$_{ab}$	6:53$_a$	6:45$_a$	9:04$_b$
Electronic media	6:50$_a$	7:35$_b$	10:00$_c$	6:26$_a$	7:43$_b$	6:44$_{ab}$	6:14$_a$	6:11$_a$	8:19$_b$

[a] See note to Table A.9.3.1.

Appendix 9.4: Heavy and Light Media Exposure

Table A.9.4.1. *Average Overall Exposure to All Media* Except Television
by Low, Moderate, and High TV Use (average time spent using; hr:min)

	Low TV	Moderate TV	High TV
Age in years			
8–10	$3:11_a$	$3:43_a$	$5:11_b$
11–14	$4:00_a$	$4:08_a$	$5:17_b$
15–18	4:50	4:35	5:23
Gender			
Girls	$4:13_a$	$15:30_a$	$15:47_b$
Boys	$4:05_a$	$4:07_a$	$5:17_b$
Race/ethnicity			
White	$4:05_a$	$3:59_a$	$5:14_b$
Black	4:51	4:28	5:14
Hispanic	4:43	4:20	5:27
Income[a]			
Low	$3:54_a$	$4:31_a$	$5:55_b$
Middle	$4:27_{ac}$	$4:16_{ab}$	$5:07_c$
High	$3:56_a$	$3:49_a$	$5:05_b$
Parent education			
HS or less	$4:25_{ac}$	$3:49_{ab}$	$5:18_c$
Some college	4:07	4:37	4:38
College or more	$4:07_a$	$6:38_a$	$12:10_b$

[a] See note to Table A.3.1.4.

Table A.9.4.2. *Average Overall Exposure to All Media* Except Print *by Low, Moderate, and High Print Use (average time spent using; hr:min)*

	Low Print	Moderate Print	High Print
Age in years			
8–10	5:47$_a$	5:54$_a$	7:39$_b$
11–14	7:04$_a$	6:58$_{ab}$	8:08$_c$
15–18	5:47$_a$	6:22$_a$	8:06$_b$
Gender			
Girls	5:56$_a$	6:24$_a$	7:35$_b$
Boys	6:34$_a$	6:35$_a$	8:23$_b$
Race/ethnicity			
White	5:58$_a$	5:58$_a$	7:13$_b$
Black	7:16$_a$	8:05$_a$	9:50$_b$
Hispanic	7:26	7:23	9:28
Income[a]			
Low	6:24$_a$	7:05$_a$	8:47$_b$
Moderate	6:32$_a$	6:43$_a$	8:07$_b$
High	5:52$_a$	5:56$_a$	7:20$_b$
Parent education			
HS or less	6:24$_a$	7:05$_a$	8:47$_b$
Some college	6:22$_a$	6:35$_a$	6:42$_b$
College or more	6:16$_{ac}$	6:20$_{ab}$	7:08$_c$

[a] See note to Table A.3.1.4.

Table A.9.4.3. *Average Overall Exposure to All Media* Except Computers *by Low, Moderate, and High Computer Use (average time spent using; hr:min)*

	Low computer	Moderate computer	High computer
Age in years			
8–10	$6{:}28_a$	$6{:}10_a$	$10{:}49_b$
11–14	$6{:}46_a$	$7{:}06_a$	$10{:}08_b$
15–18	$6{:}26_a$	$6{:}40_a$	$8{:}10_b$
Gender			
Girls	$6{:}25_a$	$7{:}02_a$	$9{:}08_b$
Boys	$6{:}43_a$	$6{:}22_a$	$9{:}57_b$
Race/ethnicity			
White	$6{:}02_a$	$6{:}08_a$	$8{:}59_b$
Black	$7{:}56_a$	$8{:}23_a$	$11{:}53_b$
Hispanic	$7{:}16_a$	$8{:}38_{ab}$	$9{:}56_b$
Income[a]			
Low	$7{:}15_a$	$7{:}50_a$	$10{:}10_b$
Moderate	$6{:}43_a$	$6{:}58_a$	$9{:}32_b$
High	$5{:}50_a$	$6{:}08_a$	$9{:}28_b$
Parent education			
HS or less	$6{:}59_a$	$7{:}37_a$	$10{:}13_b$
Some college	$7{:}03_a$	$7{:}02_a$	$9{:}02_b$
College or more	$6{:}08_a$	$6{:}11_a$	$9{:}22_b$

[a] See note to Table A.3.1.4.

Table A.9.4.4. *Proportion of 8- to 18-year-olds Earning Mostly A and B Grades in School in Relation to Amount of Exposure to Print, Television, and Computers (%)*

	Level of media exposure		
Amount of exposure to:	Low	Moderate	High
Print	61_a	69_b	75_c
Television	68_{ab}	71_a	64_b
Computers	65_a	76_b	69_a

Note: Self-reported grades.

APPENDIX 9.5: CHARACTERISTICS OF MEDIA USER TYPES

Table A.9.5.1. *Media Use Clusters*

	Media Lite	Interactor	VidKid	Restricted	Indifferent	Enthusiast	Total
Recreational media (hr:min)							
Total TV	1:32	2:50	3:54	2:26	2:24	5:18	3:05
Videotapes, prerecorded	0:06	0:16	0:18	0:07	0:06	0:32	0:14
Videotapes, movies	0:09	0:34	0:33	0:26	0:09	0:55	0:27
Videogames	0:07	0:26	0:36	0:18	0:15	0:52	0:26
Movies	0:03	0:13	0:24	0:12	0:04	0:49	0:18
Books for enjoyment	0:23	0:26	0:18	0:20	0:13	0:28	0:21
Magazines	0:07	0:19	0:15	0:15	0:11	0:22	0:15
Newspapers	0:03	0:09	0:06	0:07	0:07	0:11	0:07
CDs/tapes	0:35	0:55	1:11	0:59	0:59	1:34	1:02
Radio	0:25	0:45	1:05	0:34	0:45	1:03	0:46
Computer: chat	0:00	0:04	0:02	0:06	0:03	0:13	0:05
Computer: games	0:04	0:18	0:07	0:08	0:05	0:27	0:12
Computer: web	0:02	0:10	0:03	0:07	0:04	0:15	0:07
Computer: e-mail	0:01	0:05	0:01	0:04	0:03	0:09	0:04
Total media use	**3:38**	**7:29**	**8:52**	**6:08**	**5:29**	**13:07**	**7:29**

Combined recreational media (hr:min)

Total TV and prerecorded videotapes	1:38	3:06	4:13	2:33	2:30	5:50	3:31
Videotapes, movies	0:09	0:34	0:33	0:26	0:09	0:55	0:29
Movies	0:03	0:13	0:24	0:12	0:04	0:49	0:2C
Video games	0:07	0:26	0:36	0:18	0:15	0:52	0:27
Reading (books for enjoyment, mags, newspaper)	0:34	0:54	0:40	0:42	0:31	1:01	0:45
CDs/tapes/radio	0:60	1:40	2:16	1:32	1:44	2:38	1:53
Computer for recreation	0:08	0:37	0:12	0:25	0:16	1:03	0:31

Types of recreational media use (hr:min)

Interactive: requiring user participation (video games, computer)	0:15	1:03	0:48	0:43	0:31	1:55	0:58
Noninteractive: screen media, watching only (TV, videotapes, movies)	1:50	3:52	5:09	3:11	2:43	7:34	4:21
Interactive, nondigital: reading (books for enjoyment, magazines, newspapers)	0:34	0:54	0:40	0:42	0:31	1:01	0:45
Listening (CDs, tapes, radio)	0:60	1:40	2:16	1:32	1:44	2:38	1:53
Number of types of media used	2.45	4.63	3.99	4.16	3.10	5.07	3.88

(continued)

Table A.9.5.1. (continued)

	Media Lite	Interactor	VidKid	Restricted	Indifferent	Enthusiast	Total
Proportion who did each activity (%)							
Total TV & videotaped TV	67	96	96	90	81	97	87
Video games	12	49	45	42	25	71	41
Movies and videotaped movies	16	56	51	41	16	78	43
Reading	61	94	84	89	68	90	80
CDs/tapes and radio	65	94	91	93	82	97	86
Computer for recreation	25	68	25	55	37	71	47
Bedroom access: Proportion who have in bedroom (%)							
TV	32	31	72	65	91	96	65
VCR	13	13	33	27	55	67	36
CDs or tapes	79	84	78	92	96	96	88
Radio	74	83	79	90	96	93	86
Computer	10	14	3	21	26	47	21
Video game	19	19	40	44	63	79	45
Cable or satellite	8	7	18	24	50	60	29
Premium channels	2	2	7	11	24	39	15
CD-Rom	4	10	1	11	20	37	14
Internet	2	5	1	6	13	29	10

Home access: Proportion who have in home (%)

Computer	63	88	22	92	82	89	73
Video game	64	76	71	90	92	93	81
Cable or satellite	61	74	43	81	81	89	74
Premium channels	22	41	22	50	62	70	45
CD-Rom	48	78	11	83	71	83	63
Internet	31	57	4	69	52	69	47
Average number of TVs in home	2.3	2.2	2.8	4.2	3.9	3.7	3.1

TV environment (%)

TV on in home "most of the time"	30	37	59	24	62	63	47
TV usually on during meals	45	56	91	33	87	76	65
Have rules about TV	58	41	24	68	14	29	38
More than half of TV time alone (of those who watched)	17	28	38	19	60	51	37
Mainly channel surfing (of those who watched)	9	7	8	9	12	18	11

(continued)

Table A.9.5.1. (*continued*)

	Media Lite	Interactor	VidKid	Restricted	Indifferent	Enthusiast	Total
Mainly switched back and forth (of those who watched)	19	33	35	28	38	40	33
Mainly watched one show (of those who watched)	72	60	57	63	50	43	56
Personality (%)							
TV is entertaining "most of the time"	50	49	58	55	54	64	55
TV just killing time "never"	19	16	21	15	14	17	17
TV learn interesting things "most of the time"	21	20	25	15	13	28	20
Computer is entertaining "most of the time"	45	59	44	50	47	65	42
Computer just killing time "never"	43	31	52	29	31	35	37
Computer learn interesting things "most of the time"	24	26	28	28	26	36	28
Mean contentedness score	18.9	18.8	18.6	19.4	19.0	18.7	18.9
High contentedness	20	19	23	12	17	23	19
Medium contentedness	61	65	61	67	65	60	63

Low contentedness	19	17	16	22	18	17	18
Have lots of friends "a lot like me"	53	61	59	64	66	67	62
Get along well with parents "a lot like me"	58	54	56	58	52	50	55
Often bored "not at all like me"	19	16	17	13	14	16	16
Sad and unhappy "not at all like me"	34	35	38	40	40	47	39
Happy at school "a lot like me"	44	38	43	44	37	38	41
Get into trouble "not at all like me"	52	50	48	60	54	43	51
Cluster demographics (%)							
Girls	55	49	54	47	51	38	49
Boys	45	51	47	53	49	62	51
8–10 years	39	30	29	25	17	23	27
11–14 years	33	34	35	47	42	49	40
15–18 years	28	36	36	28	41	29	33
Percent hispanic	14	10	21	8	11	16	13
Percent black	6	9	24	9	16	22	14
Percent white	67	69	42	74	65	54	62
Single-parent	18	19	31	11	18	20	19

(continued)

Table A.9.5.1. (continued)

	Media Lite	Interactor	VidKid	Restricted	Indifferent	Enthusiast	Total
Only child	20	17	29	17	30	28	24
Urban	30	32	36	31	30	38	33
Suburban	39	36	37	44	42	39	39
Rural	31	32	27	25	28	23	28
Good grades	67	65	55	68	67	62	64
Fair or poor grades	25	28	40	23	29	32	30
Parent education: HS or less	34	24	49	19	28	26	30
Parent education: College or more	54	62	33	59	51	55	53
Mean income of school[a]	$35,805	$36,609	$32,562	$39,446	$36,113	$34,458	$35,790
Percent low income	20	14	28	11	22	22	20
Percent medium income	43	47	49	44	42	46	45
Percent high income	37	40	23	45	36	32	35
Number	366	313	303	301	357	374	2013
Percent of 8 to 18-year-old	18%	16%	15%	15%	18%	19%	100%

[a] See note to Table A.3.1.4.

REFERENCES

Abelman, R. (1990). Determinants of parental mediation of children's television viewing. In J. Bryant (Ed.), *Television and the American family* (pp. 311–326). Hillsdale, N.J.: Erlbaum.

Anderson, D. R., & Collins, P. A. (1988). *The impact on children's education: Television's influence on cognitive development.* Washington, D.C.: U.S. Department of Education.

Anderson, D. R., & Lorch, E. P. (1983). Looking at television: Action or reaction? In J. Bryant & D. R. Anderson (Eds.), *Children's understanding of television: Research on attention and comprehension* (pp. 1–34). New York: Academic Press.

Anderson, R. C., Hiebert, E. H., Scott, J. A., & Wilkinson, I. A. G. (1985). *Becoming a nation of readers.* Washington, D.C.: U.S. Department of Education.

Arnett, J. (1991). Adolescence and heavy metal music: From the mouths of metalheads. *Youth and Society, 23(1),* 76–98.

Bandura, A. (1986). *Social foundations of thought and action: A social cognitive theory.* Englewood Cliffs, N.J.: Prentice-Hall.

Bandura, A. (2002). Social cognitive theory of mass communication. In J. Bryant and D. Zillman (Eds.), *Media effects: Advances in theory and research,* 2nd ed., (pp. 121–153). Mahwah, N.J.: Erlbaum.

Bennahum, D. S. (1999). The new generation gap. *The Washington Post,* October 20, p. A-41.

Berkowitz, L. (1984). Some effects of thoughts on anti- and prosocial influences of media events: A cognitive neo-association analysis. *Psychological Bulletin, 95,* 410–427.

Bickham, D. S., Wright, J. C., & Huston, A. C. (2001). Attention, comprehension, and the educational influences of television. In

D. G. Singer & J. L. Singer (Eds.), *Handbook of children and the media* (pp. 101–119). Thousand Oaks, Calif.: Sage.

Bower, R. T. (1973). *Television and the public.* New York: Holt, Rinehart and Winston.

Bower, R. T. (1985). *The changing television audience in America.* New York: Columbia University Press.

Brown, J. D., Childers, K., Bauman, K., & Koch, G. (1990). The influence of new media and family structure on young adolescents' television and radio use. *Communication Research, 17,* 65–82.

Burk, R., & Grinder, R. (1966). Personality-oriented themes and listening patterns in teen-age music and their relation to certain academic and peer variables. *School Review, 74,* 196–211.

Bushman, B. J., & Anderson, C. A. (2001). Media violence and the American public: Scientific facts versus media misinformation. *American Psychologist, 56,* 477–489.

Calvert, S. (1999). *Children's journeys through the information age.* Boston: McGraw-Hill.

Carey, J. (1969). Changing courtship patterns in the popular song. *American Journal of Sociology, 4,* 720–731.

Center for Media Education (2001). *TeenSites.com: A field guide to the new digital landscape.* Washington, D.C.: Author.

Chaffee, S. H., McLeod, J. M., & Atkin, C. K. (1971). Parental influences on adolescent media use. *American Behavioral Scientist, 14,* 323–340.

Chall, J. S. (1983). *Stages of reading development.* New York: McGraw-Hill.

Charters, W. W. (1933). *Motion pictures and youth: A summary.* New York: Macmillan.

Cheskin Research & Cyberteens.com (1999). *Teens and the future of the web.* Redwood Shores, Calif.: Author. Http://www.Cheskin.com/think/studies/netteens.html (accessed August 5, 2001).

Christenson, P. (1994). Childhood patterns of music use and preferences. *Communication Reports, 7(2),* 136–144.

Christenson, P., & Peterson, J. (1988). Genre and gender in the structure of music preferences. *Communication Research, 15,* 327–343.

Christenson, P., & Roberts, D. F. (1983). The role of television in the formation of children's social attitudes. In M. J. A. Howe (Ed.). *Learning from television: Psychological and educational research* (pp. 77–99). London: Academic Press.

Christenson, P., & Roberts, D. F. (1998). *It's not only rock and roll: Popular music in the lives of adolescents*. Cresskill, N.J.: Hampton Press.

Coffin, T. (1955). Television's impact on society. *American Psychologist, 10*, 630–641.

Comstock, G. (1991). *Television and the American child*. San Diego, Calif.: Academic Press.

Comstock, G., Chaffee, S., Katzman, N., McCombs, M., & Roberts, D. F. (1978). *Television and human behavior*. New York: Columbia University Press.

Comstock, G., & Scharrer, E. (1999). *Television: What's on, who's watching, and what it means*. San Diego, Calif.: Academic Press.

Csikszentmihalyi, M., & Kubey, R. (2002). Television addiction is no mere metaphor. *Scientific American* (February), 74–80.

Dornbusch, S. M., Ritter, P. L., Leiderman, P. H., Roberts, D. F., & Fraleigh, M. J. (1987). The relation of parenting style to adolescent school performance. *Child Development, 58*, 1244–1257.

Dorr, A., & Kunkel, D. (1990). Children and the media environment: Change and constancy amid change. *Communication Research, 17*, 5–25.

Evans, E. D., Rutberg, J., Sather, C., & Turner, C. (1991). Content analysis of contemporary teen magazines for adolescent females. *Youth & Society, 23(1)*, 99–120.

Federman, J., Carbone, S., Chen, H., & Munn, W. (1996). *The social effects of electronic interactive games: An annotated bibliography*. Studio City, Calif.: Mediascope.

Feldman, S. S., & Elliott, G. R. (1990). *At the threshold: The developing adolescent*. Cambridge, Mass.: Harvard University Press.

Foehr, U. G., Rideout, V., & Miller, C. (2001). Children and the TV ratings system: A national study. In B. Greenberg (Ed.), *The alphabet soup of television program ratings: Y-G-PG-V-S-D-14-FV-MA-7-L* (pp. 139–150). Cresskill, N.J.: Hampton Press.

Foley, K. (2000). Wall Street Journal asks: How many teens online, and how much do they spend? *eMarketer*, February 8. Http://www.emarketer.com (accessed July 15, 2001).

Funk, J. B. (1993). Reevaluating the impact of video games. *Clinical Pediatrics, 32(2)*, 86–90.

Funk, J. B., & Buchman, D. D. (1996). Playing violent video and computer games and adolescent self concept. *Journal of Communication, 46(2)*, 19–32.

Funk, J. B., Buchman, D. D., & Germann, J. N. (2000). Preference for violent electronic games, self-concept, and gender differences in young children. *American Journal of Orthopsychiatry, 70,* 233–241.

Gans, H. (1967). *Popular culture and high culture: An analysis and evaluation of taste.* New York: Basic Books.

Garner, A., Sterk, H. M., & Adams, S. (1998). Narrative analysis of sexual etiquette in teenage magazines. *Journal of Communication, 48(4),* 59–78.

Gerbner, G., & Gross, L. (1976). Living with television: The violence profile. *Journal of Communication, 26(2),* 173–199.

Gerbner, G., Gross, L., Morgan, M. & Signorielli, N. (1981). A curious journey into the scary world of Paul Hirsch. *Communication Research, 8,* 39–72.

Gerbner, G., Gross, L., Morgan, M., Signorielli, N., & Shanahan, J. (2002). Growing up with television: Cultivation processes. In J. Bryant & D. Zillmann (Eds.), *Media effects: Advances in theory and research,* 2nd ed. (pp. 43–67). Mahwah, N.J.: Erlbaum.

Greenberg, B. S., Ku, L., & Li, H. (1989). *Young people and their orientation to the mass media: An international study. Study #2: United States.* East Lansing: College of Communication Arts and Sciences, Michigan State University.

Harris, J. R. (1998). *The nurture assumption: Why children turn out the way they do.* New York: Free Press.

Harris, M. B., & Williams, R. (1985). Video games and school performance. *Education, 105(3),* 306–309.

Hirsch, P. (1980). The "scary world" of the nonviewer and other anomalies: A reanalysis of Gerbner et al.'s findings of cultivation analysis. *Communication Research, 7,* 403–456.

Hodge, R., & Tripp, D. (1986). *Children and television.* Cambridge, U.K.: Polity Press.

Horatio Alger Foundation (1996). *The mood of American youth.* Alexandria, Va.: Horatio Alger Association of Distinguished Americans.

Horton, D., & Wohl, R. R. (1956). Mass communication and parasocial interaction. *Psychiatry, 19,* 215–229.

Huston, A. C., Donnerstein, E., Fairchild, H., Feshbach, N. D., et al. (1992). *Big world, small screen: The role of television in American society.* Lincoln: University of Nebraska Press.

Internetnews.com (1988). Study shows two-thirds of all teenagers now wired. Available at www.internetnews.com, accessed February 5, 2000.

Jackson, S., & Rodriguez-Tomé, H. (Eds.) (1993). *Adolescence and its social worlds*. Hove, U.K.: Erlbaum.

Jo, E., & Berkowitz, L. (1994). A priming effect analysis of media influences: An update. In J. Bryant and D. Zillmann (Eds.), *Media effects: Advances in theory and research* (pp. 43–60). Hillsdale, N.J.: Erlbaum.

Johnston, J. W. C. (1974). Social integration and mass media use among adolescents: A case study. In J. G. Blumler & E. Katz (Eds.), *The uses of mass communications: Current perspectives on gratifications research* (pp. 35–47). Beverly Hills, Calif.: Sage.

Josephson, W. L. (1987). Television violence and children's aggression: Testing the priming, social script, and disinhibition predictions. *Journal of Personality and Social Psychology, 53*, 882–890.

Kaiser Family Foundation (2001). *Generation Rx.com: How young people use the Internet for health information*. Menlo Park, Calif.: Author.

Kaiser Family Foundation & YM Magazine (1998). *Teens talk about dating, intimacy and their sexual experiences*. Menlo Park, Calif.: Authors.

Kane, M. (2001). Study: Internet use steals TV time. *CNET News.Com.http://news.com.com/2100-1023-276358.html* (accessed July 22, 2002).

Kirchler, E., Palomari, A., & Pombeni, M. (1993). Developmental tasks and adolescents' relationships with their peers and their family. In S. Jackson & H. Rodriguez-Tome (Eds.), *Adolescence and its social worlds* (pp. 145–167). Hove, U.K.: Erlbaum.

Klein, A. (2001). Internet use seems to cut into TV time. *The Washington Post*, November 29, 2001, p. E-1.

Kubey, R., & Czikszentmihalyi, M. (1990). *Television and the quality of life: How viewing shapes everyday experience*. Hillsdale, N.J.: Erlbaum.

Kubey, R., & Larson, R. (1990). The use and experience of the new video among children and young adolescents. *Communication Research, 17*, 107–130.

Kubey, R. W. (1986). Television use in everyday life: Coping with unstructured time. *Journal of Communication, 36(3)*, 108–123.

Larson, R., & Kubey, R. (1983). Television and music: Contrasting media in adolescent life. *Youth and Society, 15*, 13–31.

Larson, R., Kubey, R., & Colletti, J. (1989). Changing channels: Early adolescent media choices and shifting investments in family and friends. *Journal of Youth and Adolescence, 18*, 583–599.

Lenhart, A., Rainie, L., & Lewis, O. (2001). *Teenage life online: The rise of the instant message generation and the Internet's impact on friendships and family relationships*. Washington, D.C.: Pew Foundation, June.

Lieberman, D., A., Chaffee, S. H., & Roberts, D. F. (1988). Computers, mass media, and schooling: Functional equivalence in uses of new media. *Social Science Computer Review, 6,* 224–241.

Lin, S., & Lepper, M. R. (1987). Correlates of children's usage of videogames and computers. *Journal of Applied Social Psychology, 17(1),* 72–93.

Lyle, J., & Hoffman, H. R. (1972a). Children's use of television and other media. In E. A. Rubinstein, G. A. Comstock, & J. P. Murray (Eds.), *Television and social behavior,* vol. 4: *Television in day-to-day life: Patterns of use* (pp. 129–256). Washington, D.C.: U.S. Government Printing Office.

Lyle, J., & Hoffman, H. R. (1972b). Explorations in patterns of television viewing by pre-school age children. In E. A. Rubinstein, G. A. Comstock, & J. P. Murray (Eds.), *Television and social Behavior,* vol. 4: *Television in day-to-day life: Patterns of use* (pp. 257–273). Washington, D.C.: U.S. Government Printing Office.

Lyness, P. (1952). The place of the mass media in the lives of boys and girls. *Journalism Quarterly, 29,* 43–54.

Maccoby, E. E. (1951). Television: Its impact on school children. *Public Opinion Quarterly, 15,* 421–444.

Maccoby, E. E. (1954). Why do children watch television? *Public Opinion Quarterly, 18,* 239–244.

McIntyre, J. J., & Teevan, J. J., Jr. (1972). Television violence and deviant behavior. In G. A. Comstock and E. A. Rubinstein (Eds.), *Television and Social Behavior,* vol. 3: *Television and adolescent aggressiveness* (pp. 173–238). Washington, D.C.: U.S. Government Printing Office.

Medrich, E. A. (1979). Constant television: A background to daily life. *Journal of Communication, 29(3),* 171–176.

Medrich, E. A., Roizen, J. A., Rubin, V., & Buckley, S. (1982). *The serious business of growing up: A study of children's lives outside school.* Berkeley: University of California Press.

Meyrowitz, J. (1994). Medium theory. In D. Crowley & D. Mitchell (Eds.). *Communication theory today* (pp. 50–77). Stanford, Calif.: Stanford University Press.

Morgan, M., Alexander, A., Shanahan, J., & Harris, C. (1990). Adolescents, VCRs, and the family environment. *Communication Research, 17,* 83–106.

Mutz, D. C., Roberts, D. F., & van Vuuren, D. P. (1993). Reconsidering the displacement hypothesis: Television's influence on children's time use. *Communication Research, 20,* 51–75.

National Center for Education Statistics (1999). *Internet access in public schools and classrooms: 1994–98.* Available at *http://nces.ed.gov/pubs/1999017.html* (accessed February16, 2000).

National Public Radio, Kaiser Family Foundation, & Harvard University Kennedy School of Government (2000). *National survey of kids on technology.* Washington, D.C.: Authors.

National Telecommunications and Information Administration (1998). *Falling through the net II: New data on the digital divide.* Washington, D.C.: U.S. Department of Commerce.

National Telecommunications and Information Administration (1999). *Falling through the net: Defining the digital divide.* Washington, D.C.: U.S. Department of Commerce.

Neuman, S. B. (1986). The home environment and fifth-grade students' leisure reading. *Elementary School Journal, 86,* 335–343.

Neuman, S. B. (1988). The displacement effect: Assessing the relation between television viewing and reading performance. *Reading Research and Instruction, 25,* 173–183.

Neuman, S. B. (1995). *Literacy in the television age,* 2nd ed. Norwood, N.J.: Ablex.

Newburger, E. C. (2001). *Home computers and Internet use in the United States: August 2000.* (Special Studies – P23-207). Washington, D.C.: U.S. Department of Commerce, Economics and Statistics Administration, U.S. Census Bureau.

Newspaper Advertising Bureau (1978). *Children, mothers, and newspapers.* New York: Newspaper Advertising Bureau.

Oldenburg, D. (1995). The electronic gender gap. *The Washington Post,* November 24, p. D-5.

Paik, H. (2001). The history of children's use of electronic media. In D. G. Singer & J. L. Singer (Eds.). *Handbook of children and the media* (pp. 7–27). Thousand Oaks, Calif.: Sage.

Paik, H., & Comstock, G. (1994). The effects of television violence on anti-social behavior: A meta-analysis. *Communication Research, 21,* 516–546.

Pecora, N. O. (1998). *The business of children's entertainment.* New York: Guilford Press.

Perse, E. M., & Rubin, R. B. (1989). Attribution in social and parasocial relationships. *Communication Research, 16,* 59–77.

Postman, N. (1985). *Amusing ourselves to death: Public discourse in the age of show business*. New York: Viking Press.

Potter, W. J. (1993). Cultivation theory and research: A conceptual critique. *Human Communication Research, 19*, 564–601.

Potter, W. J. (1998). *Media literacy*, 2nd ed. Thousand Oaks, Calif.: Sage.

RIAA (2002). *The recording industry association of America 2001 consumer profile*. Available at www.riaa.org/pdf/2001 consumerprofile.pdf (accessed July 8, 2002).

Rice, R. (1980). The content of popular recordings. *Popular Music and Society, 7(2)*, 140–158.

Roberts, D. F. (1993). Adolescents and the mass media: From "Leave It to Beaver" to "Beverly Hills 90210." *Teacher's College Record, 94*, 629–643.

Roberts, D. F. (2001). Media and youth: Access, exposure, and privatization. *Journal of Adolescent Health, 27(2)*, supplement, 8–14.

Roberts, D. F. (2003). From Plato's Republic to Hillary's village: Children and the changing media environment. In R. P. Weissberg, H. J. Walberg, M. U. O'Brien, and C. B. Kuster (Eds.), *Long-term trends in the well-being of children and youth* (pp. 255–276). Washington, D.C.: Child Welfare League of America Press (2003).

Roberts, D. F., Bachen, C. M., Hornby, M. C., & Hernandez-Ramos, P. (1984). Reading and television: Predictors of reading achievement at different age levels. *Communication Research, 11*, 9–50.

Roberts, D. F., & Henriksen, L. (1990). *Music listening vs. television viewing among older adolescents*. Paper presented at the annual meetings of the International Communication Association, Dublin, Ireland, June.

Roberts, D. F., & Maccoby, N. (1985). Effects of mass communication. In G. Lindzey & E. Aronson (Eds.), *Handbook of social psychology*, 3rd ed., vol. 2: *Special fields and applicatons* (pp. 539–598). New York: Random House.

Robinson, J. P., & Godbey, G. (1997). *Time for life: The surprising ways Americans use their time*. University Park: Pennsylvania State University Press.

Roe, K. (1987). The school and music in adolescent socialization. In J. Lull (Ed.), *Popular music and communication* (pp. 212–230). Beverly Hills, Calif.: Sage.

Roper Starch Worldwide Inc. (1999). *The America Online/Roper Starch youth cyberstudy 1999*. New York: Author (www.corp.aol.com/press/study/youthstudy.pdf).

Rubin, A. M., Perse, E. M., & Powell, R. A. (1985). Loneliness, parasocial interaction, and local television news viewing. *Human Communication Research, 12(2)*, 155–180.

Salomon, G. (1979). Shape, not only content: How media symbols partake in the development of abilities. In E. Wartella (Ed.), *Children communicating: Media and development of thought, speech, understanding* (pp. 53–82). Beverly Hills, Calif.: Sage.

Sarkar, P. (2001). More than half U.S. homes are wired. *San Jose Mercury News*, September 6, pp. C1, C3.

Schramm, W. (1945). Reading and listening patterns of American university students. *Journalism Quarterly, 22*, 23–33.

Schramm, W., Lyle, J., & Parker, E. B. (1961). *Television in the lives of our children*. Stanford, Calif.: Stanford University Press.

Stanger, J. D. (1997). *Television in the home: The 1997 survey of parents and children* (Survey No. 2). Philadelphia: Annenberg Public Policy Center of the University of Pennsylvania.

Stanger, J. D. (1998). *Television in the home 1998: The third annual national survey of parents and children* (Survey No. 4). Philedelphia: Annenberg Public Policy Center of the University of Pennsylvania.

Stanger, J., & Gridina, N. (1999). *Media in the home 1999: The fourth annual survey of parents and children* (Survey No. 5). Philadelphia: Annenberg Public Policy Center of the University of Pennsylvania.

Starker, S. (1989). *Evil influences: Crusades against the mass media*. New Brunswick, Conn.: Transaction.

Strasburger, V. C., & Wilson, B. J. (2002). *Children, adolescents, & the media*. Thousand Oaks, Calif.: Sage.

Steiner, G. A. (1963). *The people look at television: A study of audience attitudes*. New York: Alfred A. Knopf.

Subrahmanyam, K., Kraut, R., Greenfield, P., & Gross, E. (2001). New forms of electronic media: The impact of interactive games and the Internet on cognition, socialization, and behavior. In D. G. Singer and J. L. Singer (Eds.), *Handbook of children and the media* (pp. 73–99). Thousand Oaks, Calif.: Sage.

Tanaka, J. (1996). No boys allowed. *Newsweek*, October 28, pp. 82–84.

Tangney, J. P. (1988). Aspects of the family and children's television viewing content preferences. *Child Development, 59*, 1070–1079.

Tangney, J. P., & Feshbach, S. (1988). Children's television-viewing frequency: Individual differences and demographic correlates. *Personality and Social Psychology Bulletin, 14*, 145–158.

Teens spend $155 billion in 2000 (2001). Teenage Research Unlimited press release; http//www.teenresearch.com/Prview.cfm?edit_id=75 (accessed August 23, 2001).

Thompson, B. (1999). Kids.commerce: The brave new world of marketing to children. *Washington Post Magazine*, October 24, pp. 10–14, 25–29, 32–34.

Timmer, S. G., Eccles, J., & O'Brien, J. (1985). How children use time. In F. T. Juster & F. Stafford (Eds.), *Time, goods, and well being* (pp. 353–382). Ann Arbor, Mich.: Survey Research Center.

UCLA (2000). *The UCLA Internet report: Surveying the digital future*. Los Angeles: UCLA Center for Communication Policy.

UCLA (2001). *The UCLA Internet report 2001: Surveying the digital future, year two*. Los Angeles: UCLA Center for Communication Policy.

Van Evra, J. (1998). *Television and child development*, 2nd ed. Mahwah, N.J.: Erlbaum.

Venes, R. (1999). As it gradually gnaws away at the total audience, the Net is threatening traditional media. *New Media Age*, April 22, Media, pp. 12–14.

Warner, C. (1984). *Dimensions of appeal in popular music: A new factor-analytic approach to classifying music*. Paper presented at the annual meeting of the Speech Communication Association, Chicago, November.

Wartella, E. (1986). Getting to know you: How children make sense of television. In G. Gumpert and R. Cathcart (Eds.), *Inter/media: Interpersonal communication in a media world*, 3rd ed. (pp. 537–549). New York: Oxford University Press.

Wartella, E., Heintz, K., Aidman, A., & Mazzarella, S. (1990). Television and beyond: Children's video media in one community. *Communication Research, 17*, 45–64.

Wartella, E., O'Keefe, B., & Scantlin, R. (2000). *Children and interactive media: A compendium of current research and directions for the future*. New York: Markle Foundation.

Wartella, E., & Reeves, B. (1987). Communication and children. In C. R. Berger and S. H. Chaffee (Eds.), *Handbook of communication science* (pp. 619–650). Newbury Park, Calif.: Sage.

Weiss, W. (1969). Effects of the mass media of communication. In G. Lindzey & Elliot Aronson (Eds.), *The handbook of social psychology*, 2nd ed., vol. 5: *Applied social psychology* (pp. 77–195). Reading, Mass.: Addison-Wesley.

Williams, P. A., Haertel, E. H., Hartel, G. D., & Walberg, H. J. (1982). The impact of leisure-time television on school learning: A research synthesis. *American Educational Research Journal, 19*, 19–50.

Winn, M. (1985). *The plug-in drug: Television, children, and the family*, rev. ed. New York: Penguin Books.

Witty, P. (1967). Children of the television era. *Elementary English, 44*, 528–535.

Zillmann, D. (1988). Mood management: Using entertainment to full advantage. In D. Pearl, L. Bouthilet, and J. Lazar (Eds.), *Television and behavior: Ten years of scientific inquiry and implications for the eighties. Technical reviews* (vol. 2, pp. 53–67). Washington, D.C.: U.S. Government Printing Office.

Zillmann, D. (1999). Exemplification theory: Judging the whole by some of its parts. *Media Psychology, 1*, 69–94.

Zillmann, D. (2002). Exemplification theory of media influence. In J. Bryant and D. Zillmann (Eds.), *Media effects: Advances in theory and research*, 2nd ed. (pp. 19–41). Mahwah, N.J.: Erlbaum.

Author Index

Subject Index

academic performance: affected by media exposure, 173–4; computer exposure and, 349; measurement of, 171–2; media exposure and, 171–4, 179; print exposure and, 349; TV exposure and, 349

age: identification of subgroups, 26–8; primary independent variable, 26

attitudes toward media, 200–1; age and, 263; measures of, 22–3; parent education and, 195; *see also* attitudes toward television

attitudes toward television: ethnicity and, 265; family composition and, 268; gender and, 264; income and, 266; parent education and, 267; residence and, 269

audio access, *see* media access

audio exposure: age and, 85–9, 270; amount of, 85–6; background function of, 84–5; content of, 87–8; defined, 84; ethnicity and, 89, 272; family composition and, 275; gender and, 88–9, 271; income and, 89–90, 273; measurement of, 84–5; music as primary content, 87; parent education and, 90, 274; residence and, 276; *see also* music preferences

audio exposure, previous research: age and, 10; ethnicity and, 10; radio genres, amount, 277

bedroom media: access to, 29, 55; age and, 42–3, 192; amount, 42, 191–2; ethnicity and, 46–8, 192, 226; family composition and, 229; gender and, 43–4, 225; historical comparisons, 42; income and, 44–6, 192, 227; measure of, 22; parent education and, 44–6, 192, 228; residence and, 230; *see also* bedroom television

bedroom television: screen exposure and, 68; solitary viewing and, 76, 79

book exposure, *see* print exposure

book genres, 209